STRATEGIC ALLIANCE MANAGEMENT

Brian Tjemkes, Pepijn Vos and Koen Burgers

Routledge
Taylor & Francis Group

LONDON AND NEW YORK

First published 2012
by Routledge
2 Park Square, Milton Park, Abingdon, Oxon OX14 4RN

Simultaneously published in the USA and Canada
by Routledge

711 Third Avenue, New York, NY 10017

Routledge is an imprint of the Taylor & Francis Group, an informa business

© 2012 Brian Tjemkes, Pepijn Vos and Koen Burgers

British Library Cataloguing in Publication Data
A catalogue record for this book is available from the British Library

Library of Congress Cataloging in Publication Data
Tjemkes, Brian, 1973-
   Strategic alliance management / Brian Tjemkes, Pepijn Vos and Koen
   Burgers.
      p. cm.
   Includes bibliographical references and index.
   1. Strategic alliances (Business) I. Vos, Pepijn. II. Burgers, Koen. III. Title.
   HD69.S8T59 2012
   658'.046—dc23

                                                                2011033911

ISBN: 978-0-415-68128-5 (hbk)
ISBN: 978-0-415-68129-2 (pbk)
ISBN: 978-0-203-12794-0 (ebk)

Typeset in Bembo
by RefineCatch Limited, Bungay, Suffolk

STRATEGIC ALLIANCE MANAGEMENT

Strategic alliances – voluntary, long-term collaborations between firms to achieve their objectives – are attracting increasing attention in business schools because of their growing prevalence among organizations today.

Mastering the art of managing strategic alliances allows firms to radically improve their performance and this book provides a detailed, evidence-based approach outlining the design, management and evaluation of these alliances. Elaborating on the decision-making structures apparent during each stage in the alliance life-cycle and in elucidating cases from across the world, *Strategic Alliance Management* offers a systematic framework that provides insights into the development and deployment of alliances.

Concluding with the three alliance paradoxes managers must address to design and manage their alliances effectively and efficiently, this text offers a profound vision of the key decision-making rationales and processes inherently related to strategic alliances. As such, it will be required reading for students studying the subject and a valuable supplementary reading source to those studying strategic management more generally.

Brian Tjemkes is Assistant Professor of Management and Organization at VU University Amsterdam, the Netherlands.

Pepijn Vos is Researcher Consultant in the field of innovation and alliance management at TNO, the Netherlands.

Koen Burgers is a Ph.D candidate at Nyenrode University, the Netherlands.

CONTENTS

FIGURES

TABLES

BOXES

PREFACE

Strategic alliances have become cornerstones for the competitive strategy of many firms, enabling those firms to achieve objectives that otherwise would be difficult to realize. Unsurprisingly, the increase in alliance activity over the last few decades has occurred in parallel to enormous growth in academic and managerial attention in the subject. Paradoxically, however, firms' increased focus on and use of alliances is paralleled by moderate-to-high alliance failure rates over the same period. With a few exceptions, firms appear unable to manage their alliances successfully.

This book attempts to synthesize academic insights with managerial experience via a 'guided tour' of various aspects of strategic alliance management. Building on an academically grounded alliance development framework, the book elaborates on unique decision-making situations tied to alliance development stages. In recognition of the fact that distinct alliance objectives, alliance partners, and alliance context constitute unique management challenges, the book also elaborates on these specific conditions. Furthermore, the ability to create successful alliances, which reflects learning about alliance management and leveraging alliance knowledge inside the company, is an alliance capability. The book looks in detail at alliance capabilities, which contribute to successful strategic alliance management. The conclusion builds on these insights by discussing three alliance paradoxes that are inherently tied to strategic alliances. The intended result is a more comprehensive book than has previously been available, which acknowledges that decision-making constitutes a critical success condition.

The book is written with an even-handed appreciation for theory and practice. Readers possessing management knowledge, combined with the book's logic, concepts, and implications, will be able to absorb the information. Readers are assumed to have a basic understanding of strategic management and organizations, obtained either through study or experience. Therefore, students participating in advanced courses in graduate and MBA programmes in business schools will find this book useful, as will professionals seeking a deeper understanding of the subject.

In preparing this book, the authors have received considerable assistance from colleagues who provided detailed feedback on our treatment of the academic literature, alliance experts who reviewed our decision-making steps, and executives who provided us with relevant examples. We specifically acknowledge the companies and alliance managers that have provided insights, examples and feedback on the case material. Thanks are due to Hans de Roos (KLM), Frits Zegeling (Grolsch), Rose Verdurmen (TNT), Jaap Lombaers (Holst Centre), Michiel Jansen (NAM), Berry Vetjens (TNO), Nathalie van Schie (TNO) and Ron van Vianen and Peter van Duijn (Hoogendoorn). We also appreciate the support of staff of the VU University, Nyenrode University, TNO and Kirkman Company, who offered us critical reflections on earlier drafts of the book. We also thank Elisabeth Caswell and James Morrison, whose text editing has been invaluable, as well as Terry Clague and Alexander Krause, who provided editorial assistance in the preparation of the final manuscript. Although we received much-appreciated support in writing the book, any errors remain the responsibility of the authors. Enjoy reading.

Brian Tjemkes, *Amsterdam*
Pepijn Vos, *The Hague*
Koen Burgers, *Baarn*

1

STRATEGIC ALLIANCE MANAGEMENT

In the early industrial age, firms created value by transforming raw materials into finished products. The economy was based primarily on tangible resources – inventory, land, factories, equipment – and a firm could formulate and execute its business strategy by operating autonomously and interacting with its environment through market transactions. But times have changed. In the current information age, businesses must create and deploy intangible resources, including employee skills, information technologies and corporate culture, to encourage innovation and improve their competitive strength. Value does not reside in any individual intangible resource, however. Rather, it arises from the entire set of resources and the strategy that links them. Valuable resources cannot be considered separately from the organizations in which they are embedded. In turn, to develop and maintain competitive advantages, many firms turn increasingly to alliances; instead of just acquiring resources, they enjoy the benefits of combining their own resources with the assets of others.

Alliances thus have become cornerstones of the competitive strategy of many firms, enabling them to achieve objectives that otherwise would be difficult to realize. For example, alliances provide firms with an opportunity to increase their innovative capacity, improve their market response, achieve efficiency and share investment risks with partner firms. Yet this increased focus on and use of alliances by firms is paralleled by empirical research that indicates moderate to high alliance failure rates. Extant academic and professional literature indicates that to reap the benefits from alliances, firms must overcome internal and external adversities by efficiently and effectively managing their alliances. Even as alliance literature offers a vast amount of theoretical and practical insights though, it lacks any systematic framework for decision-making. Such a framework would be of great benefit to decision makers by enabling them to manage their alliances systematically and aim toward success.

Accordingly, the objective of this book is to connect existing theoretical and practical insights and thereby present a much needed, coherent and academically grounded development framework of strategic alliance management. The framework focuses on unique decision-making situations tied to the management of alliances as they progress from formation to termination. Our unique alliance development framework is also grounded in theoretical perspectives (i.e. know-what), supported by practice-oriented decision-making guidelines (i.e. know-how), and illustrated by real-life alliance cases. It also incorporates both generic and specific decision-making situations tied to unique alliance conditions. Before we proceed to introduce our Alliance Development Framework though, we establish a foundation for this book in this opening chapter. To this end, we first outline our book's scope and provide a clear definition of an alliance. In the following two sections, we elaborate on why firms increasingly use alliances as instruments to develop and sustain a competitive advantage, as well as the causes for alliance failure. In the final section, after explaining the need for a book on strategic alliance management, we present the structure of the book.

The meaning of an alliance

An alliance is a voluntary, long-term, contractual relationship between two or more autonomous and independent organizations (i.e. firms), designed to achieve mutual and individual objectives by sharing and/or creating resources (Ariño *et al.* 2001 p. 110; Gulati 1995b p. 621). This definition encompasses inter-organizational relationships, such as joint ventures, purchase partnerships, research and development partnerships, co-makerships, co-creation efforts, multi-partner alliances, public–private partnerships and consortia, but it excludes arrangements such as simple market transactions, mergers and acquisitions. In Table 1.1, we list examples of alliances consistent with our definition.

Four important implications derive from this definition. First, an alliance is an instrument that firms use to achieve their objectives, ultimately to develop and sustain their competitive advantage (Ireland *et al.* 2002). Therefore, alliance management constitutes a strategic activity within firms. Second, the definition indicates that an alliance consists of two or more firms, which remain independent organizational entities but connect voluntarily through an alliance contract. Although alliances thus offer firms flexibility in achieving their objectives, they also represent relatively unstable organizational arrangements, because there is an absence of hierarchical governance (Litwak and Hylton 1962). Third, as critical resources get exchanged, firms engaged in alliances grow increasingly dependent on each other to realize their joint and individual objectives. This situation implies that firms must manage their alliances proactively to resolve any tension between cooperative forces focused on value creation and competitive forces oriented toward value appropriation (Dyer *et al.* 2008). Fourth, our definition implies that alliances are transitional entities, because firms can dissolve them at any convenient time. The threat of premature termination requires systematic management attention to resolve any emerging adversities.

TABLE 1.1 Examples of alliances

Alliance	Description
Takeda–Eli-Lilly	In 1998, Japan's Takeda and the US firm Eli Lilly established a pharmaceutical joint venture. Takeda's US company co-promoted Eli Lilly's insulin product and received fees based on net sales of the products; the joint venture also covered the distribution of Takeda's insulin sensitivity enhancer, ACTOS™. The alliance was successful, and in 2003, Eli Lilly and Takeda signed another agreement for joint development and co-marketing of another diabetes medicine in the Japanese market. In 2006, Takeda acquired the joint venture, as agreed in the original contract.
Saab–BMW	Loss-making Saab, bought in 2010 by Dutch Spyker from US-based General Motors, aimed to improve its car sales by adding a fourth, smaller car line to its three existing lines. Saab formed an alliance with BMW, an established German automotive manufacturer, to obtain necessary parts and technology and thereby triple its sales volume. The biggest costs for a car manufacturer are marketing and development; sharing development efforts would quickly cut costs. After the alliance announcement, Spyker's stock jumped 36.5% to a five-month high, after having lost almost one-third its value since Spyker had bought Saab.
Star Alliance	The Star Alliance is a global airline network, established in 1997 as the first alliance to offer customers worldwide reach. Members include Singapore Airlines, Air China, Continental Airlines, Lufthansa and Scandinavian Airlines. TAM Airlines, the leading Brazilian carrier, joined in mid-2010, inserting the world's longest running airline alliance firmly onto the South American continent. TAM Airlines' participation is the end result of a process that began in 2006, with informal negotiations followed by actions to align operating processes and an official announcement of membership in 2008.
Apple–Google	During the mid-2000s, Apple and Google formed several (project-based) alliances to increase their market power and counter their largest competitor, Microsoft. Apple is renowned for its innovative capability in information and communication technology, including laptops (iMac) and mobile phones (iPhone). Google is the market leader in the Internet search market and has developed other services, including Google Earth and Gmail. These partnerships succeeded until Google announced its Android, a smartphone operating system designed to compete with Apple's iPhone. Google also unveiled Chrome, an operating system designed to compete with Microsoft that has begun to compete with Apple's iPad. In response, Apple launched a counter-attack and rejected Google Voice. As of 2010, the alliance has reached a breaking point, with insiders suggesting that Apple was seeking collaboration with Microsoft.

Sources: Iphone Magazine (2010); SAAB Newsroom (2010); Star Alliance (2011); Sterling (2010); Takeda (2007).

Compared with other organizational entities such as stand-alone organizations, alliances thus represent unique arrangements with specific management challenges. For example, interdependent parties in alliances must develop joint business propositions, share control and management, accept overlapping roles and responsibilities, engage in adaptation through mutual cooperation, install internal and proactive monitoring mechanisms and develop long-term incentive systems. If alliances are relatively unstable and complex entities though, the question emerges: Why do firms engage in alliance activity?

Alliance activity

Alliances are critical weapons in firms' competitive arsenals, and in recent decades, alliance activity has increased substantially. According to Kang and Sakai (2001), the number of alliances in 1999 was six times higher than a decade before. Duysters *et al.* (1999) report a similar exponential increase in strategic technology alliances during the period 1970–1996, and Anand and Khanna (2000) count, during 1990–1993, more than 9,000 alliances just in the US manufacturing sector. On the basis of their research, Dyer *et al.* (2001) conclude that in 2001, the top 500 global businesses averaged 60 major alliances each. De Man (2005) reports the number of alliances by high-tech companies during the period 1998–2002: IBM (168), Cisco (56), Eli Lilly (40), and Philips–EU (61). Furthermore, the impact of alliances appears to be growing steadily. As Harbison and Pekar (1998) find, the percentage of the annual revenue of the 1,000 largest US companies earned from alliances grew from less than 2 per cent in 1980 to 19 per cent by 1996 and was expected to reach 35 per cent by 2002. With respect to predictions for the future, survey research indicates that managers consider alliances primary vehicles for growth (Schifrin 2001). These illustrations imply that firms cannot create value on a stand-alone basis; the way business is conducted today is based on partnerships.

The rationales for engaging in alliances shift with economic and industry developments (Doz and Hamel 1998). During the 1970s for example, firms focused on product performance (i.e. efficiency and quality) and engaged in alliances to obtain access to technology and new domestic and international markets, as well as to realize market stability. During the 1980s, the focus shifted to obtaining flexible market positions, as continuing globalization, increasing competition and more demanding customers required firms to become flexible. Their alliances provided flexibility, deployed to build industry stature, consolidate industry positions and gain economies of scale and scope. Then during the 1990s and 2000s, firms switched their attention to learning and capability development for innovation; they began using alliances to ensure a constant stream of prospects for advancing technology, proactively maximize value, optimize their total cost for product or customer segments and gain an ability to respond to changing internal and external conditions. More recent upsurges in alliance activity appear triggered by a focus on corporate social responsibility: alliances help firms comply with institutional and market demands for sustainability. Regardless of the rationale, though, the strategic value of alliances is apparent, especially in a contemporary context of rapidly growing and changing markets, global competition, network organizations and dynamic, complex, expensive technologies.

Today alliances represent strategic instruments that offer various advantages (see Table 1.2). Firms enter alliances to access valuable and complementary resources they do not already possess (Das and Teng 2000b), including capital, technology and specialized knowledge. To expand product volume and achieve economies of scale, firms also establish partnerships. Furthermore, they might engage in alliances to reduce operational and strategic risks, accelerate internal growth or increase speed to market. Alliances also can function as learning vehicles, providing a means to obtain, exchange and harvest knowledge (Lubatkin *et al.* 2001). They can even shift external dependencies to the firm's advantage by blocking competitors or inducing group-to-group competition (Gimeno 2004). If an alliance offers legitimacy and reputation effects (Stuart 2000), it can reinforce the firm's corporate social responsibility policies

TABLE 1.2 Advantages and disadvantages of alliances

Advantages	*Disadvantages*
− *Access to resources*: Firms form alliances to gain access to capital, specialized skills, market and technological knowledge, or production facilities, which can help them focus on core competences.	− *Loss of proprietary information*: Proprietary information can be lost to a partner who is a competitor or eventually will become one.
− *Economies of scale*: High fixed costs require firms to collaborate to expand production volume.	− *Management complexities*: Because alliances require the combined effort of multiple firms, they entail coordination complexities, often resulting in conflicts, frustrations and costly delays.
− *Risk and cost sharing*: Alliances enable firms to share the risk and cost of particular investments.	− *Financial and organizational risks*: The opportunistic behaviour of partners can undermine the value creation logic of an alliance. Inter-organizational routines also may make it difficult for a firm to act independently.
− *Access to a (foreign) market*: Partnering with another firm is often the only way to obtain access to a (foreign) market.	
− *Learning*: Alliances offer firms an opportunity to learn from their partners; for example lean manufacturing, product development, management know-how or technology capabilities.	− *Risk of becoming dependent*: A power imbalance arises if one partner becomes overly dependent on the other. This situation increases the risk of opportunism, exploitation, and (hostile) acquisitions.
	− *Loss of decision autonomy*: Joint planning and decision making may result in a loss of decision-making autonomy and control.
− *Speed to market*: Firms with complementary skills collaborate to increase speed to market and capture first-mover advantages.	− *Loss of flexibility*: Establishing an alliance with one partner may prevent partnerships with other potential firms.

(Continued)

TABLE 1.2 *(Continued)*

Advantages	*Disadvantages*
– *Reputation*: Firms form alliances to increase their reputation and legitimization. Lobbying activities and collective pressure prompt governments to adopt policies that favour specific industries.	– *Antitrust implications*: The benefits of alliances disappear if they are challenged on antitrust grounds. Some countries have strict regulations that prohibit certain business relationships.
– *Neutralizing or blocking competitors*: Firms can gain competencies and market power to neutralize or block the moves of a competitor (e.g. entry barriers).	– *Learning barriers*: Although alliances provide access to knowledge, learning barriers may make it difficult to integrate and exploit new knowledge.
– *Assessing acquisition partner*: Alliances offer a way to know a potential acquisition candidate better and decrease information asymmetry.	– *Long-term viability*: Despite predetermined objectives and end dates, internal and external contingencies often cause premature termination.
– *Flexibility*: Alliances provide more flexibility than hierarchies and markets and are subject to less regulation than mergers and acquisitions.	

Source: Adapted from Barringer and Harrison (2000).

and lobbying activities (London *et al.* 2006). Finally, alliances offer a way to assess potential acquisition partners, in that shared experiences reduce the costs related to integration. Thus alliances provide more flexibility than hierarchies or markets and are subject to less regulation than mergers and acquisitions.

However, alliance activity creates several disadvantages. For example, firms may lose proprietary information to a competitor, which weakens their competitive advantage (Kale *et al.* 2000); the managerial complexities due to reciprocal and interdependent relationships may create substantial coordination costs that jeopardize joint value creation (Gulati and Singh 1998); their voluntarily collaboration increases the risk of opportunistic conduct, which undermines value appropriation efforts (Wathne and Heide 2000); firms can become locked into a relationship, reducing their bargaining power; and the loss of decision autonomy could inhibit the firm's ability to steer the alliance toward its own objectives (Glaister *et al.* 2003), just as the loss of organizational flexibility may restrain its ability to pursue alternative, potentially more valuable arrangements. Furthermore, laws and regulations often inhibit an alliance's potential (Oxley 1999), and inter-firm learning may be difficult due to learning barriers that limit a firm's absorptive capacity (Hamel 1991). Finally, unforeseen internal and external contingencies constitute a threat to long-term stability (Das and Teng 2000a).

Alliance failure

Paradoxically, even as firms increase their focus on and use of alliances, their failure rates seem to keep climbing (Hoang and Rothaermel 2005; Pekar and Allio 1994). Researchers report failure rates as high as 70 per cent (Harrigan 1988), though in other settings, Franko (1971) and Killing (1983) find 24 and 30 per cent premature alliance dissolutions, respectively. Porter (1987) considers 33 randomly chosen US firms, a sample that produced a dissolution rate of 50.3 per cent during 1950–1986. Kok and Wildeman (1997) and Dacin *et al.* (1997) calculate approximately 60 per cent failure rates for alliances, whereas Park and Ungson (1997) find a dissolution rate of 43 per cent during 1979–1995 among a US–Japanese sample. De Man (2005) reports an average failure rate of 52 per cent for a sample of 140 European and US firms. These reports in combination confirm that even if firms consider alliances attractive methods to achieve their objectives, they are subject to widespread failure and premature dissolution.

A plethora of factors contribute to or inhibit the achievement of superior performance (Hoffmann and Schlosser 2001; Robson *et al.* 2002). For example, the success or failure of alliances might be attributed to environmental contingencies (Koza and Lewin 1998), the cultural distance between partners (Barkema *et al.* 1996), broad or narrow alliance scopes (Khanna 1998), the alliance contract (Hagedoorn and Hesen 2007), the governance form adopted (Sampson 2004a), emerging alliance instability (Das and Teng 2000a), management control (Yan and Gray 1994), the quality of the working relationship (Ariño *et al.* 2001) or learning processes (Lane *et al.* 2001). We postulate that whereas premature dissolution results from mismanagement and ad hoc decision making, alliance success stems from the adoption of a systematic approach to alliance management.

Specifically, we address three key reasons that encompass this plethora of potential deal breakers. First, failure stems from a lack of understanding of the potential pitfalls and hazards that pertain to the different alliance development stages. Alliances typically develop through a sequence of stages, and during each, partner firms direct their attention to specific design and management decisions. For example, during the alliance strategy formulation stage, decisions should focus on developing a business proposition and selecting an appropriate governance mode (i.e. make, buy or ally). But during the alliance management stage, decisions instead must focus on the day-to-day operations. Second, failure can be attributed to an unawareness of the unique challenges imposed on them by different alliance objectives, diverging partner firm characteristics and unique alliance contexts. For example, whereas learning alliances require firms to focus on knowledge sharing and protection mechanisms, co-branding alliances necessitate that they direct their attention toward reputation management. Third, alliance failure is more likely when firms neglect the institutionalization of their alliance know-how and know-what – which we refer to as alliance capabilities. For example, firms that possess strong alliance capabilities, implying that they have invested in an alliance function, databases and checklists, tend to outperform firms without these capabilities.

To reap the benefits from alliances, firms must deal systematically with these three issues, which will enable them to achieve, efficiently and effectively, a good design and management approach to their alliance relationships. Observing the high failure rates in practice, it seems, however, that firms are not sufficiently prepared. Therefore we need an academically grounded framework that offers a coherent understanding of the unique nature of strategic alliance management.

An academically grounded alliance development framework

Before and during alliance development, managers confront varied, unique decision-making situations. Each situation requires that firms conceptualize it in terms of problem, solutions and implementation. That is, firms must tackle any situation by defining the problem, developing a set of solutions, selecting one solution, and then implementing it efficiently and effectively. To this end, they need to be aware of decision-making rationales, that is, the underlying principles, guidelines and theories that may inform their decision. Academic research is rife with theories that attempt to explain these decision-making rationales; we draw on theories from alliance literature to discuss the decision-making content, the alternatives, and the theoretical rationales for these various alternatives. In addition, decision makers in firms must understand the necessary steps for arriving at an appropriate solution, which we refer to as decision-making steps. Management literature is informative in this context. By combining these varied concepts and research streams, we propose an academically grounded framework for strategic alliance management that consists of three main parts: (1) alliance development stages, (2) unique decision-making situations, and (3) alliance capabilities.

Alliance development stages

The foundation details the development stages through which alliances progress. Building on prior alliance development literature (D'Aunno and Zuckerman 1987; Das and Teng 2002; Dyer *et al.* 2001; Kanter 1994), we distinguish seven stages: (1) alliance strategy formulation, (2) alliance partner selection, (3) alliance negotiation, (4) alliance design, (5) alliance management, (6) alliance evaluation and (7) alliance termination (see Figure 1.1). Each development stage depicts a specific decision-making situation that requires unique know-what and know-how. An alliance transforms and proceeds to the next stage only after it has achieved the objectives of the preceding stage. Thus, each development stage is characterized by specific issues and requires specific decision-making rationales and steps.

Alliances are however purposeful entities that can learn and adapt to changing circumstances indicating that alliance development also entails a repetitive sequence of goal formulation, implementation, and modification, based on lessons learned or changed intentions among the partner firms (Ariño and de la Torre 1998). The alliance development framework incorporates a cyclical approach, such that the seven stages remain interlinked through learning and adaptation. All decisions made in one stage have effects on subsequent stages, and alliance development can

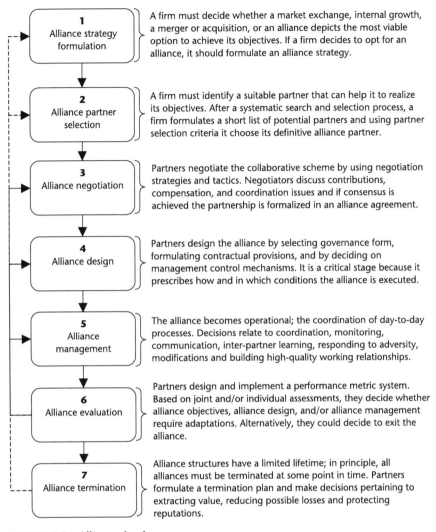

FIGURE 1.1   Alliance development stages

follow an iterative development path, such that stages may be revisited if needed. Alliance failure often results when organizations skip one or more stages and/or managers fail to complete their decision-making tasks for each development stage. Management thus plays a critical role (i.e. decision making) in successful alliances, as organizations must be actively managed and guided through various stages to increase chances for success.

Chapters 2 to 8 present the foundation of our alliance development framework and details, for each development stage, the content and steps associated with decision-making situations. Before engaging in an alliance, a firm must conduct a strategic analysis to determine the appropriate governance mode (Chapter 2). A firm then conducts a partner analysis to select an appropriate partner (Chapter

3). Building on these two pre-design stages, the firm starts alliance negotiations (Chapter 4), with the result that the outcomes of the negotiations are formalized in an alliance design (Chapter 5), which provides the foundation for alliance management (Chapter 6). As the alliance develops, performance assessments are required to monitor the relationship's progress (Chapter 7) and the firm must manage the alliance dissolution too (Chapter 8).

Unique decision-making situations

Because each alliance is surrounded by unique circumstances, we augment our framework by elaborating on unique decision-making situations. Distinct alliance objectives, alliances with different types of partners and specific alliance contexts are likely to require idiosyncratic know-what and know-how, so we must offer more detail in our framework. We first focus on alliance objectives and their management challenges, as distinct alliance objectives impose constraints on decision-making within each alliance development stage. We detail on supplier alliances (Chapter 9), learning alliances (Chapter 10), and co-branding alliances (Chapter 11). In addition, the impact of partner characteristics on decision-making is discussed, as diverging philosophies, orientations and backgrounds between partners constitute a potential barrier to effective decision-making. We detail on international alliances (Chapter 11), asymmetrical alliances (Chapter 12), cross-sector alliances (Chapter 13) and multi-partner alliances (Chapter 14). Furthermore the alliance context is critical, as conditions outside the alliance tend to obstruct or accelerate alliance-decision making. Therefore, specific attention is given to alliance portfolios (Chapter 16), alliance networks (Chapter 17) and alliance co-evolution (Chapter 18). Other alliance objectives, partner characteristics and alliance contexts may affect strategic alliance management as well, but we suggest that taken together these chapters present a coherent overview covering a wide-range of topics. All chapters are replete with illustrative case descriptions.

Alliance capabilities

The ability to create successful alliances, which reflects learning about alliance management and then leveraging alliance knowledge within the company, constitutes an alliance capability. To build alliance capabilities, organizations must not only learn and manage alliances but also exploit their own alliance competences appropriately. Firms that capitalize on their prior experience with alliances likely develop and deploy their alliance capabilities, and, therefore tend to outperform firms without alliance experience or capabilities. Chapter 19 defines alliance capabilities, details why they are important, describes decision-making in terms of building and deploying alliance capabilities, and ends with a case illustration.

Whereas the preceding chapters offer knowledge about strategic alliance management, we acknowledge that high-performing alliances require more than preset solutions. In Chapter 20, we postulate that, in addition to academic

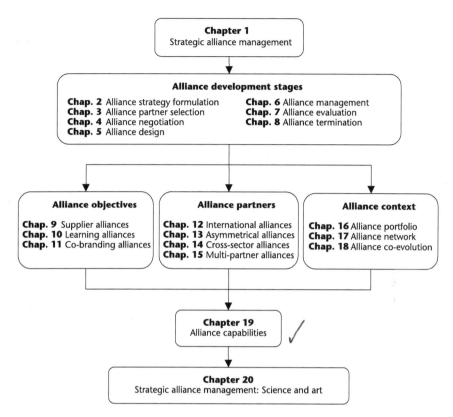

FIGURE 1.2   Structure of the book

knowledge, a manager's experience, expertise and creativity are critical to resolve three paradoxes inherently tied to alliance relationships. That is, alliance managers need to deal with three pairs of contending forces: cooperative versus competitive, economic versus social and deliberate versus emergent. We provide an understanding in how managers can resolve these alliance paradoxes. We conclude the book with themes likely to become salient to the future of strategic alliance management. Taken together, an advanced introduction to the science and art of strategic alliances, this book takes readers on a guided tour of strategic alliance management, as we depict in Figure 1.2.

2

ALLIANCE STRATEGY FORMULATION

During the alliance strategy formulation stage, a firm decides which governance mode is appropriate for realizing its objectives, that is, how it will organize the procurement of its desired resources. We distinguish three prototypical types: 'make', such that firms gather resources internally through inter-unit exchanges or through mergers and acquisitions; 'buy', which means firms procure resources through discrete market transactions organized by simple contracts; and 'ally', which refers to alliance arrangements organized through complex contracts with external parties to procure resources. This chapter is divided as follows: to inform their decisions about alliance strategy formulation, managers must understand the difference between alternative governance modes (first section) and comprehend the rationales underpinning each of them (second section). When a firm adopts the ally governance mode, it also must formulate an alliance strategy to detail the requirements that the alliance should meet. We therefore wind up this chapter with three sections describing a set of decision-making steps, a summary for alliance strategy formulation and a case illustration.

Three prototypical governance modes

In the context of governance modes, a firm's boundary pertains to its demarcation from its external environment, though these boundaries are constantly subject to change as firms rearrange their portfolios of activities to achieve their objectives. Such restructuring occurs through three types of prototypical governance modes that define exchanges and that we compare in Table 2.1: make, buy, and ally[1] (Gulati and Nickerson 2008).

The 'make' governance mode indicates that firms seek to realize their objectives through internal procurement (Gulati and Nickerson 2008). For example, in inter-unit exchanges firms autonomously invest in and develop their existing resources and capabilities to market their products and services. Prior to their internal procurement though, some firms internalize previously external resources by engaging in mergers and acquisitions. In such a transaction, two firms agree to integrate their operations because they possess resources that, when combined, create synergies. Through internal procurement, organizations obtain property rights and thus a competitive advantage, because they can develop products and services out of sight of competitors. In this case, they also might attain control over their margins and markets. However, the 'make' decision imposes hazards on the firm, in that it might increase the level of bureaucracy because the firm has full control over an activity (Williamson 1991). It also reduces flexibility; building or integrating new resources requires substantial investments, which may be difficult to recoup if the firm fails.

The 'buy' governance mode instead implies that firms procure resources through discrete market transactions, organized in the form of a simple contract. Market transactions are well suited to exchanging commodities, because 'supply and demand' governs the exchange. The exchange is organized by price (Powell 1990), so the level of organizational and financial integration between the transacting firms is low. Because markets process information efficiently, buyers gain good access to different types of relevant information, including prices, alternative suppliers and quality. However, market transactions also involve potential hazards. The main disadvantage of the 'buy' governance mode therefore pertains to the opposing objectives of the transacting organizations: The buying firm aims to lower costs, whereas the selling organization hopes to increase revenues. The conflict may induce opportunistic behaviour and increase transaction costs. Furthermore, markets may fail in response to the uncertainty surrounding the supply of resources; information asymmetries between buyers and suppliers may result in higher prices; and suppliers may use their market power to increase their margins.

Finally, the third governance mode, 'ally', suggests that firms establish alliances with external parties to obtain access to desired resources. Alliances provide a viable alternative when internal and external conditions lead the firm to desire some degree of control over the resources but not to internalize them. For example, when markets fail, firms may use an alliance to obtain access to external resources. Alliances offer several advantages: An alliance governance mode enables a firm to access complementary resources, without obtaining proprietary rights. It provides the firm with speed and flexibility in obtaining access and exploiting desired resources. Furthermore, through collaborations, firms can share investments, which may reduce risk. However, sharing resources may also impose the risk of creating increased competition. Furthermore, it may be difficult to integrate learning into the firm, and the long-term viability of an alliance is questionable. When partners have reaped the benefits from the relationship, they are then likely to terminate it.

The three governance modes offer alternative strategic options for building and sustaining a competitive advantage. However, it is also important to note the plethora of intermediate governance forms on the make–buy continuum (Powell 1990). For example, alliances constitute a hybrid governance mode between hierarchy and market exchanges, whereas joint ventures (i.e. where two firms establish a new

TABLE 2.1 Prototypical governance modes: Make, buy, and ally

	Make	Buy	Ally
Form	Internal growth	Market	Alliance
Description	Activities and resources developed internally	Activities and resources procured through a market transaction	Access to activities and resources obtained through collaboration with external firm(s)
Coordination	Hierarchy	Price	Relational (supplemented with hierarchical and price)
Characteristics	– No or limited interdependencies with external organizations – Full control over resources	– Low interdependencies with external organizations – Full control over all resources	– High interdependencies with external organizations – Partial control over all resources
Advantages	– Proprietary rights and ownership – Protecting and building competences – Adaptation to internal and external demands	– Quick access to commodities – Efficient information processing – High powered incentives	– Quick access to complementary resources – Speed and flexibility – Shared investments and risks
Downside	– Slow and costly development – Uncertainty – Limited growth and expansion	– High transaction costs due to market failure – High uncertainty – Inseparability of resources – Information asymmetries – Subject to market power	– Shared returns – Lack of control – Questionable long-term viability – Difficult to integrate learning – Need for performance monitoring

Additional "Merger & acquisition" form details (under Make/Buy spectrum):

Merger & acquisition — Activities and resources internalized through a transaction in which two firms agree to merge. Coordination: Hierarchy.
Characteristics: – Relatively few interdependencies with external organizations after integration – Full control over resources.
Advantages: – Quick access to similar markets – Authority over activity – Tax benefits – Small impact on industry capacity – Building competences.
Downside: – Required finances – Complex negotiation and integration challenges – Bureaucracy – Loss of flexibility and high risk – High failure costs.

Sources: Gulati and Nickerson (2008); Powell (1990); Williamson (1991).

organizational entity) tend to verge on hierarchical governance. In contrast, licence agreements are more closely associated with market exchange. Despite these varied intermediate forms, the logic for choosing a governance mode can rely mainly on the three prototypical types.

Governance mode rationales

Numerous theoretical perspectives permeate alliance literature, providing rationales for cooperative strategies and governance mode decisions. Contingent on a theory's assumptions and related key constructs, each theory provides alternative explanations. For reasons of parsimony, we focus here on seven theoretical perspectives that tend to dominate alliance literature: (1) transaction cost economics, (2) the resource-based view, (3) resource dependence, (4) strategic management theory, (5) social network theory, (6) the organizational learning perspective, and (7) institutional theory.

Transaction cost economics (TCE)

TCE offers a coherent framework for exploring choices of governance modes (Williamson 1975; Williamson 1991). It stresses efficiency and cost minimization rationales for cooperation and advances insights by recognizing the role of partners' motives, the nature of the investments and the specific character of the transactions. It states that transaction costs should be minimized when a governance mode matches the transaction exchange conditions. These costs of running the economic system include both ex-ante and ex-post costs (Williamson 1985). The ex-ante costs relate mainly to drafting, negotiating and safeguarding a contractual agreement; whereas the ex-post costs entail the time and resources invested in repairing misalignments and bonding. In this sense, transaction costs differ from production costs, which are generated from the primary functions of the organization, that is, producing goods and services.

Two assumptions and three exchange conditions constitute the core of TCE logic. The first assumption involves opportunism, or behaviour that is self-interested and deceptive. The logic thus holds that managers are inclined to break, whether implicitly and explicitly, the rules that govern a transaction. A second assumption refers to bounded rationality. That is, despite the firm's efforts to deal with complexity and unpredictability, managers have only limited ability to plan for the future and predict various contingencies that may arise. The potential for opportunistic behaviour and the constraints of bounded rationality pose severe problems for governing transactions, because they drive transaction costs higher and require firms to protect themselves against exploitation. Accordingly, TCE predicts that distinct transactions with variations in frequency, asset specificity and uncertainty demand alternative governance modes to be organized efficiently. Frequency refers to the number of exchanges that constitute the transaction. Asset specificity occurs when investments specifically support an exchange relationship, such that if the relationship were to be terminated, the value of these assets would be largely lost. Finally, uncertainty implies that the consequences of a situation are unpredictable.

If market transactions dominate, exchanges are likely to be straightforward and non-repetitive and require few transaction-specific investments. In such conditions, the market itself, backed by contract law, can provide effective safeguards. However, if transactions produce uncertain outcomes, recur frequently, and require substantial investments (i.e. asset specificity), they can be organized more efficiently through hierarchical governance. The transaction costs for market exchanges are greater than those of long-term relational exchanges, so increased transaction costs should prompt a shift from external to internal governance. A vulnerable firm that lacks information its exchange partners already have may benefit similarly from internalizing transactions or activities. However, if a transaction involves mixed asset specificity and recurs, an alliance, a form of hybrid governance, is likely to be the appropriate governance mode. Such hybrid governance modes demand mutual dependence, mutual commitments to resource contributions, and accepted compensation mechanisms. Although alliances thus offer advantages, including the avoidance of uncertainty caused by market failure, their uneasy control position implies an inherent instability.

Critics of TCE also refer to governance mode decisions, however (see e.g. David and Han 2004; Ghoshal and Moran 1996; Weitz and Jap 1995; de Wulf and Odekerken-Schroder 2001):

1. Studies that draw on different conceptualizations of asset specificity and uncertainty produce some mixed results. Masten *et al.* (1991) find that vertical integration in the shipbuilding industry became more likely in the presence of relationship-specific human capital, but Joskow's (1985) research suggests that physical and site specificity increase the length of contracts among coal suppliers. Moreover, TCE fails to recognize the potential value of transaction-specific investments (Madhok and Tallman 1998), even if the value creation potential of an alliance outweighs the costs associated with coordination and protection. In contrast with TCE-based predictions, Russo (1992) indicates that uncertainty relates negatively to backward integration, even as Poppo and Zenger (2002) argue that when uncertainty interacts with asset specificity and relational norms, the likelihood of relational exchanges increases. Clearly more empirical testing is called for.

2. TCE may place too much emphasis on opportunistic behaviour (Ghoshal and Moran 1996), neglecting the role of relational governance (Heide and John 1992) and emphasizing hierarchical control as a protection against opportunism, even if trust reduces transaction costs and makes alliances more suitable governance modes.

3. Only limited evidence really shows that governance modes aligned with exchange conditions outperform misaligned governance modes (David and Han 2004), such as when Sampson (2004a) reveals that governance modes designed to match the predictions of TCE experience improved innovation performance compared with misaligned governance modes.

Resource-based view (RBV)

A firm can maximize its value by pooling and exploiting its valuable resources. According to the RBV, firms attempt to find an optimal resource boundary that ensures the value of their resources is realized best, compared with other resource combinations (Barney 1991). A competitive advantage results when the firm can implement a value-creating strategy (Hitt *et al.* 2000) that is not being implemented simultaneously by its (potential) competitors. Specifically, a competitive advantage requires the firm to possess valuable, scarce, not imitable and non-substitutable resources. Such characteristics also imply that the resources are difficult to move across firm boundaries, such that they constitute barriers to external procurement. Thus market exchanges are not pivotal in the RBV; resources subject to such transactions tend instead to be available, mobile and imitable, and their acquisition does not increase the firm's competitive advantage. If all desirable resources were available for acquisition through market exchange at fair prices, it would be unwise for firms to get involved in alliances, which usually entail high governance costs and some sacrifice of organizational control. Therefore, the RBV seems particularly appropriate for examining alliances or mergers and acquisitions; firms engage in boundary-spanning activities to access and obtain resources that they do not own but need in order to strengthen their competitive position.

In turn the RBV defines both merger and acquisitions and alliances as strategies for gaining access to other firms' resources, for the purpose of bringing them together and attaining otherwise unavailable value (Das and Teng 2000b). When a firm does not possess the entire bundle of resources and capabilities it needs, markets cannot bundle the required resources or alternatives to attaining those resources are too costly, then it engages in mergers and acquisitions, or alliances. Mergers and acquisitions and alliances work toward the same overall objective, namely, obtaining resources, but the RBV suggest that two conditions particularly favour alliances. First, an alliance constitutes a more viable alternative when not all the resources owned by the target are valuable to the firm. Second, disposing of redundant or less valuable resources induces a cost, because such resources may be tied to the desired resources. Alliances enable the focal firm to obtain only its desired resources, while bypassing undesired ones.

Furthermore, unlike mergers and acquisitions, alliances enable firms to protect their own valuable resources. For example, if a firm wants to exploit certain resources but lacks the competences to do so, alliances help them retain those resources and capitalize on their value, only temporarily giving up control. The firm retains its access to its valuable resources and can exploit them for future internal development. Alliances thus form when the realized value of resources contributed to the alliance is greater than their value when realized through internal uses or relinquishment. This scenario is especially likely for resources characterized by imperfect mobility; resources which are inimitable and non-substitutable.

Of course, with respect to governance mode decisions, there are also criticisms of the RBV. First, even though prior RBV research offers a plethora of resources (e.g.

reputation, culture, brands, organizational routines) that might contribute to a firm's competitive advantage, systematic empirical testing of their impact on governance decisions is relatively scarce (see for an exception Villalonga and McGahan 2005). Second, the RBV primarily focuses on the possession of resources, not the costs of resource deployment, even though using resources, whether autonomously or collaboratively, imposes coordination and value appropriation costs. Although a complete RBV theory related to governance decisions is thus lacking (Das and Teng 2000b), we note that it contributes valuable insights to value creation within alliances. For a coherent RBV, further substantial conceptual and empirical research is required.

Resource dependence perspective (RDP)

The RDP is rooted in an open system framework: firms are embedded sets of relationships, which render them dependent on their external environment (Pfeffer and Salancik 1978). According to Aldrich and Pfeffer (1976), firms cannot generate all the resources or functions they need to maintain themselves, so they must enter into transactions and relations with external actors that can supply those required resources. A firm's ability to control external resources determines its survival and provides power over external parties. Power originates through resource scarcity, which reflects three sources. First, the importance of an external resource – or the extent to which the firm needs the resource to survive – reduces a firm's relative power. In particular, intangible resources such as patents, trademarks, market or technological know-how, and human competences tend to be pivotal, whereas tangible resources, such as commodities, can be effectively obtained through market exchanges. Second, a firm's discretion over the resource allocation and use (e.g. ownership rights, access) increases its relative power. Third, the extent to which desired resources can be substituted by alternative resources decreases the firm's relative power. With this focus on desired resources, the RDP contributes insights into why firms engage in mergers and acquisitions and alliances.

At the heart of the RDP rests the notion that two firms prefer to avoid becoming dependent on each other's resources (Blankenburg Holm et al. 1999). To reduce uncertainty and increase its relative power, a firm may seek to become autonomous by managing its external relationships with a two-fold strategy to acquire control over (1) critical resources to decrease dependence on other firms and (2) resources that increase the dependence of other firms on it. Mergers and acquisitions and alliances can help execute this dual strategy. When firms ally to obtain access to critical resources, their long-term relationship probably enables them to exercise some degree of external control, though mergers and acquisitions should be preferable when the firm needs more control over its partner (Finkelstein 1997). Alliances provide a firm with more flexibility and options to scale investments up or down; mergers and acquisitions offer more control over joint resources (Yin and Shanley 2008). With flexible arrangements, firms can take advantage of changed circumstances, but they lose the capability to exploit opportunities. Commitment and control over resources offer other benefits, but again at a cost: the potential loss of investment and foregone opportunities. Thus, though resource scarcity may encourage competition between firms, it also may stimulate cooperation, producing mergers and acquisitions that aim to increase command over external resources or alliances based on mutual support rather than domination.

We also note two main limitations of the RDP. First, despite the intuitive understanding it offers of rationales for distinct governance modes, strong empirical evidence about the distinct conditions that favour specific governance modes remains lacking (Fink *et al.* 2006). For example, internalizing resources through mergers and acquisitions could increase independence, but it may also impose high costs, because acquiring capabilities tends to be expensive, and integrating capabilities takes time and effort. Similarly, obtaining resources through market exchange increases a firm's dependence on its external environment, yet the costs are relatively low. Second, the RDP tends to neglect the importance of prior relationships, even though social connectedness may affect alliance formation decisions (Gulati 1995b). An account that focuses only on interdependence cannot explain how firms learn about new alliances and overcome the threats of partnerships. The RDP implicitly assumes that all information is freely available and equally accessible and thus that firms have equal opportunities to ally. Despite these critiques, the RDP provides a clear indication that a firm's survival depends on its ability to command external resources. A firm is effective when it resolves the trade-off between flexibility (i.e. market exchange and alliance) and commitment (i.e. internalization), while also satisfying the demands of partners in its environment on which it relies most, and which contribute most to its existence.

Strategic management theory (SMT)

To maximize their competitive strength, firms may adopt distinct governance modes, though their underlying motives tend to converge. Therefore, the SMT imagines the governance mode decision as a trade-off among distinct strategic motives, even if the strategic motives identified by SMT literature tend to be similar across modes. For example, Walter and Barney (1990) provide a list of strategic drivers for mergers and acquisitions, and Glaister and Buckley (1996) issue a similar list of strategic (and learning) motives that drive alliance formation. For parsimony, we focus on key strategic motives for alliances.

In this setting, the SMT cites the need for prospective partners to achieve synergies across their business strategies, such that an alliance can contribute to the realization of their strategic objectives. Reasons to establish partnerships are vast: short-term efficiency, resource access, market position, geographical expansion, risk reduction, competitive blockades, economies of scale, speed to market, minimized transaction costs, shared investments and so on. To organize these reasons, Barringer and Harrison (2000) divide the strategic motives to form alliances into four internally focused categories:

1. *Increase market power.* By erecting entry barriers or forming clusters with other firms, alliances enable firms to adopt monopoly-like behaviour and increase their market power.
2. *Increase political power.* Individual firms team up to influence governing bodies more effectively, whether nationally or internationally.
3. *Increase efficiency.* Being able to tap into others' resources and share the load can result in significant reductions of costs and economies of scale. Such partnerships often focus on production, though they also might include marketing or even pre-competitive research.
4. *Differentiation.* Partnerships within and across sectors in pursuit of new customers and innovation enable firms to differentiate offers from those of competitors.

Faulkner (1995) also recognizes external strategic motives. For example, globalization and regionalization increase international turbulence and uncertainty, such that firms confront the need for vast (financial) resources to deal with technological changes and shorter product life cycles.

Burgeoning literature on strategic management thus offers many relevant insights, including analyses of the reasons for establishing alliances, alliance objectives, and areas of potential conflict. Despite this focus on strategic motives, few studies provide clear-cut insights into governance mode decisions. Whereas the breadth of SMT constitutes one of its greatest strengths, it also represents its greatest weakness: motivations arising from nearly all other perspectives can be incorporated into the SMT, and its underlying logic could be applied to any governance mode. For example, realizing economies of scale implies forward/backward integration through mergers and acquisitions and alliances, as also explained by TCE. Increasing political power reflects an institutional stream of thought, and obtaining and accessing resources relates to the RBV. Thus though the SMT provides theoretical and managerial insights in the strategic rationales that underlie alliance formation, its primary contribution is its pragmatism.

Social network theory (SNT)

The social context that surrounds prior alliances influences alliance formation decisions (Gulati 1995b). Thus SNT views firms not as stand-alone entities but rather according to their location within the network of inter-organizational relationships that determine their success and survival. Although SNT has not developed sufficiently to inform governance mode decisions, it asserts that a firm's social network facilitates new alliances by providing valuable information about the location of critical resources and the partner's reliability. Repeated collaborations might provide information that helps firms learn about new opportunities and enhance their trust in current and potential partners, though indirect relationships through common partners also function as important referral mechanisms. Recognizing the ambiguities and uncertainty associated with alliances, access to valuable information thus might lower search costs and alleviate risks of opportunism, which can make firms more likely to enter alliances.

In the social network, potential partners become aware of one another's existence, as well as their needs, capabilities and alliance requirements. Social networks also provide information about partners' reliability. For example, a partner that behaves opportunistically imposes greater risk on any firm that enters into an alliance with it, but a rich social network contains clues about past behaviours, so the firm can incorporate the partner's network reputation into its alliance formation decision. Although SNT thus offers a novel view on alliance formation, we find again that the empirical evidence is virtually absent, in this case with regard to how distinct social network resources prompt distinct governance mode decisions. For example, are firms with central positions in an inter-firm network, which gives them access to high-quality information (i.e. superior network resources), more inclined to establish hierarchical governance modes, compared with firms with more peripheral network positions? Yet SNT offers a relevant explanation for the emergence of alliances: social networks (of prior alliances) function as conduits for valuable information and thus play an important role in shaping future alliance formation.

Organizational learning perspective (OLP)

Firms might enter into partnerships primarily to learn new skills or acquire tacit knowledge (Hamel 1991). According to the OLP, firms form alliances because the superior knowledge they can gain will enhance their competitive position. Firms that place a high priority on the acquisition of intangible knowledge (e.g. technological know-how) are likely to consider alliances important instruments, because in alliances, learning occurs on both macro and micro levels (Knight 2002). At the macro level, alliances provide a means for firms to share and acquire knowledge, which may improve their competitiveness and profitability. At the micro level of analysis, interpersonal links offer members of the firms an opportunity to share and learn skills from one another. That is, alliances might add value to firms by providing (1) the possibility for firm innovation and enhancement and (2) employees with the chance to exchange professional practices that can show them how to perform their tasks better.

In terms of governance mode preferences though, OLP insights are less conclusive. In general, hierarchical governance modes appear more appropriate for learning rather than market exchanges, because learning requires long-term and frequent interactions. However, alliances constitute a particularly effective means for knowledge exchange, particularly if that knowledge cannot be obtained easily in the market (Mowery et al. 1996) or internally developed. An alliance is preferable if the desired knowledge is tacit and difficult to evaluate; internal learning may prevent novel insights. Thus a firm that wants to learn a particular skill stands a better chance of doing so if it forms an alliance with an expert firm and can absorb external knowledge (Deeds and Hill 1996). Yet OLP neglects the costs and risks of learning through alliances. In particular, knowledge transfers demand substantial investments in training, education, relationship building and organizational adaptations (Lane and Lubatkin 1998). The risks pertain primarily to the unwanted transfer of proprietary knowledge, because firms in a learning alliance may compete for valuable knowledge (Hamel 1991). Thus, the gains from learning alliances must be balanced against the pains of the dilution of firm-specific resources, the deterioration of integrative capabilities and the high demands on management attention.

Institutional theory (IT)

With an open system perspective, IT states that firms are strongly influenced by their external environments (Scott 2003). Influenced by economic factors, such as industry regulations, rival behaviour, and socially constructed norms and beliefs, firms organize their boundary-spanning activities to mimic other firms. That is, firms pursue activities that increase their legitimacy and cause them to appear in agreement with the prevailing rules, requirements, and norms in their business environments (Dimaggio and Powell 1983), as these rules establish bases for production, exchange, and distribution. With this logic, IT can answer how and why firms adopt distinct governance modes, such as alliances for example. In particular, this school of thought states that alliances aim for legitimacy and social approval, rather than effectiveness or efficiency. Legitimacy in the alliance process helps ensure that the initiative receives a certain level of acceptance; without it, the initiative is unlikely to persist. Such legitimacy can be enhanced by governance mode decisions, because partnering with well-known, reputed partners improve the focal firm's reputation or congruence with prevailing norms. Common alliance practices thus emerge as collaborating becomes a more widely accepted and desirable phenomenon, and firms copy rivals in their use of this strategy (Teng 2005).

When social behaviour becomes accepted, it turns into an institution, and institutions give industry members a clearly laid route to success and lead to a bandwagon effect (Venkatraman *et al.* 1994). Pangarkar and Klein (1998) suggest that bandwagon pressures, which they capture as the proportion of firms in a peer group that undertake alliances and their average number of alliances, influence both the probability and number of alliances a firm undertakes. Such bandwagon pressures also imply a lack of clarity in the firm's cost–benefit calculations. Confronted with bandwagon pressure, firms are likely to adopt the alliance behaviours modelled by their peers indiscriminately to ensure legitimacy, without considering the actual outcomes of their alliance partnerships. Alternatively, this pressure might induce firms to hire managers with similar industry backgrounds and experiences, who are familiar with industry practices.

Beyond bandwagon pressures, firms may engage in status-driven imitations of their peers, especially the alliance behaviour performed by large and prestigious firms. Partnering with an organization that promotes socially desirable objectives may enhance a firm's reputation more widely; high-profile charitable organizations thus can benefit from such a legitimacy strategy. This view of strategic alliances implies a process of mimetic isomorphism: firms follow established rules and norms and copy, consciously or not, the strategies of their successful peers. The resulting legitimacy and reputation can open doors to other relationships that help the firm gain access to additional critical resources.

The IT thus offers a narrow, behaviourally oriented explanation of alliance formation (Barringer and Harrison, 2000). It cannot determine why particular governance modes exist or why firms engage in boundary-spanning activities that deviate from the status quo. Furthermore, if every firm adopts similar governance modes, there is little opportunity for sustainable competitive advantage. In the biotechnology field for example, alliance-based competition has become prevalent, such that firms may experience difficulty in differentiating themselves through alliances. However, IT advances literature with its assertion that firms form alliances to respond to bandwagon pressure and obtain social approval and legitimacy, rather than to realize economic outcomes.

Overview

This concise overview of theoretical perspectives on governance mode decisions reveals the varied and numerous insights have been produced, ranging from economic to behavioural motives (see Table 2.2). Among the economic explanations, TCE focuses on cost minimization, whereas the RBV emphasizes value creation. At the other end of the spectrum, IT offers a behavioural explanation: firms' behaviour is guided by their legitimacy motives. The OLP also adopts a behavioural explanation but also suggests economic undertones with its proposal that inter-firm learning enables firms to reduce costs and improve profitability. The RDP, SMT and SNT fall in the middle of this spectrum. The RDP originates in organizational theory but adopts economic explanations to explain why firms engage in alliances, namely, to gain control over scarce resources. In contrast, the SMT is primarily economically based, but recent studies have incorporated behavioural motives, such as inter-firm learning. Finally, the SNT emphasizes behavioural explanations but also incorporates economic arguments to explain the influence of network resources on alliance formation.

Academics and managers can certainly benefit from considering each theoretical perspective, but by blending them, they also might obtain a more useful understanding of governance mode decisions. For example, if we combine TCE with OLP explanations, we might predict that inter-firm learning will reduce transaction costs (Nooteboom 2004). A blend of OLP with SNT, as exemplified by Powell et al. (1996), indicates that industries with widely dispersed sources of expertise require learning in networks rather than in individual firms. Augmenting TCE with the RBV suggests that cost minimization and value maximization together drive governance mode decisions (Zajac and Olsen 1993). The SNT may be especially open to combinations with other perspectives, such as TCE and RDP, because then it can illustrate how firms create and manage alliances as strategic responses to competitive uncertainties. The IT school of thought also accords with

TABLE 2.2 Theoretical perspectives: Alliance formation

	Transaction cost economics	Resource-based view	Resource dependence perspective	Strategic management theory	Social network theory	Organizational learning perspective	Institutional theory
Description	Firms organize their boundary-spanning activities to minimize transaction costs	Firms organize their boundary-spanning activities to maximize value creation	Firms engage in resource exchanges with external parties to reduce uncertainty and obtain control	Firms forge alliances to achieve synergies between business strategies	Inter-firm networks constitute conduits of information, shaping alliance decisions	Firms engage in inter-firm learning to improve their (core) competences	Firms organize their boundary-spanning activities to conform with prevailing norms imposed by their environment
Alliance formation logic	Alliances reduce uncertainty caused by market failure and reduce costs associated with hierarchy	Alliances create value when procurement of resources is difficult through market or internal development	Alliances enable firms to minimize dependence on external parties or maximize control over scare resources	Alliances enable firms to build and sustain a competitive advantage	Firms use network resources, such as reputation and referral, to inform alliance formation	Alliances function as learning vehicles to access, obtain and exploit (intangible) knowledge	Firms form alliances to obtain legitimization by mimicking competitors' alliance behaviour
Limitations	Neglects social context and value creation motives	Neglects costs and investments of resource deployment	Neglects social context in which exchanges are embedded	Encompasses a variety of strategic motives, tied to other perspectives	Neglects other prototypical types of governance modes	Neglects costs and investments required to enable inter-firm learning	Neglects alternative motives, including economic and strategic
Examples	Toyota supports alliances with key suppliers through co-location	KLM and Northwest integrate Trans-Atlantic airline routes and destinations	Nokia forms alliance with Microsoft to secure access to mobile phone operating system	Google partners with Apple to increase market and block main competitor: Microsoft	Eli-Lilly uses information obtained via its network to select partners and forge new alliances	Mercedes and Swatch exchange technological knowledge to develop SMART	Biotech firms collectively adopt alliances as competitive strategy

Gulati's (1995) findings that alliances form within partner firms' social networks; for example, the strength of a firm's reputation and closeness in the network of past alliances are strong predictors of alliance formation, and the likelihood of alliance formation also relates positively to the complementarity of the partners' capabilities, status similarity, and social capital arising from direct and indirect collaborative experiences. Finally, SMT provides a more holistic perspective and potentially could incorporate elements from the other perspectives. Building on this observation, we outline some managerial implications in the next section.

Alliance strategy formulation: Decision-making steps

During alliance strategy formulation, firms must decide which governance mode fits their objectives and situation. However, governance mode decisions are complex, because firms confront a plethora of reasons, occasionally opposing, that provide support for a specific governance mode. To organize decision-making, we suggest that alliance strategy formulation overall comprises five sequential decision-making steps (see Figure 2.1). If, after careful analysis, a firm prefers an 'ally' governance mode, it must then explicate its alliance strategy and prepare for partner selection.

Step 1: Strategy development

A firm first must decide on its strategy, derived from its mission and its vision. The strategy describes how the firm aims to achieve its long-term objectives. To realize

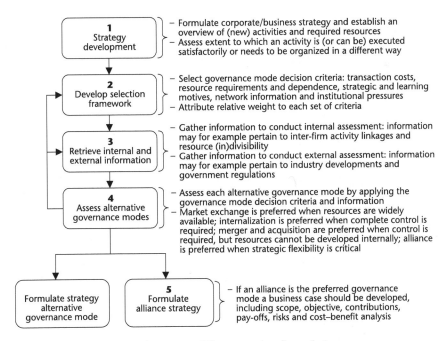

FIGURE 2.1   Decision-making steps: Alliance strategy formulation

those objectives, the firm chooses some primary activities, new and/or existing ones, and identifies resources needed to execute these activities. In turn, a firm must determine the extent to which it is able to execute these activities satisfactorily. Such an overview should grant insights into the objective(s), required tasks, and feasibility to perform the activity. Once a firm has a complete overview, it may enter the next step.

Step 2: Develop a governance mode selection framework

To evaluate and decide on an appropriate governance mode for a specific activity, selected from the overview, it should be clear which decision criteria apply and how they affect the governance mode decision. In particular, decision criteria might be organized according to the theoretical perspectives presented in this chapter. Thus the analysis might include:

1. Transaction-based motives, such as the frequency of the activity, uncertainty surrounding the activity, and degree of asset specificity; an alliance is preferred when a transaction is recurring, surrounded by moderate uncertainty, and requires mixed alliance-specific investments.
2. Resource-based motives, including the nature of existing and desired resources, divisibility of resources, and their availability; an alliance is preferred when an external party possesses valuable and scarce resources (i.e. blocking market exchange), but the desired resources are part of a larger and indivisible resource endowment (i.e. blocking a merger).
3. Dependence-based motives, such as the degree to which existing and desired resources are critical to the activity and freely available; an alliance is preferred when a firm seeks flexible control over external resources.
4. Strategic motives, such as market power, market entry, blocking competitors and international expansion: an alliance is preferred when it enables a firm to realize strategic objectives.
5. Network criteria or information about a potential partner's credibility and reliability and referrals; an alliance (partner) is preferred when a firm receives supportive information via its alliance network.
6. Institutional-based motives, incorporating criteria such as legitimacy, reputation and status; an alliance is preferred when external pressure imposes partnering as common practice.

To complement the selection framework, firms should assign each criterion a relative weight. For example, a firm might decide that obtaining legitimacy outweighs economic benefits; commanding external control over scarce resources outweighs prior established reputations; or acquiring valuable market know-how outweighs improving market position. The choice of governance mode should rely on a cost–benefit analysis of the trade-offs among distinct decision criteria.

Step 3: Retrieve internal and external information

To apply their selection framework, firms should conduct internal and external assessments to obtain the necessary information. The internal analysis involves gathering detailed information within the firm about the nature of the activity, the required resources, inter-firm activity linkages, organizational culture, and systems and procedures. An external analysis should feature information about, for example, industry developments and regulations, competitor strategies and actions, and governmental policies. Building on such information, the firm can evaluate and decide on the governance mode that is most appropriate for any selected activity.

Step 4: Assess alternative governance modes

Against the backdrop of the selection framework, supportive guidelines and gathered information about the internal and external contexts, firms must recognize that each governance mode entails its own unique advantages and disadvantages (see Table 2.1) as they decide on the most appropriate governance mode for any specific activity. In short, a market exchange is preferable when the required resources are relatively easily available, but do not necessarily enhance a firm's competitive advantage. Internal procurement or mergers and acquisitions are ideal if unified ownership and control rights permit more thorough exploitation of combined organizational resources, even if such exploitations demand higher investments (e.g. physical, human, intangible resources) and increased governance costs. Alliances, which cannot exploit joint assets as intensively as mergers and acquisitions but which offer more flexibility, are preferable if continuing cooperation is beneficial and centralized control could harm value creation. A firm might conclude this step with the following questions:

- Does the chosen governance mode generate strategic value or competitive power?
- Does it impose a risk of losing competitive strength to rivals?
- Does the mode disrupt an activity's interrelatedness with other firm's activities?

If the answers to these critical questions are unsatisfactory, a firm may need to reconsider its decision and re-engage in Steps 2 and 3. However if a firm, on the basis of extensive analysis, decides that an 'ally' governance mode is its best option, the next step is to explicate its alliance strategy.

Step 5: Formulate alliance strategy

The final step formalizes the alliance strategy. The firm should decide which external source(s) of resources it wants to deploy in support of the selected activity to attain its objectives. An alliance strategy summarizes these decisions, often formalized in the form of a business case that describes the scope of activities taken into account, the objective of the alliance, the nature of the partnership and a cost–benefit analysis.

Summary

In this chapter, we have provided overviews of the dominant theoretical perspectives that attempt to explain governance mode decisions. Transaction costs, resource synergies, dependence, informational advantages, strategic motives, inter-firm learning and institutional pressures all impact the choice between 'make', 'buy' and 'ally'. We argue that in order to arrive at a governance mode decision, executives should consider all motives. To this end, we suggest a five-step procedure for firms to help them make governance mode decisions and achieve a well-formulated alliance strategy. Much of the logic described herein however also applies to alliance-oriented governance form decisions. That is, the governance mode decision of a firm, which itself might be influenced by transaction costs, resource alignment and institutional pressures, for example, influences the firm's structural preference in terms of non-equity versus equity-based alliance agreements. We go into detail on structural preferences in Chapter 4, but a combined analysis of governance mode and structural preference may be beneficial.

Case: Shell–Gazprom

In 2010 Gazprom and Royal Dutch Shell agreed to extend their existing alliance – the Sakhalin-2 oil and gas project – and expand their cooperation in Russia and global energy markets.[2] Royal Dutch Shell is an Anglo–Dutch oil company, and has its headquarters in The Hague. Shell companies operate in more than 90 countries and territories, with businesses including oil and gas exploration and production; production and marketing of liquefied natural gas and gas to liquids; manufacturing, marketing and shipping of oil products and chemicals; and renewable energy projects. Russian Gazprom is among the world's largest energy companies; its major business lines include geological exploration, production, transportation, storage, processing and marketing of hydrocarbons, as well as the generation and marketing of heat and electric power. Gazprom's mission thus is to ensure a maximally efficient and balanced gas supply to Russian customers and reliably fulfil long-term gas export contracts.

Since 2006 Shell and Gazprom have been partners in the Sakhalin II project, which constructed Russia's first liquefied natural gas plant. However in 2006, Shell sold its controlling stake in the huge project to Gazprom, after coming under pressure from Russian officials. Specifically, the Russian government's environmental agency threatened to take legal action over alleged environmental shortcomings by Shell and its foreign partners. As a result, Gazprom took a 50 per cent equity stake plus one share in the project; Shell's stake was reduced to 27.5 per cent minus one share. But in 2009, at the height of the economic crisis, Russian Prime Minister Vladimir Putin invited Shell to participate in the Sakhalin-3 and Sakhalin-4 gas projects.

Consequently, building on their strong partnership, Shell and Gazprom agreed to strengthen their existing partnership within Russia and work together outside the country for the first time, by signing a protocol for strategic global cooperation.

The agreement establishes basic guidelines for the companies' broader collaboration. Amongst the opportunities the companies will consider are: (1) further development of bilateral cooperation in exploration and production of hydrocarbons in western Siberia and the far east of Russia and (2) cooperation in the downstream oil products business in Russia and Europe, as well as Gazprom participation in Shell upstream projects outside of Russia. In an interview on Russian state television, Alexander Medvedev, Gazprom's head of exports, said: 'We are happy to invite foreign partners to develop our fields if, in exchange, we get access to our partners' high-profile projects abroad. We know that Shell possesses good assets, which could interest us. If we find an acceptable decision for both parties, such co-operation could be expanded and include co-operation in Sakhalin.' To enact this partnership, Shell and Gazprom will set up joint working groups to push forward opportunities. The deal will pave the way for two of the world's biggest gas companies to deepen cooperation in Russia and work together in other countries as well.

Questions

1. What are (strategic) motives for Gazprom and Royal Dutch Shell to reinforce their initial alliance agreement?
2. What problems are Gazprom and Royal Dutch Shell likely to experience as the joint venture progresses? How can they overcome these problems?
3. To what extent is the alliance agreement between Gazprom and Royal Dutch Shell likely to change industry structure and competitors' strategic behaviour?

3

ALLIANCE PARTNER SELECTION

The alliance partner selection stage involves the choice of a partner or group of partners with which a firm seeks to realize its objectives. Questions that need to be addressed during this stage include: which potential partners exist, which partner is most suitable and what are potential strengths and weaknesses of each potential partner? Answering these questions requires an understanding of the notion of partner fit – that is, of the comparative inter-firm differences related to certain attributes or dimensions that continually shape the pattern of interaction between partners. If partners are highly compatible, such as in their culture or networks, they may be more likely to realize their objectives. Partner misfit instead tends to jeopardize the relationship; therefore, pre-existing knowledge about the degree and content of misfit provides valuable information for improving the design and management of any alliance. To inform their alliance partner selection, managers must understand the differences among various types of fit and comprehend the rationales that underpin partner selection (described in the first section). The following two sections provide a systematic framework containing a set of decision-making steps for alliance partner selection, along with a summary. The final section concludes with a case illustration.

Types of partner fit

In alliance literature, partner fit relies on two related concepts, each with a specific logic. The first type pertains to resource complementarity between partners as a means to enhance the alliance's collaborative effectiveness; Parkhe (1991) calls it Type I diversity. In contrast, a second type of partner fit refers to the extent to which inter-firm characteristics, including strategic, cultural, organizational and operational features, are compatible, which we refer to as partner fit compatibility and which is akin to Type II diversity. Incompatibility negatively affects alliance functioning and, without proper intervention, can result in the premature dissolution of the relationship. Both types of partner fit can explain how (mis)fit affects partners' ability to work jointly and effectively, but their underlying logic varies: complementarity functions as a rationale for alliance formation; incompatibility impedes alliance development.

Partner fit: Resource complementarity

Resource complementarity refers to the extent to which the joint use of distinct sets of resources yields a higher total return than the sum of returns earned if each set of resources were used independently (Chi 1994; Dyer and Singh 1998). In this definition, alliances give an option to a firm that lacks the entire bundle of resources and capabilities it needs to sustain a competitive edge in a particular domain of activity or the capability to develop them competitively (Mowery *et al.* 1998). Resource complementarity is thus an important partner selection criterion; a firm should prefer a potential partner that creates higher relative fit between resource foundations and resource provisions. Lambe *et al.* (2002) indicate that resource complementarity enables parties to develop an idiosyncratic resource foundation, which fosters joint value creation. According to Hitt *et al.* (2000), emerging market firms concentrate more on financial assets, technical capabilities, intangible assets and willingness to share expertise than do developed market firms. Developed market firms instead want to leverage their resources, such as local market knowledge and access, through partner selection. Thus, to increase an alliance's value creation potential, firms seek the specific partners with which they can align their particular resources.

But resource complementarity as a guiding principle constitutes a mixed blessing, because not all contributed resources can be used effectively in an alliance (Das and Teng 2000b). Consider four types of resource alignment configurations, the first pair centres on resource synergies but the second pair focuses on resource under-performance in alliances:

1.   Complementary resource alignment occurs when firms contribute dissimilar resources, because their complementarity enables them to create synergy and capitalize on non-redundant distinctive competences.
2.   Supplementary resource alignment occurs when firms supply similar resources to an alliance, such as to obtain economies of scale, increase their market power, or supply financial resources, essential to the formation of an alliance.
3.   Surplus resource alignment suggests that firms contribute dissimilar resources that are not utilized fully. For example, a firm could contribute more manufacturing capacity than needed. Such slack resources may be redundant, though the surplus also might provide protection against future contingencies.
4.   Wasteful resource alignment occurs when similar resources under-perform. For example, managerial know-how cannot be integrated in another firm, such that it simply becomes an additional cost of the alliance.

In addition, though resource complementarity might reduce the risk of opportunistic behaviour and goal conflicts, because the long-term value creation is likely to outweigh the short-term rewards, it increases risks for misappropriation and unwanted knowledge spillovers. Partnering firms that contribute complementary resources confront a tempting opportunity to gather up the valuable new resources provided by their counterparts. As noted by Cohen and Levinthal (1990), overlap in knowledge resources actually improves partners' ability to absorb knowledge, and their in-depth understanding of the potential value and deployment of resources allows them to interact more and share knowledge more easily and effectively. Resource complementarity thus may stimulate inter-firm learning – which increases the likelihood of involuntary transfers of critical resources. The initial resource-based motives for value creation therefore could undermine a firm's competitive position over time. Thus, firms must consider the extent to which a partner's anticipated resource contributions will be sufficient motive to forge an alliance.

Partner fit: Compatibility

Compatibility refers to the degree to which partner firms share similar characteristics (Douma *et al.* 2000). This sort of partner fit reinforces collective strength and positively influences alliance effectiveness, because it facilitates alliance processes. For example, the propensity for opportunistic behaviour declines when the parties in an alliance have well matched firm characteristics, because compatibility increases the quality of the relationship (Saxton 1997). Furthermore, compatibility determines the extent to which organizations can get along and realize anticipated synergies to achieve alliance success, such that alliances are more successful when partners have similar cultures, asset sizes, and venture experience levels (Harrigan 1988). However, misfit jeopardizes alliance functioning by impeding inter-firm collaboration. Emphasizing compatibility during partner selection enables firms to select appropriate partners or develop and implement corrective measures if misfit occurs. We consider five types of fit: (1) strategic, (2) organizational, (3) operational, (4) cultural and (5) human (see Table 3.1).

Strategic fit

Drawing on strategic management theory, alliance research has emphasized the concept of strategic fit among partners (Douma *et al.* 2000). Highly compatible business and alliance goals, appropriate competitive positions, compatible strategic missions and visions, mutual dependence on one another's resources, similar views about present and future developments and a shared understanding of the business rationale constitute indicators of strategic fit. Appreciation by the market (i.e. financial analysts) is an important driver of such strategic fit. Thus good strategic fit is a prerequisite for any alliance, because it implies that individual interests are carefully weighed against the potential benefits and hazards of the alliance. Partners have perceived the added value for their individual businesses and recognize the

TABLE 3.1 Partner fit types

	Description	Implications
Resource complementarity	Resource alignment yields a higher return than the sum of returns if each set of resources were used independently	– Resource complementarity provides a motive for alliance formation – Threat of resource leakage and cost of non-performing resources
Strategic fit	Compatibility in partners' strategic view and orientation	– Good fit signals long-term commitment – Misfit creates strategic conflicts that undermine joint business proposition
Organizational fit	Compatibility in partners' organizational structure and routines	– Good fit reduces uncertainty about intentions, interests, and competences – Misfit undermines collective sense-making and increases risk of decision-making conflicts
Operational fit	Compatibility in partners' operational systems	– Good fit enables partners to integrate alliance activities – Misfit impedes the execution of day-to-day alliance operations
Cultural fit	Compatibility in partners' organizational culture	– Good fit stimulates joint sense-making – Misfit undermines the quality of the working relationship at different levels in the alliance
Human fit	Compatibility in partners' employee backgrounds and experiences	– Good fit stimulates trust building and interpartner learning – Misfit fosters interpersonal conflicts and impedes communication and information exchange

Sources: Douma et al. (2000); Hennart and Zeng (2005); Sarkar et al. (2001).

important role they play in terms of alliance success. Selecting a partner with good strategic fit increases the long-term value creation potential of alliances by signalling that partners have converging long-term interests and are not likely to engage in behaviour that poses a competitive threat.

A strategic misfit is a threat, however. In the long term, poorly fit partners may be less committed and allocate resources to alternative, more valuable arrangements. Signals for strategic misfit include partners acting competitively in the areas on which the alliance focuses, varying perceptions of the importance of the alliance, divergent industry visions, the pursuit of potentially conflicting alliance objectives and market rejection of the alliance. If limited strategic fit is present, firms must carefully consider whether it can be strengthened; otherwise, they should not collaborate. Corrective measures might attempt to encourage top management dialogue about the strategic vision, reduce or expand the alliance scope, realign alliance strategies, emphasize added value and communicate carefully with stakeholders about the importance of the alliance. That is, if firms pursue an alliance with poor strategic fit, they face greater demands on their alliance design and management.

Organizational fit

The degree to which partners' organizations are compatible reflects their organizational characteristics, such as management styles, operating procedures, information systems, decision-making level (e.g. centralized versus decentralized), management style (participatory versus authoritarian), and reliance on formal planning and control systems (Parkhe, 1991). Thus Douma *et al.* (2000) call organizational fit a critical factor for alliance success, one that reduces uncertainty about the partner's intentions, interests, or competences. Partners with similar organizational attributes, such as customers, manufacturing capabilities and other organizational processes, are more likely to enjoy synergies (Saxton 1997). However, alliance partners almost always differ in some organization characteristics, so the goal is to arrive at a profound understanding of these differences and initiate corrective measures.

Poor organizational fit jeopardizes alliance development and could limit partners' ability to engage in collective sense-making, joint decision-making, or inter-firm learning. If a firm with a centralized, mechanistic structure collaborates with a firm with an organic, decentralized structure, the resulting misfit impedes their constructive collaboration (Parkhe 1991). Similarly, when established firms collaborate with entrepreneurial firms, their decision-making structures do not naturally align, which often leads to conflict, misunderstanding and frustration. To overcome these potential hazards, alliance partners should anticipate organizational misfit during the alliance design and management stages and emphasize the need for flexibility and adaptation. Manageability increases with relatively simple alliance designs, characterized by limited alliance scope, few alliance partners, contracts with contingency clauses and clear task divisions. In addition, proactive alliance management, achieved by building relational capital and emphasizing constructive partner interactions, can overcome the risks associated with organizational misfit. If well managed then, organization misfit might even help partners align their organizational differences.

Operational fit

Operational fit, or firms' procedural capabilities, can be captured by effective management, operational aspects of the business model, operational standards, working procedures, and operational systems (Sarkar *et al.* 2001). Good operational fit indicates that alliance partners can collaborate effectively at the operational level, which gives alliances a better chance of success because the links between the partners' operations are transparent. For example, when two manufacturers seek to collaborate, the extent to which they can jointly create value largely depends on their ability to integrate operational facilities. With good operational fit, the partners can work together efficiently, reduce the costs required for coordination, resolve emerging operational issues quickly, and discover potential areas for improvements. Thus, good strategic and organizational fit is a prerequisite for long-term commitment; operational fit is critical for determining the extent to which alliance partners can realize the potential benefits.

Poor operational fit creates the risk that processes will stall or produce inadequate output, thus jeopardizing value creation. When the operational processes do not match, or assumptions about the capabilities and capacities of either partner go unchecked, the seeds are planted for future operational problems. They can also lead to poor communication among operational staff, which impedes quick conflict resolution. Poor operational fit creates ambiguity about each partner's roles and skills, which impedes decision-making. Furthermore, it undermines alliance leadership and performance management, both of which are required to monitor and manage the alliance's progress. However, to overcome the risks resulting from poor operational fit, potential alliance partners simply need to incorporate partner differences in their alliance design and management. Joint training and education, personnel transfer across partners and codevelopment of operational systems could prevent the emergence of any of these concerns.

Cultural fit

Partners' cultures, including their ideologies, values and practices, should not come into too much conflict (Park and Ungson 1997). Organization culture, interwoven into the very fabric of the partners, is manifest in the distribution of power and control, commitment to the alliance, openness of the organization, innovation intentions and willingness to collaborate. Cultural fit suggests that partners have sufficient awareness and flexibility to work constructively and learn from their cultural differences, to achieve strength. Cultural fit acts as a lubricant in the relationship.

A cultural misfit instead gums up the works. It can cause conflicts in corporate boardrooms, frictions at the operational level, and mistrust between the partners. Social incompatibility may lead to partners' inability to develop harmonious relationships (Sarkar *et al.* 2001). If alliance employees resist an understanding of their partner's culture, the complete failure of the alliance is likely. To deal with their different cultures, partners can adopt several approaches:

- In non-equity based alliances, partners may decide to allow the cultures to coexist.
- For joint ventures, partners might engage in a process of cultural assimilation, combining the positive elements of both cultures to develop a new culture.

In any case, the partners must initiate activities that stimulate cultural awareness, such as joint sessions, cultural training or employee transfers. If well managed, a cultural misfit may even improve alliance performance and lead to spin-offs and positive cultural changes in the partnering organizations.

Human fit

Finally, human fit refers to the degree to which individuals or teams of individuals who will work together in the alliance have converging backgrounds, experiences and personalities (Douma *et al.* 2000). Because the behaviours of employees influence profitability, customer satisfaction and other important outcomes directly, managing human fit is utterly critical. Trust building and learning between employees can ensure the development of strong relationships and high quality learning interfaces. Common backgrounds, experiences, and personalities support employees' mutual understanding, ease interactions, and streamline employee behaviour. In addition, human fit encourages collaboration in alliance teams, which often determine alliance success.

But poor human fit likely inhibits alliance progress; misunderstandings and conflicts among alliance employees undermine alliance progress. High quality interpersonal interactions are prerequisites for the transfer of tacit know-how about markets, management and technologies. To mitigate the impact of poor human fit, alliance partners should undertake human resource management activities, including formal policies and everyday practices focused on training and monitoring. Partners might reward employees by offering alliance team-based incentives tied to overall performance. In addition, motivating and retaining key employees is an important task for alliance management, to help employees adjust to new alliance environments and then interact and work effectively with employees from their new alliance partner.

Overall partner fit thus drives the partner selection stage. Complementary resources stimulate joint coordination, which increases profitability and competitive advantages. Parties should participate in learning processes to exploit these synergies, explore complementary resource strengths, and thus achieve greater alliance performance. Compatibility enables parties to cooperate efficiently and effectively; resource complementarity gives parties incentives to sacrifice their short-term individual goals to achieve long-term value creation. Partner fit in terms of compatibility also facilitates learning by creating the perception that benefits for the partner are in the best interests of the focal firm. Finally, it reduces misappropriation concerns, mitigates the risk of conflicts, contributes to the development of trust and commitment, and enables inter-partner learning. However, when confronted with an undesired misfit, firms must decide whether to continue collaborating or take appropriate measures in the design and management phase to deal with the potential hazards.

Alliance partner selection: Decision-making steps

During the alliance partner selection stage, firms identify the partner that fits best with their organization and objectives. The focus is on achieving collective alignment across the partners' resources, strategies, organizations, operations, cultures and people. To evaluate the degree of fit, and thus the feasibility of the alliance, two questions are key: how can fit be measured, and what degree of fit is required for a

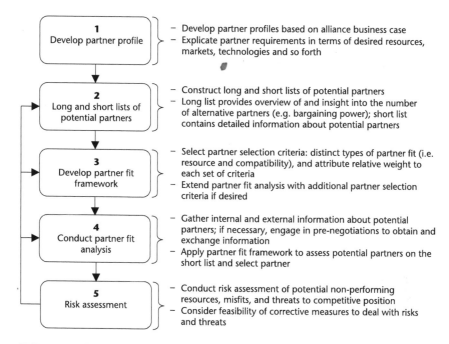

FIGURE 3.1 Decision-making steps: Alliance partner selection

successful alliance? A systematic analysis of partner fit provides clear insights into the chances for success, along with a better understanding of the nature and magnitude of corrective measures needed to mitigate negative effects. Firms must recognize though that managing partner fit effectively may require considerable investments, which implies the greater importance of careful partner selection. To this end, we suggest that alliance partner selection should involve a (repetitive) sequence of five decision-making steps (see Figure 3.1).

Step 1: Develop a partner profile

A partner profile describes the ideal alliance partner according to the firm's own requirements and intentions. It thus constitutes an important preparatory activity. The firm's intensions might be explicated partially in its business case, which is the end product of the alliance strategy formulation stage. To this end product, the firm should add generic partner fit criteria. Firms can map the important resources and competences of potential partners and how they would contribute to the alliance. Furthermore, they should explicate requirements, in terms of desired markets, products, services and technologies. They can also explicate details such as the ideal size, organization structure, reputation and image of a preferred partner. In terms of operational fit, firms should note required technologies and operational systems; cultural and human fit criteria should include optimal organizational culture and desired competences and skills. In addition, they might incorporate financial and legal criteria into partner profiles or mention a potential partner's preferred reputation in managing alliances. Developing a complete partner profile enables firms to recognize good potential partners when they appear.

Step 2: Long and short lists of potential partners

A long list of potential partners summarizes all possible partners, which is important for two reasons. First, the long list enables the firm to make informed decisions about which potential partners are appropriate. Second, it reveals the multiple alternatives available, which signals a strong bargaining position. Potential partners can be identified through different sources – intermediaries, the Internet, trade associations, business networks, conferences, line of industries or (patent) databases to name just a few. Information about foreign alliances is available from foreign investment agencies, government embassies and consulates. And a firm can seek referrals through its existing alliance partners. Even more detailed company information might be found in websites, print articles, work documents, blogs and annual reports or gathered from the insights of people in personal networks. Whereas the long list provides an overview, a short list enables firms to conduct in-depth analyses of potential partners. Scrutinizing all potential partners demands substantial resources and time. Against the backdrop of the partner selection criteria in Step 1, the firms can compare information about these potential partners to reduce their long list to the short list. This transfer demands that firms:

- Collect as much pertinent, publicly available information on potential partners as possible.
- Assess the degree to which potential partners meet the partner profile.
- Decide which potential partners are most suitable for the short list, because they can supply the desired resources and exhibit good compatibility with the firm.

Step 3: Partner fit framework

With this step, a firm develops a detailed partner fit framework to prepare for assessments of potential partners on the short list. To this end, it first explicates indicators for each type of partner fit, and then prioritizes those types by indicating their relative importance. The partner fit framework thus comprises partner dimensions, indicators, and the relative weight of each dimension:

- *Resource complementarity* indicators include the extent to which resources are complementary and anticipated resource contributions will enhance the performance of the alliance.
- *Strategic fit* indicators include alignment between partners' mission and vision, business strategy, industry threats and opportunities, technological developments, mutual dependence, strategic importance, balanced power and a win–win situation.

- *Organizational fit* entails compatibility in firm size, authority structure, decision-making approaches, planning and control systems, accounting systems, information systems, management style, and incentive systems.
- *Operational fit* includes operational standards and procedures, systems, allocation of tasks, coordination, and performance measurement.
- *Cultural fit* indicators include alignment in ideologies, values, beliefs and attitudes, as well as ethical matters and management styles. Other potential indicators might involve experience with the partner, respect and balance, ease of doing business, communication style and commitment. When considering allying abroad, issues such as the political or economic climate and national culture also should be taken into consideration.
- *Human fit* entails the 'click' in personal styles and attitudes, openness, flexibility, employment policies, reward systems, training and education.

Step 4: Partner fit analysis

Now that the partner selection criteria and the relative weight of each has been determined, the firm must reanalyse existing information and collect any additional information that might be needed. To identify the fit between the firm and its presumed partner(s), relevant, often detailed, information must be acquired about each aspect in the fit analysis framework. This information pertains not only to a potential partner but also to the focal firm. For each potential partner on the short list, relevant information can be acquired through Internet searches, annual reports and third parties. Alliance databases are also useful tools for gathering information. But the firm still needs to consider the information about itself that indicates which individuals, teams, departments or business units will be most involved to ensure that they are ready to enter an alliance. The systematic reporting of the partner fit analysis thus provides a foundation for decision-making. Such reports can include a textual partner fit report, accompanied by figures and tables.

Collecting some types of information (e.g. human, operational fit) can be cumbersome. Thus firms might agree to organize a preliminary meeting with a potential partner, in order to involve it in the partner analysis. The meeting should be clearly exploratory, but the firm also might ask the partner firm to sign a non-disclosure agreement. Such a meeting enables the firm and the potential partner to get to know each other and retrieve pertinent information. For example, they might obtain insights about both partners' strengths, personal chemistry, need to protect intellectual property and potential hazards. With the information from the fit analyses and the evaluation meetings, the firm can begin to consider seriously alliances with one or more partners.

Step 5: Risk assessment

The last step in the partner selection analysis requires the firm to conduct a risk assessment of potential partner(s). It is unlikely that a firm possesses great fit with a partner on every indicator. Rather, the evaluation helps the firm identify and discuss potential risks and hazards. Risks associated with resource complementarity primarily pertain to idle resources and the threat of resource leakage. Non- or under-performing resources hamper joint value creation, but the unwanted transfer of resources can undermine the firm's own competitive advantage. Organizational alignment risks involve incompatible organization designs (e.g. structure, decision making, management style), which may require a firm to reorganize. The operational risks refer to the costs associated with securing alignment, such as setting up new departments or units to support the alliance. Integrating control and operating systems demand additional coordination efforts. Cultural and human risks derive from incompatibilities in partners' day-to-day functioning. To develop a steady, collaborative culture, with trusting teams and committed individuals, firms should offer training and education, as well as recognize the importance of incentives. The results of this analysis can be presented in a risk-and-yield analysis, featuring an overview of partner fit criteria, the degree of fit, the associated risk and corrective measures.

Following these five steps for partner selection does not mean a clear-cut recipe for instant alliance success. Rather, by using the partner selection framework, alliance managers can better design and manage their alliances and explicate and focus their conversations with potential partners. A partner selection analysis means doing the necessary homework; occasionally, firms will need to retrace their steps. If the results of the risk assessment stage are unsatisfying and a potential partner emerges as inappropriate, the firm should reconsider Steps 2–4. At the end of the day though, the key to any alliance remains in the hand of the managers who are responsible for the next alliance development stage, for which this analysis should set the agenda: the alliance negotiation.

Summary

We have provided an overview of the drivers of alliance partner selection. Whereas partner fit in terms of resource complementarity emphasizes a value creation logic, partner fit related to compatibility functions as a lubricant for inter-firm collaboration. When confronted with an undesired misfit, firms must decide whether to continue collaborating or take appropriate measures in the design and management phase to deal with the potential hazards. We have also presented a five-step procedure for firms to use in their partner selection decisions. Its application results in the selection of a partner with which to enter into alliance negotiations. Moreover, a firm may have achieved partner fit, but as the alliance is executed, unseen contingencies, both internal and external, continuously issue challenges to the maintenance of partner fit. Without deliberate managerial action, even an alliance with an ideal partner fit can in the end produce disappointing results. To guide managerial action, firms might reapply the partner analysis framework as the alliance progresses.

Case: Grolsch

Grolsch brewery,[1] one of the oldest corporations in the Netherlands, introduced its distinctive flip-top bottle cap in 1897, which established its clear position in the beer industry and set a standard for user-friendliness and quality. Although a traditional beer bottle with a sealed cap became the norm in the twentieth century, Grolsch persisted in using its flip-top cap, retaining its distinctiveness, and enjoying domestic and international success. To date, the Netherlands remains Grolsch's core market, with some 55 per cent of total sales; North America and the United Kingdom account for the largest part of its international sales. Altogether, the company's beers sell in some 50 countries.

Grolsch operates two breweries in the Netherlands, in Groenlo and Enschede. In 1998 it decided to build a completely new brewery to replace the older sites. To design and build its new facility, Grolsch partnered with various firms, including the Italian company Sidel, which specialized in designing, installing, and manufacturing brewery lines. The actual building began in 2001, and by 2004, the first Grolsch beer was being brewed there – just in time to confront industry reports of a saturated European beer market and aggressive competitive moves, such as cost cuts.

In response, Grolsch decided to exploit its innovative experience and respond to shifting consumer demands by emphasizing innovation in its product development and marketing. In 2007 Grolsch introduced a new green bottle; it also shifted focus to appeal to the promising market of home tapping systems. After participating in the development of the PerfectDraft system, marketed by Philips and Interbrew, Grolsch recognized room for improvement. For example, following the razor market model, which sells blades separately, the home tapping system required a separate machine to cool and pressurize the beer. That is, customers had to buy the machine before they could purchase the beer. In addition, the size of the beer container (five litres) was appropriate if consumers were hosting parties or receptions but seemed quite a lot for individual consumption at home. Therefore, Grolsch aimed to develop and market a home tapping system that would be appealing for individual consumption and not require a separate machine – and would enable Grolsch to differentiate itself from competitors that sold beer only in crates. These considerations led to the project that would produce the Cheersch home tapping device: a handy two-litre plastic PET bottle with a reusable tap kit, which operates without electricity. The PET bottle can be resealed and kept inside a regular refrigerator for up to two weeks.

To launch the project, Grolsch actively shared its ideas and views with its suppliers and potential partners. Initial scepticism was the primary response, especially to the odd notion of using PET (i.e. plastic bottles). No PET-bottled beer had succeeded in the Dutch market, though it was the perfect material for a custom-made container that needed to cope with a tap-valve under high pressure but still keep the beer fresh and carbonated. The complex tapping system created further concerns. But informed by the extensive market research that Grolsch had performed, the Italian brewery construction firm Sidel began to understand and adopt the innovation.

Sidel was also active in related markets, such as soft drinks, and referred Grolsch to a PET supplier. The complex tapping system remained difficult to develop; it required a complex, three-way valve system to mix carbon dioxide with beer and then pour it into a glass. Therefore, Sidel also referred Grolsch to Coster, an Italian company with core competences in developing valve systems.

The ultimate alliance included three partners: Grolsch, Sidel and Coster. In designing the partnership, these firms actively and precisely discussed their contributions, positions and potential gains. Grolsch would provide its knowledge of brewing and the beer market; it hoped to sell more hectolitres of its beer. For Coster the valve supplier, the contribution was its knowledge of valve technology, and the gain was selling valve systems in a new market. Sidel also contributed knowledge, this time of the filler lines, and in return, it anticipated financial gains through the creation of a new filler concept for the beer market, based on PET. The alliance was formalized by the firms' CEOs, who remained actively involved throughout the alliance (pre-)formation process.

The parties also took their time during the pre-alliance formation stage, determined to build a high-quality relationship that would increase the chances of successful outcomes. Grolsch cited some key characteristics it wanted in its partners for the Cheersch project: enthusiasm, passion and faith in the innovative concept. Through intensive formal and informal communication at various levels – including strategic, organizational and operational – the partners were able to test their initial visions of markets and feasibility. The process also revealed some differences in their national and organizational cultures, which the firms worked to resolve through dialogue and collective sense-making. The chemistry among the people involved in forming the alliance spread to staff responsible for its execution. For example, engineers frequently communicated about emerging problems and solutions and had little difficulty understanding one another. As they sat together, looking for ways to produce a viable tapping concept, their enthusiasm and passions were evident, which helped the team arrive at and share ideas. The project, nicknamed Brio, never became a separate legal entity, yet the people involved commented that they felt like they worked for Brio. Alliance management also collaborated smoothly through a project management structure that superseded the individual organizational structures.

With respect to structuring the alliance, the partners refrained from forging a separate legal entity and avoided taking equity positions in one another's organizations. They discussed formalization through an equity arrangement but determined that the strategic importance did not justify such action. Instead, they created an agreement that encompassed the most important obligations and liabilities, though the alliance remained primarily governed by trust and commitment. Thus based on its confidence that the Cheersch concept would succeed, Grolsch ordered 50,000 tapping systems. This welcome signal of commitment helped the alliance resolve other issues, such as meeting market deadlines, in harmony.

The Cheersch system enjoyed a successful introduction into the Dutch market, with promising initial sales figures. But Grolsch and other competitors soon realized that home tapping systems did not offer the market growth anticipated by market research. It terminated the Cheersch project and withdrew the product from the market in early 2011. Despite this ultimate outcome, Grolsch's initiative reveals its strong commitment to entrepreneurship and innovativeness, and it established its credentials as a trustworthy and productive partner. Thus, it has provided a fruitful foundation for future projects.

Questions

1. Which types of partner fit appear in the Grolsch case, and to what extent do they represent fit or misfit?
2. The alliance partners decided to abstain from an equity arrangement or detailed contracts. Explain how the degree of partner (mis)fit may have influenced this decision.
3. The execution of the alliance was characterized by intense and constructive collaboration among the partners. Describe how the degree of partner (mis)fit affected their post-formation collaboration.

4

ALLIANCE NEGOTIATION

Alliance negotiation constitutes yet another critical stage in the alliance development framework. Many alliance initiatives are terminated before they can be executed; if they are executed, the negotiation processes and outcomes establish the foundation for the future progress of the alliance. This stage entails establishing the actual complementarities in the collaboration and defining carefully the nature and amount of resources that will be available to the partnership, the ownership, the anticipated outcomes and the contractual provisions. Because alliance partners are interdependent, reaching an agreement demands some negotiation, usually through a dialogue among representatives of partner firms, with the goal of reaching outcomes that fulfil the various interests of the partners in a way that is acceptable to everyone. Thus the key questions to be addressed during this stage refer to which negotiation outcomes will enable the alliance partners to obtain the greatest possible level of synergy, and what negotiation outcomes would provide the best deal for the partner firms. To inform their alliance negotiations, negotiators thus need a good understanding of the differences among various negotiation strategies and tactics (described in the first section), as well as how to value their resource contributions responsibly (shown in the second section). The following two sections provide a systematic framework with a set of decision-making steps for alliance negotiation and a summary. The final section concludes with a case illustration.

Negotiation behaviour

Firms establish alliances to maximize synergies by aligning potentially complementary resources. The partner firms remain independent though, so to be successful in an alliance negotiation, they must recognize their conflicting aims (Das and Kumar 2010). First, they need an outcome that maximizes the potential value of the alliance. Second, they need to protect their individual firms' interest and negotiate an outcome that maximizes value for the firm specifically. Negotiating an alliance thus entails seeking a relationship between partners that enables them to achieve business success together, without either partner needing to accept a loss of finances, identity or independence (Child and Faulkner 1998). Alliance partners should conclude their negotiations with the feeling that they have achieved a workable deal that benefits them individually as well. To resolve this conundrum, negotiation behaviour encompasses all activities exploited by negotiators during a negotiation process, with the aim of coming to terms with the negotiating partner. To this end, negotiators formulate and deploy different strategies and tactics, switching among them as alliance negotiations progress (Thompson 1990).

Negotiation strategies

A negotiation strategy reflects a party's disposition toward reconciling and integrating the interests of the partners. Prior research has remarked that negotiation strategies typically have been categorized as either integrative or distributive (Kersten 2001). Integrative negotiations address (and attempt to accommodate) the underlying interests of both parties, which is useful for generating joint gain, particularly in positive-sum negotiations. In such a negotiation situation, the amount of benefits to be divided is variable (i.e. unknown), and partners may profit without sacrifice if they can increase the overall pie. Moreover, partner interests likely converge, because their value realization depends on their long-term commitment. Integrative negotiation enables partners to solve problems, develop win–win solutions, achieve value creation, and create synergies beyond what would have been possible alone (Pruitt and Lewis 1975). When parties adopt a problem-solving orientation, they likely identify similarities in their interests and pursue common objectives (Ariño and Reuer 2004). Transparency, and the speed and reliability with which partners learn about each other's actions, also result in proposals and counter-proposals, discussions about the solutions and efforts to uncover mutual interests (Olekalns *et al.* 1996). To overcome potentially incompatible interests, negotiators seek settlements that are better for all parties involved. Integrative negotiation thus requires flexibility among parties and willingness to think creatively in order to discover efficient negotiation outcomes.

In contrast, distributive negotiation seeks to create individual gain by persuading the other party to make concessions. The focus is on securing individual interests, appropriating value through the alliance, and sharing the pie (Jap 2001), which might be appropriate if the amount of resources is fixed (i.e. a zero-sum game). Partner interests are often diametrically opposed, so they focus on the realization of immediate outcomes, even at the expense of their partner. This type of negotiation is characterized by minimal information exchanges, greater commitment to individual interests and increased hostility (Lax and Sebenius 1986). Yet it also means the exchange of information is crucial, because parties work to maximize the amount of information they receive while also minimizing the amount of information they grant (Wolfe and McGinn 2005). The parties' sole aim is to direct efforts toward negotiation outcomes that enable them to appropriate future benefits.

Building on these two dimensions, various typologies of negotiation strategies (for an overview, see Das and Kumar 2010) adopt different foci, including conflict cultures (Gelfand *et al.* 2006), negotiation models (Lewicki *et al.* 1992) and negotiation strategies (Pruitt 1983). By comparing these distinct typologies, we note five negotiation strategies that appear appropriate as categories for classifying negotiation behaviour (Child and Faulkner 1998). First, collaborating suggests concern for individual and partner interests, with a focus on problem solving. Second, competing indicates that the primary concern with individual interests leads to an attempt to force the partner to back down. Third, avoiding means that partners do not pursue either parties' interests and refuse to consider the issue. Fourth, accommodating suggests that a partner's interests are the primary concern, so the focal firm backs down. Fifth and finally, a compromising strategy indicates moderate concerns for partners' interests, such that they agree to split the difference (see Table 4.1).

TABLE 4.1 Negotiation strategies and tactics

	Description	*Tactics*	*Implications*
Collaborating	Primary concern for individual and partners' interests; focus on problem solving	Primary focus on soft tactics to build high quality working relationship; hard tactics only employed to defend interests	Strengthening of preexisting relationships; preventing conflict escalation
Competing	Primary concern for individual interests; focus on imposing outcomes on counterpart	Focus on hard tactics to exploit power advantage and obtain compliance	Jeopardizing long-term relationships; conflicts that are costly to resolve
Avoiding	Limited concern for individual and partners' interests; focus on neglecting negotiation	Limited use of tactics	Integrative solution is not achieved, likelihood of premature dissolution
Accommodating	Primary concern for partners' interests; focus on compliance with counterpart's demands	Primary focus on hard and rational tactics to deal pre-emptively with counterpart's demand	Short-term success, but risk of exploitation remains because an integrative outcome is not achieved
Compromising	Moderate concern for individual and partners' interests; focus on quick consensus solutions	Primary focus on rational tactics to obtain compliance	Short-term success, but fundamental issues persist as the alliance progresses

Sources: Das and Kumar (2010); Lax and Sebenius (1986); Rao and Schmidt (1998).

In a comparison of these negotiation approaches, collaborating seems fruitful for alliance negotiations (Das and Kumar 2010), because it maximizes the negotiation outcome through a strong focus by both parties on each other's and their own outcomes. To develop win–win alliances, partners need to negotiate generously and ensure that their partner receives a good deal, which might mean sub-optimal immediate outcomes as they lay the groundwork for long-term success. Negotiators may be more sensitive to the absence of agreement than to failure to attain an ideal agreement. With flexibility, firms are willing to back down from their initial interests and consider alternative negotiation solutions. Although collaborating cannot guarantee a successful negotiation even if employed by all partners, it is likely to result in outcomes associated with trust-building. If partners invest in relational capital during their initial alliance negotiations, they should enjoy collaborative decision making as the alliance progresses. Moreover, collaborative negotiations are often supplemented by informal, collective sense-making processes that contribute to enhance partner interactions as the alliance progresses.

Negotiation tactics

Negotiation tactics refer to the means used to execute the negotiation strategy. Parties can use a variety of negotiation instruments to achieve this objective (Lax and Sebenius 1986). For example, through communication and persuasion, a negotiator may coerce another party to accept a compensation structure that conflicts with its interests. A firm might present information in such a manner that it looks like a win–win situation, even if it benefits that focal firm primarily. Some negotiators derive power from their possession of specialized knowledge or unique information. Identifying with a charismatic person, which often relies on the negotiator's skill in building good personal relationships, also may exert influence, as can advocacy of normative conformity (i.e. claiming that a position is correct, legitimate or principled). To organize these distinct types of tactics, a three-category classification is identified: hard, soft and rational (Kipnis and Schmidt 1985; Rao and Schmidt 1998).

Hard tactics generally result when negotiators develop a subjective assessment that the counterpart will comply with their demands. This assessment causes them to develop a focus on maximizing their own value and pursuing whatever joint positive value is available. As a leading principle, they aim to fulfil self-interest by creating fear in the opposing party, using threats, demands and sanctions. Because counterparts face high costs if they fail to comply, they usually accommodate the hard negotiators' demands. This scenario also implies reduced dependency, in that the negotiator will describe the multiple alternatives available to realize its objectives, while increasing the partner's dependence and switching costs, such as by setting firm deadlines, demanding concessions, acting forcefully or threatening to terminate negotiations. Such hard influence tactics seek to weaken the other party's position, increase the credibility of the negotiator's own position and impose negotiation outcomes. In the case of conflicts, contracts supported by legal systems serve to resolve the situation. With a focus on differences, these power-based negotiations are characterized by a strong motivation to pursue individual interests at the expense of the partner.

Soft tactics instead emphasize friendliness and assume counterparts have an option of non-compliance with little cost. Thus the aim is to strive for fairness by building a high-quality relationship marked by interpersonal liking, a sense of obligation and reciprocity. Compliance through soft tactics arises because of the bilateral focus and concern for partners' interests. For example, negotiators may emphasize interdependence and actively communicate the limited number of alternatives. Another indicator of soft tactics is a willingness to make alliance-specific investments, which signals commitment and a voluntary exposure to potential exploitation (i.e. a hold-up situation). These influence tactics thus emphasize openness, informality and long time horizons. If conflicts emerge, their resolution proceeds through active consensus seeking and joint problem solving, with a focus on what partners have in common rather than their differences. Soft tactics indicate a strong motivation to seek solutions, identify a binding common objective, and a willingness to recognize both sides' interests as valid.

Rational tactics rely on logic, data and information to obtain compliance. They feature unemotional arguments, but compliance is not taken for granted. The aim is to persuade a counterpart through objective information; the logically presented facts and information cause any request to appear detailed and well prepared. The negotiator also comes off as a competent and reasonable counterpart. Gaining compliance then requires a bilateral focus and concern for partners' interests. For example, negotiators might emphasize facts and figures related to joint business development, industry dynamics and other sources of relevant information.

Negotiation dynamics

To resolve the tension between common and individual interests – and despite our distinction between them – alliance negotiations tend to feature both integrative and distributive negotiation approaches. For example, to find solutions, parties might prefer joint gain but also seek a solution that maximizes their own gain, if they can convince the partner to accept it. Switching between approaches is difficult, however; it involves role reversal by the negotiators, which may be misinterpreted. Alliance negotiations often involve a mixture of trust-building and bargaining power games, which can reinforce a perception of mixed signals about long-term commitment. In addition, adopting an integrative strategy poses a risk, because the party becomes vulnerable to opportunism in the negotiation. Being open about one's own interests and preferences to achieve joint gains might provoke a partner to adopt a distributive orientation and exploit this openness to strengthen its own position. Yet proactively adopting a distributive orientation can be perceived as hostile, which may fuel a negative escalation in the negotiation. That is, a distributive strategy may minimize vulnerability to exploitation, but it leaves significant potential joint gain on the table.

Negotiators tend to have learned about distributive strategies and hard tactics, but in alliance negotiations specifically, such tactics produce sub-optimal results. Alliances require more integrative negotiation strategies and soft tactics. A key success factor in any negotiation is recognizing the importance of the relationship, so negotiators might consider the following approaches (Das and Kumar 2010; Pruitt and Lewis 1975):

- *Super-ordinate goals.* Negotiators should focus on developing super-ordinate goals rather than pursuing individual targets. With such a focus, negotiators can resolve conflicts and seek negotiation outcomes in both partners' interests.
- *Consider interests.* Positions are the demands the negotiator makes; interests are the underlying demands. By concentrating on interests, negotiators can identify shared and incompatible interests, isolate the latter as potential deal breakers, and continue the negotiation.
- *Separate people from the problem.* Personal involvement often translates into emotions, perceptions and beliefs that deteriorate judgmental capabilities. By excluding such involvement, negotiators can focus on the problem instead of personalities.
- *Make multiple proposals.* With more than one option, the negotiator can identify what the other party values and develop creative trade-offs.
- *Engage in creative thinking.* The act of creation needs to be separate from judgments of alternatives.
- *Focus on fair.* When confronted with incompatible interests, the parties need to understand and agree on fairness criteria.
- *Work toward clarity.* Negotiators should define the scope, objectives, priorities, important tasks, milestones and performance measures for their negotiation.

Valuation

Valuing partners' resource contributions is both important and difficult (Child and Faulkner 1998). Alliance negotiations tend to be lengthy and confidential, and market mechanisms (i.e. price) are rarely appropriate for valuing resources. The future value of resource contributions is also uncertain, because value creation depends on the partners' commitment to make the alliance work. Decisions with respect to the alliance design may also affect this valuation. For example, the boundaries of an alliance are clearly demarcated in a joint venture, but non-equity alliances tend to have diffuse boundaries. And yet, an alliance negotiation absolutely necessitates resource valuation, because value assessments directly affect negotiation behaviour (Contractor and Ra 2000). In this inexact process, partners' attitudes, and the way they get managed and evolve over time, play a key role. Furthermore, valuations of contributions largely depend on the measurability of those contributions. Tangible resources such as fixed assets offer high measurability, so negotiators likely have a clear assessment of their value, perhaps based on (market) costs, uniqueness, replacement value, or net present value calculated on the basis of an expected income stream and discount rate. Working capital might be valued at face value, unless there are reasons to discount it, such as when a joint venture will incorporate bad debts. Intangible resources are difficult to measure due to their tacit nature, and their valuation is more likely to result in conflicts and disagreements between partners.

To provide some insights on valuation, Contractor (2001) distinguishes three types of intangible resources: intellectual property rights, intellectual assets and human and organizational capital. Intellectual property rights (IPR) are formally registered assets, such as patents and brand names, which makes them relatively easy to transfer among alliance partners. To value IPR, negotiators likely use a market-based benchmark. For example, it is possible to assign a value to a brand name by employing a market mechanism: firms are often willing to pay large sums to obtain the rights to such brands. Intellectual assets comprise both IPR and codified but unregistered corporate knowledge, such as drawings, software, databases, manuals and trade secrets – in written form, but deliberately not registered with government authorities. Measuring such resources becomes more difficult, as does their transferability, although it is difficult to attribute a value to such resources except perhaps through royalties and commissions for sales. Human and organizational capital refers to uncodified know-how or expertise that resides in employees' skills, routines and organizational culture. These resources are the most difficult to measure and often inseparable from the firm. For example, expertise is generally ignored in valuation exercises, even though it might constitute a key motive for forging an alliance. Technological capabilities are similarly difficult to value, due to their intangible nature, though royalties, licence agreements and discount calculations could provide some insights. Thus whereas tangible assets are often valued at their cost, the valuation of intangible assets tends to be ignored or assigned a value on the basis of equity principles (Child and Faulkner 1998).

Alliance negotiation: Decision-making steps

Negotiations in alliances must achieve win–win outcomes, because the partners ultimately seek a long-term relationship. To increase the likelihood of smooth collaboration, it is important that partners consider alliance negotiations a positive-sum game, in which integrative negotiations supported by soft tactics lead to better outcomes for all partners. Their efforts should focus on learning their partner's concerns, considering benefits and costs, becoming aware of their partner's negotiation strengths (i.e. bargaining power), and accommodating each other in valuing resource contributions. To guide successful alliance negotiations, we distinguish three negotiation stages – pre-negotiation, negotiation and post-negotiation – each with multiple steps, as we detail next.

Pre-negotiation

During the pre-negotiation stage, a firm prepares for the alliance negotiation by assembling an alliance team and formulating a negotiation strategy. In addition,

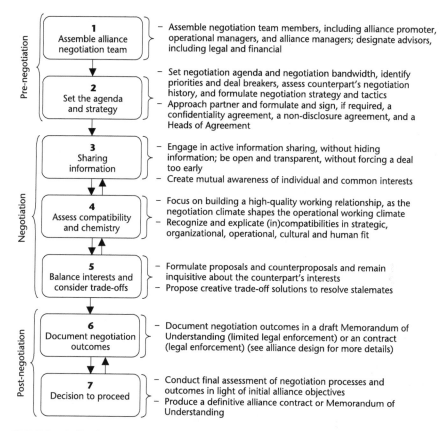

FIGURE 4.1 Decision-making steps: Alliance negotiation

each party should gather all possible information about the partner in terms of its current position, including its financial status, key capabilities, vulnerabilities, personnel, technologies and key markets. The firm might simultaneously undertake a similar analysis of its own organization to find any potential (in)compatibilities. A combination of these activities helps the firm to calculate its negotiation bandwidth, before entering the actual negotiation stage.

Step 1: Assemble alliance negotiation team

Assembling an effective alliance negotiation team can prevent the escalation of tension during negotiations, which might occur when a single negotiator becomes too emotionally involved, and loses a sense of objective judgment. All involved partners should establish their own teams, set to take part cooperatively at the negotiating table. In addition, the negotiation teams should have access to all information gathered in preceding alliance development stages (i.e. strategy formulation and partner selection). The team generally consists of an alliance promoter, senior-level managers, operational managers and alliance managers. The alliance promoter works to gain trust, support and legitimacy within the organization while also establishing the vision for the alliance, informing important actors and procuring sufficient resources within the organization. The senior managers need to take part in discussions related to financial and strategic objectives; they also can encourage firm-wide commitment to the alliance. Involving operational managers, such as division heads, financial managers and technical or marketing managers – that is, the people who will execute the alliance – gives a sense of operational fit and helps build support for decisions and trust. Finally, alliance managers, who are responsible for alliance execution and day-to-day operations, should receive support from both alliance partners and thus must be involved in the negotiations. Legal and tax professionals might help formalize partnerships, but because the main objective of the negotiation stage is to create a business framework, they rarely join the negotiation team, functioning instead as advisors, especially when the negotiation and alliance design stages are concurrent.

Step 2: Set the agenda and strategy

In the next step, but still in advance of the actual negotiation, the team attempts to set the agenda. Coming to a negotiation table without sufficient preparation can hinder both the process and its outcomes. After identifying negotiation issues, the team should establish its negotiation bandwidth to determine the worst possible condition it would accept in relation to each specific issue. The step-by-step process therefore encompasses the following:

1. Establish a list of negotiation points, including the alliance strategy and objectives, the resources provided by the different parties, protections and how to deal with changes.
2. Develop a common view of deal breakers and how to deal with them.
3. Gather information about the negotiation history of the potential partner, perhaps from network contacts, including the experience and background of its counterpart's negotiation team. When the alliance includes a foreign partner, a critical judgment relates to the level of knowledge of the foreign business culture.
4. Use this information to determine a negotiation strategy and tactics for each negotiation issue. For example, negotiating about the value of intangible resources favours an integrative strategy, whereas negotiating financial compensation benefits from a distributive strategy.

A firm may also approach its (i.e. non-disclosure agreement) counterpart and decide together to formulate and sign a confidentiality agreement to regulate the information exchanged during the negotiation and protect them from unwanted interference by external stakeholders. For example, a joint venture announcement tends to influence stockholder value, so the confidentiality agreement might prevent the parties from discussing the negotiations with stockholders or the market. In addition, the basic principles of the alliance agreement might be formalized in a letter of intent or Heads of Agreement. Such a document enables the parties to concentrate on establishing the fundamental principles of the venture, provides a basis for public announcements, helps keep negotiations moving forward and provides a draft for the definitive alliance agreement. Even when these emerge, they are rarely legally binding. During this pre-negotiation stage, parties may request due diligence, perhaps to assess financial matters and technology. The results of this exercise help negotiators assess the value of inputs, outputs and organizational requirements.

Negotiation

During the negotiation stage, negotiation teams meet in person and jointly develop an alliance roadmap by exchanging relevant information, assessing their computability and chemistry, balancing their interests and considering alternatives. We analytically distinguish these activities, but they are often simultaneous. The primary risk in this stage is that negotiators might place too much emphasis on their firms' rather than shared interests, creating tense alliance negotiations. Thus all parties should monitor actively the level of anxiety and manage it if necessary.

Step 3: Sharing information

Alliance negotiation means information sharing and the objective is two-fold: to strengthen relations between the potential partners and their negotiators, and to obtain a shared understanding of super-ordinate goals. Negotiators should expect to abide by the following rules:

- Be open and honest, because hiding relevant information could harm the negotiation process in a later stage.
- Do not force a deal by mentioning legal threats, because early meetings have softer objectives, such as getting to know each other and gaining an understanding of the other's vision of the alliance and culture.
- Balance information sharing and gathering; avoid being an open book while the other party sits silent and absorbs information.
- Share only the information that is relevant for the alliance. Remain aware of not only what is discussed but also the matters that are not discussed.

Step 4: Assess compatibility and chemistry

Good collaborations often feature partners that understand each other and the way their counterpart works. Assessing compatibility and chemistry is therefore crucial as negotiations progress. Investing in a stronger relationship pays off when more difficult negotiation issues arise, so negotiators should consider several issues. First, with regard to partner fit, they should understand the areas in which the partner firms are compatible or incompatible. For example, incompatibility might create conflict to the detriment of integrative solutions. Second, they should assess the support offered by extent senior-level and operational managers of both sides. A lack of commitment may jeopardize alliance negotiations. Third, negotiators should assess the degree to which the values and way of doing business are compatible across partners. Incompatible values may be ignored during negotiations, but they are likely to emerge and create conflicts once the alliance is executed. Collective awareness about these issues enables negotiators to develop solutions before they even arise, which contributes to a relationship based on mutual trust.

Step 5: Balancing interests and considering trade-offs

Balancing interests is a sensitive matter during alliance negotiations, which inherently involve conflicting objectives and even personal interests. Therefore, one tactic is to have one negotiation team make the first set of proposals, which prompts inquiry rather than immediate counter-proposals. The negotiation teams should be oriented toward creating win–win situations through integrative negotiations. With this orientation they also should avoid an emphasis on power or control over the negotiation, which tends to induce distributive negotiation strategies. Instead negotiators can focus on the potential for mutually beneficial agreements and try to use problem-solving strategies that support both individual organizations' goals. For example, in a careful assessment of the partner's resource contribution, the negotiator should take into account human capital, in the form of professional, expertise, reputation, and network capital. Yet this analysis also must consider the potential losses that result from investing in an alliance. Creativity also is required to determine compensation, because different alliance payments provide different incentives. For example, a lump sum fee paid at the start of the agreement might reduce long-term commitment; royalties, indexed as a percentage of alliance sales, might increase it. Dividends as returns on equity positions also function as mutual hostages. Commitment to an alliance reflects the partners' motivation to collaborate, which itself depends on the potential value of the alliances and their anticipated benefits. The goal is to build trust with the potential partner, create momentum, develop consensus and signal commitment, through both verbal and non-verbal communication.

Post-negotiation

In the last phase, the negotiation outcomes are transcribed into a legal contract that codifies each party's rights, duties and responsibilities and specifies the goals, policies and strategies underlying the anticipated cooperation. Thus a common understanding must exist regarding how the results are measured and managed. Governance structures, such as performance management, should have been discussed and accepted in the alliance economics stage, so they can be included in the documentation. Even after such documentation though, the parties must conduct a final check: does the negotiation agreement fit the original alliance objectives, and have the negotiators established a constructive working climate?

Step 6: Establish relevant documentation

The results of the negotiation are documented in a preliminary alliance contract (legally binding) or Memorandum of Understanding (limited legal enforcement), which contains an outline of the negotiated points and, if required, issues that need further negotiation. Other documented elements may include the objective and purpose of the alliance, partners' resource contributions, a draft of a potential alliance design, division of tasks and responsibilities, decision making and conflict resolutions procedures, rules and procedures in case the alliance is terminated due to unforeseen events and possible future projects for the alliance (see alliance design for more details).

Step 7: Decision to proceed

The last task means completing the alliance negotiation and deciding to initiate the next stage, alliance design. Therefore, to assess whether the objectives of the negotiation have been achieved and whether to draw up the definitive alliance contract, the negotiation teams must confirm:

- The mission statement is clearly articulated and understood by both parties.
- There is a clarity about the alliance design, including governance form, contractual provisions and management control.
- There is a clear understanding of the operational, technological, legal, marketing and decision-making procedures.
- Consensus about (resource) inputs has been reached, with balanced trade-offs between partners.
- Both parties intend to continue the alliance until objectives are achieved; however, there exists a common perception of how to deal with conflict.
- There is a clear understanding of important issues, including the protection of intellectual property or ownership rights resulting from the alliance.
- There is sufficient insight into the effect of the alliance on organizational processes (managerial, decision making, operational).
- The understanding includes the impact on certain organizational departments and units, with support gained from those affected by any potential reorganization or disruption.

Summary

In this chapter, we have provided an overview of critical issues in alliance negotiation. Resolving the inherent tension between collaboration and competition requires that negotiators understand the implications of distinct negotiation approaches and their underlying dynamics. With such understanding, negotiators can assess the implications of their behaviour, including conflict, which is generally germane to alliance negotiations. The appropriate use of negotiation strategies and tactics provides an effective mechanism for pre-emptively managing conflicts about coordination, compensation and contributions. In addition, alliance negotiations often constitute a first encounter between partners, and thus a first opportunity to develop relational norms and capital. Distributive negotiations accompanied by hard tactics may let the firm realize its negotiation objectives, but only at the expense of the counterpart and to the jeopardy of the alliance's execution. In contrast, integrative negotiations leading to win–win outcomes can reinforce initial trust and commitment. High-quality partner interactions are prerequisites for developing productive alliances, and constitute an important part of alliance management. Building on the insights presented, we distinguished three negotiation stages analytically, and suggested that negotiations proceed in this order (the stages are of course interrelated).

Moreover, we distinguish analytically and sequentially between alliance negotiation and alliance design: in practice these development stages are often concurrent. For example, negotiations could last from weeks to years – and it would not be advisable for the partners to wait to document contractual provisions determined six months previously because they want to conclude the entire negotiation stage first.

Case: Renault–Nissan

Renault,[1] the French automotive company, was founded in 1899 and now holds a leading position in the European and Latin American car markets. Throughout its history, Renault has introduced groundbreaking cars, such as the Espace and Megane Scenic. In the late 1990s, despite being in a financially sound position, Renault recognized that it needed to act if it were to remain competitive. The company was too dependent on its home market and nearby European markets. Furthermore, the merger between Daimler and Chrysler in 1998 made Renault recognize the need to economize on costs and increase its presence in the global automotive market.

Nissan Motors has produced cars since 1933 (its predecessors having done so since 1914) and has become one of the leading car manufacturers in the world. The second largest Japanese car manufacturer, after Toyota, Nissan has been able to establish strong market presence in the Japanese and Asian markets, the United States and Europe. Starting in 1991, however, Nissan was confronted with several challenges. It experienced substantial losses due to decreasing sales in key markets, it was unable to develop successful new models, it had difficulty standardizing its products, and it had a huge debt position of US$20 billion. To deal with their own adversities and changing industry and market conditions (such as over-capacity), Renault and Nissan decided to establish an alliance in 1999.

Renault's senior management realized that an attempt to acquire Nissan would be opposed by key stakeholders and the Japanese public, so it proposed an alliance between the firms, to which Nissan responded positively. Although both companies were experiencing difficulties and analysts were sceptical about the alliance, the resource and market complementarity between the two firms was high. Renault had strong marketing and design capabilities, while Nissan was renowned for its engineering capabilities. Furthermore, Renault served mainly the European and Latin American markets, while Nissan served the Japanese, Asian and North American markets. Renault sought a partner that would provide it with the opportunity to expand from a regional player into a global player, whereas Nissan was looking for a partner in a strong financial position.

Both companies realized that the cultural distance and experience in working together would both pose potential obstacles to forging a win–win partnership. Consequently, they decided to adopt a non-conventional negotiation approach. Instead of the traditional static analytical 'due diligence' approach, the partners recognized that the key to success was a climate of mutual trust and proof of both companies' ability to actually work together. Prior to the negotiations, the companies' senior management held numerous meetings in which interests and objectives were discussed. The teams were kept small, which enabled them to become acquainted and to develop a high-quality relationship. After these initial meetings, both companies selected engineers and managers to form a team that would explore concrete opportunities of collaboration and possible synergies. As a way of supporting the integrative nature of the negotiations, no formal goals were imposed on the team and team members were encouraged to let go of any cultural stereotypes. The team examined collaborative opportunities in a range of areas, such as purchasing, engines and gearboxes, car platforms, production and international markets. Based on team reports, the senior management from both firms concluded that sufficient synergies could be realized, so they decided to proceed with making a deal.

The companies signed a memorandum of understanding, through which they expressed a commitment to evaluate further possible synergies and start formal negotiations. During this period, Renault signalled its commitment by refraining to impose an equity exchange on Nissan. At that time, Nissan did not have the financial resources to fund the acquisition of Renault shares, and Renault agreed to postpone the matter. Another indication of the good relationship was the fact that Renault executives took Japanese language classes, which eased communication. However, the companies still had two issues to deal with. First, during the formal negotiations the companies had to take account of multiple stakeholders. For example, Renault was partly state-owned and had strong unions to deal with. Nissan was part of the Fuyo Keiretsu, in which its most powerful stakeholders (Fuji Bank, Industrial Bank of Japan and Dai-Ichi Metal Insurance) were organized. Second, prior to the formal negotiation, Nissan set four pre-conditions that Renault had to meet: (1) retention of the Nissan name, (2) protection of jobs, (3) support for the restructuring of the Nissan organization and (4) selection of the CEO from the Nissan organization. Renault was able to meet these pre-conditions, which allowed both firms to take the next step.

The actual negotiations benefited from prior investments in relationship building. Both companies gained an understanding about each other's backgrounds, believed in the alliance, and were fully aware of potential areas for collaboration. Instead of securing private interests and resorting to distributive tactics, both companies expressed a willingness to accommodate the other's interests. However, a serious issue emerged when Nissan asked Renault to invest US$6 billion to ease financial pressure on the company. Renault could not accommodate this request, which forced Nissan to explore other alternatives, including partnerships with DaimlerChrysler and Ford. Recognizing the importance of the Nissan alliance, Renault arranged additional financial resources and approached Nissan to restart negotiations. Nissan had experienced serious difficulties in attracting a new partner, so it complied with Renault's request. Although Renault was not able to provide conclusive financial details, it had now obtained a bargaining power advantage. However, it did not exercise this advantage, in the interests of safeguarding the important relationship between the firms. When negotiations were completed, Renault agreed to invest US$5.4 billion in exchange for 36.8 per cent of the Nissan Motor shares, 15.2 per cent of the Nissan Diesel shares, and ownership of Nissan's financial subsidiaries in Europe.

The alliance quickly proved successful. For example, Renault Mexico was established in 2000 with Nissan's support, and Renault was able to reenter the Australian market in 2001. In 2000, Nissan established a presence in Brazil with Renault's help. In 2001, both partners set up a joint purchasing organization; Renault Argentina started importing Nissans for the Argentinean market and Renault entered the Indonesian market through the local Nissan dealer network. In 2002, Nissan was able to buy a 13.5 per cent stake in Renault, which it increased later that year to 15 per cent, thereby keeping the agreements it had made earlier. Since then, the alliance has grown and proved successful.

Questions

1. Renault and Nissan adopted a non-conventional negotiation approach. How does this approach differ from a traditional approach and to what extent has it contributed to the success of the alliance?
2. How did the diverging organizational, cultural and institutional backgrounds of Renault and Nissan affect the negotiation trajectory in terms of negotiation approach, processes, and outcomes?

5

ALLIANCE DESIGN

The problem of how alliance partners can exercise sufficient control over the direction of their alliance is well recognized. In the alliance design stage, partner firms confront the challenge of designing an alliance structure that provides them with sufficient control to realize their objectives. Insufficient control limits a partner's ability not only to protect but also to use the resources it provides efficiently. Alliance partners thus are motivated to create an alliance design that fulfils the following objectives: to increase the likelihood of attaining individual and collective objectives; to create safeguards to reduce the impact of potential exchange hazards; and to increase their ability to respond to unforeseen circumstances. The guiding questions for this stage thus refer to the most suitable governance form, the required contractual provisions and the supplementary management controls to be installed. To this end, managers must understand the primary function of governance forms (shown in the first section), alliance contracts (second section), and management control (third section). In addition, the following two sections discuss how these design elements interrelate, and provide a systematic, five-step framework to assist alliance managers in their alliance design decisions. Our final two sections conclude the chapter with a summary and a case illustration.

Governance form

A governance form consists of the configuration of an alliance's structural building blocks, which aim to organize the partners' coordination and contractual enforcement legally (Williamson 1985). With minimum cost, an appropriate governance form can ensure the control that parties need before they will come to believe that engaging in the alliance will be of benefit to them (Dyer 1997). Accordingly, a governance form should align parties' interests by creating an incentive structure that stimulates the creation of long-term gains through cooperation, while reducing short-term gains from competition. An appropriate governance form also reduces the likelihood of exchange hazards, and in turn contributes positively to the likelihood of superior alliance performance. The primary purpose is to protect alliance partners against two types of exchange hazards: (1) opportunistic behaviour and (2) misappropriation of benefits.

Williamson (1975, p. 6) defines opportunistic behaviour as self-interested behaviour with guile, which may include making hollow promises or window-dressing efforts, unresponsiveness, unreasonable demands, misrepresentations of abilities, a reluctance to fulfil a commitment, withholding and incomplete disclosure of information, expropriation of know-how and/or exploitation of partner-specific assets (Williamson 1985). Various forms of opportunistic behaviour emerge in alliance contexts, including the hold-up problem (Klein *et al.* 1978), shirking (Wathne and Heide 2000) and free riding (Hennart and Zeng 2005):

- Hold-up problems arise when one party exploits the other party's dependence on the alliance, often due to the presence of assets and investments with value specific to the relationship, which thus create incentives for opportunism. If a party is tied to the alliance through specialized investments, it cannot dissolve the alliance without incurring substantial costs associated with the loss of non-recoverable investments.
- Shirking refers to situations in which one party avoids its obligations and contracted duties to increase its own short-term rewards (e.g. immediate cost saving), even though doing so imposes costs on the alliance and jeopardizes long-term value creation.
- Free riding arises when one party fails to fulfil its obligations to supply the required inputs to its partner. For example, if parties contractually agree to exploit resources but it is difficult to determine if the agreed amount or quality of resources has been provided, a party that fails to provide its share reaps additional benefits from its free riding.

After an alliance has formed, parties may have concerns about the misappropriation of their benefits too (Gulati and Singh 1998). Appropriation concerns originate from the presence of behavioural uncertainty, combined with the difficulties of specifying intellectual property rights, as well as the challenges of contractual monitoring and enforcement (Oxley 1997). Uncertainties associated with future performance and problems in observing partners' contributions aggravate the potential that a party might not receive its anticipated share of benefits. The presence of a knowledge component in an alliance raises additional appropriation concerns, because knowledge is difficult to bind, monitor and codify. A partner firm may acquire valuable knowledge that is not part of the initial alliance agreement and use it for purposes outside the alliance (Khanna 1998). As the alliance develops, the likelihood of such misappropriation may increase as a result of various internal and external dynamics (Yan and Zeng 1999), which could give rise to goal conflicts. Goal conflicts constitute a threat to alliance continuity, in that incompatible or misaligned goals reduce the incentives for parties to cooperate and contribute to the achievement of the other party's objectives.

In order to determine the extent to which they need to safeguard against exchange hazards, firms need to assess the level of governance required. A first decision relates to the type of governance form, which differs when alliance partners take actual ownership of the alliance structure (e.g. joint venture), versus when they rely on non-equity-based arrangements.

Non-equity and equity-based governance forms

A non-equity arrangement implies that the alliance agreement is organized through an alliance contract, without any transfer of equity between the partners (Pisano 1989). This type of arrangement is relatively easily established, because it relies solely on a relatively simple contractual agreement. The rules of the game are well specified, and a failure by either party to deliver on the contracted commitments can be resolved through litigation. Non-equity arrangements often involve a series of small tasks or projects, even if over a long period, but one party usually dominates, such that relationship power and information are asymmetrical. Non-equity arrangements mimic market transactions and exclude relational elements, so the contractual terms of exchange are binding and specific, and efficiencies of the market exchange enable them to maximize their profits (Ganesan 1993). Examples of such partnerships include production or marketing alliances, which offer the key advantage of speed in forging the relationship. Because of the low degree of integration and reciprocal relationships, partners can dissolve these relationships with minimal costs. However, non-equity arrangements offer only limited protection against exchange hazards and demand increasingly explicit and close controls over alliance activities and partner behaviour.

In contrast, in an equity-based arrangement, the partners transfer equity or establish a new organizational entity, called a joint venture, in which they both participate with equity (Hennart 1988). The exchange of equity thus provides an additional protection against exchange hazards, because partners become dependent on each other to achieve their objectives. Equity-based arrangements usually reflect a long-term commitment and a sense of mutual cooperation, shared risks and benefits. They are characterized by high levels of interdependence, financial and organizational integration, and often extensive contracts. The main advantage of such equity-based alliances is the partial ownership and the direct control that follows from it. Ownership also assures greater transparency in terms of shared costs, potential revenue and risks. Direct control reduces the risk of opportunistic partner behaviour, because of the higher likelihood of detection. However, equity-based alliances also require increased integration, which may cause problems in fields such as finance, human resources or information technology.

Furthermore, if equity is exchanged, firms must determine whether to opt for a minority, an equal or a majority share. If a firm has less than 50 per cent of the equity, it has less control over the alliance, acquires fewer profits and usually needs to expend more effort in lobbying activities to influence the process and results. However, the risks involved are relatively lower, the impact on the organization is smaller and the demands on management resources decline. In contrast, when the firm has more than a 50 per cent equity share, it takes more responsibility for the alliance process and invests more in the partnership; it also obtains more control over alliance processes, can push its own interests to the front and reaps a relatively larger share of the created value. Finally, in an equal share arrangement, the partners share costs and risks equally and their interest and commitment are equally important. However, this form demands complex control, agreement from all participants and a loss of speed.

A specific type of equity-based alliance is the joint venture: partner firms establish and become owners of a new independent entity. They resemble hierarchy-based organizations, such that joint ventures are subject to different problems than market exchange-type alliances, including the need to design coordination and misappropriation tactics. Setting up a separate legal entity is expensive and often time consuming; the new entity must then build its own image and reputation. Finally, flexibility is minimal, because the strong organizational and financial relationships between the partners impede either's effort to exit, possibly including high exit fees. Despite these disadvantages, joint ventures offer profit-and-loss transparency, shared and direct control through partial ownership, long-term incentives and a minimal threat to the partner firms' images in case of a reputational stumble.

Both non-equity and equity arrangements can enable firms to realize their objectives, but they do so in different ways, which influence firms' governance decisions (see Table 5.1). Non-equity arrangements enable firms to realize their objectives without resorting to full integration, such that they resemble market transactions and focus on short-term outcomes. In contrast, the degree of integration in equity-based arrangements is relatively higher, which creates stronger incentives for long-term commitments, akin to a hierarchical arrangement. Without additional measures (e.g. contractual, control mechanisms), a non-equity arrangement offers limited safeguards against exploitation and opportunistic conduct, whereas an equity arrangement provides substantial protection – though the costs associated with forging and monitoring such an equity arrangement may outweigh its benefits. Thus, both governance forms offer unique advantages, and both entail limitations. The choice of a governance form depends on the risks and level of influence a firm prefers over its alliance activities.

Governance form selection

Alliance literature draws on several theoretical perspectives to provide rationales for governance form decisions. These perspectives are similar to those in Chapter 2; for parsimony, we do not repeat an in-depth discussion of these theories here, but rather cite key implications for governance form decisions.

Transaction cost economics (TCE) notes that transaction costs are minimized when a governance form matches the exchange conditions (Williamson 1975,

TABLE 5.1 Non-equity and equity-based arrangements

	Non-equity arrangement	Equity arrangement with recurrent entity			Equity arrangement with new entity
		Minority share	Equal share	Majority share	Joint venture
Description	Agreement based on formalized alliance contract*	Firm has less than 50% equity share	Firms both have 50% equity share	Firm has more than 50% equity share	Establishment of new organizational entity
Advantages	Limited integration, keep own identity, focus on activities, flexibility, easy exit	Less risk, less organizational change and impact, less need for alliance management	Sharing cost and risks equally, equal commitment and interests	More control, push own interests, fewer debates	Transparent cost and profit sharing, risk sharing, ownership provides control and monitoring, long-term incentives, fewer reputational effects
Disadvantages	Lack of control, requires alliance management skills, risk of opportunism, good preparation and negotiation needed, less learning and synergetic benefits	Less profit, less control, more lobbying, risk of opportunism	Complex control, agreement needed at all decision points, loss of speed	Large responsibility, high investments	Difficulties with integration, transfer of staff, required set-up time, costs and legal implications to exit or amend joint venture

Note: *Franchise and (cross-) licence agreements tend to be more transactional-oriented than non-equity-based alliances

Sources: Dwyer et al. (1987); Hennart (1988); Pisano (1989).

1991). In general, when a transaction involves mixed asset specificity and is recurrent, an alliance is appropriate. Different governance form preferences thus represent responses to appropriation concerns: Firms resort to equity arrangements to reduce transaction costs when there is a risk of opportunism but not to mandate hierarchical internalization. Equity participation is a feasible counter-measure to opportunism and appropriation concerns, because opportunism by the equity partner invokes penalties in the form of the reduced value of its equity stake. In addition, asset specificity provides an important indicator of structural preference. As firms make more specialized investments, they tend to prefer equity-based arrangements, which offer protection against the exploitation of a hold-up situation. Furthermore, when creation, transfer and exploitation of knowledge are part of the alliance, an equity arrangement is preferable, because this type of joint ownership aligns partner interests and provides superior monitoring (Gulati and Singh 1998). Empirical studies generally provide support for these predictions (Osborn and Baughn 1990; Oxley 1997; Pisano 1989).

The resource-based view (RBV) emphasizes value maximization through pooling and employing valuable resources (Zajac and Olsen 1993). The resources exchanged are intimately connected with alliance performance and can determine the preferred type of alliances and chosen governance structure. The focus thus shifts from safeguarding against exchange hazards to improving knowledge flows between partner firms. In distinguishing between proprietary and knowledge-based resources (Das and Teng 2000b), a firm prefers a governance form that enables it to procure external resources without losing control over its own resources. Property-based resources are protected by property rights laws; non-equity arrangements often provide enough security for collaboration. If the exchange entails knowledge-based resources, they are less identifiable and more difficult to manage, so direct control through an equity alliance is preferable over non-equity agreements. Mellewigt and Das (2010) examine structural preferences in the German telecommunications industry and find that the exchange of knowledge-based resources tends to lead to equity agreements that safeguard against opportunism and knowledge leakage. Finally, if resource contributions become heterogeneous, the risk of unwanted resource transfers increases, a threat that can be countered by equity arrangements (Sampson 2004a).

The resource dependence perspective (RDP), concerned with a firm's external arrangements, suggests that partner firms contribute critical resources to ensure their survival (Pfeffer and Salancik 1978). When resources are not readily or sufficiently available through market exchange, firms engage in boundary-spanning activities and forge relationships with other parties in order to obtain them, and reduce external uncertainty. Non-equity-based arrangements provide more flexibility and the options to scale up or scale down an investment; equity-based arrangements offer more control over joint resources. Flexible arrangements mean that the firm can take advantage of changed circumstances, though at the cost of the extent of its capability to exploit opportunities. The more interdependent the firms are, perhaps due to their interdependencies in purchases and sales, the more likely they are to prefer an equity arrangement (Pfeffer and Nowak 1976). As the importance of the alliance increases (i.e. fewer alternatives become available), firms tend to prefer equity arrangements in order to gain more control (Blodgett 1991a).

Social network theory (SNT) states that the social context emerging from prior alliances influence governance decisions (Gulati 1995b). Repeated collaborations with the same partners provide information that helps firms learn about new opportunities, and enhances their trust in current and potential partners. Indirect relationships through common partners function as important referral mechanisms. Successive alliances reduce behavioural uncertainty and the need for more sophisticated governance forms. Trust and the development of inter-organizational routines also increase the predictability of partners firms' behaviour, which reduces the need for equity-based protection. That is, prior ties between partners reduce contracting costs and require less complex contracts; moreover, if the prior collaborations were preceded by extensive negotiations, those prior agreements can usually be embodied in new contracts at little cost. Gulati (1995a) reaffirms these claims: his study suggests that repeated alliances are less likely than other alliances to be organized using equity.

An organizational learning perspective (OLP) states that firms enter into partnerships to learn new skills or acquire tacit knowledge (Kogut 1988). The primary motive for forming alliances is that superior knowledge enhances their competitive position. In terms of governance forms, OLP suggests that equity-based arrangements are more appropriate as learning vehicles than are non-equity arrangements. If alliances involve knowledge, it can be difficult to circumscribe, monitor and codify this resource, rather than giving rise to free riding or misappropriation. Such concerns are compounded because knowledge is so difficult to value without complete information. A firm that wants to learn a particular skill thus stands a better chance of realizing this objective if it forms an equity-based arrangement, which is better equipped to handle the knowledge management processes required for knowledge creation, transfer and exploitation (Inkpen 2000). In addition, reciprocal relationships typical of equity arrangements offer better protection against knowledge spillovers.

Institutional theory (IT) argues that alliances aim for legitimacy and social approval, rather than effectiveness or efficiency. Common alliance practices emerge when collaborating becomes an accepted phenomenon, and firms copy their rivals in their use of this strategy (Venkatraman et al. 1994). In addition, entering strategic alliances increases legitimacy, because partnering with well-known and reputed partners improves the focal firm's reputation and congruence with prevailing norms in the institutional environment (Lin et al. 2009). The choice of non-equity or equity-based arrangements thus may be shaped by institutional pressures.

This concise overview of theoretical perspectives on governance form decisions summarizes the many unique insights into motives that range from economic to behavioural. Yet choosing a governance form remains relatively straightforward. A simple non-equity-based arrangement may suffice if the resources and information to be transferred are precise and highly explicit. As the alliance becomes more complex and the likelihood of exchange hazards increases, equity-based arrangements tend to be more appropriate. However, governance form is not the only decision to make when structuring an alliance. Alliance managers have considerable flexibility in designating duties and responsibilities, through alliance contracts and management control mechanisms.

Alliance contracts

An alliance contract provides a legally binding, institutional framework that codifies each party's rights, duties and responsibilities and specifies the goals, policies and strategies that underlie the anticipated cooperation (Mayer and Argyres 2004; Luo 2002). These promises or obligations to perform particular actions in the future explain the contribution of an alliance contract to alliance development and outcomes. That is, an alliance contract safeguards investments and property against misappropriation by a partner, and codifies the penalties a firm can impose on a counterpart if the latter violates the alliance agreement. An alliance contract also provides a clear overview of the tasks and responsibilities of each party, such that it also functions as a coordination mechanism. In order to cope with additional internal and external challenges that may emerge unexpectedly as the partnership unfolds, alliance contracts can enable adaptation. This so-called contingency adaptability refers to the specification of principles or guidelines that describe how to handle changing situations. Finally, an alliance contract signals commitment, as a tangible expression of trust and loyalty between partners.

The degree to which contractual terms actually appear in an alliance contract (see Table 5.2) is often referred to as contractual completeness (Luo 2002), and it directly affects alliance development and outcomes (Hagendoorn and Hesen 2007). On one end of the spectrum, contractual terms could be left wide open, such that firms have to interpret the content as relevant to the situation or renegotiate terms as necessary. On the other end, terms could be detailed closely, leaving no room for interpretation. The more complex the contract is, the greater the specification of promises, obligations and processes for dispute resolution. For example, complex contracts could specify procedures for monitoring, penalties for non-compliance, inputs to be provided, and outcomes to be delivered. As exchange hazards rise, so must contractual safeguards to reduce the threat of costs and performance losses.

The perceived risk of opportunistic behaviour is likely to determine contract completeness. However, because crafting complete contracts is costly, partners do so only when the risk of contractual breaches is high. If partners agree to make alliance-specific investments, complete contracts are needed to protect against opportunism. That is, such investments need long-term alliances to provide benefits, so the potential for threats of termination and unfavourable conditions imposed by non-investing counterparts usually demand contractual safeguarding. Performance measurement ambiguity and alliance uncertainty also necessitate contractual protections, because in these conditions, partners have incentives to limit their contributions. Whereas contract completeness deters behaviours that could jeopardize the performance of an alliance, it increases contracting costs and

TABLE 5.2 Contractual clauses

- The *spirit of the venture* or *social contract* should be embodied in the alliance contract. The parties might agree to the same terms on paper but have different expectations about how the agreement will work in practice.

- Technically, a *business plan* is not a legal document, and it is not expected that disagreements result in legal claims. It is important however to document common and individual alliance objectives.

- *Scope and exclusivity* refer to the delineation of alliance activities in terms of product, country, technology and period.

- The *governance form* should be specified in the alliance contract: non-equity or equity. It is important to specify *ownership* (if applicable). The partners may decide to equally share ownership in a joint venture. Alternatively, partners may take a majority or minority equity stake.

- *Contributions* should be specified: what each partner supplies to the alliance in terms of assets, business, services, technology and people.

- *Funding* should be specified: is initial capital provided in cash or non-cash assets, what are future legal obligations, and does the alliance require outside financing?

- *Compensation mechanisms* depict the rewards parties can expect, such as profits, royalties, dividends, or intellectual property. A hybrid compensation structure is preferred because it provides short- and long-term incentives.

- The alliance's *management structure* is usually formalized in an alliance contract. Issues include the right to appoint directors, delegates in the management team, authority given to managers from partners and reserved matters.

- *Roles, tasks and authority* specify who has the right to make decisions in which areas, and the decision-making procedures, such as majority voting, consensus, consent, blocking votes, lead partner ruling, based on proportion of investment and a 'one person, one vote' principle.

- *Protection*, such as of intellectual property rights (i.e. patents and licenses), enables firms to prevent partners from using certain organizational resources in a competitive manner.

- With *non-compete and exclusivity* clauses, partners can limit their cooperation (or the results of their cooperation) to certain products, markets, technologies, or geographical areas.

- *Adaptation and contingency* clauses provide guidelines and solutions about how partners should act when confronted with unanticipated circumstances. They may be incorporated in the contract as independent terms or as related clauses in specific areas.

- *Exit provisions* detail the consequences and obligations of parties when one or both partners want to exit the alliance. They detail implications tied to unilateral termination, such as the right to sell to a third party, put/call options in a joint venture, preemption rights, and obligations. Exit provisions also may detail exit triggers, such as insolvency, change of control and contract breaches. In joint ventures, different resolutions to buy-outs can be incorporated, including right of first refusal, right of first offer, drag along, or a shoot-out procedure.

- *Conflict resolution provisions* provide guidelines. The most effective conflict resolution strategy is joint problem solving, but procedures may also entail third-party arbitration and votes.

- An alliance's *communication structure* is often specified, because high-quality communication is critical to effective functioning. It might list different fixed contact points across different levels, boundary-spanning agents, frequency of meetings, and the ICT infrastructure.

- *Location of operation* is often specified. Activities may take place at different locations; to reduce the risk of hazards, partners need to specify the working procedures.

- Other contractual clauses may pertain to setting the *accounting principles* to be adopted by the alliance (e.g. international joint venture); the *governing law* if partners operate in different countries; *timing issues* related to third-party consent (e.g. antitrust, shareholder approval); *major contracts* with existing customers and suppliers; employees; and *taxes*.

potentially damages initial trust building. Contract completeness may thus enhance alliance performance (Poppo and Zenger 2002), but this effect really is conditional on the degree of cooperation between partners, such that when contracts are more complete, cooperation contributes more to performance (Luo 2002). Moreover, if enforcement is difficult, as in highly volatile environments, the costs of complete contracts may not outweigh their benefits.

Contract standardization implies instead the application of similar contracts or terms across a range of contractual transactions (Vlaar 2006). On a continuum, a tailored contract would represent one end, whereas the standardized contract would be the other. A tailored contract is designed especially for the alliance and tends to be fairly complex; a standard contract is intended to apply to multiple contractual relationships, so its terms are not designed for any specific collaboration (Ariño and Reuer 2004). Standardized contracts can be quickly and efficiently implemented; tailored contract can be designed according to the specific situation, allthough doing so demands significantly higher costs. The applicability of standardized contracts also depends on the variation in alliance schemes. Low variation supports opportunities for using standardized documents; high variation makes tailored contracts seem more appropriate. Poppo and Zenger (2002) thus find that firms using customized contracts can improve their alliance performance, but only if a high level of relational governance exists.

Another important distinction separates pre-specified and open-ended alliances (Reuer and Ariño 2007). When an alliance's time horizon is pre-specified, alliance managers tend to be more concerned about ownership of proprietary knowledge, disclosure of confidential information, or the means for ending the alliance. The risk of opportunistic behaviours is higher in alliances with a pre-specified duration, because the counterparts have few possibilities to reciprocate for opportunistic behaviour. Yet the costs of predicting future economic conditions for open-ended alliances and crafting appropriate contractual provisions are significant, forcing alliance managers to rely more on incomplete contracts. In open-ended alliances of long anticipated duration, the thought of future benefits safeguards against opportunism, because the 'shadow of the future' shifts dispositions toward win–win instead of win–lose perspectives (Heide and Miner 1992).

A well-designed alliance contract is thus consistent with the alliance objectives and the partners' interests, whatever those may be. Even if alliance partners have a clear understanding, however, designing an alliance contract that anticipates all possible unforeseen circumstances is simply not feasible. Alliances tend to be even more common in uncertain environments, because they offer firms flexibility. Alliance managers therefore need to balance the costs of negotiating, monitoring and enforcing alliance contracts against the threat of potential exchange hazards. They are likely to be left with the use of incomplete contracts, with their adaptation problems and room for opportunistic conduct. In this case, the governance form and alliance contract may need to be supplemented with additional management control mechanisms.

Management control

Management control in alliances refers to control mechanisms that alliance partners might use but are not likely to formalize in an alliance contract. Their primary purpose is to encourage coordination and ensure the partners achieve their predetermined objectives (Dekker 2004). Control mechanisms organize the coordination of interdependent tasks; firms might put command and authority systems in place to force their partner to comply with the tasks required to achieve alliance objectives or allocate resources even if the partner is unwilling to do so. Management control also enables a firm to acquire influence over alliance development and outcomes by installing incentive systems, standard operating procedures and conflict resolution procedures, which provide incentives to collaborate. Reducing appropriation concerns and fulfilling coordination requirements are thus critical rationales for management control. Management control may also be embodied in alliance contracts, but it extends beyond governance form; for example, control is not a strict consequence of ownership but rather results from a variety of control mechanisms.

Control modes

We begin by differentiating three control modes (Dekker 2004): output, behavioural and social. Output and behavioural control are based on formal control mechanisms, often but not necessarily incorporated into an alliance contract (Chen *et al.* 2009; Patzelt and Shepherd 2008). The former specify the objectives to be realized by the alliance and its partners, and then monitor the realization of such targets. For example, outcome controls might set alliance objectives, create incentive and reward systems and outline monitoring procedures, which together clarify mutual expectations and increase goal congruence. Behavioural control refers to how the partners should act, and monitors whether their actual behaviours comply with these predetermined behaviours. Reports, meetings, planning, operating rules and routines, standard procedures and conflict resolution procedures are typical examples. Social control mechanisms are not formalized in an alliance contract but rather reflect relational norms that guide partner firms' behaviours and result from socialization processes (Macneil 1978). Social control thus influences alliance activities through partner interactions that facilitate shared values and common understanding. It requires significant communication through organizational mechanisms such as rituals, ceremonies, teams, task forces and other socialization methods. The choice of output, behavioural or social modes of management control depends on three factors:

1. If the resources contributed to the alliance relate closely to the partner firms' core competences, the risk of misuse creates a serious threat. Firms can reduce this threat with output and behavioural controls; for example, alliance contract clauses might specify restrictions on the use of resources and establish monitoring procedures that increase detection of misuse and thus help alliance partners legally protect their contributions.

2. Alliance activities often range from achieving economies of scale to developing new concepts; the nature of these activities affects management control decisions. In alliances with clear task specialization, focused management control is desirable, preferably accompanied by dedicated output and behavioural controls.

3. When measurability of outputs is ambiguous, social control enables firms to protect themselves against misappropriation, because relational norms and capital encourage partners to act in the interest of their counterparts. If uncertainty and ambiguity surround resource contributions and outcomes are difficult to measure, social control again is most appropriate, because it reduces the risk of exchange hazards.

Control dimensions

Geringer and Hebert (1989) also identify three dimension of management control: the mechanisms alliance partners use to exercise control, the degree of control realized by the partners and the focus of the control. The mechanisms that partners use to exercise control can vary, including power, authority, or a wide range of bureaucratic, cultural and informal mechanisms. For example, Schaan (1983) suggests two main categories of control mechanisms: positive and negative. Positive control refers to mechanisms that firms employ to promote constructive behaviours, often exercised through informal mechanisms such as staffing, participation in the planning process and reporting relationships. Negative control, which relies principally on formal agreements, helps firms stop or prevent alliance partners from implementing destructive activities or decisions. In addition, Caniëls and Gelderman (2010) suggest that firms may employ administrative controls to influence decision making, enforced through contractual provisions that stipulate how to handle conflicts, the specific penalties for opportunistic behaviour and which behaviours are allowed. Bargaining power may also function as a control mechanism: A dependent partner has a strong incentive to continue the relationship, to avoid the various costs of termination, and it also avoids opportunistic behaviour for fear of retaliation by the dominant partner. All these types of control grant alliance partners influence over alliance activities, while also protecting them from opportunistic behaviours.

Next, the degree of control refers to partners' decision-making authority (Killing 1983). One partner may obtain a dominant decision-making role, perhaps through dominance in board representation, the right to veto decisions, representation in alliance management, departmentalization of activities, planning and budgeting mechanisms or performance evaluations (Makhija and Ganesh 1997). When a firm has dominant control, it can manage the alliance more easily and, for example, direct resource allocations better (Child 2002). However, partners may also share management control and play active and equal roles in making decisions. Shared control provides partners with signals of long-term commitment, eases information exchange, and enables them to deal flexibly with unforeseen circumstances, which should improve alliance outcomes (Beamish 1993). In a joint venture setting, perhaps neither partner is involved in decision making, because an independent joint venture manager enjoys decision-making autonomy. Glaister *et al.* (2003) propose that joint venture autonomy enhances alliance performance, but once performance deteriorates, parents become involved in decision-making and operations. Yet the overall empirical evidence on the required degree of decision-making authority is inconclusive: firms need to consider the alliance's circumstances carefully and make an informed decision about the degree of control they desire. Moreover, control designs in alliances may evolve over time, for example, from shared to autonomous types (Zhang and Li 2001).

The focus dimension of management control suggests that partner firms may seek to obtain control over specific alliance activities rather than control overall. Focusing management control in areas where its resources get utilized improves the firm's ability to detect misuse and free riding. Prior alliance studies thus distinguish strategic and operational control (Yan and Gray 2001); having a majority equity share tends to result in strategic control, whereas providing non-capital resources leads to operational control (Child and Yan 1999). In addition, Yan and Gray (2001) find that operational control positively influences the realization of the partner's objectives, but strategic control has no impact. Whereas ownership and overall control might provide general insights in alliance progress, focused control appears to enable firms to monitor critical alliance activities more closely.

In summary, governance form constitutes the foundation of an alliance design, but non-equity and equity arrangements also can be augmented with alliance contracts and management control mechanisms. Alliance contracts depict formalized agreements between alliance partners and detail partners' promises and obligations. However, not all design decisions can or should be formalized, in which case additional management control mechanisms, such as social and focused control, may be used to develop a coherent alliance design.

Structural configuration

Despite even their best efforts to deal with complexity and unpredictability, managers remain limited in their ability to plan for the future and predict the various contingencies that may arise, which creates the need for contracting and formalization. However, limited information may also result in misaligned governance forms or incomplete contracts, because it is too costly for managers to negotiate and write claims that fully describe each party's responsibilities and rights for all contingencies that could reasonably occur during the alliance. When new circumstances arise, a contract must specify, in its adaptation clauses, how to deal with them; otherwise, the parties will need to engage in costly renegotiations or terminate the alliance prematurely. Accordingly, alliance partners need a balance across governance form, alliance contract and management control to minimize the costs of negotiating, contracting and monitoring, while still providing sufficient coordination and protection against exchange hazards (Das and Rahman 2001).

BOX 5.1 ALLIANCE MIRROR DESIGN

A widely adopted alliance design is the mirror structure design, also known as the multiple points of contact model, which aligns governance form, alliance contract and management control. In a mirror structure, the partner firms mirror each other, such that at each organizational level, representatives are appointed to participate in the alliance management. The resultant structure covers strategic, tactical, and operational levels of the organizations. The strategic direction of the alliance is managed by executives from all participating organizations, who form an executive board (with cross-board positions) or oversight committee. Their primary role is to provide the strategic direction for the alliance and guard its fit with the strategic targets of their organization. Involvement in the day-to-day practices of the alliance is generally low. In addition, an alliance steering committee is installed and depending on the size and scope of the alliance, it might consist of a strategic and an operational management team. The strategic management team focuses on translating the strategic direction provided by the executive board into plans and priorities. Often members of the management team conduct periodic meetings to discuss the operational direction of the alliance and resolve issues. If the management team cannot resolve issues or conflicts, the matter goes to the executive board, which makes the final decision. On a day-to-day basis, the alliance is managed by representatives from the participating organizations who are directly involved with its activities. Sometimes specific groups work on specific assignments or projects. The operational management team then acts as a steering committee for working groups.

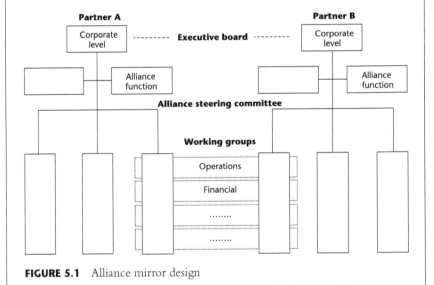

FIGURE 5.1 Alliance mirror design

We suggest that firms can design an optimal structural configuration (see Box 5.1) with a constellation of mutually supportive structural safeguards, including governance form, contractual provisions and management control mechanisms. Equity arrangements outperform non-equity arrangements with respect to reducing the likelihood of exchange hazards, but decisions about contractual design and management control also affect the likelihood of exchange hazards. Alliance partners may agree about hybrid compensation structures, share decision-making rights or commit themselves to non-recoverable investments, which in combination create reciprocal relationships akin to hierarchical control, though without resorting to equity-based arrangements. Furthermore, they may install management control mechanisms, such as shared decision making, monitoring, and mimicking hierarchical elements. This type of quasi-hierarchical control reduces parties' vulnerability to exchange hazards and enables them to protect individual interests, potentially rendering an equity governance form redundant.

Child (2002) reaffirms this view by revealing various successful structural configurations within the context of international joint ventures. Joint ventures with a majority foreign equity share that receive heavy support from the foreign parent and give local managers an active role outperform similar joint ventures with minimal local manager contribution. Joint ventures with equal equity stakes tend to perform well when they also feature shared management and aligned goals; joint ventures with a minority equity share experience higher performance when the foreign partner has operational control. In summary, designing alliances requires managers to resolve a series of trade-offs rather than seeking a single, ultimate alliance design.

Alliance design: Decision-making steps

In the preceding chapter, we focused on alliance negotiations and processes resulting in alliance outcomes. In the alliance design stage, firms formalize these outcomes. Consistent with win–win negotiations, a definitive formalized alliance design enables partners to realize common objectives, while also protecting individual interests. The focus is on designing an alliance structure, with a governance form, contractual provisions, and management control that aligns partners' objectives and offers a constructive foundation for executing the alliance. But what should be formalized in an alliance design, how, and for what reasons? To resolve these questions, we propose a (repetitive) sequence of five decision-making steps (see Figure 5.2).

Step 1: Negotiation and documentation

Alliance negotiation and alliance design are often executed concurrently. As the negotiation progresses, negotiators draft documents that provide initial input, prior to the definitive alliance agreement. Building on the pre-negotiation outcomes, the first document is a confidentiality agreement that details the rules of engagement

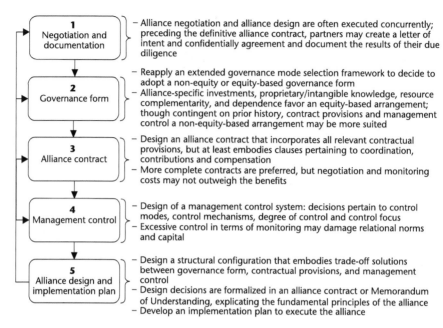

FIGURE 5.2 Decision-making steps: Alliance design

and regulates the information exchange between partners. The next document to be drafted in the alliance design stage is the Heads of Agreement. This brief document establishes the (commercial) fundamentals of the alliance. It is not a legal document but rather a road map that nurtures communication between negotiation parties. The negotiators should discuss the terms of this document, including at least the following issues:

- Spirit of the alliance, including shared values and visions.
- Fundamentals of the alliance, including alliance objectives, scope, location of operation, and exclusivity of negotiations.
- Anticipated contributions and the partners' provision of resources in terms of tangible (e.g. financial) and intangible (e.g. know-how) assets.
- Anticipated compensation, including reward mechanisms described in terms of royalties, fees, lump-sum payments and dividends, as well as ownership and rights over technologies developed by the alliance, their use (e.g. licensing), and future developments.
- Coordination and tentative ideas about governance form, contractual provisions, and management control mechanisms, including the management and communication structure.
- Public announcements that detail who will release a press release announcing the alliance to inform external stakeholders and when this will be done; stock exchange regulations that must be adhered to.

- Other agreements, including product development, pricing, cost sharing of marketing campaigns, marketing rights of products and technologies in case the partnership ends, and legal, tax and financial matters.

Step 2: Governance form

An appropriate alliance governance form provides control and conditions – that is, a context for executing the alliance successfully. The guidelines for the proper governance form are not straightforward. Negotiators must find the delicate balance across negotiation, contracting, and monitoring costs to protect their interests and anticipated benefits. Furthermore, governance form decisions should be aligned with decisions about contractual provisions and management control mechanisms. To discuss some of these considerations, we simplify matters by taking a one-sided perspective, such that we note non-equity arrangements are preferred when a firm:

- Expects to make limited alliance-specific investments; otherwise, an equity-based arrangement is more appropriate, because it offers better protection against exploitation.
- Expects to supply primarily property-based rather than knowledge-based resources; otherwise, an equity-based arrangement offers better protection against knowledge leaks.
- Considers the alliance of moderate strategic importance; otherwise, an equity-based arrangement better protects against the unwanted transfer of critical resources.
- Expects that the degree of required learning is low; otherwise, an equity-based arrangement is beneficial by functioning as a learning vehicle.
- Possesses a history of collaboration with this partner; otherwise, an equity-based arrangement is more appropriate, because trust and inter-organizational routines have not yet been developed.

In addition to the choice between non-equity and equity-based arrangements, various types of equity-based arrangements might be chosen. For example, a joint venture is preferable if the firm seeks to divest resources but wants to continue exploiting their value. Protection of the market and the firm's reputation may prompt firms to adopt a joint venture form or separate out risky investments. The choice of minority versus majority equity-based arrangements depends on the importance of the relationship to the firm, and its desire to possess ownership and exercise influence.

Step 3: Contractual provisions

A governance form alone is not sufficient to govern an alliance. Alliance partners can augment their selected governance form with contractual provisions, whose choice and content can alter the initial governance form decision. That is, using negotiation about the content of the specific contractual provisions, a firm can acquire strategic and organizational control and decision-making authority, in which case the equity-based governance form may become obsolete. Resource contributions vulnerable to exploitation also could be protected with non-exclusive protection provisions. A reward system with ex-ante and residual sharing would provide long-term incentives to partners to remain committed; however, an absence of adequate contractual protection may suggest that equity governance is more appropriate to safeguard the firm's interests. The more complete an alliance contract is, the less need for equity-based governance forms, as reinforced by a mutual history of collaboration. However, at the least, the contractual provisions should include:

- A business plan specifying the alliance's common and individual objectives.
- The governance form, whether non-equity or equity-based.
- The alliance's management structure in terms of board representations, decision-making rights, veto decisions, and the alliance steering committee.
- Partners' resource contributions, including both property-based and knowledge-based resources.
- Clauses specifying compensation mechanisms, such as royalties, dividends, and lump sum payments.
- Non-compete and exclusivity clauses that specify target markets and the use of technologies.
- Protection clauses, including intellectual property rights, patents and licences.
- Conflict resolution techniques, such as arbitration and mediation.
- Exit clauses, including triggers of termination and termination trajectories.
- Regulations for accounting principles and timing issues, contracts with existing customers and suppliers, employees and taxes.

Step 4: Management control

Alliance partners might also supplement an alliance design with management control mechanisms that are not formalized in an alliance contract. It is important to recall the spirit of collaboration when deciding on management control mechanisms. Control systems should not be based on who has more or less control, but rather on the right persons or organization to control a specific area, based on their abilities or experience, the possession of appropriate tools to exercise control and control of the moment. Ill-designed management control systems may suggest the appearance of control, but in reality, they provide inaccurate information and tend to jeopardize the quality of the working relationship. Management control might include the following:

- Modes of management control: contingent on the alliance objectives and initial design decisions, partner firms may use a combination of outcome, behavioural and social controls to monitor partners' behaviour and alliance progress.

- Mechanisms of management control: partners may use combinations of positive and negative controls, and employ administrative or power-based control.
- Degree of management control: partners need to consider in which areas they require dominant control or whether shared management is more likely to foster alliance performance.
- Focus of management control: partners may install focused control in critical areas that appear vulnerable to misappropriation.

Depending on the management control system, firms should make an organizational chart that depicts the different roles, functions and reporting directions for each firm. In addition, they can specify meeting frequency and communication and reporting systems.

Step 5: Alliance design and implementation

Building on these preceding decisions, alliance partners should evaluate the definitive alliance design: does the alliance design provide sufficient incentives and enforcement for long-term commitment, while protecting the partners' individual interests? If so, these decisions should be clearly documented in the alliance contract (or Memorandum of Understanding), which guides its execution. Choosing an alliance design without paying sufficient attention to the implementation plan is like starting a business without a business plan. The implementation plan guides operational processes and should include the following issues:

- Time span for achieving alliance objectives and performance metrics system.
- Personnel plans to allocate the roles to key persons involved in the alliance; training and education of personnel and personnel rotation programmes.
- Resource plans to secure timely resource provisions after the alliance starts (e.g. funding, patents, software systems).
- Marketing plan to secure the integration of sales and service systems and joint distribution.
- Operational plans to support operational linkages between the firms and enable the integration of business processes.
- Communication plan to identify requirements for effective formal and informal communication during all stages of the alliance, including briefings with operational managers and reporting to executive managers.
- Contingency plan that specifies responses when dealing with unforeseen circumstances, such as product launches and market failure.

Summary

We have provided an overview of three structural building blocks of alliance design: governance form, alliance contract and management control. Each block of alliance design functions to align partners' interests, enable coordination and reduce the risk of exchange hazards. Rather than considering them as discrete one-off decisions, we present them as interrelated. Governance form decisions affect the content of contractual provisions, and vice versa. Deficiencies in an alliance contract may be overcome through management control mechanisms. Alliance negotiators should account for these relationships when negotiating the alliance design. To this end, we have provided a five-step procedure for firms that may assist them in alliance design decisions and prepare the partners to execute the alliance. However, alliance design alone is insufficient to secure coordination and protection against exchange hazards. Alliance management and in particular relational governance also offers a critical coordination mechanism. In the next chapter, we thus elaborate on alliance management.

Case: Nokia–Microsoft

The Finnish company Nokia[1] was founded in 1865 as a ground wood pulp mill, and grew to become a global corporation with a prominent position in the global telecommunications industry. The company has been able to establish its leading position through easy-to-use phones aimed at individual consumers and businesses. However, the telecommunications industry has become more competitive over the last decade, with rapid technology developments in both software- and hardware-fuelled innovations. For example, innovative Smartphones integrate various forms of data communications into one device and have become the standard. In addition, the market has seen new entrants, such as HTC and Apple with its iPhone, as well as new operating systems, including Google's Android and Apple's iOS. These developments caused Nokia to start losing market share in 2010, primarily due to the fact that its phones lacked the design edge and were not as easy to use compared to rivals' phones. Nokia had to re-evaluate its strategic direction. At the same time, Microsoft was looking for ways to re-enter the mobile market. It had developed a new operating system, Windows Phone 7, that had been received reasonably well by critics, but although Microsoft forged distribution deals with LG, Samsung and Sony Ericsson, it needed a major manufacturer to commoditize its operating system.

In February 2011, Nokia and Microsoft announced a strategic (contractual) partnership that aimed to compete more effectively against Apple and Google in the fight for Smartphone dominance. The Heads of Agreement stipulated that Nokia and Microsoft agreed to create market-leading mobile products and services jointly that were designed to offer consumers, operators and developers unrivalled choice and opportunity. Because each company generally focuses on its core competences, the partnership created the opportunity to launch a new global mobile ecosystem that enabled rapid time-to-market execution.

Ahead of schedule, in April 2011, Nokia and Microsoft signed a definitive agreement containing numerous contractual provisions, some of which are outlined below. Nokia and Microsoft agreed to exploit their complementary assets to design, develop and market productivity solutions for mobile devices for professionals. The agreement stipulated that Nokia would gain access to the Windows Phone 7 operating system, which it would use as its primary operating system. This would enable the partners to reach more price points, market segments and geographic locations. However, the agreement also stipulated that the Windows Phone 7 operating system would remain available to Samsung, LG and Sony Ericsson. In addition, Nokia would deliver mapping, navigation and certain location-based services to the Windows Phone system. It would build innovation on top of the Windows Phone platform in areas such as imaging, while also contributing expertise on hardware design and language support, and helping to drive the development of the Windows Phone platform. Microsoft would provide Bing search services across the Nokia device portfolio, as well as contributing strength in productivity, advertising, gaming, social media and a variety of other services. The combination of navigation with advertising and search function would enable better monetization of Nokia's navigation assets and completely new forms of advertising revenue. Through joint developing and application sourcing, the partners intend to support the creation of new local and global applications, including making the Windows Phone developer registration free for all Nokia developers. In addition, the partners agreed to open a new Nokia-branded global application store that would leverage the Windows Marketplace infrastructure. Nokia is also expected to contribute its operator billing system expertise to allow participants of the Windows Phone ecosystem to take advantage of Nokia's billing agreements with 112 operators in 36 markets.

The partnership agreement also contained multiple contractual provisions regarding the financial pay-off. Microsoft would receive a running royalty for the Windows Mobile platform. This fee takes into account the predicted volume of phones and joint collaborative efforts, as well as the engineering work done by both companies. In return, Microsoft pays Nokia for its contribution to the development of the Microsoft platform and other Microsoft services. Microsoft also pays Nokia for the right to use its intellectual properties, which enables Nokia to reduce operating expenses. Therefore, the partnership provides multiple opportunities for revenue sharing from a combination of services, such as location-based assets with Microsoft's search and advertising platform. Although the figures have not been made public, the total deal is likely to involve billions of dollars.

The partnership agreement also contained a clause related to the division of tasks and co-branding. This clause states that Microsoft and Nokia are each responsible for different pieces of software and hardware; this differs from the Google–Apple partnership, for which operations are more integrated. Nokia and Microsoft also agreed to co-brand on several instances, such as Nokia Search, powered by Bing, and Bing maps, powered by Nokia. The partnership agreement also included a provision (known as a 'forward-looking statement'), which provides, for example, that the companies anticipate changes in leadership and operational structure. The companies reached agreement on Nokia's collaboration with Intel, which is called MeeGo. This would become a long-term open-source project (that is, sidelined) along with Symbian, which would be used on mid-range Nokia phones. Furthermore, Nokia agreed to restructure its organization into two distinct business units: Smart Devices and Mobile Phones. Smart Devices includes Windows Phone,

Symbian and MeeGo devices, while Mobile Phones concentrates on Nokia's feature and lower-end phones. Other statements tap into a variety of unforeseen circumstances that could affect the viability of the alliance, including the partners' ability to innovate, develop, execute and commercialize new technologies, products and services, and the outcome of pending and threatened litigation (such as Nokia's patent dispute with Apple).

Questions

1. Explain why the pay-off structure in the Nokia–Microsoft alliance is likely to contribute to the alliance's success.
2. What other contractual provisions and management control mechanisms could be used to support the partnership?

6

ALLIANCE MANAGEMENT

The alliance management stage confronts alliance partners with the ultimate challenge: to put the negotiation agreement, including their alliance design decisions, into practice. The partners must deploy their resource contributions, implement coordination mechanisms, act on expressed commitments and begin to execute the tasks assigned to them. This stage also introduces partners to new uncertainties and ambiguities, emerging from both internal and external contingencies. The primary task of alliance management is thus to monitor and coordinate alliance activities to the purpose of creating value-creating conditions and mitigating the potential threat of exchange hazards. The decisions made during the preceding alliance development stages may ease the task of alliance management, but as the relationship unfolds the focus should be on day-to-day coordination, related to partners' ability to align their contributions and efforts to ensure efficiency and effectiveness. To inform their alliance management, managers need to recognize how to deploy a range of soft approaches (shown in the first section). Our following two sections provide detail on the relationship between alliance design and alliance management, and a systematic framework and decision-making steps for alliance management. Our final two sections conclude with a summary and a case illustration.

Alliance management approaches

Alliance management encompasses both organizational and inter-organizational routines, systems and procedures that make an alliance work (or not). Its objective is to optimize conditions to enable communication, conflict resolution, decision making and evaluation, which in turn foster alliance performance (Ireland *et al.* 2002). Yet an alliance's value creation potential is continuously at risk. Environmental conditions such as industry dynamics, regulations and laws could pose a threat or provide an opportunity – for example, the industrial and political environment

TABLE 6.1 Four alliance management approaches

	Relational governance	*Conflict management*	*Response strategies*	*Inter-partner learning*
Description	Social institutions that govern and guide alliance partners to behave in a mutually beneficial manner	Conflicts are inherently tied to alliances and tend to hinder alliance collaboration and outcomes	Adversities require managers to react with relationship-preserving or -destroying response strategies	A regular and repeatable pattern of routines, supporting knowledge and information transfer
Logic	Relational norms and relational capital functions as self-enforcing governance mechanisms	The impact of dysfunctional conflicts needs to be mitigated; functional conflicts should be exploited	Understanding the range of responses and their causes enables alliance partners to predict response strategies	Learning about partners reduces costs and increase ease of adaptation in the alliance
Implications	Protects alliance partners against misappropriation and opportunism and functions as a lubricant for cooperation and adaptation	Active conflict management enables alliance partners to improve the quality of alliance processes	Improved resource allocation as firm can anticipate partners' responses to adversity	Increases likelihood of alliance success, specifically in terms of learning objectives
Downside	Requires investments; an optimal alliance governance form does not exist	Requires substantial investments; misuse may exacerbate tensions	Requires further validation; governance and outcome implications are unclear	Potential threat of knowledge leakage; learning requires substantial investments

may render an alliance agreement obsolete or competitors may introduce new technologies that force alliance partners to reconsider their alliance contract. Changes within the partners' firms also create dynamics that demand active alliance management. Internal reorganizations, corporate strategy shifts or transitions in the board of directors may hinder alliance progress. Furthermore, causes endogenous to the alliance can prompt managerial action: the alliance's performance might fall below initial expectations, the partners may update their expectations, or the governance form may become inefficient. We previously explicated how alliance design can safeguard against unforeseen circumstances, but here we discuss four alliance management approaches that suggest unique perspectives on how to deal with the soft side of alliance management: (1) relational governance, (2) conflict management, (3) response strategies and (4) inter-partner learning (see Table 6.1).

Relational governance theory (RGT)

Relational governance theory (RGT) offers a valuable complement to classical contracting (Macneil 1978) by emphasizing the importance of social and relational processes as building blocks of efficient and effective alliances. Classical contract law relied primarily on the legal framework as a mechanism to plan exchanges, (re)negotiate contracts and resolve contractual conflicts; RGT considers legal mechanisms costly in terms of resources and time. Alternatively, relational governance thus governs and guides parties such that they behave in a mutually beneficial manner because of their common understanding of relational norms and relational capital.

Relational norms rest on the premise that for alliance contracts to function, a set of common unwritten social rules must exist to describe the unwritten social rules that guide partner firms' behaviours in particular situations and enhance cooperation and outcomes. Relational norms generally pertain to notions of flexibility, solidarity and information exchange (Heide and John 1992). Flexibility implies that partners expect to make adjustments in their ongoing relationship in order to fit changing circumstances; it facilitates adaptation to unforeseen contingencies. Solidarity norms pertain to partners' anticipation of efforts to preserve the relationship; they signal commitment to continuing the relationship. Information exchange norms mean that parties will provide certain information that might help their partner, such that it facilitates problem solving and adaptation. In alliances with high levels of relational norms, partners can respond effectively to environmental contingencies, extend the time horizon for evaluating the outcomes of their relationships, and refrain from relationship-damaging behaviours (Palmatier et al. 2007). Relational norms promote collaboration, which operates as a safeguard that allows the parties to work on the relationship and respond to problematic situations without continuously referring to a contract. Thus normative behaviours operate as self-enforcing governance mechanisms, such that managers respond to good social relationships by acting to support the relationship. When relational norms are absent, however, managers are likely to respond to poor social relationships with uncooperative behaviours. In the resulting destructive interaction pattern, partners may engage in repeated efforts to exploit their counterpart's vulnerability by behaving opportunistically in order to extract additional rewards.

Relational capital is a response to the inadequacies of contracts that enables alliance partners to deal with their bounded rationality and opportunism (White et al. 2007). It refers to the extent to which parties feel comfortable, rely on trust in their dealings with one another, and commit to the relationship (Ariño et al. 2001). Trust reflects the willingness of a party to be vulnerable to the actions of another party (see Box 6.1), with the expectation that the other party will perform a particular action important to the party that employs trust, irrespective of its ability to monitor or control that other party. Trust-based relational capital contributes to a freer, greater exchange of information and know-how, because decision makers do not worry about protecting themselves from opportunistic behaviour. In turn, commitment refers to an expectation that behaviours will be directed toward relationship maintenance, with a high value placed on the joint relationship. Greater commitment enables both parties to achieve individual and joint goals without raising the spectre of opportunism. Because more committed partners exert effort and balance short-term problems with long-term goal achievement, higher levels of commitment should be associated with partnership success. If they have a good relationship, the parties might discuss and resolve their potential tensions, such that relational capital attenuates concerns about goal conflicts, opportunism and misappropriation. As a critical catalyst of alliance progress, it encourages economically efficient alliances, even in conditions of uncertainty, ambiguity or incomplete information (Palmatier *et al.* 2007).

Relational governance (i.e. relational norms and capital) thus emerges in alliances that include socialization between the partners, which itself results in shared beliefs and values, and influences partners' behaviour so as to increase commitment to the alliance (Das and Teng 2001). However, relational capital focuses on expectations of partner behaviour, whereas relational norms are mechanisms to influence behaviour.

BOX 6.1 TYPES OF TRUST

The alliance literature identifies different types of trust:

- Trust as a structural component resulting, for example, from alliance-specific investments, which create a mutual hostage situation.
- Trust as a behavioural component, referring to the degree of confidence that individual partners have in their mutual reliability and integrity.
- Knowledge-based trust emerges through partner interactions as they learn about each other and develop trust around norms of equity.
- Deterrence-based trust entails utilitarian considerations that lead a firm to believe that a partner will not engage in opportunistic behaviour because of the costly sanctions that are likely to arise.
- Good-will trust refers to the belief that a partner intends to allocate its resources and capabilities rather than engage in opportunistic conduct.
- Competence trust pertains to the belief that a partner does possess enough resources and capabilities to meet the agreements of the alliance contract.
- Calculative trust entails the belief that the possible gains realized through the alliance outweigh the possible costs.

Sources: Boersma *et al.* (2003); Das and Teng (2001); Gulati (1995); Madhok (1995).

Frequent and successful partner interactions might drive the development of close personal relationships that contribute to relational capital building, but these interactions also reinforce the development of relational norms. These different concepts still tend to have similar implications for alliance management, however, such that in an alliance characterized by relational governance, alliance partners are more willing to accommodate one another's needs and overcome adversity. Accordingly, they can implement necessary adjustments to the alliance and rebalance the alliance system, such that parties are confident that any changes are in their interests. Furthermore, relational governance pushes parties to focus on mutually beneficial strategies, rather than exploitation and misappropriation, by shifting their focus from self-centred behaviours toward behaviours that foster unity through common responsibilities. Tensions that arise in the course of the relationship thus will be treated as joint concerns; counterparts maintain agreements, perform competently and behave honourably, even without explicit promises or performance guarantees (Boersma *et al.* 2003). The task for alliance management is to reinforce the priority of investing in the development of relational norms and capital.

Yet relational governance also suffers several disadvantages. A good relationship eliminates costly contracts and coordination mechanisms, by reducing the need to monitor partners' behaviour (Dyer 1997). But building a high quality relationship also demands time and resources, without any guarantee that the counterpart will cooperate (Ariño *et al.* 2001). Furthermore, despite widespread recognition of the importance of relational governance, prior research has not prescribed the optimal types of governance for dealing with specific exchange characteristics. Research that examines relationships between relational governance and other alliance variables (e.g. contracts, alliance-specific investments) has tended to produce fragmented findings (Palmatier *et al.* 2007). With the conceptual framework provided in extant relational governance literature, however, we provide insights into the dimensions and dynamics that underlie alliances, as well as the belief structures and activities necessary for successful alliance relationships (see Box 6.2 for a more recent view).

Conflict management

Conflicts in alliances pertain to a perceived divergence of interests, or the belief that partners' current aspirations cannot be achieved simultaneously (White *et al.* 2007). Conflict is generally imagined as destructive, because it creates negative reactions that can intensify partner tensions (Peng and Shenkar 2002). Moreover, conflicts induce heightened competitive processes, create misperceptions of alliance progress and stimulate a sense of the inequitable distribution of alliance outcomes. They also can give rise to distrust and anxiety, reduce the level of cooperation and efficient integration of activities, and hamper alliance performance (Ding 1997). When conflict leads to overt aggression or passive resistance, it harms alliance performance in another way. Thus dysfunctional conflicts have negative effects in terms of strategic alliance collaboration and partners who perceive them tend to consider themselves obstructed from achieving their objectives.

BOX 6.2 ORGANIZATIONAL JUSTICE

Recent alliance research has drawn on equity and organizational justice theory to explain alliance behaviour. Organizational justice theory states that (in) equity, (in)justice, or (un)fairness affect the behaviour of alliance partners. Inequity exists when the perceived inputs and/or outcomes for one firm are inconsistent with the perceived inputs and/or outcomes of the partner firm. Perceived inequities lead exchange partners to feel as though they are being under- or over-rewarded, then affect their behaviours in subsequent periods by encouraging parties to change their inputs, which likely results in suspicion and mistrust by the exchange partner. Equitable outcomes instead create confidence that the parties will not take advantage of each other but rather are concerned about the other's welfare. For example, Scheer *et al.* (2003) thus find that Dutch automobile dealers react adversely to positive and negative inequities in their relationships with automobile suppliers, and Luo (2005) shows that alliance profitability increases when parties share their perceptions of procedural justice, especially compared with situations marked by asymmetrical perceptions. Despite recent advances more research is needed to achieve coherent explanations for alliance behaviour.

Sources: Greenberg (1987); Luo (2005); Scheer *et al.* (2003).

Dysfunctional conflicts arise for various reasons. Ring and Van de Ven (1994) argue that coordination and efficiency concerns due to opportunism and injustice are responsible for inter-partner conflict, but Khanna (1998) cites incompatibilities between private and common benefits. Das and Teng (2002) also suggest that conflicts result from misfit across organizational routines, technologies, decision-making styles and preferences; emerging private interests and opportunistic behaviour; or fierce competitions outside the alliance. White *et al.* (2007) instead attribute conflicts to cultural differences between partners engaged in international alliances. Thus, the initial alliance conditions and internal and external contingencies induce conflicts and require a response from alliance managers.

To deal with conflict, researchers propose various conflict resolution strategies – some of which are akin to negotiation strategies. Bradford *et al.* (2004) thus distinguish among collaboration (explore integrative solutions), accommodation (accept counterparts' perspective) and confrontation (advocacy of one perspective), whereas White and colleagues (2007) distinguish a harmony strategy, which stresses cooperative behaviour, from a confrontation strategy, with a focus on competitive behaviour, and from a regulatory strategy, stressing rule-based behaviour. Lin and Germain (1998) present problem solving (seeking mutually satisfying solutions), compromising (seeking middle ground), forcing (imposing solution) and legalistic (resorting to contract) strategies. However, conflict resolution tends to be conditional on the type of strategy used and its match with the type of conflict at issue. Lin and Germain (1998) thus reveal that a problem-solving strategy improves joint venture performance, but a legalistic strategy has a negative influence. According to Bradford *et al.* (2004), a collaborative conflict reduction strategy thus reduces the negative effect of conflicts for relational and task conflicts, but an accommodation strategy only reduces relational conflicts, the confrontation conflict strategy only reduces task conflicts, and any misalignment exacerbates the impact of conflicts.

In all these classifications, however, the apparently destructive nature of conflicts is primary, even if other studies suggest that conflicts may not be very detrimental to alliances. Functional conflicts create a positive effect and a constructive contribution to the collaboration (Morgan and Hunt 1994), because such conflicts stimulate interactions among alliance partners. Knowledge sharing and creation results from functional conflict in trusting conditions, because trust improves the quality of dialogue and discussions in the alliance (Panteli and Sockalingam 2005). Refusing to discuss conflicts means inhibiting creativity and innovation. Any conflicts resolved amicably can be regarded as functional, because they ultimately prevent stagnation, stimulate interest and curiosity, and provide a means to resolve the conflicts, which then increases productivity. Functional conflicts also might initiate a critical review of past actions, more frequent and effective communications between alliance partners, a more equitable distribution of system resources, and standardization of the conflict resolution modes available.

Active management of conflicts thus forces alliance members to disagree and debate the merits of their alternative solutions, which can mitigate the negative effects of conflicts and exploit their beneficial aspects. However, if conflicts cannot be resolved, tensions escalate and the dissolution of the partnership becomes inevitable. Despite the importance of dealing actively with conflicts, we also need to consider the hazards associated with conflict management. It demands substantial investments, during both the formation and management stages. Designing conflict resolution mechanisms ex ante and applying them ex post is particularly costly. The misuse of conflict resolution techniques may also have detrimental consequences for alliance continuity. If managers employ force or confrontation to resolve an inter-partner conflict, they may even contribute to conflict escalation instead of resolution.

Response strategies[1]

As alliances progress, partners firms deploy a wide range of response strategies to solve adverse situations (Ariño and de la Torre 1998). Response strategies entail relationship-focused reactions that managers use to resolve dissatisfying situations, such as economic under-performance and poor working relationships (Tjemkes and Furrer 2010). Response strategy research provides a particularly deep understanding of a broader range of relationship-destroying and relationship-preserving responses and their antecedents. Therefore, understanding response strategy behaviour is critical for alliance management, as anticipating partners' response behaviour enables alliance managers to allocate resources efficiently and effectively to either restore a relationship or gradually disengage from it.

Hirschman (1970) initially identifies exit, voice and loyalty as three alternative responses to organizational decline, organized along a constructive–destructive dimension. Extending Hirschman's framework with a fourth strategy – namely neglect (Farrell 1983; Rusbult *et al.* 1982) – results in the EVLN (exit–voice–loyalty–neglect) typology. The EVLN typology represents a parsimonious conceptualization of response strategies and derives its strength from the underlying two-dimensional structure into which the four response strategies are organized. This structure contains an active–passive dimension and a constructive–destructive dimension, with the four response strategies located in quadrants: exit as active–destructive, voice as active–constructive, loyalty as passive–constructive, and neglect as passive–destructive. More recent alliance research has refined and increased the number of response strategies to the seven listed below (Tjemkes and Furrer 2011):

- Exit indicates a disinclination to continue the current alliance and reflects the most destructive response. Managers using this response do not see any possibility of dealing effectively with the adverse situation.
- Opportunism entails an active intention to increase benefits from the alliance in ways that are explicitly or implicitly prohibited. Managers using this response seek to improve their performance covertly.
- Aggressive voice consists of persistent efforts to solve an adverse situation, regardless of the partner's ideas. Managers using an aggressive voice impose their views forcefully and actively on their counterparts, without necessarily trying to avoid conflict.
- Creative voice refers to voicing novel and potentially useful ideas in an attempt to overcome an adverse situation unilaterally, by proposing constructive solutions.
- Considerate voice represents an attempt to change the situation by communicating in a relationship-preserving manner. Alliance managers consider their own concerns as well as those of their partner by discussing the situation with the intention of developing mutually satisfactory solutions.
- Patience (which replaces loyalty) involves silently abiding the issues, with the hope that things will improve in the future. Alliance managers voluntarily ignore the issue and expect the adverse situation to resolve itself.
- Neglect means allowing an alliance to deteriorate. A neglectful alliance manager expends minimal effort in maintaining the partnership, and ignores possible ways to solve the situation, leading to the eventual dissolution of the alliance.

Three distinct factors explain why alliance managers prefer distinct response strategies: individual-level, alliance-level and environmental-level determinants (Tjemkes and Furrer 2011). At the individual level, alliance managers' personal characteristics influence their decision making in general and their use of response strategy in particular. For example, managers' locus of control and risk aversion tends to influence their response strategy preferences. Internally oriented alliance managers, who believe in their power over events, are likely to adopt active response strategies, whereas externally-oriented managers, believing they have little or no control over events, use passive strategies. Risk aversion reflects attitudes toward risk and also influences response strategy preferences. Risk-averse alliance managers might prefer relatively low risks and place greater emphasis on negative consequences, which might lead them to prefer a constructive response (such as the creative voice). In contrast, risk-prone managers facing adverse situations are more likely to engage in more risky response strategies, such as an aggressive voice and opportunism.

Building on social exchange theory (Blau 1964) and interdependence theory (Thibaut and Kelley 1959), response strategy research proposes that response preferences depend on alliance-level exchange variables (Geyskens and Steenkamp 2000; Ping 1993; Tjemkes and Furrer 2010). For example, economic satisfaction pertains to managers' evaluations of the financial outcomes of an alliance. Economic under-performance indicates that alliance managers perceive a discrepancy between prior expectations and desired financial results, which requires an active response (for example, opportunism and the considerate voice), to resolve the adversity rapidly. In contrast, economically satisfied managers prefer passive responses. Social satisfaction, on the other hand, pertains to managers' evaluations of the psycho-social aspects of an alliance. Low social satisfaction creates greater suspicion about a counterpart's intentions and reduces managers' expectations of the relationship's potential future benefits. Therefore, managers who are dissatisfied with relationship quality within the alliance may terminate it rather than try to save it through constructive responses. Managers who are satisfied with the relationship, meanwhile, tend to appreciate contact with their counterparts and are more likely to use constructive response strategies. The presence of exit barriers is also influential; unilateral, alliance-specific investments trigger constructive response strategies and inhibit destructive strategies. This is because constructive responses reduce the risk of losing the investments if the relationship terminates prematurely. In an adverse situation without alternatives, managers have strong incentives to make the current alliance work and are likely to respond actively and constructively to improve the situation.

Competitive intensity and technological change are environmental-level antecedents of response strategy preference. Competitive intensity is the degree of rivalry between competitors in an industry, characterized by industry-wide use of tactics such as aggressive pricing, high levels of advertising, product introductions or adding services to prevent customers from switching to competitors. Firms that operate in industries with high levels of competitive intensity must preserve the quality of their existing alliances in order to secure the resources they provide, which increases the likelihood of constructive strategies, such as the creative voice. In contrast, firms in industries characterized by low competitive intensity are more willing to put the alliance relationship at risk and opt for destructive response strategies, such as exit, opportunism or neglect. Technological turbulence refers to the unpredictability and rate of change of technology in the external environment.

In an environment with low turbulence, a firm may benefit from close relationships with alliance partners, so it relies on and preserves these relationships through constructive responses to develop and diffuse innovations. In markets with high technological turbulence, on the other hand, product and process technologies are relatively unstable. Firms have need for emerging capabilities possessed by alternative partners, which means they are more likely to use destructive responses in existing relationships.

In addition to these three levels of determinants, alliance partners may also develop dynamic interaction patterns of actions–reactions in such a way that they use response strategies to address their partner's behaviour. Such patterns are governed by the principle of complementarity, in that correspondence occurs on the constructive–destructive dimension (constructive strategies invite constructive strategies; destructive strategies invite destructive strategies). The active–passive dimension is marked by reciprocity (active strategies invite passive strategies; passive strategies invite active strategies). Although correspondence and reciprocity are distinct interaction patterns, the combination of the two governs strategic alliance development over time. For example, Ariño and de la Torre's (1998) case study of two firms engaged in an international joint venture provides anecdotal evidence that a larger (smaller) discrepancy in efficiency and equity perceptions makes the relationship more (less) likely to deteriorate through reciprocal destructive behaviour. Combining both patterns could lead to either a self-sustaining, reinforcing system of collaborating and commitment, or a downward spiral of conflictual collaboration and alliance termination.

In summary, response strategy research has advanced alliance management by presenting a coherent typology of relationship-destroying and relationship-preserving response strategies, as well as their causes. The typology improves decision-making in ongoing alliances, as it enables alliance managers to recognize, and therefore anticipate, partner firms' actions in a timely manner. However, two issues warrant further exploration. In the context of alliances, responses to adversity do not occur in a governance vacuum. Whereas deterrence mechanisms such as contracts, mutual hostages, and monitoring are designed to reduce the likelihood of destructive responses, mechanisms such as participative decision making and revenue sharing stimulate constructive responses. The fact that alliance design characteristics are incomplete in nature means they leave room for various response strategy interaction patterns; therefore the relationship between alliance design and response strategies needs to be better understood. Furthermore, to avoid premature alliance termination and anticipate the impact of response strategy use, there is a need for greater insight into the short- and long-term performance implications of using response strategies.

Inter-partner learning

In the context of alliance management, inter-partner learning refers the extent to which partner firms create a regular and repeatable pattern of routines that support knowledge and information transfer (Chai 2003). As the relationship unfolds and parties develop and deploy learning processes, they can exchange knowledge and information more easily (Simonin 1999). Learning about and with the partner entails knowledge and information transfers, both of which facilitate alliance management. As firms learn about their alliance partners, they learn how to interface and communicate with them (Cummings and Teng 2003). This type of learning involves the process rather than the content of learning (that is, inter-firm learning), which allows partners to revisit and revise their expectations and to gain a deeper understanding of their counterparts. In removing information processing barriers between parties, there are three reasons supporting the claim that inter-partner learning fosters alliance success: (1) increased openness, (2) transfer of tacit knowledge and (3) reduced risk of exchange hazards.

Inter-partner learning encourages relationship openness, which is the extent to which parties are willing and able to share information and communicate openly (Inkpen 2000). Extensive communication contributes to meaningful and timely information sharing. For example, by transferring staff, document exchange, setting up joint teams and developing best practice guidelines, partners' knowledge transfer mechanisms contribute to the quality, variety and amount of information shared (Chai 2003). Openness also helps parties learn about how to work together and increases awareness of their individual interests, which contributes to a climate that eases alliance management.

Inter-partner learning reduces the difficulties implicit in the transfer of tacit knowledge (Simonin 1999). The fact that tacit knowledge is specific to its context makes it difficult to formalize and communicate (Nonaka 1994). The 'sticky' nature of such knowledge means the incremental cost of transferring it in a form that is usable by the recipient is high. Learning enables parties to reduce the costs associated with finding and accessing different types of valuable knowledge, and also motivates them to participate and openly share valuable knowledge. Furthermore, learning helps parties to acquire the subjective viewpoints of their partners and develop a common language. Thus, inter-partner learning enhances partners' awareness, which teaches them how to make the alliance work.

As uncertainty about the performance of the alliance grows, so too does the risk of exchange hazards. However, inter-partner learning decreases the likelihood of opportunistic behaviour, goal conflicts, and appropriation and spill-over concerns, because it constitutes an informal feedback mechanism that provides partners with signals about one another's conduct; in other words, it increases the risk of detection. Inter-partner learning also eases the distribution and interpretation of knowledge and information, which motivates parties to participate and share openly strategic intents, resources and knowledge, thereby pre-emptively reducing the risk of undesirable spillovers, free-riding behaviour and expensive conflict resolution tactics (Dyer and Nobeoka 2000).

In conclusion, as partners learn in collaboration, they become aware and recognize the need to overcome differences in their structure, processes and routines, or ways to combine these resources constructively in order to make cooperation more efficient (Doz 1996). However, inter-partner learning also presents some risks. First, openness constitutes a threat, in that the partner firm could take advantage and act opportunistically. For example, it might use acquired information to appropriate proprietary knowledge, but withhold its own relevant information. Second, initiating learning processes requires substantial investments, such as employee transfers, joint product information sessions and the codification of implicit know-how demand time, energy and resources. There are currently no clear guidelines to inform alliance managers how to seek a balance between the potential benefits and the associated costs.

Alliance design and alliance management

Hennart (2006) argues that crafting an initial alliance structure is both easier and more crucial than its ex-post management. In contrast, de Rond and Bouchikhi (2004) postulate that an understanding of alliance performance requires a rich and detailed account of alliance management. Doz (1996) takes the middle ground, claiming that both alliance design and alliance management are critical to alliance success. Parties in failing alliances were unable to overcome initial design flaws, whereas those in successful alliances made adaptations to the ongoing relationship. The observation that alliance structure and alliance processes both matter is in line with conclusions from prior alliance research (Contractor 2005). It is likely that structural decisions and management decisions directly and interactively influence alliance outcomes. Although conclusive evidence is not yet available, some relevant insights have emerged regarding the relationship between alliance design and management.

One stream of studies reflects the ongoing debate about the substitutive or complementary relationship between contractual and relational governance. Proponents of substitution assert that relational governance operates as a self-enforcing safeguard that is effective and less costly than contractual governance. When firms work together, they build trust across individual members of the contracting firms, rendering contracts obsolete. In an examination of business alliances, Lee and Cavusgil (2006) find that relational-based governance is more effective than contractual-based governance in strengthening the inter-firm partnership, stabilizing the alliance and facilitating knowledge transfers. The positive effects of relational-based governance increase under the pressure of greater environmental turbulence. Aulakh *et al.* (1996) reveal that monitoring mechanisms and relational norms determine trust, and that higher levels of trust positively influence sales growth and market share relative to competitors in cross-border partnerships. In contrast, advocates of complementarity argue that alliance success depends on the alignment between contractual and relational governance, which, if properly aligned, reinforce each other. Poppo and Zenger (2002) report that complementing customized contracts with relational governance results in higher levels of alliance performance. Similarly, Luo (2002) shows that contract completeness guides the course of operations, that ex-post cooperation can overcome the limitations of contracts, and that both drive alliance performance independently and interactively.

However, this debate remains unresolved, even as studies consistently suggest that the relationship between contractual and relational governance depends on the type and level of trust (Lui and Ngo 2004), the completeness of the contract (Luo 2002), the alliance development stage (Jap and Ganesan 2000) and environmental dynamics (Lee and Cavusgil 2006). Therefore, alliance managers must seek a balance between contractual and relational governance.

Other studies have noted the relationships among initial formation conditions, post-formation processes, and alliance outcomes. In a retailer–supplier setting, Jap and Ganesan (2000) found that a retailer's specialized investments exert a negative effect on its perceptions of supplier commitment. A supplier's specialized investments and relational norms, on the other hand, increase the retailer's perception of supplier commitment, and explicit contracts are associated with perceptions of low supplier commitment. Furthermore, the retailer's perceptions of supplier commitment increase its evaluations of supplier performance and satisfaction, but relate negatively to conflict. These findings also correspond with results reported by Doz (1996) and Lane *et al.* (2001) that learning performance benefits are derived from the combination of initial conditions and post-formation processes. However, Tjemkes (2008) reports that the impact of alliance design on alliance performance depends on the alliance objective: a direct effect for financial objectives, a fully mediated effect through relational processes for learning objectives and a partially mediated effect through relational processes for strategic objectives. This suggests that alliance design functions as an architecture for alliance management, but also that the more detailed and complex an alliance design is, the less latitude alliance managers have to steer alliance progress. This discussion leads to the three following main conclusions:

1. Alliance management is critical to the effective functioning of alliances, in that it compels alliance partners to manage discrepancies, adversities and tensions.
2. Alliance management requires decisions that directly affect alliance continuity expectations, mainly through building and deploying relational governance, engaging in active conflict management, formulating and implementing response strategies to adversity and learning about partners, in order to manage the alliance successfully.
3. The related decisions are not discrete or stand-alone choices; their results are likely to interact. Moreover, alliance management can be constrained and/ or facilitated by initial alliance design decisions. Successful alliances overcome alliance design flaws through alliance management.

Alliance management: Decision-making steps

Alliances progress across management intervention cycles, instigated by the monitoring of outcome and process discrepancies; and by initiatives to deal with these discrepancies, and if required to develop, communicate and implement

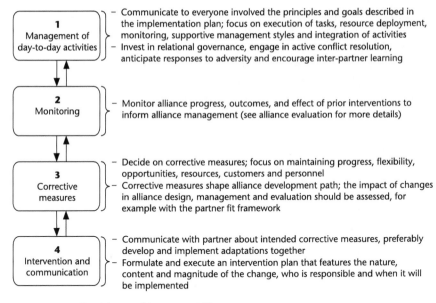

FIGURE 6.1   Decision-making steps: Alliance management

corrective measures. In turn, by monitoring, alliance managers are able to see the effect of these measures. That is, systematic attention should be given to monitoring the alliance's progress, as well as any internal and external conditions that might threaten its success. Using the results of such monitoring, alliance managers can assess the extent to which unforeseen circumstances are, or could become, a threat or an opportunity. Guided by these assessments, the manager then must decide whether to take corrective action. If interventions are required, the manager can decide where to focus those, which mechanisms are appropriate and who is responsible for implementing the corrective measures. To facilitate such complex and difficult activities, we present five steps that should inform decision making during alliance management stage (see Figure 6.1).

Step 1: Managing day-to-day activities

The first priority of alliance management is to get the alliance started, mainly by focusing on the daily activities agreed on in the alliance negotiation and design stages. Managers must understand the expectations, the new processes and the activities associated with the alliance. The principles and goals described in the implementation plan therefore should be executed visibly and, if necessary, reviewed or altered. For example, alliance managers are responsible for ensuring that all involved staff members understand their role and tasks in the alliance, and that alliance operations are integrated according to plan. Management styles should adopt a 'big picture' attitude, eliminate any 'us versus them' thinking, and keep motivation high.

Frequent communication across alliance teams, such as through meetings or joint training, can help encourage their common perceptions. Communications that even go beyond alliance issues also are essential for replenishing the reservoir of relational capital. In addition, emerging tension and conflicts should be dealt with proactively. The impact of destructive conflicts, such as disagreements about appropriation, must be mitigated, but constructive conflict, such as cultural differences, should be exploited effectively. Understanding potential responses should be the goal of any alliance manager, because predicting whether partners will respond actively–passively or constructively–destructively will help managers steer their alliances by dealing promptly with expectation discrepancies. Finally, a persistent focus on inter-partner learning enables managers to identify potential hazards and to come to adequate solutions.

Step 2: Monitoring the alliance

To identify potential threats to alliance continuity in a timely manner, it is important to monitor alliance outcomes and processes. We elaborate on the design and use of performance metric systems in Chapter 7, but in particular, managers should attend to:

- *External threats and opportunities.* Are there any external developments (e.g. in the partners' organization or broader environment) that might harm or reinforce the alliance's value creation potential?
- *Alliance performance.* Has the alliance realized outcomes efficiently in terms of financial profits, learning and competitiveness? Is the alliance growing as expected? Is the distribution of outcomes equitable?
- *Relational processes.* Are partners satisfied with the quality of the working relationship and alliance staff? In the case of conflicts, are they resolved properly? And are the partners flexible in accommodating necessary adaptations?
- *Alliance partner.* Does the partner still believe in the importance of the alliance? Changes in the partner's environment could have altered its view of the alliance.

Step 3: Decide on corrective measure(s)

Based on their assessments, alliance managers must decide if, and if so, which corrective measures to take to ensure the alliance continues to operate efficiently and effectively. Consistent with the prescriptions provided through the book, alliance adaptations might target alliance design, such as the board composition of a joint venture, compensation structure, task division, decision making and alliance management itself, including relational governance, conflict resolution and inter-partner learning. In addition, modifications may be required in the performance metric system due to emerging objectives. To overcome identified problem areas (or address opportunities) in the alliance, managers should recognize that discrepancies in outcomes and processes may evoke partner responses ranging from dysfunctional, which ultimately leads to alliance termination, to more functional reactions aimed at minimizing the damage and preventing reoccurrence. When deciding on the nature, content, and timing of a corrective measures, alliance managers should thus consider:

- *Flexibility.* Any action should preserve the flexibility of the alliance.
- *Opportunities.* Actions are needed not only to solve problems, but also to create new opportunities.
- *Resources.* Avoid exhausting available resources with actions, and pay close attention to the costs and benefits when making investments.
- *Field of intervention.* An action in any particular field (e.g. operational unit, team) requires a clear understanding of the effects on other fields.
- *Key personnel.* Determine who will take the actions and who will be most affected by those actions.

Corrective measures shape the developmental path of an alliance; such that each response to an outcome and/or process discrepancies has multiple repercussions. Assessing the possible implications is important, as it provides information to managers whether to proceed to implementation or to abstain from management interventions, such that they continue the alliance but adopt diminished expectations. It is important to recognize that design modifications are likely to affect, for example, alliance processes, thus potential adaptations should be assessed while considering the trade-off between contractual and relational governance. To anticipate the impact of corrective measures, alliance managers could use the partner fit framework (see Chapter 3). For example, managers may ask the following questions:

- To what extent do adaptations affect resource contributions and the alliance's value creation potential (i.e. resource complementarity)?
- To what extent do changes affect partners' strategic visions (i.e. strategic fit)?
- To what extent are decision-making structures, control systems and performance metrics affected by intended changes (i.e. organizational fit)?
- To what extent are cultural differences resolved through managerial intervention (i.e. cultural fit)?
- To what extent do changes influence operational procedures, systems and task allocation (i.e. operational fit)?
- Do interventions affect personal interactions between alliance staff from the partners (i.e. human fit)?

Step 4: Intervention and communication

Building on the prior assessments, it is critical that alliance managers formulate and implement an intervention plan that features at least the nature, content and magnitude of the change, who is responsible and when it will be implemented. Communication processes underlie most alliance functions, so communication behaviour is critical to successful implementation. Providing advance warning of intended adaptations to an alliance partner is important, because management interventions that could be viewed as a betrayal of joint interests (whether intentional or circumstantial) must be preceded by ample notice and appropriate explanations. For example, joint decisions to restructure or discontinue alliance activities presumably cause partners to initiate a dialogue about value creation, value appropriation and fairness, considering the value of each partner's contribution. This dialogue could result in a renegotiation of the value appropriation clauses of the alliance, such that it creates a new balance, acceptable to the partners, and reflect changes in the external environment. Moreover, joint participation in decision making, planning and goal setting ensures that required information is timely, accurate, adequate and credible. Alternatively, although under certain circumstances unilateral alliance adaptations signal long-term commitment, more often one-sided enforced modifications trigger an escalating spiral of destructive behaviours ultimately resulting in premature dissolution of the alliance. Therefore, we recommend preparing and implementing modifications jointly, for example by actively engaging the alliance partner in alliance monitoring (i.e. step 2).

Summary

In this chapter, we have noted the soft side of strategic alliances. Alliance management is responsible for executing the alliance design and governing day-to-day operations. The main objective is to advance alliance progress and if required initiate corrective measures. To this end, partner firms may invest in relational governance, use conflict resolution techniques, respond adequately to adversities and stimulate inter-partner learning. However, the bandwidth of the management effort depends on the alliance design, because the structural design, such as contractual clauses, decision-making authority and monitoring mechanism constrain or facilitate a firm's ability to initiate and execute alliance management. Alliance management is also difficult because of its inherently unstable nature; it requires substantial investment in terms of resources, energy and time. To assist alliance managers to maintain viable alliances, we have provided a five-step procedure that enables them to determine the cause of dissatisfaction, develop appropriate responses, assess the impact of potential corrective measures and execute an intervention.

Case: TNO–Hoogendoorn

TNO is a Dutch-based knowledge organization that applies scientific knowledge to strengthen the innovative power of industry and government, which it does by assisting in the various stages of product development, from idea generation to implementation and testing. Hoogendoorn is an expert in glasshouse horticulture, and its computers and software have controlled a wide range of climatic conditions for over 40 years. Hoogendoorn markets its horticultural computers across the world through a global network that is constantly kept up to date with new and innovative product developments. In 2005, TNO and a business unit of Hoogendoorn called Growth Management started to collaborate on a new innovative product: Sensiplant.[2]

Hoogendoorn and TNO signed a letter of intent in July 2005, and expressed their intention to proceed with the product development roadmap, to the point that an agreement between the two parties would be set for further commercialization of the Sensiplant project. Sensiplant is an information system based on wireless technology that measures the soil humidity of pot plants. Sensiplant's self-organizing wireless network makes the system unique, and the communication of the system is based on a self-organizing protocol patented by TNO. Hoogendoorn is responsible for the provision of the required hardware, as well as the sales, marketing and distribution of the product.

Between 2005 and 2007, TNO developed the technology further and in 2007 the alliance to commercialize the technology became formally effective. A core part of the alliance agreement pertained to TNO licensing its proprietary technology to Hoogendoorn. Some issues however emerged straight away. TNO demanded that Hoogendoorn paid an annual fee, even if sales were below expectations. Although the request was met with resistance, Hoogendoorn complied after extensive negotiations. The development of Sensiplant also had its challenges. Although the hardware seemed to work, the software contained several bugs, which were caused by changes in the initial hardware conditions. To resolve these adversities, a third party, MUCO, was approached. The addition of MUCO to the alliance fixed the hardware and software issues, but also complicated alliance management, as TNO alliance managers perceived that the other two partners were working against it. In addition, tension developed between TNO and Hoogendoorn as the latter decided unilaterally to postpone the release of version 1.0, following initial tests that revealed customers were dissatisfied with Sensiplant's technical performance.

Despite the setbacks, in 2008, version 1.1 of Sensiplant was fully operational, and Hoogendoorn was ready to launch it on the market. The release of the 1.1 version again created conflicts, as Hoogendoorn launched the product internationally, despite contractual clauses stipulating that the Dutch market would be approached first. In addition, the alliance came under pressure as customers provided serious negative feedback about the product. Complaints about cabling, hardware and software reached the partners. However, TNO decided to resolve these issues harmoniously and assist Hoogendoorn in any way it could. This proactive approach and building on customer feedback resulted in the release of version 1.2.

TNO was under the impression that version 1.2 was selling successfully. However, it was unexpectedly informed by Hoogendoorn that it had stopped selling Sensiplant, because of customer complaints and a large discrepancy between sales targets and actual outcomes. At this time, two Hoogendoorn managers who had been involved in the project from its inception also left the company. A new team was forged to focus on the future of Sensiplant and two future directions were identified in early 2009: either the project was to be terminated or the product would undergo an upgrade. Convinced about the product's potential, Hoogendoorn created a crisis team that searched for a solution, and the R&D department of the company started to investigate various technical options.

On the TNO side, however, some frustrations started to emerge as the software had worked well for a while and TNO was keen to sign the user acceptance: a formal document stating that (1) a group of users who tested Sensiplant confirm its proper working and (2) that the product is ready to be launched commercially. But, confronted with market uncertainties, Hoogendoorn procrastinated about signing it.

Up until this point, TNO had been very flexible because it was important for them to have a commercially viable product. Thus, TNO imposed some pressure on Hoogendoorn and the user acceptance was signed at a meeting in mid 2009. Following this meeting, one manager from TNO and one from Hoogendoorn developed a plan to launch Sensiplant version 1.3. However, another setback confronted the partners, as the manufacturer of the hardware went bankrupt. Nonetheless, both parties were committed to the product's success and they agreed to postpone the launch. Despite Hoogendoorn again confronting problems in product development, prior experience gave them sufficient confidence in marketability of the product.

The economic crisis in 2008–2009 made TNO and Hoogendoorn shift their attention to the financial side of the project. The partners decided to adjust the payment scheme to accommodate Hoogendoorn's acute financial needs. TNO complied with this new arrangement, as it deemed the long-term relationship with Hoogendoorn more important than immediate financial returns. In 2010, TNO and Hoogendoorn arrived at the conclusion that Sensiplant was not a commercially viable product; it seemed to be a 'nice to have' product, but not a 'need to have' one. Furthermore, new and cheaper technologies had entered the market. Consequently, Hoogendoorn decided to stop investing in Sensiplant and to sell the remaining stored products (system modules). TNO and Hoogendoorn decided to dissolve the alliance and both parties incurred their financial losses.

Questions

1. Explain why TNO and Hoogendoorn continued the alliance, despite dissatisfactory economic performance.
2. Describe the alliance's development. How did alliance management affect the partner interaction pattern?

7

ALLIANCE EVALUATION

To maintain effective alliances, alliance partners must evaluate alliance performance continuously; monitoring provides the firms with the necessary information to take appropriate actions, whether doing nothing, adapting the alliance design and management or terminating the relationship. Alliance evaluation is complex, however, owing primarily to the multifaceted nature of alliance performance. Most alliance managers focus on intentional outcomes, but they often neglect assessments of emergent objectives, relational processes and intangible outcomes. Furthermore, they tend to use generic metrics, whereas to be effective, performance metrics should align with unique alliance characteristics. An ill-designed performance metric system increases the risk of erroneous decision making, such that alliances might be continued when they should be terminated, and vice versa. To develop and use performance metric systems, alliance managers must thus understand the nature of alliance performance and the issues associated with metrics (shown in the introductory section). Obtaining insights into various performance metric approaches supports the development of a balanced performance metric system (shown in the following section). The following provide a systematic framework with a set of decision-making steps for alliance evaluation and provide a summary before concluding with some case illustrations.

Issues with alliance performance and metrics

How alliance partners assess and react to discrepancies between their expectations and realized outcomes shapes the developmental path of the alliance; alliance evaluation thus is a critical, complex activity. To deal with the complexities surrounding alliance evaluation, it is important to understand the multifaceted nature of alliance performance, or the degree of accomplishment of goals – be they common or private, initial or emergent – and the extent to which the pattern of interactions is acceptable

TABLE 7.1 Issues with performance metrics

	Description	Solution
Common and private benefits	Alliance outcomes pertain to shared and individual objectives	Use measures that provide a combined picture of alliance partners' shared and individual objectives
Multi-faceted nature	Objectives differ across partners, alliances are forged with multiple objectives, and alliance processes affect objective realization	Use measures that capture both alliance outcomes (e.g. financial, strategic and learning) and alliance processes (e.g. relational)
Time horizon	Objective achievement occurs at different time horizons, and new objectives may emerge	Identify prospective (input) and output indicators and update performance metrics if necessary
Intangible outcomes	Intangible outcomes are difficult to value and quantify	Identify realistic and quantifiable proxies for intangible outcomes; in addition use prospective and process metrics
Management control	Management control mechanisms and performance metrics may be disconnected	When selecting management control mechanism, immediately attribute appropriate metrics
Alliance types	Different alliance conditions require different types of metric systems	Use generic performance metric template and adapt to the unique context of the alliance
Measurement norms	Expectations tend to be unique for each alliance and differ across partners	Provide a systematic framework for the interpretation of measures

Sources: Ariño (2003); Kumar and Nti (1998); Perkmann et al. (2011).

to both partners (Ariño 2003). From this definition, we derive seven issues that may impede alliance managers' ability to judge alliance performance (see Table 7.1).

Common benefits often constitute an important rationale for alliance formation, related to the partners' shared alliance objectives (Khanna 1998). Performance metrics should therefore assess the extent to which partners create value jointly; these objectives might pertain to profits, market share or product innovation. A set of shared metrics helps alliance managers to ensure that both partners address alliance adaptations and continually work to maintain alignment with regard to managing the alliance. Private benefits, on the other hand, depict individual objectives and pertain to the transfer of knowledge and resources from one partner to another, with the aim of exploiting activities that may not be part of the initial agreement. Alliances in which partners do not recognize the importance of individual metrics endanger their success, in that awareness of individual interests allows the partners to look for ways to add value for their partner. Of course, too much emphasis on individual metrics at the expense of shared metrics will lead to disappointing results, especially if success depends on both partners' contributions. Partners who fail to distinguish between common and private benefits, and forsake metrics in order to capture the extent to which their partners create and appropriate value will typically find themselves working at cross-purposes.

In the complex organizational arrangements that define alliances, firm objectives often depend on a combination of motives (Kogut 1988). Any performance metric system thus must account for partners attempting to pursue multiple goals. Even if partners' objectives converge, they may forge an alliance to realize multiple objectives simultaneously. Thus, outcome metrics might entail the extent to which partners achieve economic, strategic and learning objectives. In addition, process metrics relate to the partners' satisfaction with interaction patterns (Kumar and Nti 1998). Performance metric systems should account for relational processes by explicitly incorporating metrics that capture partner dynamics. Moreover, the presence of multiple objectives may set the stage for conflicts, influencing the way partners interact. Patterns of interaction then influence the ability to realize objectives. That is, due to the interrelatedness between outcomes and process, a performance metric system should account for the multifaceted nature of alliance outcomes and processes.

Given the long time horizons of most alliances, the benefits of collaborations can be realized only after a considerable time. Therefore, effective performance metric systems should feature prospective indicators that predict the value of benefits over time (Anderson 1990). Outcome measures reflect the intended outcome of a process; prospective indicators reflect the aspects that appear causally related to certain desired outcomes (Perkmann *et al.* 2011). Such input-oriented indicators overcome the disadvantages of outcome metrics, in which the outcomes may be delayed, which implies that information to inform corrective measures arrives too late. In addition, partners often establish alliances with predefined, intentional objectives, but as the alliance progresses, new objectives may emerge, which should be assessed accordingly. For example, if a business alliance transforms into a learning alliance, the metrics should shift from financial to learning metrics. However, knowledge creation is difficult to specify ex ante, so the performance metric system should be supplemented with prospective indicators, such as R&D spending and patenting records.

When alliance outcomes are intangible, as they often are, they are not amenable to direct measurement. For example, R&D alliances focus on generating new knowledge that is relatively far from commercialization, so the value of any project is difficult to assess; it remains uncertain whether the created knowledge will have any future commercial value. Even if it is clear that the knowledge has some value, it remains difficult to quantify. The challenge for performance management, then, is to define metrics that approximate the value of intangible outputs. In addition, the use of prospective and process metrics should result in timely and reliable information.

Management control mechanisms enable alliance partners to monitor each other's behaviours and the alliance's progress. To be effective, alliance control should align with the performance metrics. For example, formalized output control might be captured with outcome metrics. Behavioural control mechanisms can be operationalized through outcome and process metrics; effective social control mechanisms (i.e. relational governance) should be accompanied by process metrics. Setting up a management control system during the alliance design stage without simultaneously defining the nature, content and target of its performance metrics is likely to lead to flawed management decisions.

Alliances also can be classified in different ways, such as exploitation or exploration, cross-border or domestic, and equity or non-equity structures. Accordingly, these various types should be subject to different dynamics that influence the choice of performance metrics. Alliances are also often surrounded by environmental uncertainty, which reduces the meaning and validity of short-term, quantitative indices of performance and hinders the use of outcome metrics. Anderson (1990) argues that manufacturing-based joint ventures operating in stable environments can benefit from outcome metrics, but R&D joint ventures operating in dynamic environments will benefit more from input (i.e. prospective) metrics. Thus performance metrics should align with not just alliance strategies (Cravens et al. 2000) but also alliance type, governance form and other relevant characteristics.

Assessments often rely on subjective evaluations of the alliance partner's satisfaction with the process and outcomes. Even if alliance managers are clear about the alliance objectives, such clarity is difficult to communicate to operational staff if the metrics are not well defined and formalized. Formalized metrics enable better coordination, legitimization, control and learning compared with ad hoc usages (Vlaar et al. 2007). Therefore, managers must articulate their goals, set targets and incorporate metrics into their management reports. Moreover, alliance managers should formulate reference values and targets for comparisons with actual performance metrics. Targets can be based on managerial experience, historical performance or other alliances. Subjective assessment will always have a role, but to measure complex alliance processes, it is sensible to complement it with objective measures.

A useful performance metric system addresses all these features. Performance metrics provide a way to assess the progress of an alliance over time in terms of specific activities that can be quantified in some form (see also Box 7.1). No single measure can represent all the salient aspects, so a set of measures is usually required in an effective performance metric system.

Performance metric approaches

A principal motivation for using performance metrics is the notion that only a collection of conceptually sound measures can properly align firm efforts with its objectives (Kaplan et al. 2010). We focus on five performance approaches that together constitute the foundation for a generic performance metric system: (1) economic, (2) strategic, (3) operational, (4) learning and (5) relational (see Table 7.2).

Economic approach

An economic approach provides insights into the economic value of the relationship and the effectiveness of the underlying business processes (Büchel and Thuy 2001).

BOX 7.1   DEVELOPMENT AND IMPLEMENTATION METRICS

During alliance formation, firms formulate an alliance strategy, select a partner, engage in alliance negotiations, and design the alliance. These stages likely require different sets of metrics than the alliance post-formation stage, when alliance management executes the alliance agreement. During the formation stages, metrics should focus on the vision, strategy alignment, pre-launch development, strategic fit, planning, selection, structuring, negotiation and team selection. These development metrics should give partner firms and stakeholders a clear understanding of why the alliance is valuable. In contrast, the implementation metrics might focus on execution, implementation, remediation, restructuring, re-evaluation, renegotiation, relaunch and termination. These metrics provide systematic and coherent information to the persons responsible for alliance operations, which are often not the same as the persons responsible for its formation.

Source: Segil (1998).

The purpose is to assess whether an alliance is increasing the economic value of the partner firms. The theoretical foundation for this economic approach is founded on the theory of financial and capital markets, and involves measures such as return on investment, net yearly profit and increases in shareholder value. Economic metrics reflect the fulfilment of economic goals and enable managers to consider the value of the partnership relative to alternative arrangements. Because of their economic foundation, financial benefits are relatively easy to specify and anticipate ex ante compared with other types of metrics. Furthermore, financial metrics have a short-term time horizon and are outcome oriented (Anderson 1990), which implies that alliance partners are more likely to anticipate immediate financial returns after the alliance is implemented. Such metrics can be captured with quantitative indicators, including profits, cost reductions, cash flows and revenues.

Under-performance on financial metrics suggests either that the alliance is not realizing its economic potential or that a partner firm is unable to appropriate its share of financial outcomes. To improve financial performance, partners should focus on underlying causes, which may relate to the alliance objectives, design or management, such as when joint product and service offerings fail to meet customer demands. The design of the alliance may hinder profit generation if the costs associated with this negotiation, alliance formation and monitoring outweigh its benefits. In terms of execution, economic under-performance may result from an under-supply of resources, wastefulness, failure to execute specific tasks or withholding of important information. If an alliance is generating economic benefits, however, an inequitable appropriation may also need to be resolved by renegotiating the alliance's compensation structure. A shift in the predetermined

TABLE 7.2 Five performance metrics approaches

	Economic	Strategic	Operational	Learning	Relational
Focus	Economic value	Strategic value	Operational value	Learning outcomes and processes	Relational processes
Charac-teristics	Easy to specify, short-term, output oriented	More difficult to specify, long-term, output oriented	Easy to specify, short-term, output and process oriented	Very difficult to specify, medium-term, input, output, and process oriented	Difficult to specify, medium-term, process oriented
Indicators	Profits, costs, revenues, return on investments	Market share, business opportunities, competitive position, risk reduction	Operating efficiency, production times, product quality, customer retention, satisfaction	Managerial, market, technological and product know-how; explicit and tacit knowledge exchange	Trust, commitment, harmony, integrity, opportunism, flexibility, solidarity

Sources: Büchel and Thuy (2001); Segil (1998).

distribution rules (e.g. royalty fees) could result in a fairer distribution of financial outcomes.

Strategic approach

Insight into the strategic value of the relationship reflects the long-term viability of the alliance. Akin to financial metrics, a strategic approach emphasizes output criteria, though it considers outputs over a longer timeframe (Büchel and Thuy 2001). Such metrics are more difficult to specify and value, because uncertainty increases the time required to achieve these objectives. The metrics offer measures of effectiveness that go beyond the exclusive use of financial metrics and target factors that, if well managed, result in superior strategic performance. They focus on the core competences that a firm possesses or wants to develop, and seek to provide information about how much the alliance assists in this effort. Strategic metrics can be captured with both qualitative and quantitative indicators, such as new business opportunities, market share or power, reputation, competitive position, resource protection and risk reduction.

Under-performance on strategic metrics suggests that the business logic supporting the alliance is poorly developed and requires adaptation, or even termination, of the partnership. Strategic metrics may also illuminate whether a firm's competitive advantage is at risk through resource leakage. For example, a firm's counterpart could be appropriating proprietary know-how to strengthen its core competences, or behaving opportunistically and withholding critical information to gain a strategic advantage over its counterparts, which would be explicit through the use of strategic metrics.

Operational approach

Insight into operational performance is important, because it taps directly into the alliance's functioning. That is, information obtained through operational metrics provides an indication of the efficiency and effectiveness of the primary processes. An operational approach focuses on output and process criteria, but differs from the economic and strategic approaches in that it consists of metrics that capture day-to-day operations. Such metrics are relatively easy to specify, because they are output-oriented and can be captured by both qualitative and quantitative indicators. Contingent on the alliance objectives, metrics tapping the production process might describe product lead times, product quality or operational efficiency; marketing efforts can be measured with indicators such as customer retention, customer satisfaction and customer service.

Operational under-performance indicates that alliance partners are not sufficiently committed to making the alliance work on a daily basis. Alternatively, the alliance partners may possess insufficient operational fit, which they can deal with through interventions targeted at aligning the operational processes of the partners. In addition, firms may reconsider the division of operational tasks and adapt their management control mechanisms.

Learning approach

Whereas the first three approaches offer a diverse set of metrics, they are unsuited to capturing inter-firm learning. Alliances often provide vehicles for acquiring and sharing knowledge between partners; learning metrics take account of both learning objectives and learning processes, which support these ends (Büchel and Thuy 2001). Because of their medium- to long-term orientations, learning outcomes are relatively difficult to specify and value (Contractor 2001). For example, an ex-ante assessment of the value of market, technological and production know-how and managerial skills is complicated, because their commercial value depends on the exploitation of such knowledge. It is thus difficult, if not impossible, to determine the amount of knowledge creation – let alone formalize parties' claims to this realized knowledge – and distribute it according to a predetermined rule. Learning metrics combine input- and output-oriented notions with a process-oriented approach, and they are best captured by qualitative indicators, such as the transfer of knowledge about production processes, marketing know-how, managerial techniques, technological know-how and product development know-how.

Learning under-performance may be attributed to a poorly designed alliance structure. For example, the initial alliance design might not enhance knowledge creation and/or enable partners to exchange knowledge. Taking the perspective of a single firm, under-performance could also signal that it is leaking valuable knowledge to a partner, without acquiring knowledge in turn. Interventions may target alliance scope, in that a broader alliance scope increases opportunities to learn, whereas a narrow alliance scope limits knowledge creation and unwanted transfer. Partners may also reconsider the distribution of tasks and/or redesign their management control system. For example, shared decision making and joint tasks foster learning, but one-sided decision-making and task specialization inhibit learning. Partners may invest in relational governance, because high-quality working relationships facilitate inter-firm learning while also functioning as a safeguard against misappropriation.

Relational approach

Insight into relational metrics is critical; alliance partners' behaviours function as a lubricant for alliance development. To this end, a relational approach focuses on the conduct of the participants in an alliance. Rather than emphasizing output and results, it addresses behaviours and ongoing processes within the alliance (Büchel and Thuy 2001). These process-oriented metrics enable the firm to evaluate its relationship status, guided by the assumption that high-quality partner interaction patterns will support the firm's alliance success (Kale *et al.* 2000). Measuring the status of the relationship enables the firm to obtain information about its partner's behavioural disposition toward the relationship, such that the firm can take corrective actions to deal with adverse situations, including opportunistic behaviour, asymmetrical inter-partner learning and conflict (Segil 1998). Essential indicators include the development of trust, commitment, transparency, ability to deal with conflicts and harmony between the partners. Such metrics tend to be more subjective and tacit in nature, so they must be captured by qualitative indicators.

Under-performance on relational metrics suggests that partners have not developed sufficient relational norms and/or capital. A primary cause stems from the alliance negotiation and design stages. Distributive negotiation reinforced by hard negotiation tactics may produce a satisfactory negotiation outcome, but damage the quality of the working relationship. Similarly, an alliance design could protect one firm's interest (e.g. task specialization) but simultaneously signal distrust to the alliance partner. Repairing damaged working relationships is difficult and demands substantial time and energy. During the alliance management stage, partner firms can demonstrate their commitment with cooperative renegotiations, proactive conflict resolution, and constructive responses to adversity.

Drawing on the similarities and differences across these five metric approaches, we suggest that together they provide a foundation for a coherent performance metric system, akin to a balanced scorecard (Kaplan *et al.* 2010). Strategic metrics focus on long-term value creation within the alliance and provide important information for various stakeholders, including top management and external parties. The long-term orientation of these metrics enables alliance managers to reconsider the alliance's design and management in light of alternative strategies and other partnerships. Financial metrics provide insights into an alliance's short-term outcomes: is the alliance contributing economic value to the firm? Operational metrics provide information about the day-to-day operations, enabling alliance managers to initiate interventions in the alliance's primary business processes. Learning metrics fulfil a two-fold function: they provide insights into the partners' ability to learn with and from each other, and they reveal the degree to which alliance partners realize their learning objectives. Relational metrics provide insight into the quality of the interpersonal and inter-partner working relationship. A balanced performance metric system that contains all five approaches would provide alliance managers with a comprehensive, systematic understanding of alliance progress and outcomes (see Box 7.2).

BOX 7.2 BALANCED PERFORMANCE METRICS IN THE DUTCH SHIPBUILDING INDUSTRY

The Dutch shipbuilding industry installed a performance metric program which aims to enhance its global competitiveness. The primary objective of the program is the continuous improvement of supply chain performance. By establishing category teams, a shipbuilder clusters all relevant functional domains in the ship-building process to align suppliers with its goals; the key objective is to prevent sub-optimization in the supply chain. A balanced set of performance indi-cators is used, comprising five pillars of strategic competitiveness: (1) quality, (2) logistics, (3) innovation, (4) flexibility and (5) total cost. During workshops, both the category teams and suppliers participate in designing the key performance indicators. Most key performance indicators tend to be standard, thus the development of the metric system is neither firm nor relationship-specific, ruling out possible competitive interests. Through the co-creation of performance metrics by both the shipbuilders and their suppliers, involvement improves, which offers an important advantage for implementing the change list approach throughout the supply chain. During the implementation, the standard set of performance metrics is made specific to each supplier through the creation of a supplier profile. This profile describes target performance on specific metrics across all five strategic pillars, which provides insight into the performance requests for both shipbuilder and supplier. Actual performance is then measured. The parties together determine improvements to close the gap between required and actual performance. Improvement plans and progress on specific initiatives are discussed regularly in meetings. Through an action learning approach, the performance metric system itself is evaluated regularly by the supply chain members, which results in a culture in which continuous improvement is the norm.

Alliance evaluation: Decision-making steps

The main advantage of a comprehensive, balanced performance metric system is that when it is appropriately formulated, implemented and interpreted, it provides alliance partners with relevant, reliable and detailed information about alliance performance. It typically comprises several metrics, standards for performance measurement, measurement techniques, frequency and timing of measurement and reporting, and a reporting format. If metric scores deviate from expectations, partner firms may develop corrective actions to steer the alliance toward its objectives. Although the formulation and implementation of metrics may be lengthy, clear metric procedures actually accelerate alliance development rather than slowing it. However, alliance managers should seek to minimize the administrative burden involved in operating such a system by tailoring their performance metrics to each alliance. Developing and implementing a performance metric system thus consists of four consecutive stages: (1) formulating, (2) implementing, (3) interpreting and (4) assessment (see Figure 7.1).

Step 1: Formulating a performance metric system

A systematic approach to performance metrics enables alliance partners to monitor the alliance's progress and obtain relevant, timely and frequent information that constructively improves the alliance's design and management. In contrast, an unstructured approach will lead to unreliable, inefficient performance metrics. The full burden falls on the alliance manager, who may or may not have experience designing metric systems and is likely to be preoccupied with day-to-day operations. An unstructured approach also misses opportunities to leverage experience and know-how across the firm, which may benefit its other alliances. More important,

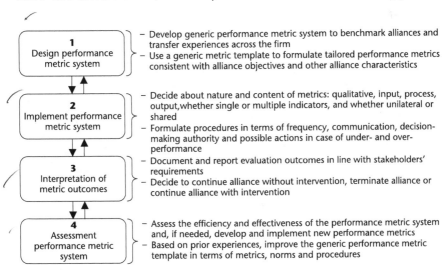

FIGURE 7.1 Decision-making steps: Alliance evaluation

it keeps firms from comparing their performance across alliances, and thus from engaging in active alliance portfolio management.

To overcome these issues, firms should adopt a structured approach to performance metrics, including an alliance scorecard template and illustrative metrics. The template should be repeatable, proactive and open to sharing, because predetermined metric types allow firms to tailor their metrics to an alliance while still retaining the possibility of comparing performance across partnerships. In addition, guidelines regarding which metrics are most appropriate in different alliance settings are invaluable to alliance managers. Even though standardized performance metric systems require ex-ante investments, the benefits, in terms of benchmarking and learning across alliances, are likely to outweigh the costs.

Building on the performance metric template, the firm can transform its alliance approach into clear, measurable alliance goals and then match performance metrics to them. For example, if a firm aims to realize financial objectives, its performance metric system should incorporate financial metrics, which may include profitability, costs, revenues, and returns on investment. If a firm seeks to realize learning objectives, the metric system may contain learning metrics, including output-oriented metrics such as acquired market know-how, management competences and technological expertise; process-oriented metrics, such as the partner's learning ability and knowledge transfer; and prospective metrics such as R&D spending. In addition, a firm should consider other unique alliance characteristics. Learning alliances with exploration objectives tend to achieve superior performance according to learning and relational metrics; business alliances with exploitation objectives, on the other hand, require financial and strategic metrics. Equity-based governance forms often build financial metrics into their very design so as to achieve government approval and meet accounting laws and regulations. However, such regulations do not apply to non-equity-based governance forms, so partner firms in such alliances should build similar metrics into their systems.

Step 2: Implementing the performance metric system

After having developed a tailored performance metric system, the firm should make several decisions in preparation for the implementation step. First, for each type of metric, it should determine the appropriate nature of the metric, and for each indicator, it should make a decision about whether prospective, outcome, process, quantitative or qualitative metrics are preferable. Financial metrics are quantitative in nature and best captured with indicators, such as profitability, that may be part of the firm's accounting system. Relational metrics are subjective in nature and therefore captured with qualitative metrics. For example, perceptual judgments might reveal the degree to which partners trust each other or behave dishonestly and opportunistically. Strategic and learning metrics might be assessed using both quantitative (e.g. market share) and qualitative (e.g. competitive strength) metrics.

Second, procedural decisions involve the frequency of assessment, communication and decision-making authority. Although a performance metric system is preferably comprehensive, partner firms may decide to use single indicators to keep the metric system manageable. That is, multiple metrics may create information overload, which hampers effective decision making. Partner firms also need to decide whether to align their metrics and engage in joint efforts to monitor the alliance, or to implement individual metric systems. Sharing information about metric assessment reduces the magnitude and nature of conflicts, because partners engage in mutual sense making. However, individual metric systems may provide more necessary information regarding how to steer the alliance toward the firm's individual objectives. Alliance partners must also decide on the frequency of the evaluation; they might conduct individual assessments once per month, but undertake joint assessments on a quarterly basis. Such procedural decisions thus reinforce a comprehensive performance metric system, because they stimulate joint sense making, create transparency and signal a willingness to work together in the alliance.

Third, the sources of data must be determined. In many cases, data required for financial, strategic and operational metrics can be retrieved from extant systems, including project management tools and customer relationship systems owned by one partner or the other. If necessary, partners should modify their individual systems and/or build new joint systems to provide the necessary information for assessing the alliance. A questionnaire also might be circulated periodically to all staff involved in the alliance. Learning and relational metrics have a subjective element; the outcomes and processes captured may not be apparent immediately. To address this problem, staff members involved in the alliance might compile qualitative, narrative reports, preferably supplemented by quantitative metrics, although the focus is on linking outcomes directly to inputs. Checking survey and qualitative reports at different time intervals provides a proxy for whether and to what degree outcomes and processes meet their targets.

Step 3: Interpreting metric outcomes

During the third step, the data obtained should be processed and interpreted. After applying the metrics to an alliance, partner firms can write a report with all relevant information that contains multiple sections with different information for the various stakeholders. Top executives require aggregated information to assess the value of the alliance; operational staff need detailed information to optimize the alliance design and management. The use of reports in combination with a structured agenda and decision-making tools ensures that the information is used adequately to support dialogue, collective sense making and decisions about what to do. It is the responsibility of alliance managers (from both partners) to organize meetings and prepare the metric report.

Using the metric report and progress meetings, these managers can arrive at decisions about corrective measures. A broad range of responses and adaptations is possible, but they consist of three generic types: continue without intervention, continue with intervention, and terminate the alliance. If only minimal discrepancies between expectations and actual outcomes emerge, alliance management may decide to continue the alliance in a similar fashion. In contrast, a greater discrepancy between expected and realized profitability may trigger renegotiations about the distribution of costs and revenues; an indication of partner distrust could trigger initiatives to change the management style from task-focused to problem solving. If discrepancies between expectations and realized outcomes become substantial and span multiple metrics, alliance partners could decide to terminate the relationship. For example, if the alliance under-performs economically and the partners distrust each other, the preferred alternative may be termination. To anticipate these critical decisions, the alliance manager may explicate the implications of performance discrepancies ex ante, using the following guiding questions:

- What actions will be initiated if the alliance under-performs on some metrics but over-performs on others?
- Is there a minimum level of required performance on certain metrics, regardless of performance on other metrics?
- What conditions will result in the decision to terminate the alliance rather than initiating alliance adaptations (e.g. shift in alliance objectives)?
- If the alliance fulfils its objectives, what actions will be initiated?

Step 4: Assessment of performance metric system

Conversations about the efficiency and effectiveness of the performance metric system are integral to the use of performance metrics, and if necessary, the metric system should be adapted to new circumstances. As an alliance progresses, new objectives may emerge, and assessments of the metric system could indicate the need to incorporate new metrics. Furthermore, based on the firm's experiences, the generic performance template might be improved with the addition of new or reformulated metrics and new reference targets. The procedures surrounding performance metrics also could be altered, such as by changing their frequency and improving the reporting format.

Summary

The ability of an organization to measure the health of its alliances through consistent and appropriate performance assessments is an important predictor of alliance success. Alliances that thrive tend to assess their performance using a balanced performance metric system that includes financial, strategic, operational, learning and relational measures, and that features milestones that partners can easily evaluate and track to intervene immediately if performance does not live up to expectations. Systematic monitoring also comprises outcome and process metrics that enable alliance managers to monitor alliance progress systematically and retrieve relevant, reliable, and timely information to inform decision making. The incorporation of prospective indicators allows for ongoing monitoring, and enables timely interventions over the alliance's progress. Although alliance performance, the value it generates and the direct and indirect benefits for individual partners are difficult to capture, balanced performance metrics systems can help alliance managers articulate, explicate and quantify objectives. Especially in situations in which goals vary among the alliance partners, developing and implementing a balanced performance metric system jointly deals pre-emptively with potential conflicts over alliance progress and outcomes. Armed with a performance metric system, partners can decide whether to continue the relationship and which adaptations to make, or else choose to terminate the relationship.

Three case illustrations

Organon–Uriach[1]

In July 2004, Organon and Uriach announced a collaboration designed to discover and develop therapeutics for inflammatory disorders. Organon creates and markets prescription medicines that aim to improve the health and quality of human life; it was a business unit of Akzo Nobel, the largest Dutch pharmaceutical firm. By combining its independent growth with business partnerships, Organon strives to remain a leader in each of its core therapeutic fields, namely, reproductive medicine, psychiatry and anaesthesia. Its products sell in more than 100 countries, and more than 60 of these countries host an Organon subsidiary. Uriach is a private Spanish pharmaceutical company, established in 1838, with a broad commercial presence in Spain and a world-class R&D centre that focuses on the early stages of drug development, particularly to treat inflammation disorders.

The alliance focus was a collaborative discovery programme, in which lead compounds would be further developed and commercialized worldwide by Organon. The collaboration constituted a new and complementary addition to Organon's immunology research strategy, such that it could combine its R&D expertise with expertise in the discovery and early development of kinase inhibitors. The non-equity agreement made Organon responsible for the preclinical and clinical development of the portfolio and granted it worldwide commercialization rights for any resulting products. The alliance also added to Organon's strategic focus on alliance partnerships and licensing opportunities as a means to boost its drug pipeline.

Organon represented a valuable partner because of its worldwide reputation and development of a family of kinase inhibitors, which offer significant potential for helping patients who are affected by inflammatory conditions. Organon's global commercial reach, combined with its expertise and commitment to the project, as well as the clear synergies between the objectives of both companies, prompted Uriach to seek this alliance. The collaboration was yet another example of Uriach's goal: to forge long-lasting partnerships with other companies and develop potential drug candidates originated at Uriach. Uriach received an upfront payment, as well as milestone payments at various stages of development and royalties on future product sales. Uriach also negotiated an option to commercialize one of Organon's late-stage products in the Spanish market.

LG Philips (LPD)[2]

LG Philips Displays (LPD) was a joint venture between LG Electronics and Philips Electronics, which formally began operations in 2001. LG Electronics was a global leader and technology innovator in consumer electronics, mobile communications and home appliances. Philips was a world leader in the healthcare, lifestyle and lighting markets; it integrates technologies and design into people-centric solutions, based on fundamental customer insights. The alliance marries LG's world-class technology and Philips' reputation and global marketing network to create a powerful synergy effect. A prior joint venture between Philips and LG from 1999 featured a 50:50 agreement to manufacture TFT-LCD screens.

LDP specialized in the production of CRT screens for televisions and computers. With more than 36,000 employees and 34 plants in Europe, Asia and the United States, LPD produced 71 million units annually, equal to approximately 28 per cent of the global market. The motives for this joint venture were straightforward: LG and Philips both sought to achieve economies of scale by combining their manufacturing capacities. Together they created a global player that could serve customers in a multitude of countries. In terms of the available purchase and marketing synergies, as well as the alignment across product portfolios, LDP was able to improve its innovative capacity. Each partner contributed assets of $2.651 million, for which they received stocks of $1.296 million and a fee of $1.355 million in cash. LDP obtained credit facilities from a banking consortium and used these funds to fulfil its obligation to the parent companies.

However, promising outlooks for the CRT market required LPD, soon after its establishment, to reorganize and attract additional funding. In addition, other concerns emerged, such as the high turnover of operational management, a high cost per unit, tensions due to different decision-making structures (i.e. LG centralized, Philips decentralized), a lack of willingness to invest further, and language and cultural barriers. Unable to deal with these problems, LPD filed for bankruptcy in 2006, leaving the partners and other stakeholders (banks, suppliers) subject to substantial losses.

L'Oréal–Uemura[3]

In 2000, the French L'Oréal Group and Shu Uemura Cosmetics signed an agreement in which L'Oréal's Japanese subsidiary, Nihon L'Oréal K.K., acquired 35 per cent equity stake in Shu Uemura Cosmetics. L'Oréal had maintained a presence in Japan for more than 35 years and created its subsidiary Nihon L'Oréal in 1996 to group all its cosmetic brands – including L'Oréal, Lancôme, Helena Rubinstein, Biotherm, Ralph Lauren, Giorgio Armani, Lanvin fragrances, Redken and Maybelline – under a single corporate banner. Shu Uemura Cosmetics, which carries the name of its founder, has pioneered not only the art of make-up but also the development of advanced skin cleansing and treatment products, making it one of the most celebrated cosmetics brands in Japan. It sells in more than 100 department stores and its own boutiques; other lines appear in leading beauty salons. Outside Japan, it appears in 25 countries; 75 per cent of these sales come from southeast Asia.

For Shu Uemura Cosmetics, the alliance agreement fulfilled two objectives: access to L'Oréal's resources to reinforce its already strong position in Japan, and reliance on the L'Oréal group's R&D and marketing strength and worldwide network to establish it among the world's leading cosmetic brands. Shu Uemura remained an authentic Japanese brand, however, with its international development conceived and piloted from Tokyo. As was the case for the L'Oréal group's US brands, which have retained their full national identity and integrity, the Shu Uemura brand retained its Japanese creativity and flair and even helped the group establish a third creative centre in Tokyo (alongside Paris and New York). For the L'Oréal group, this agreement strengthened its growing position in Japan, particularly in terms of selective department store distribution, and provided it with a modern, highly creative brand in its global portfolio, its first from Japan.

Questions

1. How and why should the design of performance metrics systems for these three alliances differ?
2. How and why should the implementation of the performance metrics systems for these three alliances differ?

8

ALLIANCE TERMINATION

Because alliance termination is an intrinsic part of the alliance lifecycle, it must be managed actively. Alliances by definition are temporary organizational arrangements, which means alliance management should focus on not only their formation and management but also on their conclusion or termination. Termination creates a complicated burden for alliance managers, who must dismantle financial and organizational relationships, recover alliance-specific investments, value and redistribute tangible and intangible assets, and safeguard their firm against damage to its reputation. Yet many managers still get caught off guard by the prospect of termination and are ill-prepared to deal with the tensions and uncertainties associated with (premature) alliance dissolution. The objective of the alliance termination stage is to organize an exit that offers favourable outcomes to all parties, while simultaneously considering the complexity of the process in terms of key actions and stakeholders, the social and economic costs, and its speed and ease. To inform decision making about alliance termination, our first section suggests that managers should distinguish different types of termination, which enables them to plan the termination during the preceding alliance development stages (shown in the second section). Our following sections provide a systematic framework with a set of four decision-making steps for alliance termination and a summary before we conclude with a case illustration.

Alliance termination types, trajectories and motives

Prior literature on alliance termination tends to focus on its reasons and contrast termination with longevity (Park and Russo 1996). An enduring alliance seemingly offers a valid proxy for alliance success, whereas termination is associated with failure. However, this view of termination ignores common situations, such as those in which firms form short-term alliances to achieve specific or immediate goals and then deliberately end them once the alliances fulfil their purposes or reach a preset date. Of course, alliance failure may also result when alliances do not or cease to achieve their goals, objectives and/or performance expectations (Reuer and Zollo 2005). In this case, alliance termination refers to the dissolution of the relationship because one or more partners withdraws. Before detailing their trajectories, it therefore is important to elaborate on the varied alliance termination types.

Types of alliance termination

Many extant studies inaccurately equate alliance termination with failure and alliance longevity with success (Makino *et al.* 2007). However, we propose that alliance termination could be considered a success when the relationship is ended intentionally, whereas failure relates to unintended termination. An alliance termination is intended and occurs because the initial alliance purposes have been achieved, the aim for which the relationship was established no longer exists, the alliance goals have been met, or the contract date is due. An unintended termination may come about before partner firms achieve the initial purposes of the alliance, in which case the performance expectations have not been met. Unintended termination also may occur after the alliance has realized its initial purpose, in the sense that the alliance might have continued even though it had ceased to produce value (Patzelt and Shepherd 2008).

Alternatively, alliance termination can be defined as a change in structure, such as when partners switch governance modes (i.e. make, buy or ally) or forms (i.e. non-equity or equity-based) (Makino *et al.* 2007). Some partners internalize alliance activities and acquire complete control, such as when one partner takes over a joint venture and turns it into a wholly-owned subsidiary. Other partners divest themselves of alliance activities, perhaps by selling them to their counterpart or through liquidation (Hennart *et al.* 1998). Furthermore, firms may seek new alliance partners or forge new alliances with the same partners. If a firm chooses to take an equity share in its partner, it turns a non-equity-based arrangement into an equity arrangement. In all these situations, the original agreement ceases to exist, but because firms often adopt alternative strategies to realize their performance objectives, the alliance termination does not necessarily constitute failure, especially if the change is in line with the long-term objectives of at least one partner (Peng and Shenkar 2002).

Termination trajectories

Over its trajectory, an alliance termination disconnects former alliance partners by cutting their active links, resource ties and employee bonds. Their business exchanges also start to decline, with weaker resource ties. However, interactions in terms of communication, coordination and adaptation may intensify temporarily, because firms must adjust to the decline in their exchange activities, as well as negotiating the contract disengagement, proprietary rights, and final invoices. These termination discussions often require a great deal of time and considerable adaptations by both parties. The complexity of such disengagement trajectories reflects the status of alliances as strategic and economic arrangements embedded in social relationships; the combination may determine the degree to which partners perceive the termination process and its outcomes favourably (Giller and Matear 2001).

When an alliance is dissolved at a preset date or has fulfilled its initial purpose, partners tend to accommodate each other's exit. They agree to the end; therefore the relatively easy termination trajectory should result in favourable termination outcomes. This natural ending integrates decisions by all parties in the relationship, such that their interests are likely to be taken into account (Halinen and Tahtinen 2002). Even if the alliance termination is unexpected, partners may agree to dissolve the relationship, which reduces any adverse impact of potential conflicts. Rather, the partners tend to facilitate the disintegration of financial and organizational relationships, as well as the recovery of alliance-specific investments and the redistribution of valuable knowledge and resources. The negative impact on the firm's reputation thus is limited.

In contrast, unilateral, unintended termination tends to create tension and conflict. Without mutual involvement, the one-sided decision gets forced onto other parties, because the alliance partners do not share the conviction that ending the relationship is in the best interest of everyone. Terminating relationships in these conditions may require a lengthy, expensive process with high risk. The firms involved might be forced to buy out stakes, possibly at a significant premium, pay switching fees, or expend significant amounts to safeguard their interests and resources. Moreover, a unilateral ending provides the terminating partner with an advantage, because it can prepare for its disengagement in advance (e.g. act opportunistically, exploit alliance-specific investments), before its counterpart can react. However, such a firm would be likely to suffer reputation damages, limiting its access to future alliance relationships. Unilateral exits also impose the risk of conflict escalation and may require arbitration by an outside party.

In some cases, partner disagreements about alliance termination resort to litigation. If one alliance partner violates the alliance contract, the disadvantaged firm may consider a court battle its best alternative. However, litigation means greatly increased termination costs: hiring lawyers, consulting with legal experts and paying for other legal and court costs. In addition, the outcomes of legislative processes are inherently uncertain, and a final decision may be pending for years. Accordingly many firms turn to voluntary arbitration, using a mediator or independent third party to resolve their conflicts. A mediation procedure offers flexibility and tends to result in tailored solutions, which are rarely feasible through litigation. The use of an outside third party suggests that partners agree ex ante to comply with the provided solutions. Mediation is thus preferable to litigation, for both its time and its cost savings. Mediation procedures also tend to be confidential, so they have limited adverse impacts on the partners' reputations, whereas the probability of favourable termination outcomes increases.

Motives for premature alliance termination

Although an alliance might end upon preset contract dates or objective attainment, reports indicate that 30–90 per cent of alliances are actually dissolved prematurely (Inkpen and Beamish 1997; Makino *et al.* 2007; Park and Ungson 1997). A firm remains in an alliance as long as it perceives the situation as an efficient and equitable organizational form for its purposes. On the one hand, a firm may end an alliance when it creates insufficient value, because the firm perceives that it could appropriate more value through an alternative arrangement form. On the other hand, performance differentials between alliance partners could lead a firm to end an alliance when it is not appropriating a fair share of the created value relative to its contribution. In general then, the reasons for premature alliance termination consist of three sets of factors: (1) structural deficiencies, (2) process deficiencies and (3) unforeseen external circumstances.

During the alliance formation stage, firms establish alliances to achieve their objectives, select a partner, engage in negotiation and formalize the initial alliance design. A firm may have selected a partner with poor fit, which increases the probability of opportunistic behaviour, knowledge spillovers, and goal conflicts (Douma *et al.* 2000), which then foster alliance instability and eventually dissolution. Park and Russo (1996) find that alliances between direct competitors are more likely to fail. Distributive alliance negotiations also increase the risk of dissolution, because firms impose unrealistic demands on their counterparts (Rao and Schmidt 1998), and even if such negotiations reach a satisfactory conclusion, they tend to reduce long-term commitment. The alliance structure might offer insufficient coordination or protection against exchange hazards, which also increases the risk of premature alliance termination. For example, unfavourable termination outcomes are more likely if research alliances, which require strong protection against knowledge leakage, are governed by a non-equity arrangement (Reuer and Zollo 2005).

During the execution stages, parties need to focus on managing alliance processes, such that neglecting to invest in relational and learning processes could undermine alliance continuity. For example, relational norms reinforced by a high-quality, trust-based working relationship tend to mitigate the adverse implications of poor economic performance on partners' inclination to end the relationship (Ariño and de la Torre 1998). In addition, alliance studies reveal that learning races by firms that compete to acquire each other's knowledge (Hamel 1991) and the convergence of partners' capabilities over time (Nakamura *et al.* 1996) both adversely affect alliance continuity. Thus mismanaging a partner's learning intentions and outcomes may trigger premature alliance termination (Doz 1996).

Beyond structural and process deficiencies, alliance studies have indicated that unforeseen external circumstances can trigger dissolution. Changes in the broader environment, such as shifts in foreign direct investment policies or new technologies, may make the alliance obsolete (Makino *et al.* 2007). According to Kogut (1989), changing partner rivalry, due to shifts in industry concentration, increases the likelihood of joint venture dissolution. Changes within the partners firms' organization can have similar effects (Koza and Lewin 1998). For example, internal reorganization, changing corporate strategies, new resource needs, a weaker financial position or new members on the board of directors may prompt firms to terminate.

Thus research has identified a plethora of factors, across levels of analysis, that might explain premature alliance termination. We suggest, however, that decisions and (in)action by alliance managers at various points during the alliance development stages constitute the main sources. Managers therefore should be advised to prepare a termination trajectory to prevent costly separations and avoid the risk of losing valuable assets due to opportunistic advances by partners to appropriate value at the expense of both counterparts and the alliance. Irrespective of the type of ending, a clear and systematic termination plan is required from the outset.

Planning alliance termination

Although alliance termination is the last stage in the alliance development framework, attention to it should be a priority in the preceding alliance development stages. Such attention often seems contradictory in the honeymoon stages of the alliance. Enamoured of each other and what they can do together, new partners rarely consider breaking up (Gulati et al. 2008), leading them to accept vague terms and conditions and develop a false sense of agreement. During the alliance design and negotiation stages, alliance managers should instead take some time to think about the uncertainties that lie ahead, and their consequences for the relationship. In addition, as the alliance unfolds, effective evaluations can issue early warnings, provide sufficient time to initiate corrections, and avoid premature dissolution.

During the alliance strategy formulation stage, firms should mark out the path for its failure (Wittmann 2007). For example, prematurely formed alliances that represent simply responses to competitors' actions increase the likelihood of premature dissolution. When top management sees competitors forging alliances, they may tend to seek out their own portfolio of alliances, such that the alliance becomes a goal, rather than a means to realize performance objectives. Without alliance prioritization strategies, alliance termination also becomes more likely. Rather, firms need to prioritize alliances and allocate resources based on their propensity to contribute to their competitive advantage. The specific prioritization (e.g. strategic, tactical, operational) should match the counterpart's prioritization. Finally, ambiguous performance expectations can foster premature termination. Without performance targets, it is impossible to determine whether the alliance is creating value or simply draining resources.

During the alliance partner selection stage firms begin screening potential partners. Choosing the right partners based on good partner fit is critical for alliance continuity (Douma et al. 2000), but blind spots that fall outside the primary evaluation criteria may also lead to premature alliance termination. The identification of wasteful and surplus resources and their impact on alliance development constitute particularly pertinent hazards. For example, when a firm over-commits its resources to the alliance, managers develop varying perceptions of the equitable distribution of value, because they are likely to count both utilized and unutilized resources in their calculations, whereas partners view any surplus and wasteful resources as insignificant with regard to value. These disparate views on value distribution will increase alliance instability. More objective reflection, or taking the partner's perspective, may help managers sharpen their partner selection skills to such an extent that they provide a solid foundation for the collaborative scheme.

The alliance termination planning in the alliance negotiation and design stages preferably entails a broad set of contingency-based exit provisions in the alliance contract to support a well-structured exit. Exit provisions pertain to the conditions in which partners may dissolve the relationship unilaterally, the costs involved in doing so, and the conflict resolution and exit procedures (Gulati *et al.* 2008). A clear and mutually agreed set of exit provisions and the ex-post conditions for activating them can help prevent devastating and opportunistic behaviour, should the alliance need to be terminated. Partners also should work to make the exit easy, rather than imposing legal constraints on counterparts. Gulati *et al.* (2008) suggest that symmetric provisions (i.e. no penalties) allow for a smooth exit by both partners, because they both can end the relationship without substantial termination costs and then attempt to achieve their objectives through alternative means. Such symmetric exit provisions also are comparatively easier to enforce when all partners involved face substantial termination costs and the alliance is progressing successfully. Another tactic, the buy-out premium, can trigger firms to continue an alliance until it has realized its initial objectives. However, the stipulation of easy exit provisions for only one partner offers no rationale for either partner to avoid jeopardizing their joint value creation. Yet such asymmetric exit provisions may be required if the alliance features dependence asymmetry. The dependent partner is always more exposed to the negative consequences of alliance termination than the independent partner, so inhibiting the latter's exit by imposing an asymmetrical exit provision provides a safety buffer for the dependent partner. In addition, exit provisions should detail situations in which one partner breaches the contract. If in violation, the partner should be penalized accordingly, and specific contractual elements in the alliance contract should stipulate procedures and timelines, and guide partners in any situations in which contract violations are ambiguous. Asymmetric exit provisions should also apply when a firm ends a relationship because it has changed its corporate strategy. If partners are engaged in an alliance and their strategies diverge, they may suffer alliance tensions and disrupted collaborative processes. In this situation, termination blockades result from transition costs. For example, the remaining firm should be compensated if its counterpart unilaterally ends the relationship.

In formulating exit provisions, alliance partners should realize that easy exit provisions provide flexibility, but this free opportunity to exist also could stimulate opportunistic behaviour. In unstable relationships that either partner could exit at any time, neither partner is willing to make relationship-specific investments. Yet challenging exit provisions, even though they signal long-term commitment and can enhance relationship building, pose the risk that partners become locked in to an alliance that is not longer providing value. Finally, irrespective of their nature, exit provisions should be agreed on and embodied in the alliance contract at the outset. However, even with great detail, no alliance contract can capture all unforeseen contingencies, so too much time spent formulating a complete contract might be wasteful or scare away a potential partner. Instead, partners should develop clear consensus performance metrics, monitor them as the alliance progresses and tie the exit provisions to these metrics.

In the alliance management stage, the available alliance contract might include alliance termination provisions – or not. Seldom do alliance managers take part in the preceding negotiations, so they have no insight into the contingencies that led to the specific provisions or ownership of the alliance termination provisions. In general, then, alliance managers should participate early in the alliance formation process, so that they gain some ownership of the alliance agreement and the termination provisions. However as Gulati and colleagues (2008) realize, fierce negotiations can damage relational quality among alliance managers. Instead of active participation, the emphasis should be on involving these alliance managers through active communication. Then the managers can increase the likelihood of a smooth exit by investing their time and effort in building relational norms and capital. When confronted with alliance termination, a good working relationship mitigates conflict, because partners expect fair, harmonious communication. These post-formation processes are thus critical for organizing alliance endings with favourable outcomes.

Through alliance evaluation, firms can prepare for alliance termination in several ways. Systematic performance evaluations provide information about outcome and process discrepancies, which informs managers about alliance status (Kumar and Nti 1998). A firm will be well equipped for the future if it remains constantly alert to internal and external events that might threaten alliance continuity. Attending to less noticeable exit communication strategies, such reduced contacts and investments, enable the partner to determine the danger of break up and take actions to repair the relationship. For example, it may proactively commission legal experts to assess exit provisions or make unilateral investments to demonstrate commitment. A balanced performance metric system enables the firm to anticipate a partner's intention to end the relationship, then prepare an adequate response and economize on termination costs.

Alliance termination: Decision-making steps

For the effective management of alliances, managers should know not only how to establish and maintain alliances but also how to end them. Termination costs demand that alliance managers carefully plan and execute their alliance exits. Alliances tend to involve intensive, complex structures that tap the internal

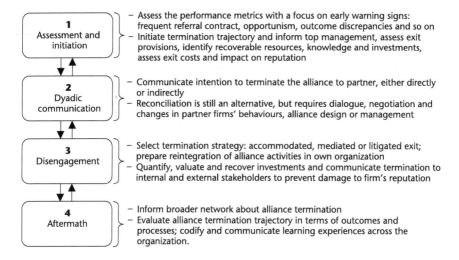

FIGURE 8.1 Decision-making steps: Alliance termination

organizations of the alliance partners. Their termination therefore requires particular effort and attention from management. Alliance managers might consider
a four-step trajectory for a smooth exit: (1) assessment and initiation, (2) dyadic
communication, (3) disengagement and (4) aftermath (see Figure 8.1).

Step 1: Assessment and initiation

During the assessment and initiation steps, a partner firm evaluates the alliance, its
future and how it might end. We have previously elaborated on the importance of
a balanced performance metric system, because it alerts managers to early warning
signs and symptoms associated with deteriorating relationships. For example,
frequent references to alliance contracts, in particular their exit provisions, signal
trouble in the relationship. A metric system also details progress toward the initial
alliance objectives and thus the appropriate course of action for managers. Because
termination is a last resort, managers should assess the conditions creating the
current situation and determine whether they might change them. But if the firm
perceives the alliance is not as successful as expected, no longer fits with its long-
term objectives, includes too many differences between the partners, has realized its
objectives or has reached its preset ending date, it needs to end. If the termination
is unintended, relationship repair through corrective measures could still be viable;
however, repeated failed attempts to modify behaviours imply that the relationship
is unsalvageable. In this case, the following steps are necessary:

- Inform top management about the intention to end the alliance.
- Intensify monitoring (of partner) to explicate and substantiate rationales
  behind termination intentions.

- Organize assessment of (contingency) exit provisions by legal experts. Alliance contracts often contain several exit provisions, such that a given clause gets activated in specific situations. Which exit provisions apply to the current situation, and what are its implications in terms of property rights, penalties, and so forth?
- Obtain an overview of resources deployed in the alliance and the degree to which they are recoverable.
- Assess the impact of the alliance termination on the internal organization, including required organizational adaptations, transfer of staff and reputation.
- Prepare strategic analyses to organize alliance activities through alternative arrangements, including internalization, merger and acquisition, market exchange or new alliance partners.

Step 2: Dyadic communication

During the dyadic communication step, a firm communicates the intention to terminate the alliance to the partner. Depending on the quality of the working relationship and the alliance infrastructure, a partner may communicate directly or indirectly. In a disguised exit, the firm hopes to end the alliance but hides its real intentions to coerce the partner into doing the terminating. For example, it might increase the partner's costs so much that it is forced to end the relationship. In a silent exit, the partners achieve an implicit understanding about the ending. Such exits are advised only if the firm realistically anticipates losing vital resources if it notifies its partner of its true intentions. However, in a revocable exit, the disengaging firm notes its willingness to alter its termination decision after a joint discussion. Depending on the communication style and the quality of the working relationship, partners could reach agreement through communication that repairs the relationship. Finally, a firm may communicate its intention to exit directly, presented as a final and irrevocable decision. If some relational capital has built up, most firms notify their partners of their intention prior to the actual exit. At this point, the partners might opt for a chosen termination, in which they agree jointly to end the alliance, or instead engage in a forced ending, in which one partner imposes its decision on the other. This critical distinction affects the likelihood of conflict, although regardless of how they get there, partners next enter the disengagement stage.

Step 3: Disengagement

The disengagement step often starts concurrently with the dyadic communication step, and induces a fundamental transition in the partners' definition of the relationship. Resource exchange and communication start to decline, and ties begin to weaken. Depending on the quality of the established termination provisions, negotiations may be required to determine the contract end, final invoices, copyrights or intellectual property rights. Disengagement discussions often require time and considerable adaptations by both parties, though if the procedures, terms and conditions already have been agreed on, the process is more predictable and smoother. Some critical issues include:

- Quantification and valuation of unilateral and bilateral alliance-specific investments, proprietary knowledge and resources and other resource commitments. Tangible assets and resource are relatively easy to value, but most alliance managers find it difficult to value the in- and outflow of resources and value from and to counterparts. Alliance managers should move beyond the boundaries of the alliance to consider the impact on their firms' other lines of business too.
- Preparation to reintegrate resources and alliance activities into the organization. For example, firms may reorganize internal decision making; relocate staff; realign financial, human resource, and operational systems; or redistribute released resources and knowledge.
- Depending on the disengagement process, the need to communicate to internal and external stakeholders that the alliance is about to end. Adequate and timely information is important to limit the possible adverse impact on partner firms' reputations, which strike the path for future alliances.

The alliance disengagement step reveals the level of difficulty of ending the relationship. An uncontested termination suggests the alliance partners do not blame each other but rather acknowledge changed circumstances or needs as the cause. In contrast, a contested termination indicates that one partner refuses to dissolve the alliance, despite its counterpart's desire to do so. It thus appears that alliance managers can follow one of three disengagement trajectories:

1. Accommodated exit: the alliance partners agree that termination is in order and emerging issues and conflicts, if applicable, are resolved using pre-specified procedures.
2. Mediated exit: the alliance partners tend to disagree on alliance termination issues, but can reconcile their conflicts. Firms voluntarily submit other conflicts to an independent third party to accelerate the end of the alliance.
3. Litigated exit: the alliance partners fiercely disagree on alliance termination, and conflicts are irreconcilable. Firms, voluntarily or involuntarily, resort to arbitration and litigation to enforce alliance termination.

Each ending has different implications for alliance termination outcomes and processes. The complexity, in terms of conflict resolution and people involved, increases from accommodated exit to litigated exit. Thus internal conflict procedures specifying the time and management level needed to resolve conflicts are sufficient to guide an accommodated exit, whereas a litigated exit demands more time, energy and resources. The termination costs, both economic and social, vary from minimal for accommodated exit to moderate and substantial for mediated and litigated exit, respectively. Uncertainty, procrastination and complexity also tend to increase when alliance partners prefer a litigated exit to mediated and accommodated exits. However, some circumstances (e.g. persistent conflicts, hostility) may make an accommodated exit impossible and a litigated exit unavoidable.

Step 4: Aftermath

In the aftermath all resource and personal ties have been disconnected. The partners need an ex-post facto account of the relationship break-up to disseminate, both within the firm and to involved external parties. With this account, the partners can build their alliance capabilities and protect their reputations. Learning from alliance termination, particularly failure, is very important to firms entering into new alliance negotiations; after a failure, many firms tend to be conservative and cautious, seeking better protection. They may also be less likely to trust other parties, or demand more contractual provisions and extensive monitoring. Such excessive controls can increase protection but also jeopardize an alliance before it begins. Through network communications, alliance partners can also inform other parties in the broader network about their efforts, which should reinforce their existing relationships and attract prospective new partners. Thus ex-partners should consider the consequences of their break-up.

Careful planning and execution of the termination process should also acknowledge that termination is not necessarily unavoidable; there are ample opportunities for reconciliation. Yet as dissolution tends to become the primary process, these opportunities diminish rapidly over time. For example, initial monitoring of alliance progress focuses on alliance continuation, but once they enter the process of termination, partners are likely to focus on dissimilarities and discrepancies that prompt termination. Moreover, a public announcement makes the chances of reconciliation and relationship repair slim.

Summary

Unlike extant alliance termination literature that tends to equate termination with alliance failure, we have presented a more fine-grained view: Alliance termination can be intended or unintended. An intended termination is in order when the alliance has fulfilled its initial purpose or reached a preset termination date. Unintended termination instead indicates that the alliance ends before realizing its objectives or is ended long after it ceased to produce value. In addition, alliance termination may result from structural changes in the alliance governance, such that a plethora of internal deficiencies and external contingencies can prompt alliance termination. Termination suggests some erroneous managerial (in)action, so we also have argued that preparing for alliance termination starts during the alliance strategy formulation stage and proceeds during subsequent stages. Salient issues that managers need to consider include type of termination, termination trajectories, termination planning, the necessity for exit provisions, the importance of relational norms and capital, and continuous monitoring. To guide alliance managers through the complexities surrounding termination, we presented a four-step termination trajectory.

Case: Wahaha–Danone

The Wahaha joint venture[1] (JV) was established in February 1996, with three alliance partners: Hangzhou Wahaha Food Group (Wahaha Group), the French corporation Danone Group, and the Hong Kong corporation Bai Fu Qin, also known as Baifu. Danone and Baifu did not invest directly in the JV but established Jin Jia Investment, a Singapore corporation (Jinjia). With the formation of the JV, Wahaha Group owned 49 per cent of the shares, and Jinjia owned 51 per cent. As stipulated in the joint venture contract, the JV and its subsidiaries would enjoy exclusive rights to the production, distribution and sale of food and beverage products under the Wahaha brand name.

At the time the JV formed, Wahaha Group obtained an appraisal of its trademark valuing it at RMB100 million (US$13.2 million). The trademark was its sole contribution, and in turn Jinjia contributed RMB500 million (US$66.1 million) in cash. The Wahaha Group also agreed to observe non-competing obligations and thus not to use the trademark for any independent business activity or allow it to be used by any other entity. From the Wahaha Group's point of view, it was the majority shareholder: 49 per cent compared with Danone's 25.5 per cent and Baifu's 25.5 per cent equity stakes. With this sense of control, Wahaha Group seemed relatively unconcerned about transferring its trademark to the JV. But in 1998, Danone bought out the interest of Baifu in Jinjia, such that it effectively became the majority owner of the JV, with legal control and the right to elect the board of directors.

Whereas once Wahaha was a state-owned enterprise owned by the Hangzhou city government, after the JV formation, it converted into a private corporation. The change prompted the Wahaha Group to act to take back control of the trademark that essentially had been transferred to Danone. The trademark transfer also was rejected by China's Trademark Office, which ruled that as the well-known mark of a state-owned enterprise, the trademark belonged to the state, not the Wahaha Group, which lacked rights to transfer it to a private company. In this sense, the Wahaha Group never complied with its basic obligation to capitalize the JV. Rather than terminate, the shareholders (now Danone and Wahaha) decided to work around the issue by entering into an exclusive licence agreement for the trademark in May 1999. The licence agreement was intended to be the functional equivalent of the sale of the trademark, which created concerns that the Trademark Office would refuse to register the licence. Therefore, they registered only an abbreviated licence, which the Trademark Office accepted without ever seeing the full licence.

The Wahaha Group ultimately realized two things: (1) it had given complete control over its trademark to the joint venture, and (2) a foreign company was now in control. Danone was the majority shareholder and maintained a majority interest on the board of directors, though day-to-day management of the joint venture was delegated entirely to Wahaha. The Wahaha Group's president, Zong Qinghou, managed the JV like his personal company, filling management positions with family members and people from Wahaha Group. Under Zong's management, the JV became the largest Chinese bottled water and beverage company, with a 15 per cent market share.

Then in 2000, the Wahaha Group began to create a series of companies that sold the same products and used the Wahaha trademark, differing only in how and where the products were sold. That is, the JV's products were mostly distributed in the coastal areas, whereas the competing products were distributed in the middle and western regions. The non-JV companies appeared to be owned in part by Wahaha Group and in part by an offshore British Virgin Islands company controlled by Zong's daughter and wife. Because the products made by both companies were virtually the same, the competing firms benefited from the JV's advertising campaigns. As marketing expenses make up a substantial part of the costs in the beverage industry, the competing companies achieved higher profit margins. Danone and the Wahaha Group were clearly aware of the situation and even discussed profit sharing, though in the end they could not reach an agreement. While Danone received no benefits from the profits of these competing companies, Zong benefited indirectly, because dealers made payments to Hangzhou Wahaha Beverage Sales Ltd., a company he owned. Yet the creation of the non-JV companies clearly violated both the trademark licence and the joint venture agreement. By 2005, Danone began insisting on a 51 per cent ownership interest in the non-JV companies. Wahaha Group and Zong – at this time one of the richest men in China – refused.

Taking into consideration the long-term development of the JV, its 27,000 employees, and the tax contribution to local governments, Danone chose not to take immediate legal action, but rather entered into negotiations. On 9 December 2006, after more than six months of these negotiations, Franck Riboud, the Board Chairman of Groupe Danone, arrived in Hangzhou and signed a legal agreement with Zong that integrated the non-JVs into the JV's system. It represented a significant compromise by Danone. Sometime later, Zong breached the contract again and sent a letter to Danone rejecting the terms of the agreement; in the face of pressure from Danone, he angrily rejected this 'low price forced buyout'.

Negotiations had broken down, so both parties resorted to arbitration and litigation. Danone filed an arbitration lawsuit containing eight claims with the Stockholm Arbitration Committee, including breach of the non-competition clause. In 2007 Danone also filed a complaint with the Superior Court of the State of California (US) against Ever Maple Trading Ltd., a British Virgin Islands company, to force it to stop using the Wahaha trademark in China and cease selling Wahaha-branded products in competition with the JV. In turn, Wahaha Group applied for arbitration before the Hangzhou Arbitration Commission, asking that both trademark licence agreements be declared void. The disputes destroyed the foundation of what was until recently a very successful joint venture.

In 2009, after several failed attempts to resolve disagreements through communication and multiple court cases, Danone and Wahaha sought to settle their disagreement and halt the dozens of remaining court cases. After determining its value in the JV, Danone decided to sell its 51 per cent equity stake to Wahaha Group, thereby terminating the alliance. Danone reportedly received approximately 300 million Euros.

Questions

1. Danone gained 51 per cent ownership of the JV through a technical legal manoeuvre, yet it did not actively participate in the management of the joint venture. Explain to what extent alliance governance may facilitate or hamper alliance termination.
2. Danone and Wahaha resorted to litigation to resolve ongoing conflicts, ultimately catalyzing alliance termination. Explain whether alliance termination was avoidable, and if so, what could they have done to prevent alliance termination.
3. How and to what extent may national cultural differences have affected this alliance termination trajectory?

9

SUPPLIER ALLIANCES

In recent decades, the competitive arena of firms has become more dynamic. Markets have become fragmented, technological developments have undermined firms' competitive advantage, and customer demands are continuously changing. This has pushed firms to compete not only using their own capabilities, but with their entire supply chain, which has caused a shift from transaction-based exchanges to supplier alliances. A supplier alliance is a collaborative arrangement between a buyer and a supplying firm, formed within a supply chain setting, in which one party (i.e. buyer) transforms the output of another party (i.e. supplier) into end products. These partnerships, also referred to as purchase, vertical or buyer–supplier alliances, are forged to achieve long-term results, including enhanced market offer to customers and reduced channel costs. However, interdependencies between buyers and suppliers increase in supplier alliances, creating coordination issues and the risk of opportunistic behaviour. Accordingly, managers are confronted with a unique challenge. By establishing a supplier alliance instead of conducting a transaction-based exchange, buyers and suppliers sacrifice independence in order to improve their competitive advantage. This requires from (purchase) managers that they need to become aware, learn, and adopt alliance management practices to establish win–win supplier alliances. The first section discusses this supplier challenge and the following section elaborates on initiatives that managers can use to deal with it. In the third section, a supplier alliance is associated with the alliance development framework in order to develop guidelines for decision-making. The chapter concludes with a summary and a case illustration.

The supplier alliance challenge

The literature on buyers and suppliers has traditionally considered exchanges between suppliers and manufacturers, wholesalers and retailers, and producers and distributors as discrete market transactions (Dwyer *et al.* 1987); in other words, a buyer and a supplier exchange a commodity in return for a payment. The actual exchange is price-oriented, short in duration and negotiations are relatively simple, as promises and obligations between the partners are clear. Because no future problems are anticipated, contractual enforcement is usually sufficient to govern the exchange, supported by legislation. However, buyer–supplier exchanges can also be organized through supplier alliances (Tan 2001). These are long-term bilateral relationships between buyers and suppliers that aim to create a collaborative advantage, while also enhancing the parties' own competitive position (Nair *et al.* 2011). The exchange in a supplier alliance tends to be an ongoing process and outcomes are more difficult to specify, as the focus lies on total costs of the relationship rather than price. Along with operational and logistic characteristics, contracts also focus on more tactical and strategic elements and encompass behavioural elements. In short, whereas a traditional buyer–supplier exchange emphasizes sourcing through multiple suppliers, competitive bidding, use of short-term contracts and purchase price and quality, supplier alliances centre on one preferred supplier, the use of contingency contracts, building relational capital and long-term objectives (see Table 9.1).

From a buyer perspective, supplier alliances can yield significant benefits (Lyons *et al.* 1990). Supplier alliances reduce a buyer's uncertainty, because forging a preferred supplier relationship secures the continuous supply of critical resources. In addition, supplier alliances may also prevent competitors from obtaining access to the high-quality resources possessed by the preferred supplier. Close and intensive contact with suppliers also improves the effectiveness of R&D, which may result in shortened product development cycles, more innovative products and higher product quality. In addition, intensive collaboration with a supplier may enhance a buyer's reputation, as it may evoke positive customer responses. Working with a set of preferred suppliers also reduces operational coordination costs. When parties have increased knowledge about product specifications, production schemes and logistical requirements, this reduces a buyer's administrative overhead costs. The downside, however, is that supplier alliances can function as mobility barriers and reduce a buyer's flexibility because they impose substantial switching costs on a buyer. If a major supplier terminates the relationship, the effects can be significant. Supplier alliances also tend to increase coordination costs in order to deal with diverging objectives and backgrounds. Furthermore, buyers may need to adopt new negotiation styles, reward systems and management skills if they are to accommodate the shift from discrete market transactions to supplier alliances: this often requires changes in the internal organization.

Supplier alliances offer suppliers a stable market for their products and/or services. This, along with their long-term nature, means they enable involved parties to better plan their workforce, production and R&D, with the possibility of technical, managerial or financial assistance from their buyers. In addition, suppliers can exercise influence on a buyer's future decision-making and receive insider access on buying decisions. A supplier can become a gatekeeper for a buyer's innovations and may receive and leverage relevant information about its own competitors. However, a supplier alliance also presents costs and risks to a supplier. For example, if a supplier's autonomy decreases, it may involuntarily leak proprietary information, and its

TABLE 9.1 Two views on buyer–supplier exchanges

	Transactional exchange	*Supplier alliance*
Description	Vertical relationship with a supplier with a focus on independence and value appropriation (e.g. costs)	Vertical alliance with a supplier with a focus on interdependence and value creation (e.g. learning)
Power	Bargaining power is exercised by buyers and suppliers to realize individual outcomes	Bargaining power is managed by buyers and suppliers to realize joint outcomes
Scope	Narrow; exit is easy due to low termination costs	Broad; exit is difficult due to high termination costs
Contractual governance	Contracts have a short duration and are narrow; contingency provisions and litigation are means of resolving disputes	Contracts have long duration and are broad; broader contingency provisions and mediation are means of resolving disputes
Relational governance	Relational elements are virtually absent; power and contracts determine outcomes	Relational elements mitigate adverse implications of power asymmetries, and reduce opportunism and misappropriation
Knowledge and information	Minimal; buyer provides specifications and supplier provides technological capability	Extensive and broad; exchange of proprietary information and technological knowledge; inter-partner learning
Payment	Fixed price per unit; ex ante known; payment upon delivery	Payment based on revenue; unknown, payment conditional on success
Decision-making	Mainly autonomous; focus on protecting investments and specifications	Mainly joint decision making; focus on division of roles authority

Sources: Dwyer *et al.* (1987); Lyons *et al.* (1990).

personnel mobility may be reduced. In addition, a buyer may pressure a supplier to assume full responsibility for design, quality and costs. A supplier alliance also forces a supplier to become more transparent: for example, the supplier may be required to display cost structures, which undermines the supplier's bargaining position.

All in all, supplier alliances have the potential to contribute to partners' (that is, a buyer and a supplier) competitive positions, as they enable the parties to economize on procurement costs while helping realize their long-term objectives (see Table 9.2), such as innovation and market share. However, managing supplier alliances is more complicated than discrete market transactions, primarily due to the risks associated with the loss of interdependency, alliance-specific investments and opportunism. Thus managers of a supplier alliance are confronted with a unique challenge: in order to realize their objectives, they must collaborate closely with supply chain partners while simultaneously protecting their firm's long-term

TABLE 9.2 Examples of supplier alliances

	Description
Ford–Magma	In 2009, Ford (US) and Magma (Canada) announced an alliance to produce new battery electric vehicles (BEV). A BEV passenger car developed jointly with Magna was one element of Ford's strategy to bring BEVs to the market in 2012. The success of BEV depends partially on the Magma alliance. Magna's capabilities include the design, development and manufacture of automotive systems, assemblies, modules and components, and the engineering and assembly of complete vehicles, which complements Ford's extensive experience and global production capabilities. The BEV technology requires substantial investments and with Magma, Ford can realize its dual objective of innovation and cost reduction.
Panasonic– NETXUSA	In 2010, Panasonic System Networks Company of America, operating in home telephone systems, forged a distribution agreement with NETXUSA, a leading distributor of Voice over Internet Protocol (VoIP) products and services. Panasonic SIP Cordless System provides a simple configuration set-up tailored to the needs of small and medium business. In turn, NETXUSA offers complete preconfigured solution of IP communications products from leading technology companies. Through the supplier alliance Panasonic's SIP Cordless phone system was added to NETXUSA's extensive portfolio.
Novatel–Raven Industries	In 2011, Novatel, a leading original equipment manufacturer of precision Global Navigation Satellite System (GNSS), and Raven Industries, a leader in technology-driven agricultural field computers, controls, and GPS guidance systems, forged a strategic supplier alliance that will see Novatel's industry leading Global Navigation Satellite System positioning technology integrated into Raven's comprehensive line of precision agriculture products. The partners seek to drive new growth opportunities for both companies, and to benefit customers by achieving further efficiencies in their agricultural operations.

Sources: Ford Media Company (2009); Marketwire (2011); Open Source IP PBX (2010); Panasonic USA Pressroom (2010).

interests. This requires a fundamental shift in their management approach of buyer–supplier relationships.

Managing supplier alliances

Various organizational theories, such as transaction cost theory, the resource-based view, the relational view, resource dependence and social exchange theory, provide explanations for the design, management and performance of supplier alliances.

As previous chapters have discussed the insights of these theoretical perspectives, this chapter elaborates only on the issues upon which managers responsible for supplier alliances must focus. These are: (1) interdependency, (2) scope and intensity, (3) alliance governance, (4) alliance-specific investments and (5) collective identity.

Interdependency

Traditionally, a buyer uses its bargaining power to influence the exchange between a buyer and supplier in order to maximally support its private objectives (Dwyer *et al.* 1987). However, when buyers exercise bargaining power in supplier alliances without considering long-term implications, the alliance is likely to fail, for two reasons. First, in discrete market transactions, bargaining power can only be exercised until the execution of the transaction. In a supplier alliance, however, the impact of bargaining power stretches from the time the alliance is forged until the relationship is ended, because the distribution of benefits continues as long as the partnership progresses. However, excessive and one-sided use of bargaining power undermines the relational capital between partners, which often leads to an increased focus on self-interest and opportunistic behaviour. Second, although extant studies have assumed buyers generally possess a bargaining power advantage, which they use to extract additional concessions from their suppliers, a strong supplier may also face a large number of small buyers, providing the supplier with a bargaining power advantage (Berthon *et al.* 2003). If a buyer uses bargaining power in a supplier's market, this could lead to retaliation from the supplier that could potentially damage the buyer's interests.

Supplier alliances are unique, in that they are embedded in the value chain, though the management implications of mutual dependence and dependency asymmetry are equivalent to those discussed elsewhere (see Chapters 2 and 13). In brief, higher degrees of mutual dependence associate positively with collaborative efforts, serving to foster higher levels of alliance performance (Kumar *et al.* 1995). More specifically, within a supplier setting, mutual dependence is associated with joint coordination, quality of information exchange, use of non-coercive strategies and less punitive actions. In contrast, dependency asymmetry undermines collaborative efforts and is associated with increases in conflict, opportunism, the use of coercive strategies and unequal appropriation of benefits. This undermines the ability of a weaker party (either buyer or supplier) to realize its objectives. Parties may attempt to deal with power through offensive tactics (such as alliance-specific investments) and defensive tactics (such as contractual provisions), or they may simply accept a power asymmetry. Thus, as the interplay between mutual dependency and dependency asymmetry affects alliance development (Gulati and Sytch 2007), managers should consider the timing and content of actions to deal with interdependencies carefully.

Scope and intensity of the alliance

The scope of a supplier alliance is defined by the range of activities it includes. Though, the focus in a supplier alliance is on purchasing, the agreement may encompass other activities, such as research and development, production, marketing and sales, and distribution. For example, an automotive supplier providing specialized parts to a car manufacturer can also be involved in innovation activities and after-sales services. Despite the tendency to assume that a larger scope would be preferable to realize a wide-range of synergetic benefits, a relatively narrow scope (i.e. pure purchasing) can be beneficial in that it limits coordination costs and the risk of opportunistic behaviour (Zinn and Parasuraman 1997).

The intensity of an alliance is defined as the degree of direct involvement between partners. The number of direct interactions, the number of people collaborating, the size of investments and joint decision-making structures are all indicators of the intensity of the alliance. High-intensity alliances have a high number of cross-firm connections, which translates into increased communication and information exchange. This enables suppliers to gain insights into the objectives and specific requirements, which can lead to improved customer-specific product and/or service delivery and collaboration that improves overall supply chain performance. However, a higher level of intensity also makes it increasingly difficult for partners to terminate the supplier alliance due to higher switching costs.

Alliance governance

Transactional supplier alliances, typically used for commodity items (e.g. limited scope and intensity) tend to be organized through non-equity-based arrangements (Dwyer *et al.* 1987). Firms then depend on multiple specialized suppliers, reducing incentives to adopt equity-based governance forms. For example, Jaguar Land Rover engaged in more than £2 billion's worth of supply contracts to over 40 key strategic partners to develop its new car model: Evoque. As the scope of a supplier alliance increases, partners may prefer an equity-based arrangement to impose control, secure property rights and obtain long-term benefits. For example, EVO Electric, a pioneer in advanced electric drive solutions for the automotive sector, forged a joint venture with GKN, the world's leading supplier of automotive driveline systems and solutions. The joint venture manufactures and sells drive systems for use in hybrid and all-electric vehicles. Whereas EVO Electric supplies advanced electric drive technology and associated vehicle integration expertise, GKN invested £5m in cash and provides engineering and commercial resources for the development of EVO Electric and the joint venture.

Irrespective of the governance form, contractual and relational governance are critical to supplier alliances to enforce coordination and exploit learning effects. To protect against exchange hazards, buyers and suppliers employ alliance contracts that contain clauses related to matters such as product specifications, exclusivity, financial contributions, specialized investments and logistics. Alliance contracts allow parties to protect themselves against misuse of bargaining power and opportunistic behaviour, as contracts are intended to steer partners' behaviour towards collaboration. However, relational governance (i.e. relational norms and capital) tends to be more effective in supplier alliances, because they avoid contracting costs and are better able to anticipate potential opportunistic behaviour. For example, the buyer's dependence and the supplier's opportunism are positively related under low relational norms, and inversely related under high relational norms (Joshi and Arnold 1997). Self-enforcement also enables value-creation initiatives, including the sharing of fine-grained tacit knowledge, exchange of resources that are difficult to price, increased responsiveness and participation in innovations.

In terms of management control, assigning joint decision-making authority is critical. Because supplier alliances are often forged in dynamic industry settings, agility and responsiveness within the supply chain demands quick decision making. In addition, supplier alliances benefit from the establishment of cross-functional teams (Lyons *et al.* 1990), because such teams coordinate development and improvement across functional areas and are instrumental in the coordination and integration between a buyer and supplier. In terms of monitoring, parties may install a balanced performance metric system that captures a wide range of output indicators (e.g. price and total cost), process indicators (e.g. logistics) and behavioural indicators (e.g. acting in accordance with standard operating procedures). However, whereas output monitoring decreases partner opportunism in supplier alliances, behaviour monitoring – a more obtrusive form of control – actually increases partner opportunism (Heide *et al.* 2007).

Alliance-specific investments

Productivity gains in a supplier alliance are possible when partners are willing to make alliance-specific investments and combine resources in unique ways (Dyer 1996). Bilateral alliance-specific investments function as a mutual hostage that prompts partners to exploit a collaborative advantage (Jap 1999), as parties voluntarily create and accept mutual dependence. For example, partners might engage in performance improvement programmes, requiring parties to make alliance-specific investments in process, technology and personnel. This translates to increased transparency between parties and a better ability to provide customer-specific performance. For example, manufacturers and suppliers often work together to accommodate stringent Just-in-Time logistical demands and specialized technological interfacing ensures the distribution of planning information and forecasts. Within the automotive industry, part suppliers often make physical investments, such as locating their factories in close proximity to an automotive manufacturer. Thus, partners in a supplier alliance tend to benefit from tailored investments in assets, personnel and sites.

When one party makes alliance-specific investments in a supplier alliance, it loses some of its bargaining power and may fall victim to opportunistic behaviour by the other party (Klein *et al.* 1978). Alliance-specific investments cause switching costs to increase, which reduces the likelihood that the relationship might be ended by the party that has to incur those costs (a hold-up situation). In an adversarial context, parties make unilateral investments to enhance their own competence selfishly, which usually has a detrimental effect on the relationship (Nair *et al.* 2011). However, unilateral investments may also signal commitment to maintaining the relationship (Gulati *et al.* 1994), as they rebalance a dependence asymmetry by voluntarily creating a hostage situation. For example, Jap and Ganesan (2000) find that, whereas alliance-specific investments made by a buyer influences its perceptions of supplier commitment negatively, specialized investments by a supplier increases the buyer's perception of supplier commitment. Thus, buyers and suppliers may expand or limit their degree of alliance-specific investments in order to create favourable exchange conditions. To avoid the adverse implications of potential hold-up situations, alliance partners may install monitoring systems, enforce relational governance and invest in goal congruence.

Collective identity

Creating a collective identity within a supplier alliance can help stimulate alliance performance (Ireland and Webb 2007). A strong collective identity among representatives of buyers and suppliers tends to reduce conflicts. The presence of a collective identity suggests that individuals reduce ambiguity and promote self-enhancement and that partners share goals, visions and working principles. Collective identity creates social cohesion amongst the team members and leads to greater cooperation within the supplier alliance. A higher level of shared identity in supplier alliances allows for increased transparency and knowledge sharing, which results in improved performance, thereby increasing trust. This facilitates further development of the relationship because firms will feel an intrinsic responsibility to contribute to the well-being of the group. To this end, boundary-spanning agents are critical for the creation of a collective identity. Close interaction between representatives from each party enhances information exchange related to buyers' and suppliers' motivations, strategic direction and supporting visions. Boundary-spanning agents are especially valuable in dynamic situations, which are characterized by a high degree of uncertainty, because they allow for faster decision making and act as a network broker within their organizations, allowing the partnership to prosper effectively from the knowledge base and the competences that firms possess. With a collective identity, a supplier alliance may also become a competitive entity in which collaboration is supported, potentially extending beyond the alliance to the entire supply chain.

Supplier alliances: Decision-making steps

The increased focus on core competences and greater reliance on more flexible structures has led to suppliers playing a greater role and has changed how suppliers are managed. The emphasis shifts from market transactions to strategic supplier alliances. The key advantages of supplier alliances compared to transaction-oriented exchanges is that they reduce transaction costs; encourage coordination and communication, which translates into lower manufacturing and labour costs and improved quality, improved predictability and supply assurance; and they engender a long-term perspective that limits opportunism, exploitation and misappropriation.

TABLE 9.3 Managing supplier alliances

	Description	Implications
Interdependency	A shift is required from a focus on autonomy and independence to managing and accepting interdependencies	Mutual dependence reinforces collaborative efforts; dependence asymmetry reinforces competitive efforts, if not curbed
Scope and intensity	Scope entails the range of activities in an alliance, whereas intensity refers the degree of involvement and integration	A broad scope offers more opportunities for synergy; narrow scope limits opportunism; high involvement enhances information exchange; low involvement facilitates easy exit
Alliance governance	Pure supplier alliances tend to be non-equity-based; increasing scope and intensity favour equity-based arrangements	Irrespective of governance form, contractual provisions (e.g. exclusivity) and relational capital (e.g. trust) are critical
Alliance-specific investments	Supplier alliances benefit from alliance-specific investments in assets, personnel and sites	Trade-off between unilateral and bilateral investments to reinforce synergies and curb one-sided exploitation and opportunism
Collective identity	Collective identity between partners stimulates joint-sense making, social cohesiveness, and performance	Boundary-spanning agents are critical in supplier alliances, as they function as creators and protectors of collective identity

To provide a coherent set of guidelines for establishing successful supplier alliances (from a buyer's view), decisions at each stage of the alliance development framework are elaborated on next (see Figure 9.1).

Step 1: Alliance strategy formulation

During the alliance strategy formulation stage, firms decide whether a supplier alliance depicts an appropriate governance mode to procure critical resources. In addition to the generic rationales discussed in preceding chapters, such as transaction costs, resource complementarity and learning, a firm may focus on buyer–supplier dependence in order to decide whether a supplier alliance is the appropriate governance mode to meet the firm's objectives:

- Internalizing resources and activities (e.g. merger) may appear to be a viable way to reduce uncertainty and secure continued provision of critical supplies. However, firms are often unable to obtain a degree of specialization that is similar to that of autonomous suppliers, which is required to exploit learning effects in terms of efficiency and innovation.

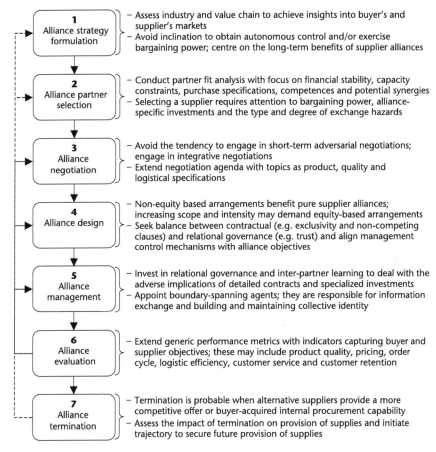

FIGURE 9.1 Alliance development framework: Supplier alliances

- Commoditized resources can be easily procured through market transactions. In a situation in which reciprocal effects are limited and synergies are not expected, a market transaction constitutes a viable option. Buyers (suppliers) use bargaining power to optimize margins at the expense of suppliers (buyers), which yields short-term benefits.
- Through an alliance, buyers seek to obtain control over the procurement of supplies without internalizing potentially unproductive resources and activities. More specifically, when a supplier contributes directly to the value-creating potential of a buyer and the latter depends on a stable supply to execute its primary processes, a supplier alliance tend to be a viable option. In these situations (i.e. the presence of a strategic supplier) buyers and suppliers expect reciprocal effects, such as by exploiting complementary resources. Buyers (suppliers) make decisions during the subsequent alliance development stages in order to optimize long-term benefits.

Step 2: Alliance partner selection

During the partner selection stage, a firm selects a (preferred) supplier with which to establish a long-term partnership. A buyer should look for a purchasing solution that includes the best products or services to meet the set requirements at an appropriate price level and in keeping with the company's demands for quality, quantity, (speed of) delivery, flexibility and total costs. In this phase, potential partners consider obligations, benefits, and burdens and trial purchases may take place. In addition to generic partner fit criteria, specific questions may help a buyer to select a supplier:

- *Financial stability.* Is the supplier financially healthy? For example, does it have sufficient working capital to carry out the order, and is it sufficiently solvent to endure a downturn in demand?
- *Ability to do the job.* Is the supplier capable of providing the agreed product or service? What methods or systems does the supplier use to manage its production process? Is the supplier's quality assurance system sufficient?
- *Capacity constraint.* Does the supplier have the capacity to carry out the order?
- *Clarity of purchase specification.* Does the supplier fully understand the product specifications? Misunderstanding in this area can be the greatest cause of delay and extra costs.
- *Ease of doing business.* Is the supplier easy to deal with and approachable if things go wrong?
- *Potential synergies.* Do the buyer and the suppliers complement or substitute each other in a manner that could lead to other potentially beneficial synergies? Besides the delivery of a product or a service, the alliance with a supplier or a buyer might build on these potential synergies.

Step 3: Alliance negotiation

During the alliance negotiation stage, emphasis is placed on getting the suppliers involved in planning and understanding the buyer's long-term goals (e.g. quality and customer retention). However, there may be some initial resistance to alliance negotiations, as supplier alliances tend to threaten the independence that buyers and suppliers value highly. Exercising bargaining power through coercive strategies to enforce a counterpart's compliance could be appropriate in a transactional exchanges, but it tends to undermine the joint value creation logic of a supplier alliance and may even result in a premature breakdown. Prompted by purchase experiences, negotiators may be inclined to use bargaining strategies that characterize market transactions and, therefore, do not match the sought-after alliance-type relationship. It is important, however, that short-term adversarial bargaining is supplemented with mutual benefit bargaining aimed at realizing long-term super-ordinate goals. A supplier alliance is unlikely to develop successfully without bilateral communication of requirements, issues, inputs and priorities, all of which contribute to the development of a collective identity. Negotiators should emphasize their mutual long-term interests and commitments in an open and transparent setting. For example, parties may signal commitment to their channel partners by employing well trained personnel, participating in buyers' or suppliers' councils, granting exclusive territories, offering exclusive distribution and investing in alliance-specific assets. Non-coercive strategies tend to be more effective. Therefore, accounting for bargaining power differences is critical to achieving favourable individual and joint outcomes during supplier alliance negotiations.

Step 4: Alliance design

The design of a supplier alliance is critical to its success or failure. Effective governance mechanisms have the potential to generate favourable outcomes, not only by lowering transaction costs, but also by influencing knowledge-sharing activities. Given that supplier alliances often constitute non-equity arrangements, firms must consider the following factors:

- *Intensity and scope of the supplier alliance.* Suppliers are likely to assume greater responsibilities in supplier alliances, including areas like product design, prototype development, engineering service, manufacturing and assembly. This could lead to an erosion of in-depth knowledge and experience for the buyer, leaving it exposed to potential opportunistic behaviour by the supplier. As the scope and intensity increase, additional coordination and protection is required against exchange hazards.
- *The degree of contractual and relational governance.* Parties must find a balance between contractual and relational governance mechanisms. Decisions related to designing governance mechanisms tend to be influenced by market characteristics. For example, is the supplier alliance forged in a buyer's market or a supplier's market? In a buyer's market, suppliers will tend to strive for contract completeness, while in a supplier's market, buyers will be inclined to use complete contracts. Depending on the degree of contract completeness, parties must invest in relational norms and capital if they are to curb opportunism.
- *The degree of alliance-specific investments.* To curb the adverse implications of dependency asymmetry, parties may commit to bilateral or unilateral alliance-specific investments (such as assets, personnel, and geographical vicinity). Such investments function as a signal of commitment, as parties voluntarily create and accept a mutual hostage situation.
- *The degree of management control.* Joint decision making, designated representatives functioning as boundary spanners and the installation of cross-functional and cross-firm teams enables buyers and suppliers to communicate effectively, exchange relevant knowledge and information and develop working routines. Whereas outcome monitoring enables partners to steer the alliance towards their objectives, behavioural monitoring tends to increase opportunistic conduct if it is not accompanied by relational governance.

Step 5: Alliance management

Alliance management, in addition to day-to-day operations, should invest in developing a collective identity and mechanisms that enforce relational governance. Boundary-spanning representatives play an important role in establishing a shared identity, which is created by extensive communication and interaction. Furthermore, by investing in relational norms and relational capital, buyers and suppliers establish higher levels of trust, commitment and flexibility. Higher levels of relational capital facilitate knowledge sharing and protect against opportunistic behaviour, enabling the alliance to become increasingly effective and efficient, possibily leading to increased rewards. Joint sense making takes place using cross-firm communicative structures, which also involve discussion and decisions regarding corrective measures to resolve outcome and process discrepancies.

Step 6: Alliance evaluation

Supplier alliances are set up to reach certain objectives, and alliance evaluation allows for timely steering of activities or even a decision to terminate the collaborative scheme. As a supplier alliance progresses, the nature of relationship may change. Learning may lead to the development of competences and other resources, thereby changing the power balance between parties, which could impact the distribution of benefits. A shifting power balance may undermine the day-to-day operations and cause alliance performance to deteriorate. This means that adaptability is an important aspect, as internal and external forces can strain the relationship, including increased transaction costs, emerging alternative suppliers and changing organizational needs. Effective evaluation and communication structures are required in order for parties to be able to adjust structures with mutual consent. This will reflect the dynamic progression of the alliance and keep the alliance on track to meet its objectives. Indicators that are typical of supplier alliances include price (per unit), total cost (per unit), product and process quality, logistical efficiency and customer service and retention.

Step 7: Alliance termination

A supplier alliance ends if the supplier no longer has strategic value. This could occur (1) because other suppliers have the ability to supply the same products or services, or (2) because the buyer has acquired the capability to supply the critical resources for him or herself. Another reason for termination could be if misconduct by either the supplier or the buyer caused damage to the reputation of the other party. Since parties work with each other in one supply chain, their resource provision or usage is likely to be critical for the parties involved. Therefore, ending the alliance may be caused by a halt in supply or demand. This may require buyers to find other sources of supply. If possible, a buyer may use a fallback scenario in which a dual source strategy can be employed that allows another supplier to take over. For a supplier, the end of an alliance may require it to look for other buyers.

Summary

Increasingly, firms have to be agile in order to respond to continuously changing internal and external conditions. To this end, transaction-based supplier exchanges characterized by market transactions are increasingly being replaced by supplier alliances. Supplier alliances secure the provision of critical resources, and buyers and suppliers use these partnerships to enhance their competitive positions. Alliances allow buyers and suppliers to realize long-term objectives such as improved market offerings, reduced supply channel costs and enhanced opportunities to develop and launch innovations. Unlike traditional bargain-driven supplier exchanges, however, supplier alliances also impose switching costs and reduce flexibility for both suppliers and buyers, and the increased entanglement (that is lock-in) mean that opportunistic behaviour can have much worse repercussions. In addition to generic alliance guidelines, managers can steer supplier alliances to success by paying particular attention to the interdependence relationship, the scope and intensity of the supplier alliance; the balance between contractual and relational governance; the size of alliance-specific investments; and to building a collective identity.

Case: NAM

In October 1933, N.V. De Bataafsche Petroleum Maatschappij (now Royal Dutch Shell) offered the Standard Oil Company of New Jersey (now ExxonMobil) the opportunity to pool oil exploitation interests in the Netherlands on a 50:50 basis. The offer was accepted in 1938. However, because of the Second World War, it took until 1947 to formalize the arrangement by forging the Nederlandse Aardolie Maatschappij (NAM).[1] In 1948, NAM discovered natural gas in the Dutch town of Coevorden. Just over 10 years later, NAM discovered the Groningen natural gas field near Slochteren, one of the largest on-shore natural gas fields in the world. That discovery led to the establishment of the so-called 'Gasgebouw' in 1963, the objective of which was to exploit the Groningen gas reserves. Gasgebouw was a partnership between NAM, the Dutch State Mines NV (now Energie Beheer Nederland BV) and the newly formed gas marketing and transportation company Gasunie. Twenty-nine gas locations and six metering stations were developed in the 1960s and 1970s to exploit the Groningen gas field.

After 30 years of operation, renovation of the facilities was necessary to ensure compliance with the latest environmental standards and operational requirements. A major and complex renovation project had to be undertaken while still meeting the Groningen field's contractual production obligations. It was clear that the competences required to execute the renovation project would not be available within the NAM organization, and contractors (that is, suppliers) were considered to play an important role. However, instead of engaging in competitive bidding procedures with multiple parties, and to reduce complexity, NAM decided to opt for an integrated entity that would accept responsibility for execution of the entire project. Furthermore, due to the strategic value of the Groningen gas field and the scope of the programme, NAM also wanted to avoid a 'hit-and-run' mentality, as it was important to meet the objectives that had been set for continuous gas production and costs reductions while executing the renovation. One implication was that ongoing maintenance had to be done by the same party responsible for the renovation, although these activities would be organized in two separate agreements. Another implication was that both the NAM and its subcontractor would have to make considerable alliance-specific investments. The upshot was that a long-term supplier alliance was deemed the most viable option.

Partners were pre-selected based on their experience, size and innovative capacity. NAM insisted that consortia would be formed if partners were unable to deliver the project alone. All parties in a consortium had to share liabilities, which stimulated partnership and commitment within the consortium. Three consortia were asked to produce a conceptual design, based on a NAM reference case and functional specifications. NAM was pleasantly surprised with the level of innovation in the designs. Based on a functional tender, the consortium Stork GLT was awarded the contract due to having the best performance on quality, integrated approach and costs.

The Stork GLT consortium consisted of Stork Comprimo, Stork Weson, Delaval Stork, Siemens AG and Yokogawa. Stork Comprimo was later taken over by Jacobs, Stork Wesom was renamed Stork Industry Services and Delaval Stork was taken over by Siemens. The consortium was registered as a separate legal entity. An underlying Heads of Agreement specified the responsibilities and liabilities of the partners involved. Due to the complementary nature of the partners and the clear division of tasks, the consortium opted for a structure in which the five partners were responsible for their own scope of work. Together, they were responsible for renovating the Groningen Gas Field and then maintaining it.

The partnerships between NAM and Stork GLT involved high risks, which were mitigated as much as possible through detailed contracts. The contract was engineered in such a way that the incentives would stimulate cooperative behaviour from both NAM and Stork GLT. For example, a comprehensive incentive system was implemented that comprised of specific performance target incentives and procurement incentives, and rules that stated that efficiency gains would be split equally between NAM and Stork GLT. NAM intentionally decided to organize the partnership in this way, having recognized that a partnership model stimulated collaborative behaviour more than other, more traditional models. In other words, NAM refrained from using a lump sum turnkey contract and a 'cost plus' with specific key performance indicators (KPI) scorecard. These approaches would have caused issues, as they induce tendencies for dashboard management and a bonus culture, both of which are inappropriate in challenging and complex environments such as the GLT project.

Stork GLT was made responsible for the technical realization of the functional requirements set by NAM, limiting the latter's interference with technical realization. This provided more space for the consortium to develop high-quality and innovative solutions. However, it contrasted with how NAM personnel we. used to working, in terms of having operational responsibility and a hands-on, eyes-on approach. The transition required a period that extended for two to three years and required flexibility and forgiveness, but it allowed Stork GLT to capitalize on its specialism. The contract was devised in such a way that the risks associated with technical realization lay with the consortium. However, potential benefits, based on better than expected performance, were shared between the NAM and the consortium.

Parties used a well-designed governance structure to monitor progress and deal with potential conflicts. The management structure of Stork GLT was formalized and resembled a project management structure. The joint board consisted of representatives from both NAM and Stork GLT, and was responsible for decision-making related to planning, budgets, and issues. The NAM project managers and Stork GLT management worked together to execute the project and reported to the joint board. An important element in the governance structure was the one-to-one relationships between NAM 'single-point responsibilities' (SPRs) and the consortium's 'business process owners' (BPOs). These couples were formed for each specific discipline and were responsible for maintaining planning, progress, budget and execution of activities. If an issue arose that had the characteristics of a commercial discussion, it was isolated and discussed in a 'Commercial Issue Meeting' attended by NAM and Stork GLT management.

Goodwill had to be formed and maintained within the NAM and Stork GLT organizations, especially at the beginning of the project. During the project, a large amount of attention was given to informal control and behaviour. People got to know each other and working routines were crafted along the way. This translated into relatively high relational capital, which strengthened the partnership and stimulated overall performance. On a more operational level, for example, cross-firm teams were established to work together. Based on detailed project planning, project delivery was monitored, with the most important performance indicators being quality, budget, and time. The collaboration between NAM and Stork GLT has been successful. In terms of performance, nearly all of the renovated facilities have been delivered within time, budget and with zero outstanding items. The collaboration has met NAM's high expectations.

Questions

1. Explain NAM's motives to forge a supplier alliance instead of using their unique position to play off multiple suppliers against each other.
2. Explain the effectiveness of the supplier alliance's design and management.

ING ALLIANCES

In an era characterized by rapid changes and high levels of uncertainty, learning enables a firm to maintain or improve its competitive advantage. Learning allows a firm to generate new knowledge about markets, technologies, processes, product and service concepts, and business models. However, because firms may lack the internal resources they need to sustain their learning to build new competences, they forge alliances to enhance the breadth and depth of the knowledge available to them, both existing and new. In a learning alliance, two or more firms enter into a collaborative scheme to generate knowledge by sharing and combining their knowledge bases. However, in a learning alliance a firm also provide access to its counterpart, enabling the latter to acquire proprietary or valuable knowledge that is not part of the alliance agreement. Therefore, firms engaged in learning alliances must protect themselves from unwanted knowledge leakage. This situation presents firms with a specific challenge: to strike a balance between learning (i.e. accessing, internalizing and exploiting knowledge), and knowledge protection. The first section of this chapter discusses this challenge in detail. The following sections elaborate on mechanisms that stimulate or hinder learning and knowledge protection, and associate the governance of learning alliances with the alliance development framework. The chapter concludes with a summary and a case illustration.

The learning alliance challenge

A firm is likely to have one or a combination of three generic motives for establishing a learning alliance (Kogut 1988). First, the firm may not possess all of the relevant knowledge and competences it needs to realize its objectives. In such a case, alliances function as learning vehicles that enable the firm to augment its knowledge base with external knowledge. Second, it can be time-consuming and costly to develop knowledge internally. Alliances provide firms with flexible and time-efficient arrangements to develop capabilities beyond their inherited ones, cheaply and more quickly. Third, firms may have fallen into competency traps and lack the ability to develop new knowledge because they have become preoccupied with exploiting their existing knowledge. In this way, alliances enable firms to improve their innovative capacity, because exposure to different and externally sourced knowledge enhances their willingness and ability to innovate (Yli-Renko et al. 2001). Therefore, firms have compelling reasons to engage: inter-firm learning enables them to augment their (core) competences (see Table 10.1).

Instead, knowledge protection requires the safeguarding of access to the knowledge a firm possesses, so that partner firms cannot access, acquire, imitate, duplicate, expropriate, appropriate or use that knowledge for their own purposes (Lee et al. 2007). Knowledge protection can safeguard critical knowledge from involuntarily spillover, which helps the firm sustain its competitive advantage (Norman 2002). The knowledge protection methods a firm employs also function

TABLE 10.1 Examples of learning alliances

	Descriptions
Sony–Toshiba–IBM	In 2006, IBM, Sony, and Toshiba forged a 5-year joint technology development alliance to work together on fundamental research related to chip technology. Toshiba contributed cutting-edge process technology and manufacturing capabilities, Sony supplied semiconductor technologies and deep knowledge of consumer markets, and IBM contributed state-of-the-art material technology. The objective of the alliance was to develop breakthrough process technologies for the 32-nanometer generation and beyond.
Shell–Academic institutions	In 2008, Royal Dutch Shell forged six new partnerships with academic institutions (e.g. Massachusetts Institute of Technology, University of Campinas of Brazil, Institute of Microbiology, Chinese Academy of Sciences) to research and develop biofuels. The partnerships operated between 2 and 5 years and sought to explore new raw materials and biofuels production processes, while improving efficiency and reducing costs. In 2011, Shell moved into the production of today's biofuels.
Arla	Arla Foods is a global dairy company and a cooperative owned by Danish, Swedish and German dairy farmers. It has production facilities in 13 countries and sales offices in a further 20. In 2009, Arla Foods formed a research partnership with multiple partners, including the National Food Institute (responsible for the project's implementation), COOP (supplying the products to the participants), the Danish Veterinary and Food Administration (supports the project) and Lantmännen Cerealia (responsible for supplying the milk and bread). The aim of the alliance was to examine whether a low vitamin D status in the winter months can be reduced by enriching milk and bread with Vitamin D.

(Continued)

TABLE 10.1 *(Continued)*

	Descriptions
HP–Microsoft	In 2009, Hewlett-Packard (HP) and Microsoft announced a 4-year strategic global initiative to develop and deliver an end-to-end unified communications and collaboration solution. The two companies expected to invest up to an additional $180 million in product development, professional services, as well as joint sales and marketing. In 2011, they deepened their relationship with two initiatives designed to explore new enterprise computing opportunities. The Infrastructure-To-Applications (Infra2Apps) initiative is a 3-year agreement investing $250 million to simplify technology environments for businesses of all sizes. With the Unified Communications and Collaboration initiative HP and Microsoft offered innovative communications and collaboration solutions developed to harness the combined power of technology and business productivity solutions.

Sources: Arla (2011); CNN News (2008); EE Times (2006); HP Technology@work (2011); HP (2009); Partnership Shell (2011).

as safeguards against opportunistic behaviour by partners (Simonin 1999). However, knowledge protection implies several hazards. For example, explicit knowledge protection policies and procedures are likely to have negative impacts on relationship quality. If a partner protects (hides) knowledge and information, this suggests an unwillingness to devote resources to the alliance. This perception could create other barriers to the free flow of knowledge and information, such as new contractual provisions, which can increase distrust if partners equate knowledge protection with a greater risk of opportunism. Perhaps even more important, safeguards against unwanted knowledge spillover tend to impede the alliance partners' abilities to learn.

Therefore, firms that engage in a learning alliance are confronted with a unique challenge. They must design and manage an alliance to enable inter-firm learning, while simultaneously protecting themselves against the unwanted transfer of valuable knowledge (Kale *et al.* 2000). When a firm deals successfully with this challenge, it builds a learning alliance that improves its innovative capacity while also preserving its competitive advantage. However, when a firm is unable to tackle this challenge, its alliance is likely to turn into a learning race (Hamel 1991), in which partners make continuous, opportunistic efforts to outlearn each other. Such races are detrimental to alliance continuation, because once a party has achieved its learning objectives, none of the parties has any incentive to maintain the relationship (Khanna *et al.* 1998). Therefore, although learning alliances may help a firm absorb critical knowledge and develop capabilities similar to those of its partner, participation also increases the probability of the unilateral or disproportionate loss of core competences to the partner.

Managing learning alliances

Managing learning alliances requires firms to understand the mechanisms that facilitate inter-firm learning and knowledge protection. Previous literature has emphasized the importance of (1) relative absorptive capacity, (2) governance form, (3) alliance contracts, (4) relational capital, (5) knowledge characteristics, (6) knowledge practices and (7) the role that staff involved in the alliance play in these efforts (see Table 10.2).

TABLE 10.2 Managing learning alliances

	Description	Implications
Absorptive capacity	Set of organizational routines and processes that enable a firm to assess and acquire external knowledge; prerequisite to knowledge transfer and creation	Similar and high level of absorptive capacity enhances learning and reduces need for knowledge protection; protection becomes critical if absorptive capacity is uneven and in alliances between competitors
Governance form	Equity-based arrangements provide better learning and protection opportunities, but non-equity-based governance may be preferred if relational capital exists	Conditional on the governance form, supplemental design decisions are required, including alliance scope, task specialization and contractual provisions
Alliance contracts	Contractual clauses that stipulate knowledge transfer and protection are required, including patents, penalties, and nondisclosure agreements	Contracts provide protection against unwanted knowledge spillover, but over-reliance on contracts tend to damage relational capital
Relational capital	Influences partners' openness and willingness to exchange knowledge, but also functions as safeguard	Investing in relational capital is critical, as it facilitates learning and it reduces the risk of learning races and knowledge leakage
Knowledge characteristics	Tacit knowledge is often key motivation for alliance formation, but higher degrees of tacitness impede knowledge transfer	Transfer of tacit knowledge requires additional measures; if a firm possess tacit knowledge it may need to install protective measures
Knowledge practices	To manage inter-firm learning, firms need to invest in supportive organizational routines, control and coordination mechanisms	Training, education, communities of practice, knowledge systems and incentive and reward systems encourage learning
Alliance staff	Persons involved in the alliance enable learning but also constitute important protection mechanisms	Involvement of top management, alliance managers and alliance employees is required for knowledge transfer; personnel also need to be aware of their role as gatekeepers

Absorptive capacity

A firm's absorptive capacity is the organizational routines and processes that enable it to assess and acquire external knowledge and disseminate it internally (Zahra and George 2002). This capacity is the result of a prolonged process of investments and knowledge accumulation within the firm, which makes it a firm characteristic that is shaped incrementally over many years (Mowery *et al.* 1996). Absorptive capacity also plays an important role for knowledge transfers in learning alliances, because it constitutes the firm's ability to recognize the value of new knowledge, assimilate it and apply it to commercial ends (Cohen and Levinthal 1990).

However, Dyer and Singh (1998) argued that absorptive capacity varies as a function of the alliance partner. That is, a firm's ability to absorb knowledge may depend on how much its pre-alliance knowledge overlaps with that of its partner. At the most elemental level, prior knowledge might include basic skills or a shared language, as well as knowledge of the most recent scientific or technological developments in a field. Although a certain degree of overlap in basic knowledge does reinforce inter-firm learning, because both alliance partners possess a similar ability to absorb knowledge (Lane and Lubatkin 1998), partners with greater absorptive capacity are likely to learn at a faster pace. Therefore, firms that perceive the absorptive capacity of their partners as high are more protective of their knowledge (Norman 2002), because absorptive capacity asymmetry between alliance partners increases the threat of knowledge leakage (to the partner with a better ability to absorb knowledge) and learning races (Khanna *et al.* 1998). This means that awareness of the extent to which partners possess similar or different abilities to absorb knowledge is critical, particularly as it informs alliance decision-making.

The issue of relative absorptive capacity becomes even more important in learning alliances between competitors (Khanna *et al.* 1998). The competitive overlap between partners creates positive and negative incentives to transfer knowledge. High competitive overlap encourages firms to be more protective about their knowledge, because unintended knowledge transfer might endanger their own competitive advantage (Khanna *et al.* 1998). At the same time, it also facilitates knowledge transfers, because knowledge bases are likely to resemble one another (Schoenmakers and Duysters 2006), which increases each partner's ability to understand, valuate and assimilate knowledge. Although the empirical evidence is somewhat inconclusive (Chen 2004; Mowery *et al.* 1996), studies demonstrate that alliances between competitors are likely to fail (Park and Russo 1996). If such alliances are undertaken, they certainly demand more management attention.

Governance form

A firm may derive its ability to assess and acquire knowledge from its governance form decision. Equity-based alliances align the interests of partner firms and offer opportunities for knowledge transfer and protection against unintentional knowledge leakage. For example, Chen (2004) and Mowery *et al.* (1996) reveal that equity-based alliances are superior to non-equity-based alliances in terms of transferring tacit knowledge. Oxley and Wada (2009) corroborate these findings, but also found that equity-based alliances (e.g. joint ventures) limit the leakage of knowledge unrelated to the alliance relationship. Reciprocal financial and organizational relationships, which are typical of equity-based arrangements, foster the transfer of knowledge, especially tacit knowledge. However, the degree of protection in an equity-based alliance depends on the overlap between the partner's knowledge bases; knowledge diversity between partners may render an equity form obsolete because firms lack sufficient absorptive capacity (Sampson 2004b).

Decisions pertaining to the alliance design, other than its governance form, can also hinder or reinforce exposure to knowledge that is available through the relationship (Oxley and Sampson 2004; Zeng and Hennart 2002). Partners can reduce their need for knowledge transfer by limiting the alliance scope, allocating specialized tasks among the partners, and forging alliances with the purpose of knowledge access rather than knowledge acquisition. For example, two firms that forge a marketing and distribution alliance may be more successful if they exchange market know-how, but decide to divide distribution activities to prevent unwanted knowledge transfers. Therefore, alliance governance should retain the option of knowledge exchange, which is necessary to achieve learning objectives, while also controlling knowledge flows in order to protect proprietary know-how and avoid unintended outflows.

Alliance contracts

A firm wishing to protect knowledge may use certain legal mechanisms, such as patents, copyrights and alliance contracts. Intellectual property protection offers legal protection for inventions and processes (Arora and Ceccagnoli 2006). If another party uses a patented product or process without obtaining the proper authority, the patent holder may pursue legal remedies that prevent the use or sale of the product or process, and perhaps receive monetary damages for any such infringement. However, intellectual property only provides limited protection against unwanted knowledge transfer. For example, patents do not cover all categories of competitively sensitive knowledge, and over-reliance on them may leave a company vulnerable. For high-tech industries, such as electronics and semiconductors, the patent process discloses information that may enable some competitors to 'invent around' the patent. Therefore, patents have historically been most effective in industries such as pharmaceuticals and chemicals, where the physical composition of the patented products makes them difficult to imitate without violating the patent.

It is also possible to impose certain contractual and legal mechanisms to protect specific knowledge from unwanted appropriation:

- Alliance contracts might explicitly identify knowledge and information that has been designated as proprietary. Such contracts can specify what capabilities can be shared and expressly identify those that are not to be shared.

- A more active approach imposes contractual or legal penalties if an alliance partner deliberately accesses or uses knowledge inappropriately. For example, a contractual clause might specify monetary penalties or contract termination if knowledge protection agreements are violated, such as when one partner establishes itself as a direct competitor by using illegally acquired knowledge to build its own product and discloses protected alliance information to outside parties.
- A widely used approach for implementing contractual protection requires each individual alliance member to sign a non-disclosure agreement (NDA). Each member is then bound to protect designated knowledge from being disclosed to outside parties.
- Partners might reach some kind of exclusivity agreement, so that knowledge exploitation is restricted to predefined products and/or markets.
- Another protective mechanism involves employment limitations, which prohibit companies from offering jobs to the employees of an alliance partner. These limitations are usually specified for a given time period and apply to specific employees who have been involved in the alliance or have obtained relevant knowledge.

Relational capital

In a learning alliance, the willingness and ability of partners to communicate freely, share knowledge and risk unintended knowledge transfers is a result of relational capital (Hamel 1991). Trust and commitment signal a willingness to exert effort on behalf of the relationship. Furthermore, these elements increase proximity, frequency of contact and close interactions between partners, which further stimulates openness. Kale *et al.* (2000) find that relational capital based on mutual trust and interactions at the individual level create a basis for learning and know-how transfer across the exchange interface. Relational capital also fosters the accuracy, timeliness, adequacy and credibility of information exchanged. On the prevention side, relational capital mitigates the chance of a learning race, because it implies a future orientation in which partners build a relationship that can weather unanticipated problems. Relational capital also protects firms against involuntary transfers of core or proprietary knowledge to partners, and restricts opportunistic behaviour by alliance partners to prevent the leakage of critical know-how (Muthusamy and White 2005).

Knowledge characteristics

The nature of the exchanged knowledge affects each party's ability to assess and acquire knowledge (Simonin 1999). As knowledge ambiguity increases, it becomes more difficult for other firms to absorb that knowledge (Kotabe *et al.* 2003), even though the level of knowledge ambiguity may be different for explicit knowledge and for tacit knowledge. Explicit knowledge, such as checklists and blueprints, is easy to codify and can be absorbed without loss of integrity. In contrast, tacit knowledge is often complex and integrated into organizational routines, technologies and individual experiences in such a way that makes it difficult to transfer across a firm's boundaries. Tacit knowledge is more resistant to appropriation, both within and across firms (Szulanski 1996), because acquiring it requires the active involvement of the knowledge provider. According to Simonin (1999), knowledge ambiguity – which is caused by factors such as tacitness (negative), complexity (positive) and organizational distance (positive) – relates negatively to knowledge transfer. The more tacit the knowledge exchanged in an alliance, the more the firms' potential to assess and acquire the knowledge is hampered, especially if the partners do not take additional measures to facilitate its transfer. Therefore, even though tacit knowledge promises a competitive advantage and represents a key motive for learning alliance formation, it is difficult to transfer, which impedes efforts to capitalize on the alliance.

Knowledge practices

Knowledge practices involve the organizational routines, control and coordination mechanisms, and systems that firms use to manage inter-firm learning (Meier 2011). Firms that engage actively and purposefully in building and deploying such practices are more effective at transferring and creating knowledge, as they reinforce partners' motivational orientations toward learning, ensure resource allocations, raise the quality of human assets and stimulate the development of learning-based organizational climates and incentive structures (Chen 2004). The following are some of the forms of knowledge practices that can be used (Inkpen 2000; Lyles and Salk 1996):

- Personnel transfer, delegation of expatriates, training and education programmes and oversight of a partner firm's alliance managers support the transfer of knowledge.
- Proactive technology sharing, articulating goals and aligning learning strategies function as knowledge connections.
- Frequent interaction, active involvement and on-site meetings benefit knowledge exchange.
- Advisory systems, liaison functions, communities of practice and shared ICT systems enhance knowledge exchange.
- Reward and incentive programmes can be structured and implemented in such a way that performance appraisals incorporate measures of employees' efforts to learn and/or protect knowledge.

However, knowledge practices may differ for explicit and tacit knowledge transfer. According to Evangelista and Hau (2009), for example, commitment from senior management reinforces the transfer of explicit knowledge rather than tacit knowledge. Revilla *et al.* (2005) argue that firms must blend different learning approaches with distinct management styles, depending on their knowledge management objectives: a structural approach fits best with both exploitative learning with a focus on existing knowledge and strategic learning with a focus new knowledge; a social approach fits best with both interactive learning with a focus on existing knowledge and integrative learning with a focus on new knowledge. In addition, Janowicz-Panjaitan and Noorderhaven (2008) demonstrate that informal knowledge practices (such as informal meetings, spontaneous interactions, both during and outside working hours) have a positive influence on knowledge transfer, whereas formal practices (participation in joint projects, joint training sessions, organized events, etc.) have a positive but diminishing effect.

The role of staff involved in the alliance

Despite not usually being involved in the day-to-day operation of alliances, senior management often plays a significant and vital role in enabling or constraining knowledge flows. Senior managers must identify the firm's core capabilities and determine which knowledge cannot be transferred. Although senior managers may not make all such decisions themselves, they must ensure that adequate management processes exist so that appropriately designated members of the firm can make timely decisions. Senior management must also create awareness by stressing personally the importance of protecting the company's critical capabilities. They should also ensure that the required resources are allocated to protect knowledge and educate the work force. Failure to make these decisions clear and communicate them widely can cause alliance members and other employees to share information inadvertently that could harm the firm's competitive position.

Alliance managers should endorse and strengthen senior management's emphasis on the protection of core capabilities. Alliance managers may appoint or act as knowledge managers, who monitor, survey and scrutinize critical knowledge to ensure it has been classified accurately, and that alliance members and other involved employees are properly informed and educated about relevant issues. The role of a knowledge manager is usually an additional duty that is assumed by the overall alliance manager or another key manager (for example, a business coordinator or lead engineer). Alliance managers must also ensure that employees follow the guidelines and procedures established by the knowledge protection system. Finally, alliance managers might also act as consultants if employees believe the circumstances surrounding knowledge protection are vague or unclear.

In turn, these employees constitute an important knowledge protection mechanism. Knowledge leakage is often primarily dependent on the choices of individuals who work daily in the alliance and come in regular contact with alliance partners. Any point of contact between the firm's employees and its partners' employees represents an information flow that could allow the inappropriate communication of critical knowledge. One way to protect knowledge is to provide employees with education and training programmes, which are usually conducted in conjunction with the alliance manager. For employees who are indirectly involved or may only occasionally come into contact with partner employees, alliance managers must also ensure that they understand the importance of maintaining confidentiality. Firms may also require employees to report any contact with alliance partners if they believe an information issue exists. Such a report would be advisable, for example, if an employee believed an alliance partner was 'fishing around' for critical knowledge that had been marked as off-limits.

Learning alliances: Decision-making steps

A high-quality knowledge interface creates the potential for alliance partners to evaluate each other's competences, strengths and weaknesses. Such an interface enables a firm to assess the value of new knowledge and integrate this knowledge into its existing knowledge base. However, a high-quality knowledge interface also increases the degree of openness, which exposes alliance partners to the danger of losing valuable knowledge, thus creating the need for knowledge protection. To steer learning alliances toward success, we connect the governance of learning alliances to the stages of our alliance development framework (see Figure 10.1).

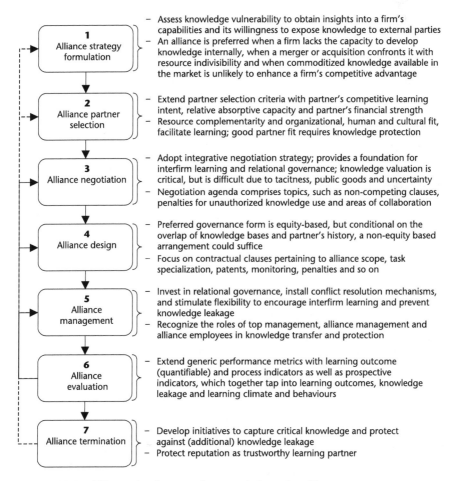

FIGURE 10.1   Alliance development framework: Learning alliances

Step 1: Alliance strategy formulation

During the alliance strategy formulation stage, firms decide whether an alliance is an appropriate governance mode for acquiring and/or developing new knowledge, technology and capabilities. From a learning alliance perspective, the objective is to obtain or access knowledge that reinforces the firm's knowledge base. To this end, a market exchange is unsuited as it means that the desired knowledge is readily available to rivals as well; commoditized knowledge is not likely to contribute to a firm's competitive advantage. When a firm recognizes that it both lacks the desired knowledge and the possibility to develop it internally (e.g. lack of know-how or too expensive) a merger or acquisition could be a viable alternative. But in most instances, resource indivisibility impedes this governance mode, as a firm is often only interested in accessing and obtaining specific knowledge, not a target's complete knowledge endowment. Alternatively, an alliance constitutes an appropriate option, as it grants access to desired knowledge while offering flexibility. For example, pharmaceuticals forge alliances with a wide-range of small bio-tech firms to access their knowledge and only acquire a bio-tech firm when it has developed a commercial viable particle for a drug.

However, exposing critical knowledge to external parties through an alliance increases the risk of unwanted spillovers, which can directly undermine a firm's competitive position. During their strategic analysis, therefore, firms must also assess their vulnerability by analysing the knowledge resources they possess, as well as the strategic relevance and transferability of that knowledge. If a firm's knowledge has strategic value and the risk of knowledge leakage is relatively high, internal development and mergers and acquisitions might become preferred alternatives, because these governance modes provide better protection. However, if the potential risks of an alliance are outweighed by its benefits, the firm should consider taking steps to protect itself. The firm must consider its decisions at the subsequent stages with great care.

Step 2: Alliance partner selection

During the partner selection stage, a firm selects the partner(s) with which it can establish the learning alliance. Partner fit must enable inter-firm learning, and resource complementarity between partners is also important. The partners' knowledge foundations should have sufficient overlap to enable knowledge transfer, but the partners should also be different enough to capitalize on learning opportunities. Organizational fit is particularly relevant, because it enables partners to build an adequate knowledge interface through compatible organizational structures and systems. Human and cultural fit, which suggest similarity between employees in terms of experience, background, education, and professional and cultural identities, are also important because they foster learning at the micro level between individuals. However, firms must be aware that, as partner fit increases, so does the need for knowledge protection.

Partner selection criteria may also include relative absorptive capacity, the learning intent of potential partners, and financial resources. If partners have differing abilities to evaluate, assess and assimilate external knowledge, this could create learning races, which are likely to lead to a premature dissolution of the alliance. Relevant indicators of absorptive capacity include existing knowledge resources, learning structures, staff competences and knowledge practices. When a potential partner has high absorptive capacity, protective measures may be required, specifically if an alliance is formed with a competitor. Knowledge leakage to a rival usually jeopardizes a firm's competitive position. Furthermore, the assessment of a partner's learning intent should reveal whether possible knowledge spillovers are likely to be exploited. However, although indirect sources of information can provide important clues about learning intent, firms must remain aware that this intent may be hidden, misrepresented or denied. For example, a systematic pattern of alliances focused on an emerging technology implies competitive learning intent. If a potential partner has such a competitive learning intent (i.e. is a direct competitor), detrimental learning races are more likely. To prevent such races, a firm should consider whether it can impose knowledge protection mechanisms on its partner without destroying the value creation potential of the alliance. In addition, financial strength of a partner may constitute a selection criterion, as building and maintaining successful learning alliances often require substantial financial investments in, for example, research centres and patenting.

Step 3: Alliance negotiation

This stage involves negotiations between alliance partners regarding scope and conditions; if the parties reach a consensus, they can formalize the outcomes in an alliance contract. When parties adopt integrative negotiation strategies, they are likely to create openness, build transparency, engage in mutual information exchange and stimulate joint problem solving, which increases the chances that they will achieve aligned interests. Furthermore, this negotiation strategy creates a solid foundation for learning alliances, which tend to have uncertain learning outcomes and depend on cooperative alliance processes. Distributive negotiation strategies, on the other hand, prevent mutually beneficial solutions and require withholding or distorting information to secure and protect individual interests. Though possessing valuable knowledge may provide a firm with a bargaining power advantage, using it to support distributive negotiation strategies undermines the knowledge creation potential of a learning alliance.

Furthermore, in order for a learning alliance to succeed, each partner must contribute some knowledge, whether it is in the form of basic research capability, product development skills, manufacturing capabilities or market know-how. An ex-ante assessment of the value of knowledge is cumbersome; it is easier to attach value to tangibles than to measure the value of intellectual capital. However, as competitive abilities increasingly come to rely on firm competences, efforts to assess their value are necessary. Firms should assess investments made in building skills that are central to their competitive advantage, and should judge the competitive consequences of a partner's development of those same skills. However, the knowledge created in an alliance often constitutes a public good, meaning that parties can appropriate knowledge and information without depleting the source during different stages of alliance development. This makes it difficult, if not impossible, to determine the amount of knowledge creation, let alone formalize parties' claims to this realized knowledge and distribute it according to a predetermined rule. In addition, a negotiation agenda may contain topics, such as non-competing provisions, penalties for unauthorized acquisition and exploitation of knowledge and the knowledge scope (i.e. the areas in which knowledge is shared).

Step 4: Alliance design

An alliance design shapes the flow of knowledge, the breadth and depth of the interaction between the two firms, and the incentives for inter-firm learning. Decisions about the knowledge interface should aim to enhance inter-firm learning by directly affecting the partners' ability to absorb knowledge and the rate of knowledge dissemination. As a result, parties should have little difficulty assessing the value and relevance of new knowledge or assimilating that knowledge into their existing knowledge stores. In addition, because an alliance design functions as a first and critical protection mechanism against knowledge leakage, it should incorporate incentives to learn and barriers to avoid knowledge leakage.

The decision regarding governance form is likely to indicate some preference for equity arrangements, because such arrangements stimulate knowledge exchanges, but still safeguard against knowledge leakages. If the partner firms have already built relational capital, perhaps through their prior collaborations, the flexibility and lower coordination costs of non-equity-based arrangements may outweigh the benefits of an equity-based form. In addition, firms must formalize contractual decisions. Contractual clauses should state that knowledge exchange is tied exclusively to non-competitive activities, is protected by patents and copyrights, or is subject to shared ownership by partners. Such restrictions limit the likelihood of competitive and opportunistic behaviour. Furthermore, partners may reduce the alliance scope (that is, market overlap in alliance and firm activities), which also minimizes the risk of leaking sensitive knowledge to another partner. Therefore, the scope of the alliance may only involve precompetitive cooperation. Contractual clauses specifying how and when partners are supposed to contribute financial resources are also critical.

In learning alliances, the potential outflow of proprietary technology is partially controlled by partitioning tasks between partners, but in turn co-specialization also impedes knowledge transfer. Sequential knowledge sharing may also help build partner trust before the partners share sensitive knowledge that could harm either firm's competitive position. For example, a firm might start by sharing older technologies and gradually start sharing newer ones over time; this approach enables firms to observe partner behaviour and secure intent. Control over human resources is also a means of protecting intellectual capital. For example, agreeing to involve senior management and operating managers in alliance formation should stimulate learning and prevent post-formation opportunistic behaviour. Because knowledge flows over learning interfaces, staff members who are directly involved in the alliance should be allocated in such a way that they constitute a collaborative membrane, maximizing the inflow of necessary knowledge while minimizing unintended outflows. Agreement on the location of the alliance is also important, as it affects partners' ability to control knowledge flows. For example, a neutral location offers partners equal opportunities to learn, whereas research activities located at one of the partner's facilities offers its counterpart a learning advantage.

Step 5: Alliance management

Within the setting of learning alliances, the alliance management stage initiates day-to-day operations that enable partner firms to create and exchange enough knowledge to obtain advantages over rivals outside the alliance, but still prevent the wholesale transfer of core skills to a partner. A critical task for management is to build relational capital, which serves two main purposes:

1.   Relational capital increases proximity, frequency of contact and close inter-actions between partners, which enables them to overcome learning barriers and embrace transparency and receptivity. Joint information processing makes partners better able to evaluate each other's competences, strengths and weaknesses, which facilitates the integration of new knowledge within a firm's existing knowledge base.
2.   Relational capital reduces the probability of distributive-oriented learning strategies that focus on securing individual interests, transfer of knowledge that is not part of the agreement, protecting proprietary knowledge and appropriating knowledge without considering the alliance's value-creation potential.

Step 6: Alliance evaluation

This stage requires a performance metric system that should include learning and relational metrics. Learning metrics should comprise of metrics capturing learning processes and outcomes, which are pivotal to steering learning alliances. Whereas process metrics, such as the learning behaviour of researchers and the number of documents exchanged, provide information about the quality and working of the knowledge infrastructure, outcome metrics, such as degree of knowledge leakage and number of commercially viable product innovations, are indicative of the alliance's success. In addition, prospective indicators, such as the patenting rate and R&D spending, are required to obtain information about the alliance's progress. Relational metrics capture the quality of the relationship and entail trust and commitment metrics. Because relational processes are critical to learning alliances, the insights that related metrics provide enable firms to enhance the alliance's learning climate: to stimulate inter-firm learning while enforcing relational protection against leakage. Taken together, learning and relational metrics provides alliance managers with relevant information to initiate adaptations to their alliance design and management.

Step 7: Alliance termination

If partners have reached this stage, it means they have decided to dissolve the alliance. Depending on the alliance contract, each firm must capture knowledge and secure it against loss. Using the performance metric system, a firm can assess the extent to which it has achieved its learning objectives. If the outcome is not satisfactory, the firm should explore possibilities to internalize critical knowledge, as well as erect additional knowledge protection barriers, if possible, to prevent the other partner from appropriating valuable knowledge. A firm also might examine contractual clauses and, if required, confront the other partner. However, for the sake of its future alliance efforts, the firm must protect its reputation as a trustworthy learning alliance partner.

Summary

Learning alliances provide platforms for the creation and application of knowledge; their essential purpose is to create, transfer, assemble, integrate and exploit knowledge assets. As such, learning alliances function as vehicles to enhance a firm's competitive advantage. However, learning alliances also present risks for a firm, as they provide partner firms with an opportunity to obtain access to knowledge that is not part of the initial alliance agreement. The risk of unwanted knowledge leakage creates the need for knowledge protection. To this end, this chapter has elaborated on mechanisms that enable or impede inter-firm learning, including absorptive capacity, alliance governance, contracts, relational capital, knowledge practices, and alliance staff. In a learning alliance, the primary task of alliance management is to achieve the delicate balance between exploiting learning opportunities and curbing learning risks. To guide decision-making we presented managerial guidelines for each alliance development stage.

Case: Holst Centre

The Holst Centre[1] is an independent open-innovation centre for R&D that develops generic technologies for wireless autonomous sensor technologies and flexible electronics. A key feature of the Holst Centre is its partnership model with industry and academia, which is based on shared development roadmaps and programmes. This kind of cross-fertilization enables the Holst Centre to tune its scientific strategy to industrial needs. The Holst Centre was set up in 2005 by

IMEC (Flanders, Belgium) and TNO (the Netherlands), with support from the Dutch Ministry of Economic Affairs and the Government of Flanders. The centre is named after Gilles Holst, a Dutch pioneer in research and development and the first director of Philips Research. Located on High-Tech Campus Eindhoven, the Holst Centre benefits from the state-of-the-art on-site facilities and has over 170 employees, representing roughly 25 nationalities and commitments from approximately 35 industrial partners.

During the 1990s and the early 2000s, Philips Research (formerly Natlab) found it increasingly difficult to provide cutting edge but affordable R&D services to the Philips product divisions. Rapid technological developments made it increasingly difficult for Philips Research to remain a front-runner in all of the necessary technology domains using only its in-house R&D resources. The future was in combining knowledge that was developed and owned by Philips with knowledge of other firms and research institutions in a more open environment. To this end, the closed 'Philips Research Campus' was transformed into the open 'High-Tech Campus Eindhoven'. Moreover, many of the Philips-owned laboratories on this campus were made accessible to third parties through a separate organization called 'MiPlaza'. Supporting activities and facilities like restaurants, sports facilities and shops were centralized in a building called 'the Strip', which became the central meeting place of the High-Tech Campus and a vital element in open communication and exchanging information. Independent organizations were set up to facilitate and orchestrate open innovation. The primary role of these organizations is to bring people and organizations together and facilitate active communication, information sharing and co-research. The most important facilitator is the Holst Centre.

At the Holst Centre, leading scientists work on research programmes together with scientists of partner companies and universities. These parties participate in research programmes facilitated by the Holst Centre to share ideas, costs and risks. Conducting the type of research in which the Holst Centre is involved requires significant investment, which may not be affordable for many firms individually. The Dutch government provides subsidies, which creates more favourable conditions for partners to join the research programmes. Another important motivation for joining research programmes at the Holst Centre is the availability of research competences that are complementary to those available at one's own organization. The Holst Centre facilitates and expands its research programmes by actively managing the partnerships.

The Holst Centre plays an active role in facilitating knowledge creation and knowledge sharing, while respecting the fact that the background knowledge of each of the participating firms may not be affected. Therefore, the Holst Centre focuses its research programmes on generic technologies for 'wireless autonomous transducer' solutions and 'systems in foil'. The Holst Centre does not engage in product development, which is left to the participating companies. The focus on this so-called 'pre-competitive research' reduces the threat of competitive interests jeopardizing the open research model. The Holst Centre also engages in active partner portfolio management. Traditional alliances tend to focus on single goals and typically consist of a fixed number of specific partners, which team up during a fixed period. Since technology development is so dynamic, various competences are required at various stages of the research programme. This might require partners to phase in or out of the research programmes. Holst Centre has implemented effective partner portfolio management structures by using research roadmaps, knowledge mapping, and partner selection strategies.

The research programmes are managed by roadmaps. Research roadmaps typically describe goals that can be realized in five to ten years, and for each roadmap work breakdown structures are provided that describe how the long-term goals are to be achieved. These research roadmaps allow the necessary research competences to be identified. The Holst Centre then approaches appropriate partners that will benefit from the shared results, are able to deliver the required competences and fit the open innovation culture within the Holst Centre. In order to build the strongest knowledge and value chains in the Holst Centre, partners must be leading players in their field. Diversity is also considered a vital asset to the research community active within the Holst Centre. This refers not only to diversity in research competences and knowledge areas, but also diversity in culture and nationality. As well as large corporations, small companies and start-ups are also partners of the Holst Centre. Research benefits from the dynamic atmosphere within the consortium.

Individual participating organizations do not have a blocking vote regarding the admission of a new partner. However, the Holst Centre communicates closely with existing participants about the admission of new participants in order to maintain the required motivation and provide reassurance that appropriate choices will be made. The Holst Centre charges entrance and participation fees, which entitle partners to non-exclusive access to the research results. When new partners step into an existing research programme, they must pay an entrance fee that increases over time to maintain a fair situation between earlier and later entrants. By paying the entrance fee, the new partners receive access to the background knowledge that was created in the research programme prior to their involvement. However, this access is limited to the background that is required to exploit the foreground (the results planned achieved during their participation).

The Holst Centre also actively helps organizations that are considering joining the consortium to establish what should be exclusive and what can be brought into the consortium. The Holst Centre provides an important assurance to participating organizations that collaboration will not endanger in-house research activities and intellectual property. Each research programme is managed by a programme manager (a Holst Centre representative), who plays an important role in preventing participation imbalances. Research contributions and transfer of research results are actively monitored. Parties are confronted if any imbalances between knowledge contributions and knowledge acquisitions are detected or suspected. Partners receive only access to the knowledge resulting from the specific programme(s) in which they participate and the Holst Centre's open innovation works only within secure environments. Not all knowledge is open to all participants and participation does involve certain obligations. In other words, the Holst Centre's open innovation is not 'public innovation'.

Questions

1. Explain the extent to which the mechanisms the Holst Centre uses to facilitate knowledge exchange and guarantee knowledge protection are effective.
2. How would these mechanisms operate in a single alliance between two partners?

11

CO-BRANDING ALLIANCES

Co-branding, co-partnering, or dual branding are all terms to refer to the act of presenting two established brand names, owned by different companies, simultaneously to customers. Such tactics have made inroads into nearly every industry, from automotive and high-tech Internet firms to banking and fast food providers. Co-branding alliances constitute a weapon for firms as they attempt to transfer the positive associations of their partners' products or brands to the newly formed co-brand, or composite brand, create synergy between existing brands, or even build up (or change) an existing brand. This avenue draws in new customers, increases brand awareness, supports customer loyalty, offers signals of quality and an image of success and binds the brand with certain emotions. Although a co-branding strategy thus can be a win–win proposition for alliance partners, even when those brands have unequal standing or brand equity in the marketplace, co-branding alliances present their own set of unique risks. For example, actions by one partner firm may damage the other's reputation, established co-brands are difficult to dismantle, and brand spillover effects may be distributed unevenly across the partners. This tension – between reaping the benefits of co-branding and simultaneously protecting firms from negative repercussions – confronts alliance managers with a unique challenge. Therefore, our first section discusses this co-branding alliance challenge and the following section elaborates mechanisms for dealing with it. We use the alliance development framework to develop managerial guidelines for co-branding alliances in the third section, and conclude with a summary and a case illustration.

The co-branding alliance challenge

A brand is the personality that identifies a product, service or company and its relationship with key constituencies, such as customers, staff, partners and investors

(Kotler 1991). In addition to a brand name, a brand may be a term, sign, symbol or drawing or some combination of these elements. The brand translates the organizational identity – the internal perception of organizations and their product and services – into terms that external stakeholders can understand, with the goal of creating a positive image. The brand also cues customers to recall images they have formed through their past experiences with brands or information they obtained about it (Swait *et al.* 1993). When further information is not available, customers can use the brand (or brand names) to make judgments about the product. Consequently, a firm hopes to position its brand in a way that make its uniqueness and value apparent to customers. As a form of communication, brands effectively communicate, consistent with firms' actions, which gives customers deeper and more meaningful consumption experiences.

To build strong brand reputations firms increasingly employ co-branding alliances, which pair two (or more) individual brands and presents them simultaneously to customers (Geylani *et al.* 2008), often in the form of a single, unique product or service (Chang and Chang 2008). Co-branding alliances link the participating brands in the mind of consumers, to enable the transfer of thoughts and feelings from one brand to another. This use of two or more brand names to introduce new products helps the partners capitalize on their combined reputations, in an attempt to achieve immediate recognition and positive evaluations by potential buyers (see Table 11.1). These immediate attitudes toward a particular co-branded alliance also influence subsequent attitudes toward the individual brands in that alliance.

TABLE 11.1 Examples of co-branding alliances

	Description
Sony–Ericsson	In 2001, the Japanese consumer electronics company Sony Corporation and the Swedish telecommunications company Ericsson established a 50:50 joint venture to manufacture mobile telephones: Sony Ericsson Mobile Communications AB. In support of the joint venture both partners halted their individual production of mobile telephones.
Columbia Pictures– Mercedes-Benz	Columbia Pictures and Mercedes-Benz agreed to use the Mercedes E500 as the hot car in the Hollywood movie Men in Black II (2002). The partnership went beyond a simple promotional tie-in. An integrated promotional campaign was launched involving events such as offering a 'Men in Black II' version of the MIB Strike Cruiser Vehicle toy produced by Hasbro; an on-line sweepstakes for five pairs of winners to receive tickets to the LA premiere of Men in Black II; and a direct marketing campaign for Mercedes-Benz customers and prospects to see Men in Black II gratis.
Bulgari–Marriott Hotels	In 2001, Marriott International formed a joint venture with Bulgari Spa to launch a new luxury hotel brand, Bulgari Hotels & Resorts. The first hotel was opened in Milan in 2004, and a second in Bali in 2006. Bulgari is the supplier of luxury goods used in guest suites.

(Continued)

TABLE 11.1 *(Continued)*

	Description
Apple's iPod	In 2005, Volkswagen was the first car manufacturer to ally with Apple, offering a free iPod with every New Beetle. Since then, other automobile manufacturers incorporated the iPod in their offerings including BMW, Audi and Honda.
Disney– McDonald's	As part of a 10-year agreement, McDonald's opened several restaurants in Disney theme parks. Toys from Disney movies, including *Finding Nemo*, *The Lion King* and *Atlantis*, appeared in McDonald's Happy Meals.

Sources: Buss (2003); Cisionwire (2001); *Economist* (1998); *Eneco Nieuws* (2011).

For example, the presence of a second brand on a product reinforces the perception of high product quality and thus higher product evaluations. Most co-branding relationships include brands with an obvious or natural relationship that has the potential to be commercially beneficial for both parties. When the target customers of each firm match, at least to some extent, customers also should accept this connection and thereby formulate associations easily.

Several motives underpin firms' decisions to forge co-branding alliances (Chang and Chang 2008; Erevelles *et al.* 2008). First, firms may find themselves unable to reach new customer segments with their individual marketing apparatus. A co-branding alliance provides access to the partner firm's marketing infrastructure, which is likely to reach somewhat different customer segments, or reaches them in a different way, increasing sales revenues. Second, marketing activities are costly, especially when they include new product development and launches. A co-branding partnership shares such marketing costs across the partners. Third, marketing activities often pose risk to individual firms, again especially when their scope includes new product development. Relying on the strength of a partner brand through a co-branding alliance, each member has a better chance of reaching its marketing goals. Fourth, a firm that aligns its brand with another is often seeking to enhance its product image and credibility, which can then improve customer confidence. These motives reflect the promise of positive spillover effects (Park *et al.* 1996): reinforcing positive reciprocal effects of co-branding on alliance partners' brands. However, co-branding alliances also may result in image impairment, if combining the two brands causes brand meaning to transfer in ways that were never intended.

In particular, a negative brand spillover effect, which represents an adverse impact of co-branding on the perceptions of stakeholders, including customers' perceptions (Park *et al.* 1996), results when firms that are incompatible in some way forge a co-branding alliance. For example, inconsistency between customers' associations for the two brands leads to a negative response if the alliance forces the customer to transfer the association of one brand to the other. A potential repositioning of a brand also could adversely influence the other party's brand.

Furthermore, such negative spillover effects often get unevenly distributed, such that one partner experiences positive repercussions, while its counterpart suffers the negative outcomes. Such an unbalanced spillover effect creates a free-riding problem; the partner experiencing positive effects lacks the incentive to accommodate any changes to address the negative effects suffered by its partner.

In addition to potential negative spillover effects, a co-branding alliance can reduce a firm's flexibility, because once this association becomes rooted in stakeholders' perceptions, it is difficult to end the partnership without incurring substantial costs. When a co-brand achieves a particular position in a market, it is difficult to knock it out of that place – and even more difficult to re-establish a single brand on its own. Furthermore, customers do not just accept that things can go wrong, and rebuilding a damaged reputation requires substantial investment. In particular, inappropriate actions by one alliance partner may have severe repercussions on its counterpart's brand, though reputation damage is also possible owing to events beyond the alliance, such as when interest groups bring pressure to bear on one of the alliance partners.

Firms engaged in a co-branding alliance thus confront unique challenges. On the one hand, they need to collaborate to strengthen their brand reputations and achieve positive spillover effects. On the other hand, these partners risk damaging their brand reputations through negative spillover effects and the potential for harmful actions by partners. Alliance partners that can deal effectively with such challenges have an opportunity to create powerful synergies that not only improve reputations but also accelerate performance. Those that fail to do so, however, are likely to damage the alliance's progress, the partners' reputations and their own brands.

Managing co-branding alliances

A wide range of co-branding alliance activities take place in the marketplace (Geylani *et al.* 2008), ranging from touting several brands in a single advertisement (e.g. joint Shell–Ferrari ads, messages about the complementary consumption of McDonald's fries and Coca-Cola) to jointly branded products (e.g. the Lexus Coach Edition, Kellogg's Healthy Choice cereal). See Box 11.1 for some other examples. Because customers seek consistency and internal harmony in their attitudes, but their evaluations of one brand are influenced by the context of another co-brand, it is important to distinguish these various types of co-branding alliances. In general, co-branding consists of four types (Chang and Chang 2008; Washburn *et al.* 2000).

First, in a joint promotion, two brands promote their products together, usually because one or both of them hopes to secure a corporate endorsement that will improve its market position. For example, cross-marketing co-branding involves the mutual promotion by two companies, such as when one company includes coupons for another company in its packaging, in return for which the other company features a promotion from the first company in its direct mailing to its client base.

BOX 11.1 ALTERNATIVE FORMS OF CO-BRANDING

Partnering charitable causes with brands has become a common practice, referred to as cause–brand alliances. Allying a cause with a familiar brand improves attitudes toward the cause if the cause is relatively unfamiliar, but it also tends to result in more favourable brand associations. Firms might also sponsor sports or the arts in an attempt to associate their brands with renowned events, athletes, artists, and celebrities. Adidas' long track record of alliances with famous athletes features partnerships with David Beckham and Lionel Messi. In addition, firms forge global co-branding alliances to obtain global coverage for their brands or use co-branding alliances to extend the number of product categories in which they are active. Philips and Nivea combined their brand names and product to mass market the Cool Skin: an electric razor that dispenses shaving lotion; Gillette M3 power shaving equipment is co-branded with Duracell batteries, both brands owned by Proctor & Gamble; the BMW–Rover alliance to develop the new Mini constituted a brand extension strategy. Although they differ in nature, these alternative forms of co-branding alliances all seek to improve competitive positions through an alignment with a prestigious partner brand.

Second, joint advertising occurs when a specific product owned by one firm appears in the advertising campaign or product of another firm. In *Austin Powers: The Spy Who Shagged Me*, a woman in a photo shoot uses a Powerbook G3 Lombard; in *Mission Impossible 2*, Anthony Hopkins' character describes the mission on a Powerbook G3 Wallstreet. Unlike joint promotion, in joint advertising partners avoid long-term or repetitive campaigns. However, both joint promotion and joint advertising are relatively easy to design and manage, as the effort is limited mainly to the firms' marketing departments.

Third, when promoting the complementary use of their products, firms endorse the brands of a distinct yet complementary product. In addition to aligning the brands, such efforts can evoke favourable responses from consumers. For example, Nike and Apple suggest using an iPod with running shoes, to encourage faster times, farther distances and personal coaching. Such complementary uses again constitute a less intensive form of collaboration, because the partner firms turn to existing products to endorse their brands.

Fourth, physical product integration or ingredient co-branding involves actual product integration. One brand, which is usually the market leader for its product, supplies that product as a component in another branded product. In one example, Bacardi and Coca-Cola provide mixers with both brand names that suggest combining their flagship products to make a rum-and-cola drink. Ingredient co-branding alliance is thus the most intensive form of collaboration, because it involves multiple departments, including product design, production and marketing.

It appears particularly common when a supplier comes under the threat of entry by a competitor, because the incumbent supplier can reduce the probability of this entry while rewarding its downstream partner with a lower price.

Managing spillover effects in co-branding alliances

The main principle behind co-branding alliances, irrespective of the type of alliance, is that the allying firms help each other to exploit their brands. The purpose of their double appeal is to capitalize on the brand value of the partner brand, to achieve immediate recognition and a positive evaluation from potential buyers. In managing co-branding alliances, firms may focus on five instruments that influence the emergence of positive and prevent the creation of negative spillover effects (Simonin and Ruth 1998): (1) brand and product fit, (2) pre-existing brand attitudes, (3) brand equity, (4) alliance partner behaviour and (5) contractual provisions (see Table 11.2).

Brand and product fit

The success of co-branding alliances primarily depends on associations that (potential) customers have with the involved brands. That is, the likelihood that consumers will purchase the new product increases when two brands fit together.

TABLE 11.2 Managing co-branding alliances

	Description	Implications
Brand and product fit	The extent to which a brands and/or products are perceived by customers to posses similar attributes	Overall cohesiveness between brands and/or products results in more favourable perceptions of the co-brand
Pre-existing brand attitudes	Initial attitudes toward an individual brand affect dispositions toward the co-branding alliance	Negative and positive pre-existing brand attitudes impact the direction and nature of brand-spillover effects
Brand equity	Set of assets and liabilities linked to a brand's name or symbol, which adds to or subtracts from the perceived brand value	Brand equity management enables partners to reinforce positive and mitigate negative brand-spillover effects
Partner's behaviour	Perceptions of partner's competence and morals are critical, as they affect perceptions of the co-brand	Incompetent (e.g. low-quality) or immoral (e.g. dishonest) behaviour result in negative brand-spillover effects
Contractual provisions	Contracts help to reduce the adverse repercussions of negative brand-spillover effects	Contracts may contain clauses related to licensing, trademarks, intellectual property, liability and exclusivity

Co-branding alliances form to increase positive perceptions of at least one of the brands involved; the presence of a second brand creates the possibility that the two brands will be perceived as similar in quality. For example, if one brand is less well known than the other, a co-branding alliance can increase assimilation, such that the image of the less well-known brand comes to align with the image of the better known brand and its values, in the minds of consumers. The existence of overall cohesiveness between the two brands makes evaluations of the brand alliance more positive and favourable than they would be if the brands and their associations were regarded as incompatible and inconsistent. Whereas perceived fit between the two brands, products, or services thus offers a predictor of alliance success, brand misfit impedes alliance performance (Chang and Chang 2008).

Brand misfit arises when customers perceive incompatibility between the alliance partners' brands. For example, if a high quality brand partners with a low cost brand, customers of the high quality brand will perceive a misfit and experience more uncertainty toward their brand, because the association allows for a transfer of uncertainty from the less reliable to the more reliable brand (Geylani *et al.* 2008). In the late 1990s, the financial services provider H&R Block partnered with Bristol-Myers Squibb in a joint promotion of tax services and Excedrin pain relievers. No one got it. That is, the co-branding alliance failed because customers did not recognize any association between the two brands. On paper, the message seemed to make sense: Both Excedrin and H&R Block could relieve the headaches associated with completing taxes. Unfortunately, customers instead perceived that H&R Block would cause migraines that only Excedrin could cure. This difference between actual and perceived meanings may have seemed difficult to anticipate in advance, but the overall lack of product or brand fit contributed to the failure of the alliance. Poor fit offers less positive attitude changes than co-branding with strong fit; it can also induce deteriorating quality perceptions and a costly erosion of brand equity.

In addition to brand fit, product fit reflects perceived compatibility in terms of the function or quality of the products offered by the alliance firms. Two brands working together should provide greater assurance about product quality than one brand on its own, and attitudes toward the brand alliance should improve even more at higher degrees of product fit. Customers see that another firm is willing to put its reputation on the line, so they develop greater trust in the product (Park *et al.* 1996). However, if no natural logic aligns the combined products, customers cannot understand the reason for the partnership. In addition, product fit matters more when the alliance lacks brand fit. That is, consumers look first for image congruence, and if it is missing, they try to find congruence on the product category level.

The selection of co-branding partners accordingly must take brand and product fit into consideration. A firm might seek a complementary partner; Park and colleagues (1996) show that the combination of two brands with complementary attribute levels leads to a composite brand extension with a better attribute profile than either a direct extension of the dominant brand or an extension with two favourable but non-complementary brands. Alternatively, a firm might seek a partner with similar brand associations, because the brands then evoke equivalent responses from customers. For example, alliance managers in the mobile telephone industry might forge co-branding alliances based on brand personality, such as sincerity, excitement, competence, sophistication and ruggedness (Chang 2009). If a firm appears exciting and competent, it might search out a partner that is sincere, sophisticated and rugged, because the resulting complementary alliance would cover all the dimensions. Or it could find another exciting and competent partner, to forge a co-branding alliance with similar attributes.

Pre-existing brand attitudes

Attitudes are relatively stable psychological constructs, so pre-existing brand attitudes tend to relate closely to post-exposure attitudes toward that same brand (Simonin and Ruth 1998). Consequently, initial negative or positive attitudes toward an individual brand often transfer to a co-brand, and vice versa. A firm with a favourable perceived brand image might thus forge a co-branding alliance with a firm that suffers from a less favourable perceived brand image, assuming brand and product fit exist, to reconcile customers' sympathetic with their adverse perceptions. Positive attitudes toward individual brands get reinforced even further when customers process favourable information about a co-branding alliance (e.g. advertisements) or enjoy positive experiences with a co-branded product. Thus a well-known, well-liked firm such as McDonald's might signal the quality of a lesser-known brand, but it must do so carefully, because in some cases, a low-quality image can have negative spillover effects on its partner. McDonald's needs thus to take great care in selecting which partners will provide co-branded foods or beverages. Aligning with a perceived low-quality brand such as Faygo could have negative effects on the McDonald's brand, so instead, it allies with Coca-Cola. Thus the negative or positive pre-existing brand attitudes of consumers determine the likelihood and direction of potential spillover effects in a co-branding alliance.

Brand equity

Brand equity refers to the set of assets and liabilities linked to a brand's name or symbol, which add to or subtract from the value provided by the branded product or service. These associations define the product in customers' minds and have powerful effects on their buying behaviour. Co-branding alliances might increase the alliance partners' brand equity. In particular, pairing a well-known brand with a less known brand will enhances the less known product's equity (Washburn et al. 2000). However, such effects demand active management if the co-branding alliance is to succeed, because brand equity is associated with critical outcomes including sales revenue, market growth and customer retention. Through careful brand equity management, firms can capitalize on positive brand spillover effects and prevent negative implications. Management attention should focus particularly on four major elements of brand equity, each of which has a powerful influence on customer perceptions:

- Brand awareness refers to the strength of the brand presence in customers' minds. It can vary from recognizing the brand to associating the brand actively with a product or product family.
- Brand loyalty refers to the tendency to be loyal to the brand, demonstrated in the form of an intention to buy the brand whenever possible. High brand loyalty also means a reduced tendency to switch between brands. This outcome is cost-effective, because it is much more difficult and expensive to attract new customers than to keep existing ones.
- Perceived brand quality indicates customers' perceptions of the overall quality or superiority of a brand relative to alternative products and influences their buying behaviours.
- Brand associations reflect non-product-related associations evoked by the brand, and can be actively influenced by marketers. For example, to encourage a sporty, youthful image, Nike frequently employs celebrity spokespersons such as Michael Jordan and Rafael Nadal, but it also establishes alliances with Apple that grant it a technical, intelligent image.

In managing brand equity a firm needs insight into the manner in which stakeholders construct perceptions; the alliance partners could execute targeted marketing initiatives to enhance those perceptions. For example, to increase brand equity, they might provide customers with greater value to ensure the value they perceive exceeds the price they paid. In addition, high-quality support services are likely to enhance brand equity; the provision of timely, reliable, accurate information, perhaps through brochures, salespeople and online channels, also tends to increase customers' perceptions. In service contexts, customers often associate employees who have superior skills with better service quality. Such management initiatives become even more important when there are differences in brand equity between the partners. In particular, a co-branding alliance may pose a potential risk for the stronger brand, whereas the weaker brand can enjoy improved product quality perceptions without having to invest in the provision of better product quality. Neglecting such inequalities over time may result in long-lasting damage to reputations.

Partners' behaviour

Brand spillover effects often reflect two primary attributes of partners' behaviour (Votolato and Unnava 2006): competence and morality. Competence is a firm's ability to deliver information about the brand promise it makes to the customer. Negative information that arises in this category might pertain to the failure to meet quality standards, according to consumers. In a co-branding alliance, such failures adversely affect both partners' reputations, but they also often are due to the deliberate actions of managers. For example, partners might demand cost savings and use substandard raw materials, such that they undermine product quality.

Morality is the representation of the firm's ethics and principles. Negative outcomes emerge when behaviours (such as dishonesty) conflict with consumers' established ethical standards. For example, the use of child labour is perceived to be immoral, so companies that engage in such methods suffer damaged reputations. When customers receive signals of such immorality, they tend to dissociate from the brand; in co-branding alliances, partners must continuously monitor their partner's behaviours and initiate behaviour changes if necessary to prevent negative spillover effects. In the mid-1990s, Intel's poorly designed microprocessors diluted its brand quality, which then spilled over to its partners Gateway and Dell, tarnishing their quality images as well. Only a few years later, after Intel corrected the problem, was it able to rebuild its quality image and allow Gateway and Dell to see a return on their investment in partnering with the microprocessor manufacturer.

Research on negative information has suggested that information about companies morality and competence affect customers' responses in different ways. Customers are more willing to forgive competence failures than moral failures, because moral standards represent hygiene factors that should be respected by every individual (Brown and Dacin 1997). Wojciszke *et al.* (1993) also argue that consumers are less forgiving of moral failures when the negative information pertains to a particular person. Votolato *et al.* (2006) find similarly that a brand may be impervious to negative publicity surrounding its partner; it suffers ill effects only if consumers come to believe that the focal brand knew of and condoned its partner's behaviour.

Contractual provisions

In co-branding alliances, licensing of one or more trademarks between the parties is common. This approach helps reduce the adverse repercussions of negative spillover effects on a firm's brand and reputation. For example, licensing provisions may include guidelines for the use of the respective brands, trademarks or other intellectual property, including the partners' proprietary rights, quality controls, continuing rights upon termination, policing and enforcement. The licensing terms generally are reciprocal, specifying that the parties may use each other's trademarks, trade names, logos and copyrights solely to perform the obligations of the co-branding alliance agreement. They also usually contain a clause that states that the use of the respective marks must be in accordance with established policies and procedures.

In addition, any trademark licensing deal embodies a contractual provision regarding the potential of product defect liability. Each company involved in a co-branding alliance deal must know that affixing their brands to the product makes them liable for product failures. Indemnification, warranty and termination clauses should be specified carefully if they are to provide any protections in worst-case product defect and liability scenarios. Furthermore, exclusivity provisions may restrict co-branding partners' rights to enter into other third-party agreements. Such provisions typically prohibit any co-branding, co-marketing or other alliance with direct competitors, in an attempt to avoid any unwanted transfer of customers' brand associations. Some co-branding alliance agreements also include restrictions on affiliations with categories of services, products or industries. The exit provisions then specify the conditions for ending the alliance by one of the partners, which might include damaging actions that lead to possible negative spillover effects. Finally, an alliance contract might include penalties for broken conditions, varying from limiting or correcting the damage to active communication or even rectification. Penalties also can be specified in monetary terms, such as settling for damages of negative spillovers.

Co-branding alliances: Decision-making steps

The core logic underpinning co-branding alliances is that alliance partners combine their brands, occasionally augmented with an existing product or service, to realize objectives such as sales revenue and market share. However, unawareness of brand and product quality misfits, pre-existing brand attitudes, brand equity asymmetry and partner's misconduct may cause serious damage to a firm's brand. Alliance managers thus need to find a way to exploit positive spillover effects while preventing the emergence of negative spillover effects. To provide guidelines for forging win–win co-branding alliances, we next elaborate on specific decisions in each stage of the alliance development framework (see Figure 11.1).

Step 1: Alliance strategy formulation

During their strategic analyses, firms should decide whether a co-branding alliance is an appropriate governance mode to realize their branding strategy. In addition to generic rationales, such as transaction costs, resource complementarity, resource dependence and learning, a firm may consider improved brand equity as its primary motive. The analysis then should focus on the value of the existing brand, stakeholder perceptions and the anticipated benefits of co-branding. If the sole purpose of the branding strategy is to exploit the combination of two brands, such as through a joint promotion, an alliance generally suffices. However, if the physical integration of products is involved, firms may prefer more hierarchical control (e.g. merger or acquisition) as a means to govern the design, production and marketing processes.

If a firm decides to forge a co-branding alliance, it must make decisions about whether it will undertake joint promotion, joint advertisement, complementary use of products and/or physical product integration. In developing their co-branding strategy, the partners should be aware that familiar brands are better stimuli in brand alliance relationships, because they have a relatively higher degree of likeability among consumers due to their pre-existing associations and possibly positive previous experiences. In addition, high awareness brands are recalled more easily and generally signal high product quality and trustworthiness.

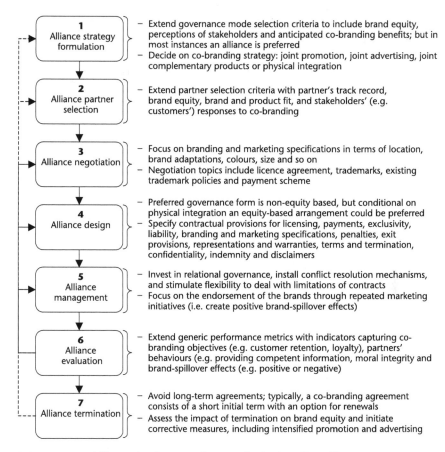

1
Alliance strategy
formulation
– Extend governance mode selection criteria to include brand equity, perceptions of stakeholders and anticipated co-branding benefits; but in most instances an alliance is preferred
– Decide on co-branding strategy: joint promotion, joint advertising, joint complementary products or physical integration

2
Alliance partner
selection
– Extend partner selection criteria with partner's track record, brand equity, brand and product fit, and stakeholders' (e.g. customers') responses to co-branding

3
Alliance negotiation
– Focus on branding and marketing specifications in terms of location, brand adaptations, colours, size and so on
– Negotiation topics include licence agreement, trademarks, existing trademark policies and payment scheme

4
Alliance design
– Preferred governance form is non-equity based, but conditional on physical integration an equity-based arrangement could be preferred
– Specify contractual provisions for licensing, payments, exclusivity, liability, branding and marketing specifications, penalties, exit provisions, representations and warranties, terms and termination, confidentiality, indemnity and disclaimers

5
Alliance
management
– Invest in relational governance, install conflict resolution mechanisms, and stimulate flexibility to deal with limitations of contracts
– Focus on the endorsement of the brands through repeated marketing initiatives (i.e. create positive brand-spillover effects)

6
Alliance
evaluation
– Extend generic performance metrics with indicators capturing co-branding objectives (e.g. customer retention, loyalty), partners' behaviours (e.g. providing competent information, moral integrity and brand-spillover effects (e.g. positive or negative)

7
Alliance termination
– Avoid long-term agreements; typically, a co-branding agreement consists of a short initial term with an option for renewals
– Assess the impact of termination on brand equity and initiate corrective measures, including intensified promotion and advertising

FIGURE 11.1 Alliance development framework: Co-branding alliances

Step 2: Alliance partner selection

During the partner selection stage, a firm selects a partner to establish a co-branding alliance. The partner chosen should be reliable and responsible. Both companies should represent the partnership responsibly, without scandals or public relations problems. For example, each firm should be comfortable with its counterpart's product safety track records and original equipment manufacturer relationships, especially if it is responsible for manufacturing or bringing goods to market. When the co-branded product features brands with inconsistent images, customers tend to regard it as inconsistent with the brands' existing products and only slightly revise their prior beliefs. The acts of each partner thus influence customer bases powerfully; a poor decision will result in failure and increase negative brand images. Anticipating both positive and negative potential spillover effects can prevent costly mistakes, which implies that partnering firms must evaluate both the actual monetary expenses involved in an alliance and the potential costs associated with the possible negative effect on their brand. Brands tell consumers who made a product and therefore whom to punish if the product fails to perform up to their expectations. The more positive the equity associated with a brand prior to the alliance, the higher the downside risk if the alliance partner proves to be a poor-quality provider. Firms must carefully weigh the costs and benefits of any alliance and consider both best-and worst-case scenarios during their due diligence process. Several questions can assist a firm in its efforts to identify and select an appropriate partner:

- What is the track record of this potential partner? Its existing brand may have prompted some association in the past, which could limit the co-branding alliance possibilities. In addition, partnering with a firm that has exhibited moral failures is likely to have negative repercussions.
- What is the brand equity of the potential partner, in terms of brand awareness, quality, loyalty and association? Partnering with a low-equity brand may create an uneven distribution of positive and negative spillover effects.
- Which brand personality dimensions are most important in a potential partner? Does the potential brand combination constitute a complementary or supplementary brand fit?
- How will customers react to the combination? Are customers able to associate the brands? If (potential) customers fail to see the connection between two brands, they will not understand the logic behind the partnership, which can ultimately lead to confusion and damage to the brand.
- If products are involved, how will customers react to product fit, and to what extent do product designs need to be altered to develop a valuable market proposition?

Step 3: Alliance negotiation

Consistent with generic guidelines, alliance negotiations should be integrative and rely on soft tactics. However, any firm might want to add branding and marketing specifications to the agenda, to ensure they determine the appearance and positioning of the respective brands in terms of location, colour, size and proximity, as well as any needed modification to existing brands. Other important topics to cover include the types of marketing initiatives employed (e.g. direct marketing), the use of each party's customer data and media campaign planning (e.g. television, print advertising, promotions). In addition, negotiations need to focus on the content and nature of licence and trademark provisions; co-branding alliances generally involve the licensing of at least one of the trademarks between the parties. Additional topics might cover payment schemes, existing licence and trademark policies or the partner's marketing contributions.

Step 4: Alliance design

A co-branding alliance design can be the key to alliance success or failure. If the sole purpose of the branding strategy is to exploit the combination of two brands, perhaps through joint promotion, a non-equity arrangement generally suffices. However, if a physical integration of products is needed, alliance partners could prefer more hierarchical control, such as through equity arrangements. The alliance governance form and management control mechanism should be consistent with generic guidelines, though the partners should place a particular focus on contractual provisions seeking to limit the adverse impact of negative spillover effects. Finally, the following contractual provisions are preferable ingredients of a successful co-branding alliance contract:

- Licensing provisions that cover guidelines for the use of the respective brands, trademarks and other intellectual property, including those for proprietary rights, quality control, continuing rights upon termination and policing and enforcement of rights.
- Product defect liability provisions, such as indemnification and warranty and termination clauses that provide protection in worst-case scenarios.
- Exclusivity provisions prohibiting co-branding, co-marketing or alliances with direct competitors.
- Penalty provisions, varying from limitations to or corrections of damage to public reputation through active communication, rectification and financial compensation.
- Exit provisions that specify the conditions in which alliance can be ended, such as when one partner engages in damaging actions and induces negative spillover effects.

Step 5: Alliance management

Although alliance contracts can increase the predictability of partner behaviour, detailed contracts also signal distrust, such that they may become a liability in co-branding alliances. Extensive contracts undermine initial trust building, reduce moral entanglements between partners and allow for opportunism. Investing in relational norms and capital is therefore critical once the co-branding alliance has been executed. In addition, interdependency between the collaborating organizations is greater than the initial scope of an alliance might reveal. For example, acts undertaken elsewhere in a partnering firm might have adverse effects on public awareness and stimulate conflicts. A closer interaction between collaborating parties can help ensure that they communicate a consistent message. However, their different organizational and cultural backgrounds are likely to give rise to varying views on the activities needed to strengthen reputations. Thus the managerial climate must leave room for active communication and sense making.

During the course of the co-branding alliance, partners may initiate joint efforts to endorse the endeavour. However, managing public awareness and strengthening reputation is not an exact science. To increase positive effects, the co-branding connection needs the benefits of repetition, appearing several times in advertising. Advertisers also should be aware of the special features of this strategy, such as the appropriate timing of the co-branding presentation or the proper ordering of images to achieve maximum brand association formulation. For example, to increase the chance of positive associations a (joint) product should be presented before the brand(s) in a joint advertisement.

Step 6: Alliance evaluation

Co-branding alliances are established to reach certain goals; alliance evaluation supports the timely revision of activities or even the decision to terminate before negative effects become overwhelming. A performance metric system might be augmented with indicators that also tap the positive and negative effects of brand spillovers. For example, some indicators might determine customers' perceptions of the co-brand, satisfaction, loyalty and retention. In addition, performance metric systems could feature indicators of the partner firms' behaviour, in terms of their morality and information competence. Another set of metrics could capture changes in partners' brand equity elements: brand name awareness, brand loyalty, perceived quality and brand associations.

Step 7: Alliance termination

The length of the agreement and the termination provisions are important, because they affect the parties' ability to escape from co-branding alliance arrangements that turn out to be harmful or that simply are not as effective or profitable as expected. Typically, a co-branding alliance agreement consists of an initial term and the option for renewal. The initial term should be relatively short (e.g. two to three years), so that the brands are not tied together for an excessive period, but long enough to establish the co-branding strategy and realize its success or potential. Incorporating exit provisions in the alliance contract also enables partners to end the alliance, without creating anger or unfavourable conditions.

Summary

Co-branding alliances combine brands and often the products of allying firms, in an attempt to realize marketing objectives such as market share, sales revenue and customer retention. Such marketing solutions may stimulate quality perceptions and provide reassurances about the true quality of a product, because brand names communicate a certain level of quality to consumers. A combination of one brand name with a reliable partner in a co-branding alliance reduces the risk to customers of buying a product. However, an ill-designed co-branding alliance will have severe repercussions for alliance partners, especially if customers transfer their negative associations to each of the partner brands. Such associations fail primarily because the value is not equitable for both brands in the relationship, the brands' values do not match or consumers have trouble understanding the alliance strategy. Through careful partner selection and contractual provisions though, partner firms can reduce the risks associated with co-branding alliances. Selecting partners with good brand and product fit and pursuing continuous investments in brand equity increase the chances of success, even as licence agreements, exclusivity provisions and termination clauses help protect the firm from liability issues and reputational damage.

Case: Capcom–Playboy

The game industry has become an increasingly interesting site for branding activities, especially as it has developed from a tightly focused niche market to a considerable mainstream industry. The size of the game industry has been estimated at $60.4 billion, and like trends in the movie industry, games now provide important platforms for companies to market their products and services. Capcom Entertainment Inc. (Capcom),[1] a worldwide developer and publisher of video games, has thus partnered with the Playboy corporation to include content from the iconic magazine publication featured in its forthcoming videogame, *Dead Rising 2*. Players that discover the presence of a *Playboy* magazine in the game receive a unique upgrade that Chuck Greene, the main character in *Dead Rising 2*, can use in his quest. Furthermore, players will encounter Playboy ads and billboards that feature specially selected issues from the magazine's 57-year history.

Founded in 1983, Capcom has created hundreds of games, including the best-selling franchises *Resident Evil*, *Street Fighter*, *Mega Man*, and *Devil May Cry*. In the action adventure game *Dead Rising 2*, the protagonist Chuck Greene must fight hordes of zombies while accomplishing specific missions to save his daughter Katey. The partnership with Playboy allows Capcom to integrate Playboy images and figures into the progress of the game, which further increases the attractiveness of the game for its primary target market: young men. For Playboy, the game offers an opportunity to increase its exposure to this similarly appealing target market. Playboy is one of the most recognized and popular consumer brands in the world, such that it can provide positive spillover effects to Capcom by coupling their images and associations.

According to Capcom, sales of *Dead Rising 2* reached more than two million copies in a matter of months. For Playboy, troubled by its declining market share, this massive exposure is valuable. Furthermore, in its connection with a hip new video game, Playboy's image gets refreshed among a younger demographic. However, none of these positive effects accrue without sufficient fit between the game and the partner brand.

For example, game characteristics and the storyboard help brands determine the level of match. Some popular games feature high levels of violence, which implies either a fit or a misfit, depending on the image of the partner brand. According to Seon King, the Senior Director of Licensing for Capcom, 'the Sin City-type environment in *Dead Rising 2*, *Fortune City*, is a natural playground for the Playboy Bunnies'. Therefore, King states, Capcom has 'integrated the Playboy brand throughout the game in ways that bring even more life to Fortune City and add to the user experience'. Although Capcom and Playboy representatives, including game developers and Playboy's marketing managers, worked hard to reach agreement on the basic storyboard and then the final product, the partnership remains limited to a single game. For that purpose though, they endorse each other's brands and participate in joint marketing activities.

Questions

1. To what extent is the alliance between Capcom and Playboy characterized by brand and product fit?
2. Which alliance partner, Capcom or Playboy, is more exposed to the risk of negative brand spillovers? Why?
3. A common way to determine financial compensation in a co-branding alliance is to divide the revenues generated by game sales. Explain how Capcom and Playboy might organize the financial structure of their co-branding alliance.

12

INTERNATIONAL ALLIANCES

Global markets, which represent the convergence of consumer demand across different societies; lowered barriers to trade and investment; the alignment of government policies; and key technological developments in information processing, communications and transportation, have prompted firms to adopt internationalization strategies to maintain their competitive advantage. Within the portfolio of competitive instruments a firm can use to discover and exploit international opportunities, international alliances have become quite prominent. They often enable firms to produce goods less expensively but with the same quality level, which improves their cost structure and/or helps them penetrate new markets to improve their profits. Although international alliances thus have grown increasingly popular, their failure rate also is extremely high. Clashing cultures are the most widely cited reasons for such failures, though cultural tensions often intertwine with other deal breakers, such as unrealistic expectations or distrust. That is, the international environments in which international alliances operate may exacerbate adverse situations or create great opportunities; in either case, their management is critical. Our first section details this unique challenge. Then we elaborate on the nature of national culture (second section) and discuss cross-cultural management approaches (third section). In the fourth section we use our alliance development framework to highlight key management issues, before concluding with a summary and a case illustration.

The international alliance challenge

International alliances (see Table 12.1), which refer to partnerships between parties located in different countries, are forged for multiple reasons (Glaister and Buckley 1996). They offer firms opportunities to gain access to knowledge and capabilities

TABLE 12.1 Examples of international alliances

	Description
Galapagos–Roche	In January 2010, the Dutch firm Galapagos (bio-tech) announced a strategic alliance with the Swiss firm Roche (pharmaceutical). The alliance expanded from a focus on small molecule and antibody approaches to include peptides in May 2010. By December 2010, it broadened to include fibrosis (i.e. the formation of scar tissue or other fibrous tissue as a result of injury or long-term inflammation). Galapagos also announced receiving 3.5 million in milestone payments.
Anheuser-Busch–Budejovicky Budvar's	In 2007, the US-based Anheuser-Busch and the Czech firm Budejovicky Budvar's put aside their long-running legal battle over the brand name Budweiser to form an historic trade alliance, in which Anheuser-Busch agreed to distribute Budweiser only in the United States. The dispute was not over yet though; Budvar's Budweiser continued to be known under the name Czechvar in the United States. Yet Budvar recognized the 'historical turning point' for the two companies, even as they continued to fight for the Budweiser trademark.
Technicolor–Canon	France's Technicolor, a leader in the field of imaging technology, formed an alliance in 2011 with Canon USA to develop a set of creative tools to facilitate the use of Canon EOS cameras for television and motion picture production. The new service incorporated Technicolor's CineStyle, an innovation that coupled with Technicolor's Digital Printer Lights™, provides a flawless workflow from photography to editorial status, for projects filmed using Canon EOS DSLR cameras.

Sources: Martino (2010); AFX News Limited (2007); Galapagos (2010); Technicolor Press Center (2011).

not currently controlled or available within their home country. International alliances also function as vehicles to enable firms to enter developing markets that may have restrictive conditions for foreign investment or gain a significant presence and greater market penetration more rapidly in new markets. Through international alliances, the partners create common and global platforms for products and services, as well as supplementing their knowledge bases with the new knowledge possessed by the foreign partner, such as when they integrate knowledge from different areas of science and technology to develop more radical innovations (Lane *et al.* 2001).

Despite the good reasons for forging international alliances they are inherently unstable, because the partners lack shared cultural norms and values (Meschi 2005; Park and Ungson 1997) – that is, these alliances feature cultural distance. Increasing cultural distance undermines the partners' interpretation of each other's strategic intents and tends to hamper their effective communication during alliance negotiations (Rao and Schmidt 1998). Many firms thus adopt alliance designs characterized by excessive governance and control to deal with the uncertainties related to different regulations, work-related values or management practices (Steensma *et al.* 2000). Even when the firms focus on governance, however, they often fail to establish effective control processes and procedures to encourage cooperation or mitigate resistance to change (Inkpen and Beamish 1997). Moreover, cultural distance tends to impede the building of trust as the partnership develops, along with inter-firm learning and knowledge sharing (Aulakh *et al.* 1996; Parkhe 1991). In general, cultural distance thus appears to affect negatively the strategic, tactical and operational processes that underlie the formation and maintenance of international alliances.

Yet some studies paint a rosier picture, in which international alliances develop into long-lasting, productive partnerships. Park and Ungson (1997) find that international joint ventures between Japanese and US parents survived longer than those between two US parents, perhaps because their prior relationships had already stimulated trust and enabled inter-firm learning, which counter-balanced any cross-cultural differences. Aulakh *et al.* (1996) show that investing in relational norms and mutual trust increases the likelihood of high-performing international partnerships. Brouthers and Bamossy (2006) reaffirm these findings and reveal that alliance processes, such as trust and commitment, constitute an important condition for developing successful international joint ventures. Although cultural distance is thus a prominent and potentially destructive factor, cross-cultural experience and management can also help firms overcome their cultural adversities and enable them to exploit cultural differences. Insights into the nature of national cultures and cross-cultural management are thus critical for successful international alliances.

The nature of national culture

National culture is ubiquitous, multidimensional, complex and pervasive. It consists of values, behavioural norms, beliefs, language, rituals governing behaviour, patterns of action, shared expectations and responses to the environment by a group that constitutes the nation. Deeply set values, norms, and priorities are thus common to members of a nation (Hofstede 1991), acquired early in life through a person's primary socialization in families, schools and social interactions. A country's culture permeates all aspects of life within that society – including the norms, values and behaviours of managers in its companies. It also constitutes an ethical habit, nurtured by repetition, tradition and example, which is manifested through images, habits and social opinions. In this role, it regulates the behaviour of people, often through communication and decision making. Because national culture is learned, however, people should be able to adapt their mental programming, regardless of their national culture. This point is important, because forging international alliances requires the managers involved to adapt their cultural dispositions to deal with cultural differences. National cultural frameworks can assist managers in this endeavour.

National cultural dimensions

Of the various national culture frameworks, including those by Trompenaars (1993) and the GLOBE study (House 2004), we turn to Hofstede's (1991) well-known framework for this chapter. Hofstede's framework has been criticized as outdated and specific to the context in which data was collected, but recent studies still maintain that the positions of the countries he established are relatively stable (Taras *et al.* 2009). Furthermore, although the development and application of various cultural frameworks remain constantly subject to controversy, they make similar contributions: namely, a better understanding of the relationship between people's cultural dispositions and their behaviour. Hofstede (1991) initially identified four cultural dimensions – individualism–collectivism, masculinity–femininity, power distance and uncertainty avoidance – to which he later added a fifth (Hofstede and Bond 1988), time orientation (Table 15.2).

Individualism–collectivism indicates the relative closeness of interpersonal relationships. It thus anticipates fundamental issues about individual motivation and place (and the management thereof), as well as about the organization and functioning of society as a whole. It pertains to people's attitudes toward relationships. People from individualistic countries, characterized by loose interpersonal ties, tend to emphasize their self-interest. But when the ties among individuals are tight (i.e. collectivism), their concern lies with the group interest. Thus alliance managers from collectivistic countries tend to be more loyal to the alliance, whereas those from individualistic countries consider the alliance as a means to an end.

The masculinity–femininity cultural dimension pertains to norms regarding an achievement motivation versus quality of life. Masculine cultures convey norms that emphasize the need for autonomy, competitiveness and assertiveness to achieve materialistic goals. In contrast, in countries with a feminine culture, the dominant norms emphasize sympathy, collaboration, the importance of relationships and helping others. Alliance managers from masculine countries tend to be more proactive in imposing their alliance solutions, if necessary with the risk of conflicts, on their counterparts, whereas managers from feminine countries tend to propose consensus-based solutions.

Power distance refers to the distribution of power within a country, as well as how societies deal with inequalities in social status. In countries with high power distance, citizens tend to accept such power inequality, whereas in low power distance countries, they emphasize equality. Therefore alliance managers from countries with high power distance tend to prefer centralization, whereas managers from low power distance countries tend to focus on empowerment.

Uncertainly avoidance pertains to people's inclination to reduce or cope with uncertainty about the future and deal with risk. High uncertainty avoidance indicates that the future is viewed as a threat, so alliance managers from these countries are less inclined to take risks. Managers from low uncertainty avoidance countries, however, tend to engage in more risky endeavours.

Finally, the time dimension entails a long- versus short-term orientation distinction, or the degree to which a society embraces a persistent devotion to traditional, forward-thinking values. With a long-term orientation, a society tends to focus on the future, but a short-term focus indicates that people focus on the present. Then alliance managers from long-term-oriented countries tend to be more patient with alliance progress, but their counterparts from short-term-oriented countries demand immediate results.

TABLE 12.2 Hofstede's five cultural dimensions

Description	Characteristics	Example
Individualism–collectivism	In individualistic cultures, relations with others should be rational, based on personal goals, and governed by cost–benefit calculations. In collectivistic cultures, relations are organized to protect group harmony and save face and avoid embarrassment.	Alliance managers from individualistic countries (e.g. US) tend to focus on individual achievements and rights; their counterparts from collectivistic cultures (e.g. Turkey) tend to emphasize joint achievements.
Masculinity–femininity	Masculine societies convey norms that emphasize the need for autonomy, competitiveness and assertive actions to achieve materialistic goals with a preference for extrinsic rewards. Feminine cultures convey norms that emphasize the need for collaboration and relationships. The dominant norms are caring for others and quality of life, with preference granted to intrinsic rewards.	Alliance managers from masculine countries (e.g. Italy) tend to focus on decisive and daring and resolve conflicts through fighting; their counterparts from feminineoriented cultures (e.g. Netherlands) tend to emphasize consensus behaviour and resolve conflicts through compromising.
Uncertainty avoidance	In cultures with high uncertainty avoidance, people seek to reduce uncertainty by planning everything carefully and relying on rules and regulations. In countries with low uncertainty avoidance, people are more willing to accept uncertainty and not afraid to take risks.	Alliance managers from high uncertainty avoidance countries (e.g. Belgium) tend to focus on incremental improvement steps guided by blueprints; their counterparts from low uncertainty avoidance cultures (e.g. Singapore) tend to accept uncertainty.

(Continued)

TABLE 12.2 *(Continued)*

Description	Characteristics	Example
Power distance	In cultures with high power distance, a belief exists that power should govern relationships; inequality in power is the basis of societal order. In cultures with low power distance, the belief is that power is a necessary evil that should be minimized and people should treat one another as equals.	Alliance managers from high power distance countries (e.g. France) tend to focus on centralized decision making; their counterparts from low power distance cultures (e.g. Denmark) tend to focus on empowerment and subscribe to management by consensus.
Time orientation	In cultures with a long-term time orientation, ordering relationships by status and observing this order, thrift, and a sense of shame are important. In cultures with a short-term orientation, personal stability, protecting face, quick results, and unimportance of status are typical.	Alliance managers from short-term oriented countries (e.g. US) tend to focus on immediate (financial) results; their counterparts from long-term oriented cultures (e.g. China) tend to focus on long-term (strategic) outcomes.

Sources: Hofstede (1991); Hofstede and Bond (1988).

When people from different countries work together, conflicts and opportunities are likely. For example, an alliance manager with an individualistic orientation might make decisions to prioritize the protection of individual profits, as justified by utilitarian principles. His or her counterpart from a collectivist culture recognizes the group as the dominant structure and therefore makes decisions to achieve consensus, protect group harmony and save face. In an international alliance, an individualistic alliance manager tends to be less concerned about process discrepancies (i.e. distrust) than the collectivist counterpart. The former manager also exhibits a low desire to understand the causes for distrust or initiate corrective measures. The collectivist manager in the meantime is viewing the process discrepancy as a barrier to alliance progress that must be resolved. These contrasting views might result in decision-making conflicts or, if properly managed, constructive dialogues. In an alliance, cultural differences therefore can function as (1) barriers to cooperation, (2) challenges to be addressed or (3) windows to unexpected opportunities (Child and Faulkner 1998).

Culture as a barrier

An international alliance brings people from different countries together in a working relationship. If they identify strongly with their national cultures, collaborating with members of other nations may constitute a threat. The participants in the international alliance may then resist changes to their structures and practices, especially those initiated to advance the alliance's progress. For example, considerable difficulties arise in international alliances featuring firms that manage and organize their employees according to masculine versus feminine orientations. In the former, managers emphasize goal achievement, completion and management action. In the latter, they will focus on mutual collaboration and a supportive working climate. It is difficult to reconcile these contrasting orientations. In turn, the cultural differences signal a loss or low level of control and a source of fundamental conflict, which leads to misunderstanding and disagreements. At a superficial level, cultural differences may entail simple misunderstandings, originating in language and behaviour differences, which are relatively easily to address as long as people are sensitive and aware. Even if a foreign alliance partner recommends different management practices, joint, open communication and dialogue can help resolve any cultural differences. At a more fundamental level though, such differences reflect conflicts in values and thus may bar the development of successful international alliances. If socially embedded values clash, they can seriously damage interpersonal collaboration.

Culture as a challenge

Beyond their roles as barriers to cooperation, cultural differences confront managers with unique challenges, including the very design of the alliance. Firms that face seemingly incomprehensible cultural differences tend to adopt excessive governance forms to obtain protection and safeguards against exchange hazards. Gulati and Singh (1998) report that the country of origin often determines the choice between minority-equity investment and joint ventures, according to the partners' different perceptions of time. For example, Japanese partners tend to adopt long time horizons when dealing with exchange hazards, in contrast with their European and US counterparts. Brouthers and Bamossy (2006) find that initial formal control by a foreign partner often benefits alliance progress, particularly if supplemented with social controls, but then as the alliance progresses, management control must be shared. Moreover, maintaining dominant formal control tends to result in under-performance by the international alliance (Fryxell et al. 2002).

Other challenges pertain to alliance negotiation and execution; cultural distance increases the likelihood of premature breakdown due to cultural conflicts. Developing a negotiation climate characterized by mutual trust is difficult for negotiators from different countries, because the probability of mutual misunderstandings, miscommunications, erroneous interpretations of proposals and personal offence tends to increase. For example, US managers might adopt soft negotiation tactics when dealing with foreign partners, but as their cultural distance increases, the likelihood of the use of hard tactics increases, because the managers perceive higher risks of opportunistic conduct and non-compliance (Rao and Schmidt 1998). In the alliance execution stage, cultural differences may result in considerable operational problems. If people involved in the alliance focus on different priorities, as reflecting their cultural orientations, any breakdown in relational norms and capital, interpersonal communication, or inter-firm learning will inhibit these partners' ability to work together. Many alliance managers just assume that their counterparts will respond similarly to a problem, but managers from masculine Japan are quick to adopt destructive response strategies, whereas managers from collectivist Turkey prefer more passive responses (Furrer *et al.* In press). Similarly, managers from individualistic cultures perceive conflict as a constructive and inevitable part of alliances, so they use dialectical inquiry and play the devil's advocate to improve decision making (Parkhe 1991). Managers from collectivistic countries would never embrace such tactics, which reduce their ability to save face and lead to vigorous and inappropriate-seeming conflicts. Furthermore, developing and implementing performance metric systems that accommodate both partners' interests is difficult in the face of vast cultural differences (Büchel and Thuy 2001).

Culture as opportunity

Differences in national culture also may constitute an opportunity. Cultural diversity enables alliance partners to build on their cultural strengths, by combining the advantageous aspects of their existing cultures into a new, improved culture. The establishment of NUMMI by Toyota and General Motors is a well-known example of the US car manufacturer's attempt to learn about the lean manufacturing methods being used so successfully in Japan. Meanwhile, Toyota gained access to information about the competitive strategies of its partner and developments within the US auto industry (Doz and Hamel 1998). Yeheskel and colleagues (2001) find that certain cultural differences (e.g. in masculinity and power distance) have negative impacts on joint venture performance, whereas others, such as individualism and uncertainty avoidance, produce positive impacts. To explain this divergence, they argue that if perceived properly, cultural differences offer a valuable asset. If alliance managers recognize the potential challenges of working with foreign partners, they should be more willing to expend effort to avoid misunderstandings, such that differences in national culture then lead to high-level communication and more sustained collaboration (Shenkar and Zeira 1992). When regarding cultural differences as an opportunity, the partners aim to harvest the benefits of the diversity in alliance partners' cultures while also building effective bridges between them.

Exploiting cultural opportunities is not always an appropriate course of action, however. Culture provides people with a sense of social cohesion (i.e. reference point) and makes them accept shared goals. Firms must therefore consider carefully the form of their international alliance. If it will entail a stand-alone entity (e.g. joint venture), partners may benefit from building a separate alliance identity that intentionally aims to meld the strengths of both partners' national cultures. However, if an alliance represents an investment opportunity, the transfer of cultural values and norms may not outweigh the potential benefits of cultural integration. Furthermore, even if alliance partners are willing to accommodate their

---

BOX 12.1   HIGH AND LOW CONTEXT CULTURES

A more parsimonious classification of national cultures entails the distinction between high and low context cultures. In a high context culture information remains tacit, and interpretation requires an understanding of the situational context. In a low context culture, information is primarily communicated in codified form, and the burden of interpretation is placed on the receiver. Most Asian cultures fall at the high context end of this continuum; North American cultures fall at the low context end. International alliances between partners that are both from either high or low context cultures are likely to experience only minor cultural adversities, but partnerships that span these categories will tend to suffer substantial cultural conflicts. In the latter case, alliance managers must adapt their communication styles to accommodate the partners.

---

partners' national cultures, they still need the opportunity to maintain their own identity.

Firms engaged in international alliances thus confront a unique challenge: They must counter the negative consequences of cultural differences, such as the greater risk of opportunistic conduct, by first recognizing the potential for cultural barriers and thereby initiating measures to avoid detrimental implications. Simultaneously, they should identify opportunities to exploit cultural diversity. To this end, alliance managers need to understand the extent to which cultural differences exist (see Box 12.1), identify whether they constitute a threat or opportunity, and assess the degree of influence of alliance acculturation. Appropriate cross-cultural management can then transform cultural differences into assets, which increase the probability of alliance success.

Managing international alliances

The management of international alliances includes activities designed to reconcile differences in the alliance partners' cultures – a prerequisite of the long-term viability of an international alliance. When different national cultures enter into a workable relationship, the alliance partners can realize their objectives with minimal tension, conflict or disagreement. This point does imply however that the original cultures should be reconciled. The more national cultures differ, the greater their impact on alliance development, and the more difficult and time-consuming management becomes. If national cultures in an alliance are deeply embedded, their attempted reconciliation with other cultures will result in resistance to change. Therefore, the active management of cultural diversity is important in alliances, and managerial attention should focus on (1) building cultural competence, (2) alliance manager selection, (3) partner selection, (4) learning and (5) the work climate.

Cultural competence

In an alliance context, cultural competence refers to the ability to interact effectively with people of different cultures, and it comprises three components. First, alliance managers must become aware of their own cultural worldview; such consciousness of their personal reactions to people who are different improves their attitudes toward cultural differences. Prior to forging an international alliance, managers must make an effort to assess the nature of their partner's cultures and the potential for adversities. Second, knowledge of different cultural practices helps alliance managers maintain consistency between their attitudes and behaviours. With cultural awareness, they can identify the implications of their (unintended) actions. Third, cross-cultural skills, such as developing cultural competences, result in an ability to understand, communicate with and effectively interact with people across cultures. Neglecting cultural differences instead results in highly unpredictable consequences. The active and constructive interaction between counterparts eases cultural harmonization and integration, because a firm with a good cultural competence can diagnose and remedy cultural differences, which enables cultural integration.

Cultural competences might be built through training or education in cross-cultural management. Training should improve managers' cultural awareness, sensitizing them to their own interpretive schemes, as well as those of their partners. It also reduces managers' natural tendency to process information automatically, so that they do not just make instantaneous judgments about their partner's intentions. Cross-cultural sensitivity and language competence in particular can increase managers' understanding of partner needs and interests, resulting in high-quality cross-cultural interactions. Other forms of beneficial education include training in the partner's country for both sides, or personnel exchanges between the alliance partners. In addition, a firm may learn from its prior international alliances and coach other alliance managers using these prior experiences. Once firms gain more experience in international business, they are more confident about operating abroad, more willing to take risks and better able to manage international alliances. Host country-specific experience is especially useful when it comes to strategic decisions, managing local labour and communicating with customers, suppliers and stakeholders. Rewards are key when building and using such cultural competences. Firms often provide training but never mandate full participation or reward employees who apply the training to their work. To manage international alliances successfully, it is utterly necessary that the involved staff and management gain sufficient understanding of their partners' cultural dispositions and recognize the value of cultural diversity.

Alliance manager selection

National cultural differences may inhibit alliance managers' ability to interact. To resolve this issue, a firm preferably should select alliance staff with open minds and flexible personalities, as well as those who demonstrate positive approaches during previous experiences in alliances or international business settings. Schneider and Barsoux (1997) propose a set of behavioural competences needed for effective intercultural performance, including linguistic ability, interpersonal (relationship) skills, cultural curiosity, ability to tolerate uncertainty and ambiguity, flexibility and patience, cultural empathy, a strong sense of self and a sense of humour. If managers lack these abilities, they need cultural training and education to help them adjust to the different national cultures. The content of such training should be up to date and realistic, with an added focus on language proficiency – insufficient comprehension of another language often creates conflicts. Trainers should preferably include native speakers of the language who maintain regular contact with their country of origin. These anticipatory trainings are both costly and time-consuming, so some firms designate alliance staff with hands-on cultural experience to conduct it. In another approach, an alliance partner sets up a team of experienced managers who take responsibility for the alliance execution in an attempt to absorb initial cultural shocks. As soon as the alliance operation is functioning smoothly, they hand it over to others who continue their work.

Finally, when evaluating employees for staffing decisions, competency models provide useful guidance that can increase the organization's ability to staff its alliances with employees who will easily adjust to and enjoy cultural diversity.

Partner selection

Partner selection confronts firms with a dilemma (Meschi 1997): is it better to collaborate with a partner with a compatible national culture, or seize an opportunity with a partner that is less compatible but immediately available? Investing too much time in seeking out a compatible partner may allow the motivation underpinning the alliance to expire. But collaborating with a partner with an incompatible culture could jeopardize any alliance outcomes anyway. For example, the immediate realization of short-term financial benefits is often difficult when cultural differences exist. Harmonizing cultural differences requires time and devoted management attention, but when the partners share at least certain aspects, their cultural integration can be accelerated. During partner selection, alliance managers thus might consider other partner selection motives. Foreign partners tend to contribute distinctive resources (Hitt *et al.* 2000), increasing the risk of exchange hazards (i.e. unwanted knowledge leakage), and greater cultural distance increases the likely preference for a marketing or supplier alliance over an innovation-oriented alliance (Kaufmann and O'Neill 2007). International alliances thus demand extensive protection against exchange hazards, which is possible through effective partner selection. A firm should select a partner by making trust and commitment the foremost priorities, because alliance partners must believe that they can depend on each other before they can possibly deal with the adverse consequences of cultural differences (Cullen *et al.* 1995).

The work climate

International alliance failure often results from the execution of the venture, rather than the rationale and resources used to form it. The parties involved might fail to develop or implement post-formation processes to overcome international barriers to success. Furthermore, a healthy working climate is critical to successful international alliances, which means partners must be able to acknowledge their differences to avoid fatal conflicts. For example, Japanese firms and foreign partners may follow similar paths to develop trust, commitment, credibility, reciprocity and benevolence, but trust tends to be more important for the former (Cullen *et al.* 1995). In this sense, cultural differences between partners tend to inhibit open and prompt communication, which is necessary to spur a process in which parties are able to examine one another's credibility and trustworthiness. Although partners with similar cultural backgrounds also tend to use similar trust forms (e.g. cognitive versus affective), they are more opportunistic when they embrace dissimilar trust forms. If cultural differences are great, partners should invest in building a high-quality working climate to prevent the emergence of inter-partner conflicts and tensions. Similarly, norms that govern giving and receiving feedback differ greatly across cultures, but regardless of culture, some feedback is necessary to achieve effective relationships. Cultural differences leave feedback communications particularly prone to misunderstandings and misinterpretations, so well designed performance management practices should be in place to ensure that employees receive the feedback they need in a culturally appropriate way. Investing in intensive cross-cultural programmes can reduce the adverse impact of cultural differences overall, as well as improve relational norms and capital, which positively influence alliance performance (Brouthers and Bamossy 2006).

International alliances: Decision-making steps

Whereas international alliances enable companies to share risks and investments, as well as obtain access to new technologies and markets, the international environments in which they operate also exacerbate the likelihood of dissatisfying economic performance, distrust between parties and premature termination. Therefore, the improper management of cultural adversities contributes to high failure rates; decision making is critical in such situations to avoid premature termination. To help steer international alliances toward greater chances for success, we next present managerial guidelines for each stage of the alliance development framework (see Figure 12.1).

Step 1: Alliance strategy formulation

During its strategic analysis, a firm decides whether an international alliance is even an appropriate governance mode, compared with international mergers and acquisitions or other forms, to realize its objectives. Before selecting a governance mode, the firm should analyse whether it possesses sufficient know-how and

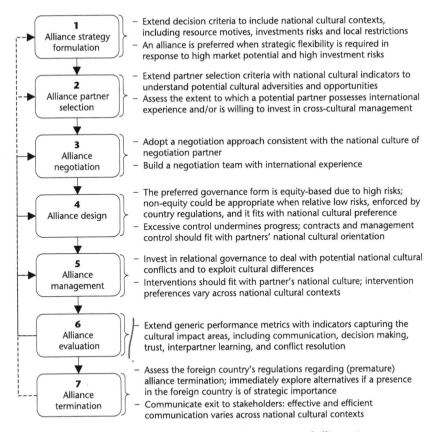

FIGURE 12.1 Alliance development framework: International alliances

know-what (i.e. cultural competence) to engage in an international endeavour. Detailed preparations in the form of cross-cultural management efforts are required in order to guarantee that the international alliance delivers on its promise. In addition to various general considerations, firms must recognize that forging an international alliance necessitates some additional, specific analyses:

- Partners of different countries often have different resource needs and offer different resources and capabilities. For example, conditional on its resource alignment, an international alliance may have a low (high) degree of resource similarity and a high (low) level of resource heterogeneity, which would suggest the appropriateness of (non) equity-based governance modes.
- Distinct countries pose different risks and challenges due to their unique appropriation regimes, regulations and industry conditions. Collaboration then may constitute an investment risk and induce additional transaction costs, which must be carefully analysed. For example, wholly owned subsidiaries are preferable to joint ventures when market potential is high, investment risks are low and local legal restrictions are comparable for both partners.

Step 2: Alliance partner selection

Differences in national culture between alliance partners could be an opportunity for or a threat to joint value creation. The partner fit framework needs sufficient indicators to be able to identify fit (or misfit) between national cultures. Against the background of a generic framework, firms also need to acquire information about the national culture of their potential partners and assess the possibility of adverse implications, as well as of potential synergies. A cultural misfit suggests that partner firms' cultures are potentially incompatible, which could be detrimental to alliance success. The greater the cultural distance, the more measures are necessary to deal with cultural barriers, which may adjust cost–benefit calculations downward. Furthermore, it is important to know upfront whether a potential partner has sufficient experience and know-how to participate in an international alliance: has the partner been involved in prior (successful) international alliances, does it offer cultural training programmes and is it willing to appoint experienced managers?

Step 3: Alliance negotiation

During the alliance negotiation stage, the firm needs to consider not only its negotiation approach but also cultural dynamics. The national culture of the partners may determine the right composition of the negotiation team, which topics to be discussed and with whom, and how to codify the results of the negotiation. Negotiators may want to adapt their strategy and tactics to the cultural context of the alliance negotiation. For example, negotiators from collectivist countries (e.g. Japan) are likely to respond adversely to hard negotiation tactics, because direct conflicts cause them to become embarrassed, whereas their counterparts from individualistic countries (e.g. United States) are better able to deal with open confrontation.

Step 4: Alliance design

International alliances may also pose additional risks, such as country-specific regulations, opportunistic behaviour, knowledge leakage and misappropriation, which necessitate additional protection. Consequently, equity arrangements (i.e. international joint ventures) supplemented with extensive contractual clauses and management control can offer a preferred governance form by functioning as a superior safeguard. However, not all international alliances include learning objectives, so sometimes excessive protections are unnecessary. Furthermore, excessive, prolonged control by a single partner tends to result in poor performance, because the costs associated with alliance design outweigh the benefits. Dominant control also reduces incentives for active participation by the counterpart in the alliance. Efforts to impose controls on a foreign partner might provoke resistance and hostility, thus undermining the development of the relational norms and capital that are so critical to success and the resolution of cultural tensions. Thus, during the alliance design stage, partners need to resolve a dilemma: how to include enough governance to secure individual interests without undermining the working relationship. Although clear-cut prescriptions are virtually impossible, some guidelines can inform the related decision making:

- Extend generic rationales for alliance design with contextual factors, such as country-specific regulations and investment risks. Some countries have strict laws and regulations that dictate acceptable alliance designs (e.g. China). Economic and social uncertainty within a country will also influence alliance design decisions.
- Alliance design preferences are likely biased by cultural orientation. Managers from countries with high uncertainty avoidance scores will focus on equity-based governance and complete alliance contracts (to reduce uncertainty), unlike managers from countries with low scores.
- Even if dominant control appears appealing (e.g. a majority joint venture), alternative design arrangements should be considered, such as non-equity-based alliances with supplemental contractual provisions and management control.

Step 5: Alliance management

An important task during the alliance management stage is to harmonize actively the national cultural differences between the partners, to the extent desired. Appropriate alliance designs should have reduced the adverse impacts of cultural distance, but these differences remain manifest in the ongoing behaviour and thinking of the people involved. Culturally specific behaviours thus can produce misunderstanding, conflicts, limited trust and learning barriers. For example, the developmental path of the international alliance depends on whether collectivist partners try to manage process discrepancies, and then the resulting response of individualist partners to these interventions as they focus instead on outcome discrepancies. In principle, the interaction could lead to the resolution of the crisis or intensify it further. To avoid such cultural-based adversities, alliance management should focus on:

- Building collaborative communication patterns and, if necessary, undertaking management interventions to improve cultural awareness through training and education.
- Interpreting constructive and destructive conflicts consistently with cultural orientations and using resolution techniques that fit the cultural context.
- Avoiding breakdowns in relational norms and capital (e.g. trust) and investing time, energy and resources to rebuild them, because strong working relationships are critical.
- Understanding that responses to adverse situations vary across countries and thus considering partners' cultural orientations while making response strategy decisions to prevent destructive spirals of partner interactions.

Step 6: Alliance evaluation

In international alliances, specific consideration should be granted to <u>performance</u> metrics that imply cross-cultural problems, such as <u>communication, conflict, trust,</u> <u>decision making and learning.</u> With such attention, the firm can monitor the process of working together and outcomes, which are pivotal for steering the international alliance. If alliance partners also intend to combine the strengths of their national cultures, they need measures that facilitate cultural integration. Also important is a consistent focus on shared goals and objectives. Certain training programmes can inform employees about the shared goals of alliance partners, but performance management systems must convince employees that the rhetoric fits the reality. Ideally, in each development stage, all involved employees will understand how their performance is being assessed, and how those performance assessments relate to the overall goals for the alliance.

Step 7: Alliance termination

Finally, and conditional on the alliance design (i.e. governance form and exit provisions) and cultural orientation of the partners, firms must decide how to terminate their international alliance to ensure favourable outcomes for all involved. Issues that the partners may need to consider include:

- Irrespective of whether the termination is intended or unintended, country-specific regulations may affect the termination trajectory. For example, legal restrictions may inhibit the acquisition or divestment of equity stakes.
- If it is of strategic importance for one partner to be present in the foreign country, it should explore alliance alternatives immediately and ensure that it capitalizes on its learning experiences.
- Cultural orientations tend to influence the effectiveness of communication strategies. For example, in collectivistic countries, saving face is critical; an abrupt, premature alliance termination will thus have serious repercussions for all parties.

Summary

International alliances confront managers with a unique challenge: the international environments in which they operate can either exacerbate adverse situations or create a new opportunity. This challenge can be addressed using time-consuming processes associated with becoming acquainted with other cultural dispositions. To reconcile cultural differences effectively, each partner must make an effort to learn the ideologies and values of its counterpart. Developing mutual understanding prompts tolerance and a proactive approach to the reconciliation. In particular, it requires a systematic assessment of the characteristics of potential international partners, a programme to deal with these cultural differences and attention to key alliance design and management dimensions, depending on the partner's nationality.

Case: Coca-Cola

The Coca-Cola Company[1] (Coca-Cola) is the world's largest non-alcoholic beverage company. Along with the Coca-Cola® trademark, which is recognized as the world's most valuable brand, the company markets four of the world's top five non-alcoholic sparkling beverage brands – including Coca-Cola®, Diet Coke®, Fanta®, and Sprite® – plus a wide range of other non-alcoholic beverages, including diet and light beverages, waters, juices and juice drinks, teas, coffees, and energy and sports drinks. Through the world's largest beverage distribution system, consumers in more than 200 countries partake of more than 1.4 billion servings of the company's beverages each day.

Over the last 60 years, Coca-Cola has actively approached the Chinese market. The company built its first bottling plant in China in the decade following the First World War, and became the first US company to distribute its products in China after the country was opened to foreign investors in 1979. Initially, Coca-Cola imported its products and was only allowed to sell them to foreigners at designated retail outlets. In addition to its wholly owned subsidiaries, Coca-Cola also initiated a partnering strategy. In 1984, the company set up its first joint venture in China, a bottling plant in Zhuhai, Guangdong Province, with the former Ministry of Light Industry. The next year, Coca-Cola obtained permission to sell its products to the Chinese people. The company also sold local brands through a 50:50 joint venture (Tianjin Jin Mei Beverage), which was established in 1993. Since then, Coca-Cola has steadily expanded its operations and now works with three bottling group partners, each of which operates a number of bottling companies in its respective franchise territories: Swire Beverages Ltd (12.5 per cent equity stake), COFCO Coca-Cola Beverages Ltd. (65 per cent equity stake), and Coca-Cola China Industries Ltd (wholly owned). The bottling group partners manufacture, sell, distribute and market branded beverages. Through intensive collaboration with its suppliers, Coca-Cola sources ingredients and develops packaging materials and promotional items; distributes and sells products; and minimizes its environmental footprint from water, energy, and packaging. To reinforce collaboration in its domestic supplier network, Coca-Cola provided its partners with financial assistance, technical advice and quality programmes. However, to maintain control over the ingredients and formulas of its drinks, Coca-Cola produces concentrates in a wholly-owned factory located in Shanghai.

After initial successes in the mid-2000s, Coca-Cola started to lose market share to local companies like Wang Lao Ji, a herbal tea producer, and was also under attack from its global rival, PepsiCo. Coca-Cola recognized that people were becoming more health-conscious and that future trends could turn them away from carbonated soft drinks altogether. In fact, Chinese consumers preferred juices and teas to colas. They bought more Sprite than Coke itself. Sprite, with its lemony taste and clear colour, is perceived as healthier than cola. One opportunity that presented itself was Chinese herbal medicines.

Coca-Cola started to explore how traditional Chinese herbal medicine could enable the company to develop and produce healthier beverages. To this end,

Coca-Cola needed to understand the ancient system of Chinese herbal medicines. If Coca-Cola could leverage Chinese expertise in traditional herbs and herbal formulas to develop a new and unique line of beverages, it should be able to drive growth in the functional drink category. Through its partnerships, Coca-Cola was able to promote holistic health beverages, thereby reclaiming market share. For example, the company introduced Yuan Ye, a beverage brewed completely from real tea-leaves, to the Chinese market. It also invested in the marketing of readymade teas, bottled water, juices, and energy drinks, including Glacéau vitamin water, Minute Maid Pulpy Super Milky, and Minute Maid Pulpy in different flavours.

In October 2007, Coca-Cola announced the official opening of the Coca-Cola Research Center for Chinese Medicine in Beijing, setting up laboratory facilities to experiment with new Chinese herbal flavours for Coke and other beverage products. Coca-Cola was the first international company to open a research centre at the China Academy of Chinese Medical Sciences, the most respected and trusted group in the field of research, education and practice in Traditional Chinese Medicine. The Academy is administered by the Ministry of Public Health and employs 3,100 professionals, including 800 doctors and professors working in 11 research institutions, five hospitals and clinics, and several educational and publishing branches. The objective was to have many combinations of these herb powders mixed into Coca-Cola products, bringing the insights and benefits of traditional Chinese herbal medicines to consumers all over the world. Dr. Huaying Zhang, the director for Coca-Cola Asia, oversaw how Coca-Cola staff worked side-by-side with researchers on collaborative projects. The centre represents an important step in strengthening the Coca-Cola innovation pipeline for beverages that contribute to wellbeing.

The success of Coca-Cola's alliance probably stems from the company's earlier lessons in China. The company has adopted the 'think local, act local' attitude and adapted its products, business and partnering strategies accordingly. It encourages local managers to develop new drinks, regional offices have the freedom to approve local initiatives, and locals have control over advertising operations. In addition, Coca-Cola recognizes that foreign firms in China must honour the ruling party and its laws.

Questions

1. One element of Coca-Cola's success in China relates to its numerous alliances with Chinese government agencies. Taking a cross-cultural perspective (that is, United States versus China), can you explain this partnering strategy?
2. When setting up the research centre, Coca-Cola recognized the importance of personal communication. Taking a cross-cultural perspective, what other initiatives could they have developed?

13

ASYMMETRICAL ALLIANCES

Alliances tend to be asymmetrical in nature, such that a dominant partner has a bargaining power advantage due to its superior resource endowments.[1] When such power asymmetries characterize the relationship, alliance partners are engaged in an asymmetrical alliance; the dominant firm can exert power, and the weaker firm risks being taken advantage of. In turn, dominant firms might appropriate the lion's share of the alliance benefits. Without proper management, power asymmetries create an eminent risk of inequitable value appropriation and sub-optimal alliance performance. Thus partners – especially weaker ones – face a unique challenge: Finding the balance between exploiting resource asymmetries to create value while still preventing the escalation that can result from power asymmetries. This chapter focuses on this asymmetrical alliance challenge (first section) and elaborates on the mechanisms that managers might use to deal with it (second section). Connecting asymmetrical alliances with the alliance development framework offers some guidelines for decision making (third section). We conclude the chapter with a summary and a case illustration.

The asymmetrical alliance challenge

Alliances are forged from resource interdependencies between firms, which provide them with an opportunity to create value jointly. However, interdependency between firms is rarely equal, so an asymmetrical alliance results (see Table 13.1), in which one (dominant) partner possesses a net bargaining power advantage, and the other (weaker) partner possesses a net bargaining power disadvantage. By combining the partners' unique resources, the alliance might enable significant advantages. However, a dominant firm with a bargaining power advantage could exercise or even just threaten to use its power to coerce the weaker firm to comply with its demands, which reduces the weaker firm's motivation to continue the

TABLE 13.1 Examples of asymmetrical alliances

	Description
Pfizer–Neurocrine	In 2002, Pfizer embarked on an alliance with Neurocrine Biosciences to develop new drugs to treat neurological and endocrine-related diseases, including Indiplon, a treatment for insomnia. The objective was to couple Neurocrine's key compound with Pfizer's robust sales and marketing power. Pfizer agreed to pay an initial payment of $100 million and up to $300 million in milestone payments, cover third-party development, marketing and commercialization costs, save for pre-specified $30 million in costs that Neurocrine incurred. Pfizer was also obligated to pay for and support the creation of a 200-person Neurocrine sales force. In turn, Pfizer obtained an exclusive licence to handle all international sales of Indiplon, with Neurocrine receiving a percentage of worldwide sales. Indiplon was originally scheduled for release sometime in 2007. However, Pfizer decided to end its relationship with Neurocrine following one non-approvable letter and one approvable letter (with stipulations) from the Federal Drug Administration (FDA). Neurocrine continued the research project alone, but announced at the end of 2007 to cease all Indiplon clinical development activities as well as all pre-commercialization activities following a letter from the FDA, which stated new requirements to obtain total approval.
Google–fulfilNET	Google is an American multinational public corporation specializing in Internet search, cloud computing and advertising technologies. Google hosts and develops a number of Internet-based services and products and generates profit primarily from advertising through its AdWords program. Since its inception Google has become a dominant global player in the Internet industry. Australian-based fulfilNET develops software solutions and provides marketing and implementation services to leading publishers. Extending a earlier partnership with Google, Australian web advertising provider fulfilNET Australia and Google agreed that fulfilNET became the only party to sell Google's AdWords service, an online advertising service, under the name of Yodel in South Africa, Ireland and the UK. The AdWords service from Google offers companies pay-per-click advertising solutions and site-targeted advertising for companies wanting to promote their services and products online. The partnership propelled the company's international expansion strategy.

Sources: Neurocrine (2002); Neurocrine (2006); Yodel (2008).

alliance (Gulati and Sytch 2007), and probably diminishes alliance performance. Even though asymmetrical alliances often offer advantages for both partners, the presence of power asymmetries tends to influence their commitment to value-creating activities.

A weaker firm forges an asymmetrical alliance because it hopes to gain access to valuable resources owned by the dominant firm. For example, manufacturers might enter into a partnership with more powerful integrators, distributors and retailers to market their products. For the dominant firm, access to the specific resources possessed by the weaker firm also constitutes a primary motivator for establishing the alliance. Pharmaceutical firms with large and established R&D centres, for example, could ally with smaller biotechnological firms that have less bargaining power but offer state-of-the-art, commercially unexploited knowledge. The weaker biotechnology firms in turn receive financing for their high-risk research programmes, and the dominant firms can continue to expand their competitive advantage. If this setting entails a low risk of misappropriation, the asymmetrical alliance represents a viable strategy for both partners.

But regardless of these strong motives for asymmetrical alliance formation, a power asymmetry inherently represents a source of alliance friction that poses a particularly stringent risk on the weaker party. That is, because the dominant partner can appropriate an unequal share of the value created by the alliance, it enjoys a better position relative to, and at the expense of, its weaker counterpart. Dominant firms may not use this power advantage to exploit their partners, but weaker firms remain subject to the threat of exploitation. The very threat is likely to increase conflicts and reduce relationship proclivity. Moreover, the presence of this threat may cause the weaker firm to react preemptively to defend itself, which creates the further risk of retaliation by its dominant counterpart, perhaps in the form of the threatened misappropriation. Thus even when both partners are fully aware of the value generated by an alliance, the asymmetrical dynamic gives rise to frustration and tension, undermines joint value creation and can harm both the weaker and the dominant firm.

Whereas asymmetrical alliances may offer significant advantages for both part-ners, the realization of benefits requires cooperative behaviour. Power asymmetry creates the risk of misappropriation by the dominant firm, which will evoke dysfunctional conflicts and translates into alliance under-performance. To deal with this challenge, managers involved in asymmetrical alliances, especially those who represent the weaker party, must learn how to defend against or neutralize the adverse impacts of power asymmetry, to ensure that their initiatives do not interfere with the collaborative efforts and benefits of the alliance.

Managing asymmetrical alliances

Bargaining power implies an ability to change multi-party agreements in one's own favour, such that individual benefits are maximized. By using their bargaining power, firms influence both the scope of activities within the alliance and the appropriation of the resulting alliance benefits (Pfeffer and Salancik 1978). Dominant firms enjoy an advantageous position; with their bargaining power, they can deploy various strategies, from non-coercive to coercive, and reap the benefits. The weaker firm suffers a great risk because of its lack of bargaining power, which minimizes its ability to prevent exploitation. A weaker firm must take a reactive position to secure its share of the value generated, and these strategies are relatively limited. Because a fair distribution of value (i.e. outcomes relative to contributions) between partner

TABLE 13.2 Managing asymmetrical alliances

	(1) Offensive tactics	*(2) Defensive tactics*	*(3) Acceptance tactics*
Logic	Seeking to (re)balance power relationship between partners; mutual dependence offers incentives to preserve alliance	Installing protection against misappropriation; being protected offers parties incentives to preserve alliance	Accepting power asymmetry and using non-power-based tactics; equitable outcomes offers incentives to preserve alliance
Goal	Change in resource–need balance	Change in alliance governance	Accepting power asymmetry
Mechanisms (examples)	Provide additional and/or intangible resources; make relationship-specific investments, inter-firm learning	Equity arrangement, contractual provisions, residual sharing, task specialization, relational capital	Trade off relative share for absolute outcome, trade off objectives, exploit spill-over and information asymmetry
Downside	May trigger retaliation by dominant firm, undermines weaker firm's position	May require extensive resources, difficult to impose contractual clauses on dominant partner	Exposure to exploitation by dominant firm as alliance progresses

firms is crucial to build stable alliances, we propose three set of tactics that weaker firms might use to deal with dominant partners: (1) offensive, (2) defensive and (3) acceptance (see Table 13.2).

Offensive tactics

Weaker firms may take a proactive stance to reduce the threat of misappropriation. In this case, their offensive tactics aim to shift the resource–need asymmetry to enhance their own relative bargaining power position (Makhija and Ganesh 1997). For example, they might proactively contribute more valuable resources to the alliance, which would increase the dependence of the dominant firm on them (Blodgett 1991b). Contributing additional or intangible resources should also enhance their bargaining position. It is unlikely that intangible resources, which are more difficult to transfer, can be seized by a dominant, more powerful firm, so the provider of these resources can protect itself from this form of opportunism (Coff 1999). Weaker firms can also increase the dependence of their dominant counterparts (i.e. reduce the dominant firm's power) by convincing them to make specialized, relationship-specific investments to signal their commitment to the relationship (Gulati et al. 1994). If a firm is tied to the alliance through specialized investments, it cannot easily dissolve that alliance without incurring significant costs and the loss of non-recoverable investments (Klein et al. 1978). Finally, learning can help a weaker firm improve its bargaining power (Hamel 1991), because acquiring knowledge from a dominant partner expands its resource base and thus reduces its dependency over time.

Yet offensive tactics also can be counter-productive, in that they ultimately decrease the weaker firm's relative power, leading eventually to a greater risk of exploitation by a dominant partner. In particular, offensive tactics can trigger retaliation, because the dominant firm is motivated to retain its strong ability to appropriate value. Furthermore, by increasing their resource contributions, weaker firms might enter into even more vulnerable positions, because they are likely to commit substantial expenditures that are open to retaliatory actions by the dominant firm. Such contributions also make the weaker firms more dependent, because they have increased their alliance-specific stake. If weaker firms instead choose a learning race (Hamel 1991), they undermine the relationship's value creation potential. Moreover, without some partner-specific absorptive capacity to acquire socially and organizationally embedded skills, expertise or tacit knowledge, learning tactics also are not particularly effective. Even when offensive tactics enhance a weaker firm's bargaining power by reducing the power asymmetry, their use ultimately may provide the dominant firm with more leverage to exploit its overall bargaining power advantage.

Defensive tactics

Defensive tactics serve rather as mechanisms to protect the firm against value misappropriation (Oxley 1997). Such tactics build on the logic that firms with superior power seek to exploit their power, so weaker partners must try to limit that exploitation by adopting a defensive, protective stance. Forms of such protection include a governance structure that prohibits the use of bargaining power or rules that guarantee an appropriate division of alliance benefits. Compared with non-equity arrangements, equity-based alliances (e.g. joint ventures) offer better protection against misappropriation (Gulati and Singh 1998), because they guarantee the weaker partner a pre-specified share of the value created, depending on their equity stake. Contractual provisions such as royalties and transfer prices offer another form of protection against misappropriation, because they summarize firms' ex-ante agreement about the ex-post distribution of value (Hagedoorn and Hesen 2007). Detailed contracts that specify, for example, the use of patents, the non-disclosure of trade secrets, exclusivity conditions and task specialization protect the firm from partner misappropriation, such as the unwanted transfer of proprietary resources or knowledge (Katila et al. 2008). In addition, firms can invest in trust- and commitment-building efforts, because relational capital tends to reduce the risk of exploitative behaviour (Kale et al. 2000).

Similarly, defensive tactics have their own limitations. Weaker firms may expose themselves to exchange hazards by using contract-based defensive tactics, in that they lack the power to coerce a dominant firm to comply. In this case, the dominant firms are more likely to obtain formal controls, to reinforce their power imbalance (Yan and Gray 2001). Moreover, weaker firms tend to prefer simpler contracts, which lack the clauses necessary to deal with unforeseen misappropriation (Ariño and Reuer 2004). More complete contracts increase contract monitoring burdens, and many weaker firms lack the resources and opportunities to monitor contract fulfilment actively. In contrast, incomplete contracts are less of a concern for dominant firms, which can just substitute their bargaining power. Relational-based defensive tactics also entail risks. A high-quality working relationship could substitute for an alliance contract (Lui and Ngo 2004), but over-reliance on relational governance leaves the weaker firm exposed to exploitation (Barney and Hansen 1994). Relationship building also is expensive and time-consuming: if it stretches its limited resources to focus on better relationships, the weaker firm could undermine its vulnerable position even further. In summary, defensive tactics may seem appealing to weaker firms, to protect themselves against misappropriation by the dominant firm, but they also have serious potential repercussions.

Acceptance tactics

As the name suggests, acceptance tactics acknowledge upfront that dominant firms are better positioned to extract value. However, they also assume that weaker firms can contribute best to establishing stable asymmetrical relationships if they accept this power difference, rather than actively addressing the power differences as the offensive and defensive tactics do. To avoid direct conflicts, weaker firms simply accept the power asymmetry and use careful tactics to appropriate value, which increases the likelihood of alliance stability. During alliance negotiations, partner firms bargain about the distribution of anticipated value, and the allocation depends primarily on the partners' relative bargaining power. The weaker firm may purposefully accept a relative smaller share in this negotiation to stimulate joint value creation, with the belief that doing so will eventually provide a larger absolute (not relative) share. In addition, it may trade off some alliance objectives, such that its financial loss is compensated by an opportunity to acquire knowledge. Finally, the weaker firm might increase its pay-off by focusing on forms of value that are difficult to specify ex ante in an alliance contract, such as knowledge spillover. If it possesses information about future circumstances, the weaker firm could strategically wait patiently to exploit its information asymmetry.

Of course, acceptance tactics also have their own limitations. Weaker firms expose themselves to future (unforeseen) exchange hazards, because the effectiveness of these tactics partially depends on the success of the alliance. For example, reaping a large absolute share, trading off between alliance objectives and exploiting information asymmetries all require that the alliance create value first. The weaker firm therefore needs to demonstrate its commitment before it can appropriate its share of value, although as the alliance progresses, the dominant firm could exploit its advantage to secure its individual interests. Despite this disadvantage, acceptance tactics help the weaker firm increase its individual benefits, just not at the expense of the dominant firm. It thus can avoid direct conflicts, prompt cooperation, focus on value creation and appropriate value without jeopardizing alliance stability.

The different properties tied to each type of tactic thus have varying implications. Offensive and defensive tactics require some bargaining power to appropriate value, and their use can clearly initiate conflicts. Acceptance tactics suggest that bargaining power is just one of multiple ways to appropriate value, and conflicts can be avoided. Acceptance of power imbalances also encourages cooperation without imposing a cost on the dominant firm, unlike tactics to manage power, which prompt competition. Although firms preferably select partners with which they can achieve a net bargaining power balance, which would reduce the need for protection, acceptance tactics make bargaining power a somewhat less important selection criteria. In turn, the degree of contractual specification can be minimized, unlike offensive and defensive tactics, which often require formalized alliance contracts (e.g. specifying resource contributions) if they are to avoid and resolve ex-post conflicts. Investing in relational norms and contributing capital increases alliance stability, especially in the context of offensive and defensive tactics, in that their effectiveness depends partially on the degree of trust and support offered by the dominant partner. In contrast, acceptance tactics require less trust and commit-ment, because implementation can be unilateral and without partner support. In practice though, weaker firms might use offensive, defensive and acceptance tactics simultaneously and interchangeably.

Asymmetrical alliances: Decision-making steps

Although asymmetrical alliances are common, they are also inherently unstable. In addition to generic guidelines, we identify several specific managerial guidelines that will enable alliance managers to turn potentially unstable asymmetrical alliances into stable ones. To this end, we discuss asymmetrical alliances in light of our alliance development framework (see Figure 13.1).

Step 1: Alliance strategy formulation

During the strategic analysis, firms decide whether an alliance is an appropriate governance mode for realizing their objectives. At this point, firms do not have any understanding of whether the potential alliance will be symmetric or not, because their relative bargaining power is a function solely of the potential partner's bargaining power. Nevertheless, given their objectives, firms identify the required resources and determine the nature and severity of interdependencies with other firms to gain access to resources that cannot be provided autonomously. Interdependency provides strong collaboration motives to capture synergies; however, increasing dependence on a potential partner could also suggest the benefits of internalizing an activity to secure the focal resources. If a firm is willing to accept some power asymmetry, however, the alliance could be the preferred

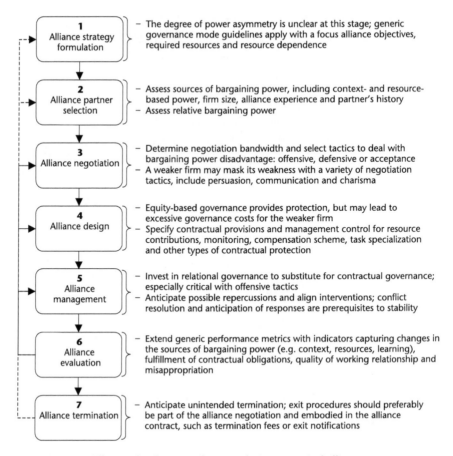

FIGURE 13.1 Alliance development framework: Asymmetrical alliances

alternative, because the costs of internalization might outweigh the potential benefits. For weaker firms these benefits probably involve access to deeper, broader resource bases and potentially advantageous reputation effects. For dominant firms, the benefits primarily pertain to specific resources that extend and enhance their competitive advantage. By allying rather than internalizing, dominant firms also minimize divestment, coordination and integration costs.

Step 2: Partner selection

During the partner selection phase, power asymmetries should be identified and analysed prior to the actual selection. Specific attention should centre on assessing the sources of bargaining power and levels of power asymmetry. In addition to partners' characteristics and motives for establishing the alliance, each firm should consider the following topics:

- Sources of partners' bargaining power, including context-based (e.g. possessing more scope to form an alliance than a potential partner) and resource-based (e.g. possessing more valuable and scarce sources than a potential partner) power.
- Other indicators of power, such as firm size (because the relative importance of alliances tends to be greater for small firms), alliance experience (which improves firms' ability to exploit power) and cultural background (because national cultural orientations may favour power use).
- The relative bargaining power of each potential partner, which reveals whether the intended alliance is asymmetrical. Such information is necessary to develop the most effective negotiation approach.

Step 3: Alliance negotiation

As the introduction to this chapter noted, asymmetrical alliances confront weaker partners with a unique challenge: to negotiate a favourable outcome without any bargaining power to make demands. Formulating a negotiation approach therefore requires substantial thought and consideration about the various tactics available, including offensive, defensive and acceptance tactics. Each tactic has unique and specific implications for the negotiation span and alliance stages. Offensive tactics demand additional resource contributions, which will increase the weaker firm's stake in the alliance. Unilateral or mutual relationship-specific investments both increase the commitments of the partnering firms and function as exit barriers. However, they also demand precise, careful negotiations and contractual specification to avoid ex-post exploitation. Similarly, defensive tactics require ex-ante agreements about ex-post benefit sharing, and their use often requires formal alliance contracts that might specify, for example, equity exchanges, royalties and trade secret protections. Acceptance tactics require that negotiators consider trade-offs between short- and long-term interests (common and private): thereby avoiding conflict with a dominant partner.

In addition, a weaker firm may use negotiation tactics to mask its weaknesses. Through communication and persuasion, a good negotiator might coerce its counterpart to accept outcomes that conflict with its own interests. A negotiator also might present information to make the outcomes seem like a win–win situation – whether they are or not. A charismatic, skilled negotiator who can build strong personal relationships may function as another influence tactic, as can consistent advocacy of normative conformity (i.e. convincing claims that a particular position is correct, legitimate or principled). However, excessive negotiation may jeopardize relational norms and capital, which are necessary to protect weaker partners from exploitation by their dominant counterparts.

Step 4: Alliance design

Equity-based arrangements provide protection against exploitation; they also can create excessive governance costs, depending on the partners' actual objectives. Partner firms should follow generic guidelines to select an appropriate governance form. Irrespective of the form they adopt, though, the alliance design stage should emphasize the alliance contract and supplemental coordination mechanisms. The preferred tactic also influences the protective measures that should be embodied in an alliance contract. Agreements about partners' resource contributions and mechanisms to monitor the fulfilment of their obligations should nearly always be specified. Formalizing their task specialization can prevent leaks of vital knowledge between partners by limiting access to strategically important competences and capabilities. Each firm thus should define which activities and processes are most vulnerable to unwanted leakage and the degree to which its partner would be able to absorb that knowledge. Provisions specifying exclusivity and non-disclosure of trade secrets should also be incorporated in any contract. By setting up incentive structures that continually reward cooperation (i.e. residual sharing), partners can develop the foundation for a stable asymmetrical alliance. Finally, alliance design should allow for intensive inter-firm contact, because strong working relationships reduce the tendency to resort to bargaining power. High-quality working relationships are generally characterized by strong bonds between the individual representatives of partnering firms, which enhances mutual trust. Thus overall the alliance contract should formalize ex-ante decisions that aim to reduce ex-post ambiguities related to the division of benefits between partners, and help mitigate ex-post repercussions of the use of bargaining power.

Step 5: Alliance management

The risk of exploitation represents a continuous threat. At any given point, a dominant firm may to decide to exploit its bargaining power advantage. Therefore, according to their alliance monitoring and evaluation efforts, weaker firms should focus on building relational norms and capital. Regardless of the governance structure or management control, partners' ability to influence each other in a relational sense is critical to effective interaction, learning, knowledge transfer and joint decision making. Because relational influence becomes manifest as mutual support, forbearance and power sharing, it may be more effective than contractual governance as a means to avoid misappropriation. Moreover, it facilitates conflict resolution and joint decision making. Other alliance processes, such as responses to adversity and inter-firm learning, also demand attention. Partners may develop an interaction pattern in response to adversity that stimulates power use, such as when dominant firms engage in opportunistic behaviour or aggressively impose solutions onto their weaker counterparts, which prompts the weaker firms to respond with similar tactics. In contrast, more constructive responses, such as seeking compromises and creative solutions, imply power avoidance. When partners organize and monitor learning processes, they also acknowledge knowledge transfer as an important source of shifts in bargaining power and conflict. Thus in addition to the generic alliance management guidelines, weaker firms should focus on conflict avoidance so as to develop stable relationships, particularly by adopting acceptance tactics.

Step 6: Alliance evaluation

In addition to generic metrics, asymmetrical alliances need a performance metric system that features metrics to capture the sources of bargaining power, including resource contributions and alternatives. For example, partner contributions may change due to learning, which directly influences the power relationship. A weaker firm needs to be aware of such shifts. Depending on the type of tactic used, weaker firms may also employ different metrics. For example, offensive tactics require active monitoring of contractual fulfilment, defensive tactics need metrics to capture relationship quality and acceptance tactics require output metrics that can capture the degree of objective achievement over time. Alliance performance metrics should also centre on alliance process execution, which may be more qualitative and thus more unambiguous than objective inputs, though these still provide valuable insights into the actual functioning of the alliance and the extent to which a firm is exploiting its counterpart. The inherently unstable nature of asymmetrical alliances means that performance metric systems should also include indicators that capture and regulate communication. Representatives of both organizations would preferably come together to evaluate performance, decide on corrective actions and communicate decisions across their organizations.

Step 7: Alliance termination

Finally, alliance termination still tends to favour the dominant party, which can use its power advantage to secure exit provisions, explore alternatives and reap the remaining value of the alliance. In an unintended termination, weaker firms might protect themselves from unilateral termination with contractual provisions that demand a termination fee if the alliance is dissolved prematurely. Advance notice agreements in an alliance contractcan also postpone any effective termination for a pre-set period of time, which allows the parties to recoup their contributions and stimulate learning to maximize the alliance benefits. Another prevention of premature, one-sided alliance termination demands relationship-specific investments by all parties. The costs of such investments should arise only with alliance termination, such that they erect a potential exit barrier. Because these precautions against unintended alliance terminations often require formalization, weaker firms should ensure that the type and content of exit provisions represent part of their negotiation agenda.

Summary

The danger of misappropriation and sub-optimal value creation makes an interesting challenge for partners in an asymmetrical alliance. They need to exploit their resource asymmetries to create value, but at the same time, they must prevent exploitative moves that often result from power asymmetries. By taking the dominant firm's perspective, most mainstream alliance research focuses on value attainment, but weaker firms can also use offensive and defensive tactics to secure their share of jointly created value – though not without some risk. These tactics demand resource commitments and increase conflict (i.e. they induce power use by the dominant firm), which may make acceptance tactics more attractive to the weaker firms. With such strategies, weaker firms acknowledge their weakness, but still extract satisfactory value and thus have good incentives to maintain their asymmetrical alliance relationships. In practice however, most firms use some combination of these tactics.

As a final note, we warn against the common misconception that power asymmetries always reflect firm size. Small firms often have strong motives to forge an alliance with larger firms, but they are not necessarily the weaker partner. Certainly larger firms tend to have more resources, can draw on more extensive partnership experience and possess more (financial) stamina to endure negative alliance outcomes or conflicts. Furthermore, alliances with larger firms tend to increase the legitimacy of smaller firms and offer them an opportunity to tap into a broader resource base, which implies a faster time to market, better ability to serve new and geographically dispersed markets and market expansion (Alvarez and Barney 2001). These trends often lead to the presumption that larger firms are always more powerful than smaller firms. But smaller firms can possess specific resources (e.g. radical innovations) with great value to a larger firm, and their organizational characteristics (e.g. an innovation focus) may appeal greatly to that larger partner. Thus a smaller firm can dominate an alliance, if it provides crucial, unique resources that the larger firm must have. In forging asymmetrical alliances, firms must therefore resist the temptation to attribute power solely on the basis of the partner's size.

Case: Disney–Pixar

In the past two decades, the world of computer animation has witnessed rapid developments. In particular, increasing technological possibilities have radically changed the style and complexity of animated films. Furthermore, the markets for these offerings keep changing too, providing great opportunities for new entrants and significant potential threats to existing industry players – such as Walt Disney,[2] the king of the animated movie industry. Familiar characters such as Oswald the Rabbit, Mickey Mouse, Donald Duck and Goofy helped Walt Disney build a business empire held up by four pillars: (1) production and distribution of animated and live action motion pictures, (2) parks and resorts, (3) consumer products (i.e. merchandising) and (4) media networks, including ABC and ESPN.

Despite the expansion of the Disney enterprise, its core remained the production of animated films. The competence underlying this core contributor also was well set: hand-drawn animated figures. In the face of a technical revolution, however, Disney found it was lacking competences to generate the sophisticated look and creative approaches that consumers were demanding. To overcome these challenges, it sought alliance partners to incorporate new animation technologies into its film production; Pixar appeared to be an excellent alliance candidate.

Begun in 1979 as the Graphics Group, Pixar was part of the Computer Division of Lucasfilm before being acquired by Apple co-founder Steve Jobs in 1986 for approximately $16 million. Pixar focused on the development of computer-animated feature films that would target all layers of a society. Its key strengths, creativity and technological ability to produce computer-animated characters and feature films, helped Pixar develop its first short film in 1987, called *Red's Dream*.

Although the companies were about to become partners with closely aligned goals, they were quite different. Pixar was a young, relatively unknown entrepreneurial company, with a culture renowned for its friendly working environment. Disney was an established multinational with a strongly hierarchical management style and a consistently financial focus. But perhaps the biggest difference was the two firms' size. Disney was a far bigger company than Pixar.

The year 1991 started poorly for Pixar, which laid off 30 employees from its computer department. But the $26 million deal it made with Disney that year to produce three computer-animated feature films improved the outlook. Despite strong income, however, the company was still losing money, and Jobs often considered selling it. As late as 1994, Jobs contemplated selling Pixar to other companies, including Microsoft. Only after confirming that Disney would distribute *Toy Story*, the first feature movie developed by the alliance, for the 1995 holiday season did he decide to give it another chance. And the film went on to gross more than $350 million worldwide.

Following this success, Pixar and Disney signed a co-production–distribution partnership in 1997, agreeing to co-produce five feature films. Disney obtained access to Pixar's technological competences and creative drive. Beyond reinvigorating the animation genre with a new visual style, the alliance allowed for more cost-efficient and easy repurposing of digital content. But perhaps most important, Pixar's films provided great storytelling, the very foundation of Disney's long-held dominance in the market. Furthermore, with its functioning alliance, Disney could neutralize potential competitors. For Pixar, the partnership with Disney meant access to the vast Disney production and distribution resources. Pixar thus could focus on its core competence: producing computer-animated films. In addition, Disney offered access to its merchandising knowledge and distribution network, so Pixar could develop and sell toys, apparel and so on.

Profits and costs were split 50:50. Disney owned all story and sequel rights and also collected a distribution fee. Pixar lived up to its end of the agreement by creating and releasing *A Bug's Life*, *Monsters Inc.*, *Finding Nemo*, *The Incredibles* and *Cars*. The alliance thus provided production capital to Pixar and distribution fees to Disney. Soon enough, however, the success of these animated films shifted Pixar's position; it no longer needed capital, because it could source production and distribution capital more cost efficiently if it worked with other studios. The disagreement that arose surrounding the release of *Toy Story 2* exemplified the deteriorating alliance conditions.

Originally *Toy Story 2* did not fall under the alliance agreement, because the intention was to release it straight to video rather than in the theatres. But Disney decided to release *Toy Story 2* as a motion picture in theatres, prompting Pixar to demand that *Toy Story 2* be counted as one of its contracted films. Disney refused. Then Pixar began questioning the equitability of its arrangements. The distribution fee was growing into an increasing problem for Pixar, in that the distribution and merchandising fees ultimately resulted in a 68:32 split of profits in Disney's favour. As Pixar voiced its concerns, Disney insisted on maintaining the initial contractual agreement and the relationship grew more contentious.

The two companies attempted to reach a new agreement in early 2004. The new deal would cover only distribution: Pixar proposed that in the revised alliance contract, it would provide full financing for its films but also be entitled to the full benefits. Disney would receive only a distribution fee of approximately 10 to 15 per cent of the gross sales. Disney rejected the proposal. In preparation for the potential fallout, Jobs announced in late 2004 that Pixar would no longer release movies in November, as Disney dictated, but would rather pursue the more lucrative early summer months, which would enable it to release the DVD versions just in time for the Christmas shopping season. The possibility that Pixar would find a more cost-efficient distribution arrangement with another studio became too great a risk for Disney, even if the new distribution arrangement yielded much lower distribution fees for it. By the time Disney came to this recognition, however, the personal relationship between Steve Jobs (owner of Pixar) and Michael Eisner (Disney CEO) had deteriorated to the point that the negotiation ultimately wound up a failure.

Pixar had grown so much by now that it could be self-supporting even after the demise of its alliance with Disney. Jobs admitted he would be on the lookout for other partners. In 2006 Disney headed off this possibility by acquiring Pixar for $7.4 billion in an all-stock deal. The acquisition was of the utmost strategic importance to Disney, not only because of where the distribution relationship with Pixar seemed headed, but also because of Pixar's potential value to Disney's entertainment brand and assets, such as its theme parks and television, that it needed to keep feeding off this valuable brand.

Questions

1. What asymmetries appear in the Disney–Pixar alliance? How do they change? To what extent do they affect the alliance's power relationship?
2. In which ways did the dynamic power relationship between Disney and Pixar, and its management, influence the alliance development?
3. Disney paid a high price to acquire Pixar. Could it have done something differently?

14

CROSS-SECTOR ALLIANCES

The challenges that societies currently face are highly complex and unprecedented. Many of these challenges, such as climate change, scarcity of natural resources, increasing globalization, terrorism, poverty and food shortages, cannot be resolved within the public sector alone. Consequently, collaboration between private firms and public organizations, such as governments, universities and non-governmental organizations (NGOs), has become increasingly important. These cross-sector alliances provide opportunities for partners to share resources and expertise, which allows more effective solutions in keeping with individual and communal objectives. However, private firms and public organizations vary in many ways, including societal function, profit and non-profit orientation, accountability and organizational backgrounds, all of which are major causes of alliance instability. If these differences are not controlled, they will negatively affect the partners' ability to realize their individual and collective alliance objectives. Thus, although cross-sector alliances can enhance a firm's competitive position, they also present a unique challenge, in that firms wishing to realize their private objectives must reconcile a wide range of differences that give rise to conflicts. The first section discusses this cross-sector alliance challenge and the second section elaborates on the mechanisms that managers can use to deal with it. Next, a cross-sector alliance is associated with the alliance development framework to develop guidelines for decision-making (described in the third section). The chapter concludes with a summary and a case illustration.

The cross-sector alliance challenge

The literature covers a wide range of cross-sector alliances (see Table 14.1), including business–community partnerships, union relationships, NGOs–business partnerships, fund-raising alliances, ethical responsibility networks, voluntary

TABLE 14.1 Examples of cross-sector alliances

	Description
BASF Plant Science– *Crop Improvement* *Research Club*	BASF Plant Science is a division of BASF (a German-based chemical) and forms the industry's leading research and technology platform on plant biotechnology activities. The Crop Improvement Research Club (CIRC) is led by the Biotechnology and Biological Sciences Research Council and constitutes the UK's largest public funder of agri-food research. In 2010, BASF Plant Science participated in the CIRC. One example of a joint project is the exploitation of a site in Hawaii, where research seeks to develop a gene discovery platform focusing on yield and quality traits in crops such as corn, soybean and rice.
Optiqua Technologies– *Nanyang Technological* *University*	Optiqua Technologies, a subsidiary of Dutch optical sensor company Optisense, is based in Singapore. It provides the international water industry with innovative products that offer high quality monitoring applications for the detection of contaminants in water. All Optiqua products are patented on lab-on-chip sensor technology. In 2011, Optiqua forged a partnership with Nanyang Technological University (Singapore) to develop the next-generation sensor technology. The objective is to enhance contaminant-detection capability, to accelerate Optiqua's R&D in biochemistry, and help Optiqua to develop innovative real-time monitoring solutions.
CARE–Cargill	CARE and Cargill formed an innovative partnership to fight poverty and long-term hunger in the developing world. CARE is a leading humanitarian organization fighting global poverty. Cargill is a multinational corporation that specializes in agriculture, food and beverage ingredients, meat products, industrial agricultural and steel products. CARE and Cargill leverage their respective strengths to improve livelihoods while at the same time improving Cargill's competitive advantage. For example, CARE partners with local Cargill teams provided training, skills development and market access for farmers; enhance education and nutritional support for children; and organize health care and safe drinking water for rural communities.

Sources: BASF News (2011); Biotechnology and Biological Sciences Research Council News (2010); *Business Week* (2010); CSIS News (2011); Eurekalert (2011); Oneworld Trust (2009); Van Voorhis (2011).

corporate code agreements and cause–brand alliances (Rondinelli and London 2003; Wood 2002). Each type of cross-sector alliance is unique and poses distinct barriers to alliance formation and management. For the sake of brevity, however, this chapter focuses on three prototypical cross-sector alliances: (1) university–industry partnership, (2) public–private partnership, and (3) non-governmental organization (NGO)–business partnership.

A university–industry partnership depicts a collaborative agreement between a private firm and a university that combines resources to create and exchange academic and experience-based knowledge (Perkmann *et al.* 2011), often to develop innovative products and services and/or develop new technologies. For example, pharmaceutical companies, such as GlaxoSmithKline and Novartis, leverage academic knowledge to acquire fundamental expertise in specific disease areas. Engineering-based companies such as Rolls-Royce work with academic departments in a variety of fields, including combustion aerodynamics and systems software engineering. Firms establish alliances with universities for a variety of reasons, all of which relate directly to their competitive position, including the ability to gain access to scientific breakthroughs, state-of-the-art information, and training and support for building in-house skills, as well as to recruit highly qualified staff, save costs by delegating research and development activities, and to economize on investments in internal facilities (Bonaccorsi and Piccaluga 2000). In contrast, universities benefit from partnerships with industry through the additional funding, direct access to hands-on knowledge and expertise, access to case material and facilities (for example, laboratory facilities) and references for future public projects (Meyer-Krahmer and Smoch 1998).

Public–private partnerships are cooperative institutional arrangements between private firms and government agencies (Kwak *et al.* 2009). Governments are challenged to act effectively in an increasingly complex society that puts a strain on available resources, while gradually reducing funding. To realize their objectives, governments depend more and more on the corporate sector. Public–private partnerships enable government agencies and private firms to work together on such projects as developing and maintaining large infrastructural projects, including roads, bridges and tunnels. Firms supply specialist construction knowledge, management skills and funding in long-term infrastructure projects commissioned by governments. In return, private sector actors agree on the commercial exploitation of the project through which they receive revenues. Public–private partnerships rebalance the division of government and private responsibilities, allowing governments to reduce spending and implement their policies simultaneously. When firms in the corporate sector assume responsibilities that were previously executed by government agencies, they tap into new markets, which leads to extra revenues.

An NGO–business partnership refers to a cooperative arrangement between a NGO and a private firm that aims to strengthen the firm's efforts to support its corporate social responsibility policies (Austin 2000) and to improve the NGO's ability to achieve its idealistic and communal objectives. The profit-oriented nature and competences of private firms makes them relatively incapable of dealing with the social and environmental demands of customers, shareholders and other stakeholders on their own. Consequently, firms forge NGO–business partnerships to develop a green image; prevent boycotts and protests, and circumvent public pressure; enhance their credibility through voluntary codes of conduct; avoid adverse publicity; improve staff morale, public affairs and public relations; and improve their credibility and positive reputation (Arya and Salk 2006; Loza 2004). NGOs, on the other hand, rely on the corporate sector primarily for funding and critical resources.

Although these three types of cross-sector alliances differ from business-to-business alliances in terms of their objectives and partner characteristics (see Table 14.2), they have three types of conflict in common that jeopardize alliance stability without adequate management. First, institutional conflicts are likely to emerge that originate in the different functions parties fulfil in society. The objectives of a firm primarily concern profit, while universities are mainly focused on knowledge production and dissemination. NGOs tend to focus on social issues (such as poverty and the suppression of minorities), while governments serve the community. In other words, there is a distinction between profit and non-profit orientation and between private and public interests. These diverging orientations affect the way representatives perceive themselves and their behaviour. Consider a large infrastructural project, such as the construction of a highway. Private firms get involved and support the construction of a highway so as to generate revenue; motorists participate constructively because such projects tend to reduce travel times, but environmentalists are likely to resist because highways often imply negative consequences for ecosystems. Thus, decision-making in cross-sector alliances is impeded owing to different institutional backgrounds.

Second, an accountability conflict may emerge, referring to differences in how partners need to deal with financial responsibilities and reporting. Universities, government agencies and NGOs rely primarily on a variety of stakeholders to provide funding. Such variety in the sources of (public) funding, along with the social pressures imposed on public organisations, increases the need for accountability and transparency, but also makes it complicated to assign accountability. In contrast, private firms are primarily accountable to owners, shareholders and external regulative entities. Partners in cross-sector alliances have varying requirements for accountability, which means that their stance toward the partnership is likely to differ in that they demand different financial infrastructures. The need to comply with distinct internal and external requirements complicates alliance design decisions as well as ex post modifications. This disparity in funding and accountability can lead to tensions between partners.

The third type of conflict is the intellectual conflict that often exists between partners in cross-sector alliances. Research institutes, in keeping with their role in society, attempt to share their research findings with a larger audience, whereas a private firm that shares intellectual property could lose its competitive edge. Similarly, knowledge and technology developed through public funding, such as the case in public–private partnerships, should be openly available (sometimes free) to the public; firms, on the other hand, would prefer to acquire and protect unique assets to strengthen their position in the market. For example, intellectual conflicts tend to characterize cross-sector alliances between pharmaceuticals and universities. Due to the high costs of R&D activities and the increasing speed of technological change, pharmaceutical companies collaborate with research institutions that possess state-of-the-art knowledge and facilities. Whereas firms strive to protect intellectual

TABLE 14.2 Types of cross-sector alliances

	Government agency	University	Non-governmental organization	Private firm
Main interest	Public	Intellectual	Charity	Profit
Main source of income	Community	Government	Donations	Customers
Time horizon	Long term	Long term	Short term	Short term
Focus	Societal and economic situation of a country or region	Knowledge production and dissemination	Societal and economic situation of a country, region, and minority groups	Discovering and exploiting market opportunities
Ranking of conflict	Accountability Institutional Intellectual	Intellectual Institutional Accountability	Institutional Accountability Intellectual	Competitive

Sources: Austin (2000); Kwak *et al.* (2009); Stafford *et al.* (2000); Wood (2002).

capital, specifically if research output undermines claims about the effectiveness of new medicines, universities are inclined to disseminate knowledge – sometimes having been forced to do so by specific legislation. Similarly, intellectual conflicts may arise in NGO–business and public–private partnerships.

In summary, partners in a cross-sector alliance face challenges that are inherently tied to this type of partnering. Differences in partners' societal functions, profit orientation, organization design and culture, and incentive systems form critical obstacles for win–win cross-sector alliances. The repercussions of these dissimilarities manifest in divergent objectives, different time horizons and context-specific languages that, if left unresolved, can lead to institutional, accountability and intellectual conflicts. For example, whereas universities are supposed to act as independent societal institutes with a long-term orientation to generate high-quality knowledge in relatively stable environments, firms operate in highly competitive environments with short-term orientations and a focus on profit making, knowledge protection and the commercial value of knowledge. Due to these differences, the objectives of all parties can be met only to a limited extent, and the challenge for alliance management is to find an optimal trade-off solution in which each party can improve its pay-off without damaging the interests of its counterpart. In other words, partners in cross-sector alliances face the challenge of reconciling private interests with communal interests.

Managing cross-sector alliances

The management of cross-sector alliances requires partners to identify differences proactively, and to understand how these differences give rise to conflicts and what initiatives they can develop to reconcile these differences in order to reduce the probability of conflicts (London *et al.* 2006). This section presents three areas that managers may focus on in order to steer their cross-sector alliance towards success. These are: (1) enforcing power neutrality, (2) creating autonomy and transparency and (3) building a culture of collaborative commitment.

Power neutrality

Heterogeneous resources, competences and alternatives make it unlikely that partners in a cross-sector alliance will have balanced power positions. However, successful cross-sector alliances are often characterized by power neutrality, which means that partners' participation in communication is democratic. All parties involved in discussions about the partnership must have an equal voice in determining the outcomes, even if one of them (often the private firm) possesses a power advantage. In order to achieve commitment and constructive collaboration, partners must create a context that is free of coercion and the fear of retaliation. To develop a platform for power-neutral discussions, partners may use defensive, offensive and acceptance tactics (see Chapter 13). However, whereas the first two tactics are likely to ignite a power struggle, the use of acceptance tactics is more likely to contribute to a stable partnership; by using acceptance tactics, partners recognize that all interests are best served on egalitarian grounds. For example, Starbucks and Conservation International formed an alliance to encourage environmentally friendly coffee. Although Starbucks' strong position in the coffee market provided it with a power advantage, it did not exercise (or threaten to exercise) this power in an attempt to hinder Conservation International's attempts to achieve its own objective (Austin 2000). Failure by any partner to realize and accept some degree of power neutrality is likely to hamper the performance of the alliance.

Autonomy and transparency

Autonomy of the partners and transparency in cross-sector alliances is important for creating a climate in which parties can deal actively with potential conflicts. Autonomy refers to the extent to which a participant should have an equal opportunity to express its interests and be able to question the assertions made by any other participant. When a partner cannot participate fully in the discussion, its autonomy becomes jeopardized, which constrains its efforts to advocate its individual or communal interests. For example, Macdonald and Chrisp (2005) described an alliance between a pharmaceutical firm and a charity organization that encouraged teenagers to lead healthier lives. One reason the alliance failed is because the pharmaceutical firm gained dominance and suppressed the charity, driving the partnership toward the achievement of its own private interests rather than being concerned with the interests of the partnership or the charity. Recognizing the need for autonomy requires managers to plan and invest resources carefully to enable and facilitate dialogue and discussion. A win–win cross-sector alliance can only be established when all partners are equally able to express their interests fully.

Transparency suggests that partners are able to communicate in such a way that makes other members aware of their positions, goals and interests. This applies not only to the partners involved in the alliances but also to external stakeholders. Although there is no clear way of guaranteeing transparency within a single discussion, ongoing interaction over time can provide the conditions in which the true motives of the stakeholders become exposed (Reynolds and Yuthas 2008). This notion of transparency conflicts somewhat with alliance practices within business-to-business settings. During alliance negotiations, for example, companies tend to withhold critical information to secure private interests. In the pharmaceutical–charity alliance described above, partners agreed openly on certain private interests (the pharmaceutical sought public relations and the charity sought funding) but the parties did not acknowledge the fact that their fundamental intentions were causing conflicts as the alliance progressed. Transparency requires an ongoing, iterative dialogue between partners and their stakeholders as discussion exposes each partner's position, interests and intentions.

A culture of collaborative commitment

In the context of cross-sector alliances, it is important that partners share fundamental values and beliefs if they are to reduce the risk of potential conflicts, or to resolve them effectively once they have emerged. A culture of collaborative commitment enables partners to become aware of and reconcile diverging values. However, it can be difficult to build and maintain a culture of collaborative commitment, because it requires staff to be aware of individual dispositions and those of their counterparts. Developing and maintaining a collaborative commitment culture does not happen by organizational decree alone. It must be interwoven into all aspects of the partner's organizations and into the alliance. This new or modified culture must start with a focus on internal and external stakeholders, as it is they who must embrace the alliance's intended direction. For example, if a firm and a university acknowledge different time horizons, they may agree to postpone publication of research output in order to provide the firm with an opportunity to exploit this knowledge by staying ahead of its competitors. Building a culture of collaborative commitment in a cross-cultural alliance requires partners to focus on the following factors.

Employees and senior management from partner organizations should support the alliance's objectives. Management plays a powerful role in the process of establishing a collaborative culture within a cross-sector alliance, as it ensures the credibility of the push for collaborative behaviour (Noble and Jones 2006). Management must be perceived to support the collaboration both publicly and privately. A project champion who supports the alliance may serve as an example to other members of the staff. In addition, designating boundary spanners enables a firm to lay a foundation for collective sense-making activities that reinforce the development of a collaborate culture. Partners should use an employment selection process for participating in the alliance in order to prevent the inclusion of people who are unsupportive of the alliance's objectives. For example, staff can be selected by conducting a test that taps into the congruency between their value systems and that of the alliance. Furthermore, the initial stage of involvement in the alliance is the best time to start instilling the collaborative commitment culture into alliance staff. It is not enough simply to impart information about the existence of collaborative values. Through training and education, alliance staff must be made aware that collaborative behaviour is the foundation for the alliance and should be manifested in all its activities. An education programme designed to understand and subsume fully the alliance philosophy on collaborative commitment practices and behaviour may fulfil this purpose. This programme should be formally endorsed by the alliance and should explain to all levels of alliance participants the importance in being collaborative, not only for the benefit of their organizations, but also to enhance alliance performance. Hence, it is desirable to establish an 'education committee' that can not only coordinate, but also monitor, the level of education and the subsequent exposure to and awareness of collaborative issues.

In addition, partners may introduce a code of conduct that serves as an instrument to enhance awareness and helps organizations reduce and/or deal with conflicts of interest in a constructive manner (Harrington 1991). Within the context of a cross-sector alliance, a code of conduct should be developed that has both an internal and external focus. An external code of collaborative commitment provides guidelines for how to interact with various stakeholders connected with the partners and the alliance. This also contributes to transparency in their communication to other members outside the alliance. An internal code targets employees who work at all levels within the alliance and aims to provide guidance to staff when they face conflicts of interest during day-to-day operations. The process of developing a collaborative culture can be enhanced only if all parties are consulted and agree on the collaborative stance of the alliance.

Cross-sector alliances: Decision-making steps

Cross-sector alliances are unique because the partners are likely to have noticeable differences in terms of their societal functions, incentive systems, organization cultures, decision-making styles, time horizons and professional languages. Cross-sector alliances are difficult to realize and tend to result in minimal joint decision making and continuity in cooperation owing to inherent conflicts between the partners. To assist alliance managers, the next section provides guidelines for each stage of the alliance development framework when forging successful cross-sector alliances (see Figure 14.1).

Step 1: Alliance strategy formulation

During the strategic analysis stage, a firm will decide whether a cross-sector alliance is an appropriate governance mode to realize its objectives. Although generic

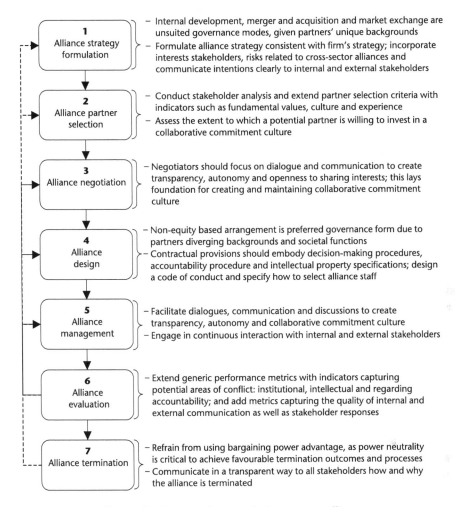

1 Alliance strategy formulation	– Internal development, merger and acquisition and market exchange are unsuited governance modes, given partners' unique backgrounds – Formulate alliance strategy consistent with firm's strategy; incorporate interests stakeholders, risks related to cross-sector alliances and communicate intentions clearly to internal and external stakeholders
2 Alliance partner selection	– Conduct stakeholder analysis and extend partner selection criteria with indicators such as fundamental values, culture and experience – Assess the extent to which a potential partner is willing to invest in a collaborative commitment culture
3 Alliance negotiation	– Negotiators should focus on dialogue and communication to create transparency, autonomy and openness to sharing interests; this lays foundation for creating and maintaining collaborative commitment culture
4 Alliance design	– Non-equity based arrangement is preferred governance form due to partners diverging backgrounds and societal functions – Contractual provisions should embody decision-making procedures, accountability procedure and intellectual property specifications; design a code of conduct and specify how to select alliance staff
5 Alliance management	– Facilitate dialogues, communication and discussions to create transparency, autonomy and collaborative commitment culture – Engage in continuous interaction with internal and external stakeholders
6 Alliance evaluation	– Extend generic performance metrics with indicators capturing potential areas of conflict: institutional, intellectual and regarding accountability; and add metrics capturing the quality of internal and external communication as well as stakeholder responses
7 Alliance termination	– Refrain from using bargaining power advantage, as power neutrality is critical to achieve favourable termination outcomes and processes – Communicate in a transparent way to all stakeholders how and why the alliance is terminated

FIGURE 14.1 Alliance development framework: Cross-sector alliances

rationales such as transaction costs, resource complementarities and resource dependence inform governance mode choice, an alliance is most likely to be the preferred alternative owing to the partners' distinct backgrounds. For example, a merger between a university and a private firm is unlikely, because the two parties fulfil different functions in society. A market exchange is also improbable because state-of-the-art academic knowledge is often not commoditized. Alternatively, a cross-sector alliance enables a firm to exploit efficiently the synergies obtained through collaboration with a public organization. However, to complete its strategic analysis a firm may wish to include a stakeholder analysis. An effective cross-sector alliance strategy fits with a firm's environment to accommodate the demands of external stakeholders, comply with social pressures and capitalize on contextual opportunities. This requires conscious decision-making, both from the private firm and from the public organization considering a cross-sector alliance. Whereas a private firm must assess the extent to which a partnership strengthens its competitive position, a public organization must evaluate whether its interests are best served by a cross-sector alliance. Moreover, public organizations must often adhere to laws and regulations that limit the room in which they can manoeuvre. Private firms must also take certain risks into account, such as changes in law, public acceptance and government. These could impact such areas as increased operating costs to comply with new laws, adverse effects on quality and service delivery and/ or additional operating costs and time delay. These aspects need to be incorporated in the strategic analysis.

Step 2: Alliance partner selection

Owing to varying interests, objectives and organizational backgrounds, partner fit can be deemed low in most cross-sector alliances. Consequently, partner selection becomes a critical activity as recognizing areas of incompatibility – which include strategic, organizational, cultural, operational and human areas – allows partners to develop corrective measures. For example, managers must consider whether the partners' organizational missions match, whether the alliance is equally important to both partners, whether partners' needs and capabilities can be integrated and whether the partners share values. In addition, partner analysis may focus on earlier partnership experience and partnering culture, as prior successful cross-sector alliances are indicative for future successes. An existing collaborative commitment culture or a willingness to build will reduce the likelihood of conflicts. More specifically, the cultural ability to appreciate different environments and the ability to adapt accordingly is an important partnering criterion. In addition, partner analysis may focus on flexibility, as the willingness of partners to adapt to existing and unforeseen circumstances is an important condition to success.

Step 3: Alliance negotiation

In order to achieve mutual collaborative commitment, partners in a cross-sector alliance must recognize the problems within their power relationship and also take precautions to neutralize power imbalances that may affect the fundamental purposes of their alliance. Thus, in addition to the generic negotiation guidelines, the negotiation approach should preferably be integrative and accompanied by soft tactics. It is important to obtain agreement on how to stimulate all participants and reward them for expressing their interests and objectives openly, as well as to make assertions and question the assertions of others. Moreover, the partners should openly explain their positions, goals, and interests, both to each other and to the 'outside world'. Such transparency and openness during alliance negotiations fosters alliance progress and performance, and firms must suppress the pressure to engage in distributive tactics. This means that partners should use acceptance tactics that recognize the fact that all interests are best served on egalitarian grounds.

Step 4: Alliance design

Like the rationale of avoiding mergers and acquisitions, cross-sector alliances tend to be most efficiently governed through non-equity-based arrangements that are supplemented with specific contractual provisions and management control. Whereas the alliance's governance form and management control mechanism should be consistent with generic guidelines in cross-sector alliance, particular focus should be given to contractual provisions and control mechanisms that deal with potential conflicts. More specifically, the following elements should be embodied in an alliance design if possible:

- Agreement on the decision-making procedures. For example, decision-making speed is critical as public and private organizations often have different requirements. Failure to manage these differences can translate into high levels of frustration, possibly damaging collaborative efforts.
- Agreement on accountability. Whereas public organizations are under public scrutiny and must adhere to laws and regulations, private firms must satisfy shareholders and other regulatory requirements.
- Contractual provisions, including communication structures, escalation pro-cedures and conflict management structures, must be designed to deal with relational risks in order to prevent potential damage to the partnership.
- Agreement on how to select and monitor employees involved the alliance. The dispositions of these employees should match the desired collaborative commitment culture. If necessary, partners should develop and implement a collaborative commitment culture programme to train and educate staff.
- The design of operational procedures must reflect the need for interaction and sense making. Therefore, working in mixed teams is preferable to working in separated teams that remain organization-specific.
- Constructing a code of collaborative commitment culture, as well as com-municating and discussing this with all participants in the alliance. Besides internal communication, it is also important to communicate the code to other stakeholders in the environment.
- Measures to ensure sufficient power neutrality. Selecting coordinators and staff who are aware of power-based behaviour makes it possible to deploy adequate counter-measures. It is also important to educate staff to be aware of the consequences of power abuse.

Step 5: Alliance management

Partnering with a non-profit organization can involve uncertainty for a firm because it requires working with institutions (e.g. government agencies) that may have complex decision-making systems and a complex set of interests and objectives. Consequently, within a cross-sector alliance, employees are challenged to deviate from their normal intra-organizational routine life, and confront a situation that often involves a new and potentially complex inter-organizational experience. In managing a cross-sector alliance, understanding the backgrounds and interests of one's partners allows participants to act and react better, which improves the management interventions and quality of the working relationship. The various motivations, organizational cultures and value patterns of the public and private sectors would be expected to give rise to management challenges that are not normally associated with private–private or public–public partnerships. This is the perfect time to try and mould employees into the alliance's culture:

- Employees should allocate sufficient time and effort to become familiar with the collaborative commitment culture, both at the start and also during execution.
- It is important to facilitate and monitor dialogue and discussion between the partners in order to create an environment that fosters autonomous behaviour. During progress meetings, for instance, the chair should ensure that participants are able to express their interests and question claims made by others.
- It is important to stimulate continuous interaction with external stakeholders based on transparency and openness. Partners may create a common website about the alliance that presents the goals, participants, their roles, events and news on a regular basis.

Step 6: Alliance evaluation

Cross-sector alliances are established to reach certain objectives. The performance metric system can be augmented with additional indicators that tap into these objectives, such as customer's awareness and funding. In addition, metrics may capture the potential conflicts that are likely to emerge. For example, indicators may concern the extent to which participants are satisfied with how they dealt with intellectual and accountability issues, how they cope with or respect each other's interests and how they handle external stakeholders. Performance metric systems may also include indicators that capture the collaborative culture; partner firms' behaviour, in terms of the extent to which management and employees behave accordingly to the collaborative commitment culture, how open communication is; and whether partners have the opportunity to express their interests and objectives. Metrics may also ascertain the extent to which partners are sufficiently transparent about their position, goals and interests to external stakeholders; and whether potential power differences have been neutralized.

Step 7: Alliance termination

The duration of the agreement and the termination provisions are important, because such items affect the parties' ability to escape from cross-sector alliance arrangements that turn out to be harmful to the business, or simply not as effective or profitable as other stakeholders might have expected. Because of the desire for transparency, it is important to communicate to the external environment why and how the alliance is being terminated. It is important to refrain from use, as retaining power neutrality will increase the likelihood of avoiding barriers for future cross-sector alliances.

Summary

Alliances between private firms and public organizations, such as governments, universities and non-governmental organizations (NGO), have become increasingly important for dealing with society's challenges. These cross-sector alliances provide opportunities to align resources to achieve individual and communal objectives. However, uncertainty and ambiguity can be expected to increase when people with different backgrounds and cultures interact with each other. A lack of mutual understanding, varying interpretations and different ways of doing things might lead to frustration that could ultimately damage and possibly jeopardize the partnership. Managers may deal with the promises and perils of cross-sector alliances by adopting a power-neutral stance, emphasizing autonomy and transparency and building a culture of collaborative commitment.

Case: World Food Programme–TNT

TNT, the Dutch-based express delivery company, has been an active partner of the United Nations World Food Program (WFP), the world's largest humanitarian aid agency, since 2002.[1] Each year, WFP provides food aid to an average of 90 million people, including 56 million children, in more than 80 countries. The struggle to feed the hungry is immense, with a billion people suffering from malnutrition. TNT Express, a global transportation company, specializes in providing delivery solutions to its customers. TNT and WFP have forged an alliance named 'Moving the World', and have committed to realizing their ambition to move the world to an era without malnutrition.

The alliance between TNT and the WFP was initiated by TNT's former CEO, Peter Bakker. While travelling, Bakker read an article about malnutrition and the severe negative impact it has on the social and economic development of Africa. Bakker recognized that the problem was not necessarily a shortage in food production, but rather an inability to distribute food across the world more evenly. Bakker also realized that TNT's competences and capacity could make a valuable contribution towards alleviating hunger. TNT realized that a cross-sector alliance would reflect positively on the company's reputation, so the primary partner selection criteria were organizational stability and good conduct; criteria that the WFP met. In addition, providing food aid requires an extensive local and political networks and specific competences and resources if it is to actually provide food aid where it is needed most; again, WFP had such knowledge.

The advantages for both organizations became clear immediately. The support of TNT has improved the WFP's ability to transport and distribute food across targeted, often underdeveloped countries. TNT's logistics knowledge and expertise enabled WFP to operate more efficiently, thereby saving costs and releasing funds that can be used to increase food aid capacity. For TNT, important motives to forge the alliance were increased goodwill and strengthened social reputation among the general public. Another important advantage was that the alliance boosted employee morale. TNT employees were motivated to set up their own initiatives in order to support Moving the World, which resulted in informal cross-functional communication, improved team spirit and a feeling of 'doing good'. Moreover, TNT used the programme to strengthen further its corporate social responsibility by generating numerous spin-off projects to reduce its carbon footprint. It did this through methods such as challenging drivers to drive in a more controlled manner ('Drive Me Challenge'). TNT was also able to strengthen its management skills through the special assignments. These varied from jointly developing logistical concepts to building a school in Africa.

The contractual basis of the alliance was kept simple. In 2002, a Memorandum of Understanding was signed, which described the basic legal contributions and liabilities for a period of five years. TNT's contributions were divided into four pillars. The first is *hands-on support*, which consists of emergency response and special assignment, in which assistance is given in both skilled specialist and resources (for example, warehouses, aircrafts, and vehicles). The emergency response agreements described in detail the specific contributions that TNT had to make, and procedures detailing the specific roles of the WFP and TNT. An important aspect within these agreements is the fact that TNT must react within 48 hours and make staff available to coordinate the following logistic effort together with WFP. The second pillar is *knowledge transfer*. TNT expertise is used to support and train WFP staff in areas such as transport optimization, fleet management, aviation and customs support. The special assignments were critical for realizing this goal. These first two pillars created intensive interaction between people from both organizations and helped bridge cultural differences and gain better understanding of the challenges faced by both organizations.

The third pillar is *transport for goods* in which TNT works together with WFP to develop sustainable development programmes for communities. The fourth pillar is *awareness and fundraising*. Employee involvement was one of the strategic goals behind the Moving the World programme. The contribution to the initial strategic goals is monitored by a yearly employee satisfaction survey that includes specific questions about Moving the World. Over 70 per cent of personnel indicated that they regard the programme as an important initiative. The encouraging results were supported by spontaneous fund-raising initiatives started by TNT employees that have so far collected more than 9 million Euros.

Despite the positive synergies, both organizations recognized the risks involved in starting up the partnership. To steer the partnership in the appropriate direction, a governance structure was set up in which a distinction was made between strategic-level management and tactical-level management. At the strategic level, the CEO of TNT and the executive director of WFP met regularly, for example, at the World

Economic Forum, to discuss the general direction of the partnership. The tactical level involves more day-to-day management of activities, often organized through special assignments. Performance management and assessment are also organized at this level.

One important challenge was to overcome the cultural and organizational differences between TNT and WFP. For example, the two organizations have different purposes: profit generation and the provision of non-profit relief. In addition, WFP is organized to swiftly respond to emerging crises. Also, WFP used to operate in situations with low financial certainty due to the organization's dependence on yearly budgets from UN member states. In contrast, TNT is a multinational, stock exchange-listed enterprise. TNT's strategic planning is extensive and the company aims to achieve operational excellence, which means that it strives for steady flows instead of peaks.

To overcome these cultural and organizational barriers, the inter-organizational special assignments played an important role. Staff from both organizations had to work together and communicate with each other. This has led to mutual understanding and respect, as well as improved working relations between the organizations. WFP understood that TNT was not in it for a quick boost to its reputation, while TNT understood that WFP had a strong history in emergency response within a very complex setting. This allowed the partnership to develop and deepen further. The main business goals of TNT are to improve employee satisfaction and management development. These goals did not require extensive marketing campaigns, which may have prompted feelings at WFP that TNT was only participating in the alliance to benefit from WFP's reputation. Also, TNT did not cut its funding for the programme, even during times of economic downturn. This was considered to be a positive sign and proof that TNT's intentions are morally founded.

Questions

1. The Moving the World alliance depicts a cross-sector alliance. How is alliance design and management different from business-to-business alliances?
2. What are the critical factors contributing to the success of the Moving the World alliance?
3. The use of special assignments fulfilled an important role for dealing with organizational and cultural differences? Explain how and why.

15

MULTI-PARTNER ALLIANCES

Multi-partner alliances (or multi-lateral alliances) are partnerships formed by more than two parties. A multi-partner alliance enables firms to align multiple sets of complementary resources, often with the aim of creating additional synergies or complying with increasing customer demands. Examples of multi-partner alliances can be found in a variety of industries, from the semiconductor and airline industries to agri-food industries. If properly managed, a multi-partner alliance strategy can be a win–win for all parties involved. However, whereas dealing with adversity is relatively straightforward in an alliance with only two partners, governance within a multi-partner alliance becomes more complex, as the one-to-one relationship is replaced by a one-to-many relationship. The increasing number of parties presents the managers involved with a particular challenge. In order to capture the potential synergies that come with a multi-partner alliance, these managers must prevent and control free-riding behaviour by their counterparts. The opening sections of this chapter explore this multi-partner alliance challenge and elaborate on the mechanisms that managers can use to deal with it. The alliance development framework is used in the following section to present specific managerial guidelines for multi-partner alliances. The chapter concludes with a summary and a case illustration.

The multi-partner alliance challenge

A multi-partner alliance is defined as a collective, voluntary organizational arrangement between more than two parties, with common objectives, joint decision-making and shared risks. These parties engage interactively in multilateral activities, such as collaborative research, development, sourcing, production, marketing and commercialization of technologies, products and/or services (Lavie *et al.* 2007; Rochemont 2010). Multi-partner alliances are typical in areas such as the airline industry. Through code-sharing, joint network coverage and joint marketing initiatives (such as frequent flyer programmes), airlines are able to increase their utilization rates and offer an increased number of destinations. Although a multi-partner alliance can be organized through an alliance contract, parties often establish a separate organizational structure in which the alliance activities are executed. Such entities are usually non-profit-oriented and participating firms pay a cost-covering fee. The main advantage of this arrangement is that it allows the partnership to enlarge easily if other parties are interested in joining. A consortium is another specific type of multi-partner alliance in which multiple parties collaborate to achieve a common goal, often related to research and development, economies of scale and setting industry standards. See Table 15.1 for examples of multi-partner alliances.

Similar to the motives behind bilateral alliances, firms form multi-partner alliances to access and complement each other's resources (García-Canal *et al.* 2003). By sharing resources across multiple partners, participants are better able to

TABLE 15.1 Examples of multi-partner alliances

	Description
SEMATECH	SEMATECH (Semiconductor Manufacturing Technology) is a consortium of American semiconductor manufacturers, which was founded in 1987. The motivation for establishing the alliance was the loss of American market share due to increased competition among Japanese manufacturers. Between 1987 and 1992, SEMATECH generated 15 patents and 36 patent applications, helped enact more than 300 industry standards, participated in 110 equipment improvement projects and joint development programs, and published more than 1,100 technical documents. In 1993, American semiconductor producers recaptured the top position in worldwide sales with 45.3% of the chip market.
Wi-Fi Alliance	In 1999, the Wi-Fi alliance was forged to test and certify the interoperability of Wireless Local Area Network (WLAN) products based on the IEEE 802.11 standard. The alliance consisted of both hardware manufacturers (such as Philips and Dell) and telecom-focused companies (such as Nokia and Ericsson), which jointly developed an industry standard.
Prominent	In 1994, as a response to declining sales, six Dutch tomato cultivators decided to cooperate and establish 'Prominent'. The goal was to increase the quality of the tomatoes and therefore increase market share in Germany, while maintaining the sustainability of the ecological system. Prominent members analysed new lighting techniques for tomato cultivation, new methods were developed to create a closed greenhouse, and a joint packaging company was forged. By creating a new company that took over non-core activities, each firm was able to concentrate on its primary function. Additional value was also created for the members through improved bargaining power. Prominent expanded and currently has 22 partners. *(Continued)*

TABLE 15.1 *(Continued)*

	Description
Blu-ray Disc Association	In 2002, a large group of companies announced the introduction of the Blu-ray Disc (BD) format, at that time the next generation in optical storage. In 2005, the Blu-ray Disc founders announced the creation of the Blu-ray Disc Association, re-incorporating the founders group, but creating a voluntary membership group that is open to any corporation or organization with an interest in creating, upholding, and/ or promoting the BD formats. The aim was to develop Blu-ray Disc specifications, ensure Blu-ray Disc products are implemented by licensees according to the specifications, promote adoption of Blu-ray Disc formats, and provide information to anyone interested in supporting Blu-ray Disc formats.

Sources: Browning *et al.* (1995); Den Hartigh *et al.* (2010); Rochemont (2010).

use their resources and improve their ability to serve a larger part of the value chain. For example, partners within co-development multi-partner alliances exchange knowledge to develop new products and/or services, thereby increasing customer value and competitive advantage. Sharing research and development activities also enables partners to divide investments over a larger number of participants and to realize economies of scale. In addition, shared procurement with multiple partners provides an opportunity to bundle volume, which translates into increased bargaining power and, consequently, lower purchase prices. Multi-partner alliances also offer opportunities in terms of network connections, as participating parties join a network that becomes a repository of resources and information about the availability and reliability of prospective partners. Multi-partner alliances are sometimes forged to enable collective lobbying to guard the interests of multiple firms or even entire industries. Through a multi-partner lobbying alliance, firms can influence political decision-making that affects a group of firms or entire industries. Multi-partner alliances also arise when industry standards are to be set. Setting an industry standard often involves substantial investments and is beyond the ability of a single firm. By participating in a multi-partner alliance, firms reduce individual costs and risks, while increasing the chance of successful market introductions.

Despite the potential advantages of multi-partner alliances, they are inherently more complex to manage than two-party alliances. A growing number of partners increases the risk of opportunistic behaviour, because the number of dyadic relationships increases geometrically as the number of partners becomes larger (García-Canal *et al.* 2003). One critical hazard concerns the danger of free-riding behaviour by partner firms, whereby a member of a group obtains benefits from group membership, but does not bear a proportional share of the costs (Albanese and Van Fleet 1985). A multi-partner alliance may generate 'collective' or 'public' goods, such as knowledge, that are accessible to all partners involved, even when they fail to fulfil their resource contributions and other obligations (Dyer and Nobeoka 2000). For example, a partner firm may willingly participate in knowledge-sharing activities to acquire knowledge and then exit the multi-partner alliance or refuse to contribute its own knowledge. The multi-partner setting reduces the guilt that a partner feels toward its counterparts when it chooses not to cooperate. This causes the risk of internal competition and conflicts between partners to increase due to diverging interests and the possibility of unsanctioned free-riding (Zeng and Chen 2003).

To deal effectively with free-riding, multi-partner alliances need specific governance mechanisms that pertain to areas such as coordination, communication and incentives schemes. Partners must strike the right balance between under-investing and over-investing in multi-partner alliances. Whereas some firms seek to free ride on their partners' investments, others end up subsidizing their partners and fail to earn an appropriate return on their investments. It is also important to identify the right time to exit a multi-partner alliance given that, unlike one-to-one alliances, a multi-partner alliance can maintain its operations even after certain members have left. Therefore, alliance managers must invest in the partnership to increase the probability of value creation, while also preventing and controlling free riding by their counterparts to avoid asymmetrical contributions and appropriation.

Managing multi-partner alliances

The main motivation behind multi-partner alliances is to capitalize on resources supplied by multiple partners, with the aim of achieving synergies that can only be realized with multiple partners. Simultaneously, however, partners must eliminate the risk of free riding pre-emptively and, if necessary, resolve (for example, through sanctions) the adverse impact of this behaviour. There are five mechanisms by which participants can achieve this two-fold objective: (1) resource complementarity, (2) task organization, (3) contractual governance, (4) relational governance and (5) orchestrator role (see Table 15.2)

Resource complementarity

The precise amount of resources that each alliance partner contributes to a multi-partner alliance depends on the competences of each partner. Preferably, each partner would contribute resources to the multi-partner alliance that their counterparts cannot provide. Partners ideally bring something unique and non-redundant to the alliance, so that the overall resource base of the alliance becomes stronger. At the same time, the fact that partners depend on each other helps prevent internal competition (Hill and Hellriegel 1994). For example, whereas one partner may provide a financial contribution, its counterparts may supply non-financial resources, such as specific material assets or tacit capabilities, deployment of personnel, machines or production facilities, and technical skills. In addition, when each party provides a unique contribution, any failure to fulfil obligations is quickly

TABLE 15.2 Managing multi-partner alliances

	Description	*Implications*
Resource complementarity	Multiple partners contribute resources to the purpose of generating synergy	Unique resource contributions reduce the risk of free-riding, whereas overlapping resource contributions encourage free-riding
Task organization	Multiple partners makes it more difficult to distinguish between individual tasks and outcomes	Designating identifiable, unique, and transparent tasks to partners reduce the risk of free-riding
Contractual governance	Multi-partner alliance tend to be organized through a non-equity based arrangement, implying a need for clear contractual specifications	Developing a transparent incentive system, demanding an entrance fee, installing a clear decision-making and monitoring structure reduce the risk of free-riding
Relational governance	Multi-partner alliance demand high-quality relational governance	Investing in relational norms to guide collaborative behaviour is imperative
Orchestrator role	An orchestrator is responsible for the pro-active management of a multi-partner alliance	Orchestrators create stability, align interests, encourage communication, and execute brand management

noticed and subject to immediate sanctioning. Unique contributions also reduce the risk of surplus and wasteful resources. In contrast, the presence of resource substitutes within a multi-partner alliance may cause tension. Resource substitution undermines power relations because partners that provide similar resources may lose their justification for being a member of the alliance. Consequently, a firm may either increase its resource contribution to signal its commitment or economize on its resource contribution and engage in free-riding behaviour. However, alliance continuity is not necessarily jeopardized, as resource contributions made by free-riding partners are substituted by the resource contributions of other partners. Nonetheless, if management does not effectively control free-riding behaviour, free-riding partners will illegitimately reap the benefits of a multi-partner alliance. Therefore, a successful multi-partner alliance is dependent on having a precise mix of partners with resources that are complementary to one another and required to realize alliance objectives.

Task organization

Increased group size reduces the perceptibility of individual contributions and tasks, which makes it more difficult to distinguish free-riding partners (Albanese and Van Fleet 1985). Therefore, it is important to translate a multi-partner alliance strategy into identifiable, unique, and transparent tasks in order to prevent free riding in multi-partner alliances. Identifiable tasks are those in which the output of the specific tasks can be identified, and tied to a specific partner. A lack of clear task definitions results in weak contracts, which allows partners to make use of ambiguity about duties and responsibilities and behave in an opportunistic manner. However, as the number of partners increases, identifying and allocating specific tasks for each member may become more hazardous and tasks may overlap across partners. The more partners involved in an alliance, the more difficult it is to formulate a specific role for each alliance partner. The risk of free riding increases if similar tasks are delegated to more than one partner, as the failure of one partner to execute a task is most likely to remain unnoticed. Moreover, this partner can still enjoy the benefits, because other parties may have completed similar tasks.

Free riding may also result from a lack of transparency in the objectives and related tasks. When tasks are not made transparent, it is difficult to monitor progress, which increases the opportunity for partners to exploit this ambiguity. Designating identifiable, unique, and transparent tasks in a multi-partner alliance prevents free riding, reduces conflicts, and stimulates collective value creation.

Contractual governance

Owing to the larger number of parties involved, multi-partner alliances are often organized through non-equity-based arrangements. However, if the number of partners increases, supplemental governance in the form of contractual provisions and management control is required (García-Canal et al. 2003). An effective and formalized incentive system can prompt parties in a multi-partner alliance to act in the interests of the collaborative arrangement (Zeng and Chen 2003). Since free-riding behaviour is essentially a result of an individual's unfavourable comparisons of benefits to costs, one major way of reducing or preventing free riding is either to improve a party's perceptions of its pay-off by increasing its share of benefits of public goods, or to decrease its costs. For example, special incentives can be offered to encourage the provision of public goods. Extrinsic incentives include additional compensation, extra time off, assignment to preferred projects, extra released time, a larger share in the public good and recognition from superiors or peers. Intrinsic incentives include the sense of achievement or satisfaction that results from completing a difficult or unique task. Another way to build long-term commitment is to ask participating firms for an entrance fee. High entrance fees represent incentives to solve any emerging adversities as participating firms are locked into the partnership.

Effective monitoring of partner behaviour (contributions and compensation) is also vital for effective management of multi-partner arrangements. These monitoring systems can act as early warning systems, since deviations are detected promptly and allow partners to impose (economic) sanctions, such as penalties. Clarity in decision-making processes is also important in order to prevent opportunistic behaviour, because a lack of clarity increases ambiguity among parties and provides opportunities to pursue separate interests covertly (Rochemont 2010). Decision-making procedures, including majority voting, consensus, blocking votes and lead partners, describe how decisions are made within the alliance. It should be clear who has the authority to make decisions and what decision-making procedures are being used or will be implemented. Without a clear decision-making structure, partners may feel isolated or ignored and may start to question whether their influence is sufficient to achieve the alliance's objectives. Financial investments may also function as a signal of commitment. In the SEMATECH alliance, for example, companies were obliged not only to contribute R&D knowledge, but also to bring financial resources. These financial resources were necessary to develop an industry standard successfully, but they also had the effect of locking in the members of the network, which can act as glue for the cooperation (Hwang and Burgers 1997). Preferably, agreements about these and other governance mechanisms should be embodied in an alliance contract.

Relational governance

A multi-partner alliance demands strong relational governance. It is impossible to safeguard every action through formal contracts, and a strong collaborative climate represents a powerful tool for managing the free-riding problem. Relational norms comprise of unwritten rules that depict how parties collaborate with each other and pertain to flexibility, solidarity and continuity expectations. Relational norms reduce self-interested behaviour and help parties understand the congruency of individual goals more easily, thereby reducing the need to resort to close formal monitoring. These norms also reduce uncertainty about potentially destructive behaviours (such as free riding) and encourage partners to act in accordance with alliance objectives. In the presence of such norms, the partnership will develop based on the principles of solidarity and fair exchange, suggesting that all partners believe that the benefits they receive from the relationship are equivalent to their contributions. Relational norms also stimulate the building of a relational capital. Based on the belief that partners will be dealt with in an equitable manner, even in ambiguous situations, relational capital will guide partners' behaviour to trust one another. They will act for the best performance of the alliance, which will lead to optimal contributions. When free-riding parties deviate from relational norms, they can be forced to leave the alliance or change their behaviour. Socialization within multi-partner alliances increases the likelihood of collective success.

Apart from formal sanctions, free-riding behaviour can be prevented by social sanctions or the threat thereof (Albanese and Van Fleet 1985). This form of sanctioning does not involve formal policies and procedures, management directives and controls; instead, it uses relational and or behavioural persuasion to enforce the conduct of partners by the other partners. In a multi-partner alliance, social sanctions are a powerful instrument with which to guide partner

behaviour since they can have significant implications for an individual partner, especially in situations in which the partner is dependent on the multi-partner
network. Collective group sanctions may then be an effective measure for resolving
conflicts, as they affect a firm's opportunities negatively over a longer period of
time. Social sanctions become more effective if the group size increases, as the
possible damage to a member's reputation is greater if more partners spread negative
word of mouth.

The orchestrator role

Maintaining a group of partners can be difficult, due to the risk of conflicting
interests. This requires active management. Whatever the governance structure, the
group of firms must have some way to coordinate actions. Without leadership, a
multi-partner alliance cannot expect to formulate and execute a consistent strategy
(Bamford and Ernst 2003). In large multi-partner alliances, this function can be
performed by orchestrators (Rochemont 2010), an active network manager
(Doz and Hamel 1998), or a strategic centre (Lorenzoni and Baden-Fuller 1995).
Effective orchestrators foster group stability by minimizing internal competition
among member firms. Having a larger number of parties in an alliance implies
diverging interests, and a key task of an orchestrator is to align member's interests
and prevent free riding by stressing the importance of collective objectives over
individual objectives. Orchestrators also engage in brand management, as many
multi-partners alliances create a unified brand in order to increase the awareness of
potential consumers. An orchestrator can promote the network brand and ensure
that all marketing activities are consistent to create a uniform appearance.

Multi-partner alliances: Decision-making steps

Value appropriation in multi-partner alliances must be considered jointly with the
value-creating strategy because the quality of the collaboration and value-sharing
rules both determine how much value the partnership can create. Alignment of
complementary resources may provide strong motivation to forge a multi-partner
allaince, but the issue of value appropriation is more salient owing to the higher
governance costs caused by the risk of free riding. In order to provide guidelines
for establishing win–win multi-partner alliances, this section elaborates on specific
decisions for multi-partner alliances at each stage of the alliance development
framework (see Figure 15.1).

Step 1: Alliance strategy formulation

During the strategic analysis, firms decide whether a multi-partner alliance is an
appropriate governance mode to realize their goals. Their focus at this stage should
be to analyse the benefits of a multi-partner alliance in comparison to alternative

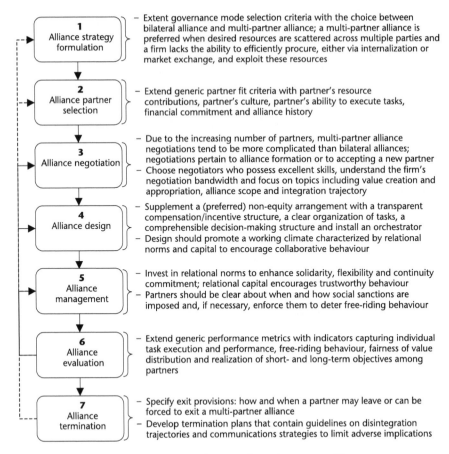

FIGURE 15.1 Alliance development framework: Multi-partner alliances

governance modes, including autonomous growth, mergers and bilateral alliances. A multi-partner alliance is a preferred governance mode when the type and magnitude of required resources extends beyond the focal firm and an alliance with a single partner. Internalization would only be a preferred alternative if a firm were able to integrate and exploit a variety of external resources efficiently; yet most firms lack this ability. In addition, desired resources are often not readily available in markets, making market exchange inappropriate. For example, developing an industry standard requires substantial investments, involves high risks, and depends on the participation and commitment of parties across the value chain. It is beyond the scope of one or two firms to develop such a standard. In such circumstances, multi-partner alliance strategies are appropriate because the probability of one firm's success depends on the resource contributions of multiple parties, including suppliers, competitors and customers. Analysis should focus on resource availability and the potential strengths, weaknesses, opportunities and threats related to participation in a multi-partner alliance.

Step 2: Alliance partner selection

During the partner selection stage, a firm either selects multiple partners to forge a multi-partner alliance or decides to participate in an existing multi-partner alliance. A key issue in both situations is assessing partner fit, as a misfit may encourage free-riding behaviour. Furthermore, it is important that partners have some degree of common objectives and shared visions on industry development; otherwise, the multi-partner alliance is likely to collapse. Next, attention should be given to resource complementarities. In a multi-partner setting, partners prefer to contribute varying resources as the level of resource uniqueness is inversely correlated with free-riding behaviour. In other words, resource substitution should be minimized, as overlap tends to lead to free-riding behaviour and dysfunctional conflicts. If overlap is inevitable, analysis of the partner firms' market positions could reveal that they serve different markets, which reduces the risk that the overlap will actually translate to dysfunctional conflicts or competition. Cultural fit between partners stimulates a collaborative culture, whereas misfit prompts a competitive culture that fuels the chance of free riding. Therefore, a cultural assessment of the potential partners is required. Another important selection criterion relates to a party's willingness to pay an entrance fee. By complying with this requirement, new partners express commitment by providing a certain contribution to a collaborative platform.

Step 3: Alliance negotiation

Negotiations in multi-partner alliances tend to be more complicated than in bilateral alliance negotiations. Because more parties are involved within the alliance, it can be more difficult to develop a collective value creation strategy and agree on the fair distribution of benefits. To this end, the role of an orchestrator becomes important. By demonstrating leadership, an orchestrator is able to influence partners positively and in a functional manner by providing a clear and enthusiastic vision, emphasizing the importance of the collective over the pursuit of individual interests. In addition to these qualities, the role of the orchestrator is critical in two separate negotiation situations that are typical for multi-partner alliances. If the multi-partner alliance is newly established, negotiating partners may benefit from appointing an orchestrator directly (or a group of people fulfilling an orchestrator's role). An orchestrator's task is to introduce the parties involved, disentangle private interests, create a shared understanding of the alliance's objectives and individual roles and responsibilities, and create common ground from which to launch the partnership. If the alliance has been operating for a while, the orchestrator represents the collective and is tasked with negotiating with any new partners and initially ascertaining the desirability of the new partner (for example, identifying the unique contribution the partner will make to realize the collective objectives). In addition, because accepting a new partner involves enlarging the group, negotiation topics and approaches may differ from the former situation. For example, negotiations may split in several phases, enabling a new partner to integrate slowly. In this way, a new partner can be brought up to standard; this prevents disturbances in the existing alliance, and existing partners postpone a definitive entry decision until the final negotiations.

Step 4: Alliance design

The focus during the alliance design stage should be on installing governance mechanisms to supplement the non-equity-based governance form through which multi-partner alliances tend to be organized. Even if partners exchange equity, these additional coordination mechanisms are necessitated, as equity alone is insufficient to protect against free riding and other types of exchange hazards. Specifically, in addition to generic guidelines, managers responsible for forging multi-partner alliances may focus on the following areas:

- A compensation structure that specifies partners' tangible (financial) and intangible (knowledge) outcomes in the short and long term. A clear compensation structure helps prevent different expectations among partners as the alliance progresses and functions as an incentive system. It preferably involves some form of advance payments (such as an entrance fee) and rules about the ex-post distribution of outcomes (for example, royalties and transfer prices). Incentives include financial benefits, a larger share in the public good, and bonuses for completing tasks. The absence of a clear incentive system increases ambiguity, which encourages free-riding behaviour.
- Task organization in terms of allocating identifiable and unique tasks to specific partners. Clear responsibility and transparency prompts responsibility and prevents free riding.
- Ideally, decision-making and communication structures and processes are designed to stimulate a collaborative working climate that provides sufficient incentives for each partner to remain committed. However, because the relative weight of one partner might differ from the next, responsibilities and authority should be adapted consistently. Voting rights can be distributed consistently with contributions, but excessive dominant control by one partner undermines collective efforts.
- Preferably, an orchestrator's function will be formalized. This could constitute a person or a team of representatives that aims to resolve conflicts originating from diverging interests, contributions, outcomes and expectations. An orchestrator is also responsible for the entrance and integration of new members.
- The monitoring of outcomes, processes and behaviours is critical for advancing the progress of multi-partner alliances. Rules and procedures should be formalized regarding how and when to act if discrepancies are detected.
- Clear exit provisions, to avoid partners being able to exit the alliance without having fulfilled their contractual obligations, which could include elements such as sharing knowledge and technologies. The absence of such provisions may lead to free-riding behaviour from the exiting partner, which could decrease the trust and commitment of the remaining partners.

Step 5: Alliance management

Alliance managers from individual partners and orchestrators representing the collective should attempt to build and maintain a healthy collaborative climate. These managers are responsible for enhancing the development of relational norms and capital between the parties involved in a multi-partner alliance. They must create a climate for building trust, and be aware of possible feelings of distrust among members in order to prevent or resolve free riding or other forms of opportunism. For example, face-to-face communication prior to formal decision making ensures that partners are motivated to participate in such meetings. In addition, management may focus on the use of social sanctions to deter partners from behaving dysfunctionally. It is the role of the orchestrator to create a system of social sanctions and a shared understanding of when these social sanctions are to be used and by whom. Social sanctions serve to weaken the reputation of the penalized parties and limit their access to vital resources, particularly when partner reputation is connected with the alliance or when there is strong partner dependency on the alliance. As the partnership progresses, under-performance might justify modifications to the alliance design, including the incentive scheme, the sanction system and group size. Clear procedures are required in order to prevent conflict, stating when procedures may become effective, who can make the appropriate decisions and what the consequences will be.

Step 6: Alliance evaluation

Although the perspective of managing partners individually, using unique tasks and measuring individual contributions, looks promising, the inherent danger is that the overall alliance performance may be overlooked, along with the potential synergies that can be realized through the collaborations between partners. Therefore, evaluation must also apply to alliance-wide performance indicators for which all partners, or a subset of partners, have specific responsibility. To this end, in addition to generic indicators, the performance metric system will preferably be augmented with indicators that capture the following factors:

- Objective and subjective indicators of multi-partner performance.
- Short- and long-term performance objectives of individual partners and the partnership.
- Fairness of value distribution across partners.
- Individual partners' task execution and performance.
- Behavioural aspects, including free-riding behaviour and other forms of opportunism.

Step 7: Alliance termination

The length of the term of the agreement is important, as are exit provisions specifying how and when partners may exit or be forced to exit. Such clauses affect parties' ability to leave a multi-partner alliance that has become unproductive. Depending on the degree of integration, a termination plan may also involve procedures and guidelines for disintegration. For example, withdrawal from a research consortium that has over 100 members is usually easier than pulling out of a highly integrated airline multi-partner alliance. Communication strategies must also be developed, because termination of the alliance or the departure of one partner may have serious repercussions for the other partners.

Summary

A multi-partner alliance can be a win–win situation for all parties involved. However, multi-partner alliances present their own set of unique risks. Whereas the likelihood of detecting free-riding behaviour is relatively high in a bilateral alliance, within a multi-partner alliance the one-to-one relationship is replaced by a one-to-many relationship, which increases the risk of undetected free-riding behaviour. Free-riding occurs when partners act opportunistically by not contributing to the alliance, while benefiting unequally from the outcomes of the alliance. In order to deal effectively with this challenge, firms may require (new) partners to supply unique resources, design alliances with sufficient protection (e.g. task organization), invest in relational governance and install an orchestrator function to coordinate alliance activities.

Case: SkyTeam

The airline industry is characterized by fierce competition between airlines and high levels of regionalization, owing to national ties between airlines and their country of origin.[1] This translates into restrictions on landing rights and routes. Despite the deregulation of recent decades, no single airline in the world is able to provide a global network. In order to build and maintain a competitive advantage, airlines circumvent these strict regulations through collaboration. For example, bilateral agreements, such as code sharing, allow airlines to share their network, which enables passengers to complete a journey involving multiple airlines using just one ticket. However, having recognized that bilateral agreements were insufficient to maintain their growth strategies, airlines started to initiate and participate in multi-partner alliances.

The establishment of the Star Alliance in 1997 by United Airlines, Lufthansa, Air Canada, Thai Airways and Scandinavian Airline System (SAS) constituted the first global airline network. The Star Alliance example was soon to be followed by the Oneworld alliance in 1999. SkyTeam was the third alliance to be created in 2000. The primary motivation for SkyTeam was to create a globe-spanning network of routes and airports. Therefore, the most important contribution that partners within the SkyTeam alliance make is their network of routes and airports. Initially, SkyTeam consisted of four founding airlines: Aeroméxico, Air France, Delta Airlines and Korean Air. In 2001, KLM merged with Air France, while in the

North American market, Northwest and Continental airlines had already formed a partnership. This partnership was expanded with Delta Airlines forming an important North American bloc. Within Europe, Air France and Alitalia were part of the SkyTeam alliance. The merger between KLM and Air France strengthened the European bloc. Combining both blocs within SkyTeam provided SkyTeam with a key asset: transatlantic routes. SkyTeam currently consists of Aeroflot, Aeroméxico, Air Europa, Air France, Alitalia, China Southern Airlines, Czech Airlines, Delta Airlines, Kenya Airways, KLM, Korean Air, TAROM and Vietnam Airlines, offering a worldwide network. This constellation of multiple airlines presented SkyTeam with the challenge of aligning varying interests and preventing dysfunctional behaviour like free riding. By carefully selecting its partners and requiring them to pay a membership fee, and incorporating active alliance management and specific decision-making structures, SkyTeam was able to assure alliance viability.

SkyTeam developed an extensive partner recruitment policy consisting of multiple stages. The primary criteria for selecting potential partners are: (1) the network the potential partners can contribute to the alliance and (2) the access a partner can provide to new markets in, for instance, developing regions and countries. In other words, SkyTeam reduced internal competition by minimizing substitution of routes and airports within the alliance. Guided by these criteria and building on the results of preliminary assessments, SkyTeam may decide to proceed to the next stage, introducing a new member of the SkyTeam alliance. During this next phase, the alliance terms and conditions are discussed. An important factor in this negotiation phase is the partner's ability to meet SkyTeam's requirements. These requirements cover aspects concerning flight safety, airline organization and IT infrastructure. The time it takes to fulfil these requirements means the negotiation phase typically takes between one and two years. Meeting these requirements sometimes requires airlines to make significant changes and investments within their organization and operations. Becoming a member of an airline alliance is often critical for long-term airline viability, so airlines are willing to make these investments. In most cases, SkyTeam appoints a buddy airline (sponsor) that helps the airline meet the SkyTeam requirements. Through this buddy system, new partnership members are introduced to partnership rules and routines, translating into easier integration within the alliance. In addition to the process of becoming a member of SkyTeam, partners must also agree to pay an alliance fee. This fee covers general alliance expenses such as marketing, communication and management costs.

SkyTeam has seen its alliance management structure develop, and a transition was made from a decentralized to a centralized management structure. During the first decade of the alliance, SkyTeam employed a decentralized management structure. Coordination of alliance activities was designated to airline managers. Whereas Oneworld and the Star Alliance opted for a more costly centralized alliance office, SkyTeam was able to economize on overhead costs. Having a limited number of partners, a decentralized management model fulfilled SkyTeam purposes. However, the increased complexity, which was mainly caused by the increased number of partners, increased the need for more centralized control. To this end, a specialized alliance office was established. Acting as an orchestrator, this office was made responsible for managing airline contributions, overall performance, collective decision-making and managing projects and analyses to identify and incorporate potential new partners.

Decision making was formalized by securing a collective competitive advantage and managing the pluralistic interests within SkyTeam. At the strategic level, the governing board consists of the CEOs of each airline, who meet twice a year and discusses general alliance developments and its strategic direction. The potential for new partners to join is also a responsibility of the governing board. Accepting a new partner requires a 'super majority' of 85 per cent, and blocking votes are not allowed. The supervisory board acts as a steering committee and is occupied with more daily affairs within the alliance, and it monitors the activities of the central alliance office. This board meets six times each year and decides on specific projects that will be executed. The alliance office is in charge of the daily monitoring of project execution and reports to the supervisory board. The chair of the alliance office is also the chair of the governing board. The alliance office monitors general airline performance and keeps track of customer complaints. If airlines are not in compliance with SkyTeam standards, the supervisory board discusses measures that will be taken to ensure airline compliance. SkyTeam has an elaborate compensation structure; based on each airline's performance, size and position, that airline receives an appropriate share of the benefits. The alliance office is responsible for maintaining the compensation structures for each airline.

SkyTeam is flourishing. Although the alliance is becoming increasingly complex as a result of its new members and a collective strategy to integrate the partner airlines further to further exploit synergies, recent reorganization of the management structure and the high maturity level of alliance procedures and relational capital have increased the chances that SkyTeam will prosper in the future.

Questions

1. Explain how competition is different in the airline industry for autonomous firms than for groups of firms connected through a multi-partner alliance.
2. Why is free riding a typical exchange hazard for multi-partner alliances? Assess the quality of the measures that SkyTeam took to prevent it.
3. Under what conditions is decentralized or centralized governance more likely to result in superior performance for individual alliance members and the multi-partner alliance?

16

ALLIANCE PORTFOLIOS

A firm may maintain multiple alliance relationships that, together, constitute a firm's alliance portfolio. By extending their focus beyond the management of single alliances to one that incorporates their alliance portfolios, firms gain additional opportunities to enhance their competitive advantage. A central issue then becomes how a firm can generate, configure and develop a high-performing alliance portfolio, as firm performance depends not only on the success or failure of single alliances, but also on the firm's bundle of alliances. To realize portfolio synergies, firms must proactively design and manage the linkages and interdependencies between their partners of different alliances. However, alliance portfolios also tend to increase management complexity, coordination costs and the risk of conflicts. To be able to realize superior portfolio performance, it is important for managers to understand what an alliance portfolio is (first section) and how to design and manage a high-performing alliance portfolio (second section). The next section of this chapter also provides a set of guidelines that explain how alliance portfolio management impacts the governance of single alliances. The chapter concludes with a summary and a case illustration.

The meaning of an alliance portfolio

Firms wishing to successfully implement strategies cannot rely on a single alliance and are increasingly using different kinds of alliances, including contractual alliances, joint ventures and consortia, to improve their competitive advantage. In addition, many firms have established alliances with customers, suppliers, competitors and other kinds of public and private organizations. The way that a focal firm organizes these intertwined relationships has a notable influence on its competitiveness, which means that a goal-oriented alliance portfolio approach could play a decisive role in firm performance (Hoffmann 2007). By adopting an alliance portfolio approach, a firm shifts its focus from single-alliance governance to systematic governance of its bundle of alliances (see Table 16.1). The argument is that firms can benefit from engaging in multiple simultaneous alliances that may not be available if the firm had only one alliance at a given point in time. In other words, the linkages

TABLE 16.1 Examples of alliance portfolios

	Description
Solazyme	Solazyme is a renewable oil and bioproducts company and a leader in industrial biotechnology. Founded in 2003 and headquartered in San Francisco, its technology allows microbes to produce oil and biomaterials in standard fermentation facilities quickly, efficiently and at large scale. To realize its objectives Solazyme depends on multiple, yet complementary, partnerships. Solazyme allies with agribusiness companies such as Bunge, an alliance that started in 2003. Bunge buys, sells, stores and transports oilseeds and grains to serve customers worldwide, processes oilseeds to make protein meal for animal feed and edible oil products for commercial customers and consumers and produces sugar and ethanol from sugarcane. In 2010 they extended the alliance to develop microbe-derived oils utilizing Brazilian sugar cane feedstock. In 2008, Solazyme partnered with Mercedes. Solazyme developed an algae oil-based biodiesel which was road tested using a Mercedes. In 2011, a partnership with Dow Chemical Company was forged to develop bio-based dielectric fluids. Dow signed a letter of intent to use up to 20 million gallons of Solazyme's algal derived oils in 2013 and up to 60 million gallons in 2015.
CPI Card Group	CPI, a global leader in financial, commercial, and identification card production and related services, offers a single source for plastic cards: from foil cards and holograms to translucent and smart cards. CPI's success depends on various intertwined partnerships. CPI forged alliances with distributors such as Keycorp Limited. In 2006, they established an alliance to manufacture MasterCard's PayPass. The issued cards were introduced into McDonald's fast food outlets. In addition, CPI maintains partnerships with security in system companies, such as INSIDE. In 2010, CPI and INSIDE introduced a next-generation, MasterCard-approved payment tag that paves the way for mobile commerce adoption by enabling any mobile device to be used to make payments anywhere using the MasterCard® PayPass™ standard. In 2011, CPI initiated partnerships with NXP Semiconductors and KSW Microtec. KSW Microtec is one of the world's leading suppliers of contactless components for applications such as Access Control and eGovernment, ePayment, eTicketing and Asset Management. NXP Semiconductors is a global semi conductor company and the partnership was forged to broaden CPI's portfolio of contactless offerings and provide customers with expanded contactless technology solutions.

Sources: Algeanews (2011); Grooms (2008); Business Wire (2011a); Energyboom (2011); PR Web (2011); Beer (2006).

and interdependencies between a firm's alliance partners provide additional opportunities for synergy.

Firms build and maintain alliance portfolios for purposes that go beyond those of entering into individual alliances. By pursuing multiple goals through a number of simultaneous alliances, firms mitigate risk and uncertainty and may obtain greater alliance benefits overall (Hoffmann 2007). For example, when suppliers provide complementary offerings, managing proactively the connections between them enables a firm to achieve economies of scale. In addition, whereas single alliances are generally considered critical mechanisms for accessing valuable resources, an alliance portfolio, and thus the simultaneous access to a broad range of valuable resources from different partners, can be an effective means of enhancing a firm's resource endowment (Lavie 2006). For example, synergies occur in an alliance portfolio when partners from different alliances are stimulated to create and exchange knowledge. Furthermore, by drawing on social network perspective, firms can use alliance portfolios to capitalize on information advantages (Parise and Casher 2003). Examples include existing portfolio partners providing valuable information about existing and potential partners. A history of joint collaboration across the portfolio reduces transaction costs and reinforces partners' reputations. Next, alliance portfolios can reinforce firms' internationalization efforts (García-Canal et al. 2002). Having international partners in the alliance portfolio could provide additional benefits, such as access to new resources, information and capabilities, that may not be available from local partners. Multiple simultaneous alliances with different partners can also help firms to create a more substantial experience base with which to accelerate institutionalization of best practices for governing alliances (Anand and Khanna 2000). Thus, a proactive alliance portfolio approach involves the creation of tighter coordination among alliance partners by exploiting interdependencies between them to achieve portfolio synergies.

However, portfolio management is more complex and demanding than governing single alliances (Parise and Casher 2003). Whereas facilitating interdependencies between partners in different alliances presents certain opportunities, it may also constrain a firm's value creation potential because these linkages expose a firm to unique hazards. Any attempt at collaboration between partners from two different alliances with opposing objectives, such as competitors in the same industry, is likely to meet resistance. The firms are probably unwilling to share valuable product, customer and market information, or new business opportunities, for fear that this information would become available to their rival. Similarly, when partners are members of competing networks or promote competing technologies, attempts by any firm to capitalize on interdependencies are most likely to cause conflict and tension. In addition, one single alliance may exhibit such high exclusivity that it prevents a firm from working effectively with other partners. For example, an alliance with a market leader may impede alliances with smaller niche players in the same product space. The partnership with the market leader is most likely to use the majority of the firm's resources, including the time of the dedicated sales force. In turn, the smaller partners may become dissatisfied with their inability to expand the alliance because of the rival partner. Thus, constraining interdependencies lead to distrust, lower transparency and decreased commitment. However, alliance portfolios with constraining interdependencies are not unheard of; a well-formulated alliance approach can curb the negative consequences.

In summary, a portfolio approach is unlike single-alliance governance in that it includes explicitly the design and management that facilitates and constrains interdependencies between partners of different alliances. Firms that embrace an alliance portfolio approach can enhance their competitiveness, as the overall value created by an alliance portfolio with adequate governance is greater than the sum of the values created by each individual alliance in the portfolio (see Box 16.1). However, whereas a proactive alliance portfolio approach involves facilitating interdependencies between partners, constraining interdependencies can undermine the realization of portfolio synergies. Firms can use portfolio design and management to deal effectively with this unique challenge.

BOX 16.1 TOYOTA'S SUPPLIERS' PORTFOLIO

In 1988, Toyota started producing cars in the United States. At this time, Toyota's suppliers had virtually no contact with each other, so Toyota formed the core of a network with bilateral arm's-length supplier relationships. Each party pursued its own individual objectives while maintaining its independence, and relationships were organized through formal contracts, the outcomes of which were determined through power. Toyota faced the challenge of how it could improve efficiency and innovation to respond to shifting customer demands. Over the next few years, Toyota implemented a learning plan consisting of three phases. Phase 1 was to develop weak ties among suppliers. In 1989, Toyota initiated a supplier association (BAMA). Phase 2 was to develop strong ties between the suppliers and Toyota. To this end, the company offered trained consultants to BAMA members at no cost. In Phase 3, to develop strong ties among suppliers, Toyota divided its suppliers into small learning teams. After the completion of its plan, Toyota had built an effective knowledge-sharing network of suppliers consisting of multilateral relationships with strong direct and indirect ties, through which explicit and tacit knowledge was exchanged. Trust between participants governed the relationship through fairness, interdependence and open informal contracts. Toyota's network solution increased its knowledge-sharing by devising methods that would motivate members to share valuable knowledge openly (while preventing undesirable spillovers to competitors), prevent free riders, and reduce the costs associated with finding and accessing different types of valuable knowledge. Toyota's network, which is characterized by a variety of institutionalized routines and a collective identity, facilitates multi-directional knowledge flows among its suppliers.

Sources: Dyer (1996); Dyer and Nobeoka (2000).

Alliance portfolio governance

The issue of alliance portfolio design and management revolves around what type of partners to incorporate in the portfolio and, in connection with this, what type of portfolio management is necessary. A first fundamental task is then formulating a portfolio strategy to the end of a goal-oriented alliance portfolio approach. Essentially, firms can use one of two different alliance portfolio strategies (Hoffmann 2007). First, firms may focus on exploration, which then makes the purpose of an alliance portfolio to acquire new resources and capabilities through alliance relationships. For example, adopting an exploration strategy suggests that alliances are used to develop new technologies, fundamentally improve product lines and develop new service offerings to meet changing customer needs. Second, an exploitation strategy relies on using existing resources efficiently and protecting competitive advantages as much as possible. An alliance portfolio then functions as a vehicle to stabilize the environment, and alliances are used to refine and leverage built-up resources. Firms can also use their alliance portfolios to seek a balance between exploration and exploitation strategies. A portfolio can provide quick and flexible access to different kinds of resources, while also reducing environmental uncertainty by developing long-term stable alliances. The key is not the success or failure of a single alliance, but whether a firm reaches its exploration and/or exploitation objectives by means of its alliance portfolio. Therefore, the design and management of the alliance portfolio is at the centre of interest (see Table 16.2).

TABLE 16.2 Alliance portfolio governance

	Portfolio design	*Portfolio management*
Objective	An efficient portfolio configuration in support of the alliance portfolio strategy	Management of inter-partner linkages between set of alliance partners
Focus	A firm's configuration of intertwined alliances in which facilitating interdependencies are maximized and constraining interdependencies minimized	Capturing portfolio synergies through active management of alliance formation and termination and coordination of inter-partner knowledge and resource flows
Mechanisms	Portfolio size – Large or small portfolios Structural: – Redundancy or non-redundancy Governance – Weak or strong ties Partner – Heterogeneous or homogeneous	Knowledge management – Develop knowledge infrastructure between alliance partners Internal coordination – Orchestration and alignment of internal organization with alliance portfolio

Sources: Parise and Casher (2003); Wassmer (2008).

Alliance portfolio design

The challenge of portfolio design is to configure a set of intertwined alliances in such a way that maximizes portfolio synergies (that is, exploits facilitating inter-dependencies) and minimizes coordination costs (that is, controls constraining interdependencies). An efficient portfolio design determines the quality, quantity and diversity of information and resources to which the focal company has access, the efficiency of getting access to these resources, and the flexibility or stability of the firm's position in the industry (Baum *et al.* 2000). Prior studies on alliance portfolio design have identified various design parameters, including (1) a size dimension, (2) a structural dimension, (3) a governance dimension and (4) a partner dimension (Jiang *et al.* 2010; Wassmer 2008, 2010).

The size dimension pertains to characteristics such as the number of alliances and partners. Some studies, primarily those that have examined entrepreneurial biotechnology firms and technological performance, suggest that larger alliance portfolios are more likely to result in portfolio synergies, such as innovation output rates (Shan *et al.* 1994). However, other studies report that once a firm's alliance portfolio has reached a certain size, any additional alliance will provide diminishing returns. For example, Deeds and Hill (1998) report a curvilinear relationship between the number of alliances held by an entrepreneurial biotechnology firm and the firm's rate of new product development. Contrary to studies that focus solely on portfolio size, this book suggests that portfolio size alone is not a sufficient predictor of portfolio performance and is outweighed by other design parameters.

The structural dimension pertains to the level of redundancy across alliances within the portfolio. Redundancy within an alliance portfolio is the result of a firm collaborating with multiple partners that make similar contributions. The main advantage is that redundancy provides a firm with multiple access points to critical resources, valuable knowledge and information about existing and potential partners. A firm itself is also more visible for firms seeking partnering opportunities (Ahuja 2000). In contrast, an alliance portfolio characterized by non-redundant relationships (that is, where each alliance makes a unique contribution), enables firms to enhance portfolio performance by leveraging and exploiting resources obtained through the few specialized alliances they have. Koka and Prescott (2008) show that, when confronted with a radical change in the environment, an entrepreneurial alliance portfolio (redundant) outperforms both a prominent alliance portfolio (non-redundant) and a hybrid configuration. This suggests that distinct structural configurations can enhance portfolio performance, yet the impact of portfolio structure is likely to be conditioned by other factors, including governance form and partner characteristics (Wassmer 2008).

The governance dimension pertains to the level of commitment, degree of integration and learning of alliances in the portfolio (Jiang *et al.* 2010); this is also referred to as tie strength. Strong ties, such as equity-based arrangements, serve as vehicles for learning and information exchange, as partners are highly inter-connected through reciprocal financial and organizational relationships (Hoffmann 2007). An alliance portfolio comprised of primarily strong ties has a positive effect on a focal firm's innovative capabilities, especially if they are trust-based, knowledge-intensive and reinforced through relationship-specific invest-ments (Capaldo 2007). Alternatively, an alliance portfolio comprised of primarily weak ties, such as non-equity-based arrangements, provides firms with strategic flexibility, as these relationships are more easily established and terminated. Firms that build a homogeneous portfolio of governance forms tend to experience higher performance (Jiang et al. 2010), as repeated experience with a specific governance form often translates into institutionalized knowledge that can be readily applied to future alliances, thereby reducing managerial costs (Sampson 2005). However, a portfolio with primarily strong ties can also have a negative effect on a focal firm's innovative capabilities by stimulating a vicious circle in which a reduced number of contacts, decreased flexibility for collaboration with new partners and diminishing responsiveness to new market trends reinforce each other. Thus, whereas hetero-geneity in governance forms within an alliance portfolio enables a firm to realize multiple objectives simultaneously, homogeneity tends to reduce coordination costs.

The partner dimension refers to partner-related characteristics, including partner industry, organizational characteristics, nationality and functional orientation (Jiang et al. 2010; Wassmer 2010). Because no single firm can possess all of the critical resources required for long-term success, an effective means of achieving a firm's objectives is to ally with partners operating in different industries. Partners from the same industry are often competitors, whose overlapping backgrounds, experiences, knowledge and technological bases may provide learning in the form of imitation and greater absorptive capacity. However, conflicts of interest do exist and learning races can happen, which increases monitoring and safeguarding costs. For example, Lavie (2007) finds that the relative bargaining power of partners in the alliance portfolio constrains the firm's appropriation capacity, especially when many of these partners compete in the focal firm's industry. However, the firm's market performance (e.g. market share) improves with the intensity of competition among partners in its alliance portfolio. In contrast, although collaboration with partners from different industries tends to increase coordination costs, owing to different routines and processes that can make collaboration difficult, it also leads to novel resources, knowledge and information. Like partner diversity within an alliance portfolio, organizational characteristics, nationality and functional orientation all have positive and negative performance implications. Consider functional orientation for example: firms employ a mixture of marketing, manufacturing and distribution alliances to broaden their market reach and enhance value creation, and for further exploitation of core competences; a primary focus on R&D alliances, on the other hand, enables firms to build new capabilities and competences. Thus, variation in partners' characteristic plays a role in determining the benefits and costs that firms derive from their alliance portfolios.

It is clear from the above discussion that each portfolio design parameter associates positively or negatively with (different types of) performance. In addition, we proffer that the portfolio design dimensions combined constitute an alliance portfolio configuration and that a configuration is 'high performing' when it supports an alliance portfolio strategy. More specifically, contrasting exploration and exploitation strategies with distinct portfolio designs leads to two generic implications:

- An exploration strategy is more likely to be effectuated when an alliance portfolio has a set of redundant alliances, primarily weak ties and diverse partner characteristics. The resulting heterogeneity increases the richness of information and resources, broadens search options, improves a firm's ability to develop new capabilities and increase its visibility in the broader industry network, which in turn enhances performance. The downside is that a firm may fall into a learning trap and the coordination costs are very high.
- An exploitation strategy is more likely to be effectuated when an alliance portfolio has a set of non-redundant alliances, strong ties and uniform partner characteristics. The resulting homogeneity enables a firm to build and leverage a specialized resource pool, exploit existing capabilities and react flexibly and quickly to changing circumstances. This may cause a firm to fall into a competence trap, but the coordination costs are relatively low.

The implications outlined above are generic (see Figure 16.1), and firms may seek alternative configurations in support of their objectives. For example, when a firm adopts an exploration strategy but seeks some degree of flexibility in its research efforts, weak ties are preferable to strong ties. However, a firm can replace weak ties with strong ties when more stability is required during the development stage. Alternatively, if an exploitation strategy requires multiple sources of resources, partner diversity is preferable to uniformity.

When seeking a balance between exploration and exploitation strategies, firms may also seek to establish an integrated or hybrid configuration, thereby simultaneously accommodating exploration and exploitation requirements. Alternatively, a firm may use a parallel configuration in which an organization develops two

   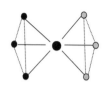   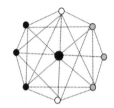

Alliances as stand-alone entities	**Alliance portfolio with exploitation orientation**	**Alliance portfolio with exploration orientation**

·········· Weak tie ——— Strong tie ● Focal firm ○ Actor type A ◐ Actor type B ● Actor type C

FIGURE 16.1   Alliance portfolio configurations

separate portfolio configurations to accommodate exploration and exploitation requirements, respectively. A firm may also use a temporal configuration in which an alliance portfolio is restructured over time to accommodate subsequent exploration and exploitation requirements; for example a portfolio configuration may evolve with a product life cycle.

The configuration of an alliance portfolio is generally not static and may actually change over time through the formation of new alliances and the termination of existing ones. Firms are often forced to change the configuration of their alliance portfolios if they are to improve their competitive position vis-à-vis their rivals in an industry, or simply to secure their competitive advantage. Adding, replacing or removing alliance partners may influence the facilitating and constraining interdependencies within the alliance portfolio. Therefore, instead of adding and removing partners opportunistically, conveniently or randomly, firms should adopt a proactive alliance portfolio approach. For example, a pharmaceutical company may envision a portfolio that consists of research and development alliances with biotech companies during the discovery stage of a drug's product life cycle, but a dramatically different portfolio involving marketing alliances with drug delivery or other pharmaceutical companies during the commercialization stages of the product's life cycle. Whereas an efficient alliance portfolio configuration can provide a firm with the desired synergetic effects, constraining interdependencies will limit willingness to share knowledge, decrease transparency, undermine communication and adversely affect trust building. To overcome these negative repercussions, firms must complement portfolio design with portfolio management.

Alliance portfolio management

Portfolio management pertains to governance of the set of alliances and the linkages between partners. The design and management of single-alliance relationships are critical; however, to secure a competitive advantage, firms must extend single-alliance governance with portfolio management. The two management factors that allow firms to maximize their return on their alliance portfolio are knowledge management and internal coordination (Parise and Casher 2003; Wassmer 2008, 2010).

When managing an alliance portfolio, it is critical to initiate some form of knowledge management targeted at knowledge creation and exchange between partners. The degree to which a firm captures, shares and leverages information and knowledge across its alliance portfolio, as well as the mechanisms it has in place to promote communication among its partners' alliance managers, has a direct effect on its performance. Examples of knowledge practices include designated project teams, a secure extranet, a directory that contains contact details, a virtual team room, joint training and education and a repository with important alliance documents. For example, Dyer and Nobeoka (2000) showed that intentionally facilitating knowledge transfer between Toyota's suppliers increased those companies' commitment to share valuable knowledge, prevented free-riding and reduced the costs associating with finding and accessing knowledge. Thus, knowledge management targeted at knowledge exchange between partners in an alliance portfolio increases awareness of partners' abilities, enables inter-firm knowledge creation and stimulates partner referral. In addition, knowledge management practices may involve intra-firm knowledge sharing, which improves insights in alliance portfolio opportunities as well as professionalism in alliance management. Instruments that can be deployed include the creation of best practices, formal and informal communication structures, the creation of communities of practice and the implementation of IT infrastructure. Knowledge management is important, therefore, as it enables firms to overcome constraining interdependencies by increasing the cohesion between partners in the alliance portfolio, which in turn allows them to exploit facilitating interdependencies.

Managing an alliance portfolio requires the internal coordination of alliance activities, which will enable a firm to orchestrate the linkages between alliance partners. Internal coordination helps firms to align the alliance portfolio strategy with the separate parts of the organization (such as corporate and business units). Most alliances are initiated on an operational level as ad hoc responses to local business issues. A business unit will forge an alliance that serves its own (business unit) objectives, often without realizing the impact this has on other parts of the organization or firm as a whole. This silo-thinking approach could create situations that are not only conflicting, but also costly. For example, when a newly formed alliance overlaps in products and markets with existing partners' businesses, a firm may incur not only increased conflict resolution costs, but may also have to bear the consequences associated with dissolving preexisting alliances. Communication structures and information exchange between managers operating at different levels and businesses allows managers to keep up to date with latest developments in strategy and adapt their alliances accordingly. Managers become informed about alliance initiatives outside their responsibility, which reduces the risk of forging alliances that undermine portfolio performance. Internal coordination also involves a systematic approach to defining and measuring portfolio performance. In addition to metrics that capture the performance of single alliances, a performance metric system should include measures of the entire portfolio's performance. Although alliance metrics may indicate that a single alliance generates superior performance, portfolio metrics may reveal that it undermines portfolio performance. Taken together, internal coordination provides a holistic approach to a firm's set of alliances, which enables the firm to identify and resolve opportunities and threats within the alliance portfolio. Some firms may establish a separate department to coordinate all these alliance-related activities.

Alliance portfolio: Decision-making steps

A traditional perspective considers alliances as isolated transactions. However, firms that adopt an alliance portfolio approach create new opportunities to improve their competitive advantage. Many firms' alliance portfolios are configured and managed inefficiently, and often represent nothing more than a random mix of strategic alliances that sometimes even have conflicting demands. In contrast, managers in firms with high-performing alliance portfolios visualize their portfolio in the context of the entire network, rather than as a series of single partnerships. These managers have a holistic visualization of the possible interdependencies among (potential) partners, which broadens their range of strategic actions. The next section connects alliance portfolio thinking to the stages of the alliance development framework depicted in Figure 16.2 in order to provide insights into the efficient governance of single alliances in light of the broader alliance portfolio.

Step 1: Alliance strategy formulation

Before managers decide which governance mode (make, ally or buy) suits their objectives, an alliance portfolio approach helps them assess the extent to which an

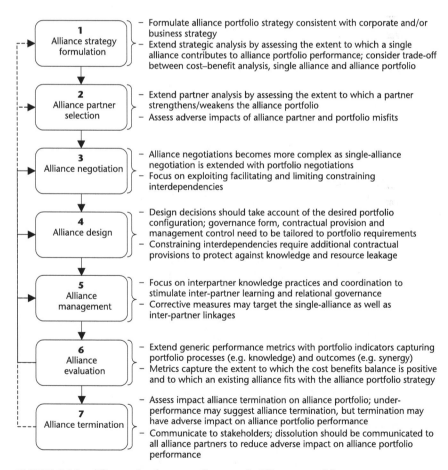

FIGURE 16.2 Alliance development framework: Alliance portfolio

alliance will strengthen the alliance portfolio (that is, facilitate interdependencies) or weaken it (that is, constrain interdependencies). Taking the alliance portfolio as a departure point, a clear alliance portfolio strategy that is consistent with a firm's corporate and/or business strategy will enable managers to determine the preferred portfolio configuration. Periodic scenario-planning exercises can be a useful tool for analysing the effects of adding, removing and replacing specific alliance partners in the alliance portfolio. Communicating the portfolio strategy across business units increases transparency and allows expectations to be managed accordingly. Managers will understand the changes being made in portfolio composition, as they will fit the portfolio strategy that has been communicated. By incorporating a portfolio approach (that is, considering the linkages between partners) in the strategic analysis, firms become aware of synergies and constraints among multiple alliance partners, which in turn inform their governance mode decision-making. That is, they understand the degree to which an alliance depicts an alternative that is preferable to internalization or market exchange.

Step 2: Alliance partner selection

Partner fit is critical when selecting a new partner. However, firms must be aware that the positive implications of good partner fit could be offset if that partner creates constraining interdependencies in the alliance portfolio. For example, although a firm and a potential partner may serve distinct markets indicative of resource complementarity, the preferred partner may possess market overlap with an existing partner in the alliance portfolio. This new partnership is therefore likely to create conflicts, as the existing partner may start to decline to share resources and knowledge. A firm that wishes to be aware of such adverse consequences asks the following questions during the partner selection phase, in addition to generic partner selection criteria:

*   To what extent does a potential partner reinforce an exploration or exploitation portfolio strategy? The firm assesses whether the intended alliance needs to be integrated in the alliance portfolio or whether it can be considered as a stand-alone alliance.
*   To what extent does a potential partner create facilitating interdependencies (that is, synergy) in the alliance portfolio? The firm assesses the extent to which existing partners and the potential partner are part of the same collaborative network, provide complementary offerings, promote similar standards or infrastructure, are willing to learn from each other and view the presence of other partners in the portfolio as a way to mitigate risks.
*   To what extent does a potential alliance partner create constraining interdependencies (that is, conflicts) in the alliance portfolio? The firm assesses the extent to which existing partners and the potential partner are members of competing collaborative networks, are strong rivals in an industry, promote competing technologies or infrastructures, and create conflict as one alliance

relationship becomes so exclusive that it prevents the firm from working effectively with the new partner (or vice versa).

• The firm compares the results of the assessments. What are the potential benefits and costs of this potential partner from a portfolio perspective? If the benefits are higher than the costs, the firm then proceeds with the alliance. If the costs are higher than the benefits, continuation depends on the cost–benefit analysis of the single alliance.

Step 3: Alliance negotiation

During the alliance negotiation stage, negotiators seek agreement on the initial alliance conditions, including topics such as compensation, contribution and coordination. By embracing an alliance portfolio approach, however, single-alliance negotiation strategies tend to become more complex, as a firm is confronted with multiple trade-offs (e.g. knowledge exchange and protection) that can be resolved by using integrative and distributive negotiation strategies interchangeably. Furthermore, the negotiation bandwidth is extended, as a firm's total value creation potential comprises the value of the single alliance and the value derived from this single alliance's embeddedness in the alliance portfolio. Transparency and openness are critical, as potential partners must understand that part of their value is generated through collaboration with other alliance partners. Awareness of potential facilitating and constraining interdependencies may also affect the negotiation process and outcomes. For example, whereas jointly identifying and discussing opportunities to create portfolio synergies creates a constructive dialogue, attempts to resolve a partner's conflicting interests with other partners may result in resistance, conflict and tension. Therefore, alliance negotiations must centre on both the alliance and the alliance portfolio.

Step 4: Alliance design

Against the background of facilitating and constraining interdependencies, managers should design alliances in such a way that maximizes potential portfolio synergy and minimizes additional governance costs. To this end, the generic guidelines for alliance design are extended with guidelines that follow from an alliance portfolio approach. If an alliance is forged to support an exploration strategy, an equity-based arrangement is preferred in order to support knowledge transfer, such that the learning from one alliance or partner can be applied to other alliances. In contrast, if an alliance is forged to support an exploitation strategy, a non-equity-based arrangement is preferred to support flexibility. In addition, an alliance design may include provisions that specify how and when a partner will collaborate with other partners in a firm's portfolio. For example, there may be a clause stating the circumstances under which partners will exchange product information and specifications. However, constraining interdependencies (such as competitors) will necessitate additional contractual provisions to protect against knowledge and resource leakage. Furthermore, an alliance design may stipulate the nature and content of knowledge management practices.

Step 5: Alliance management

During the alliance management stage, managers focus on the day-to-day operations that enable them to realize the alliance's value creation potential. In addition to stimulating inter-firm learning, resolving conflicts and initiating appropriate responses to challenges, managers must pay attention to the management of inter-firm linkages. For example, Microsoft, IBM and Oracle all provide some type of infrastructure (for example, research centres, testing facilities, training, online communities) to support knowledge exchange between developer partners. Another critical task is to build relational capital between portfolio partners. This facilitates knowledge exchange, functions as a safeguard against misappropriation and reduces the risk of opportunism. In addition, managers can fulfil the role of mediator if conflicts emerge between their alliance partners. Furthermore, based on performance assessment, managers may initiate modifications in order to enhance the performance of a single alliance as well as the portfolio.

Step 6: Alliance evaluation

Defining and measuring performance objectives for a single alliance can be a challenge for many firms. However, by adopting an alliance portfolio approach, the performance metric system should be supplemented by metrics that capture portfolio process and outcomes. For example, it is informative to look for patterns of high or low performance across alliances, which can expose areas of strength or weakness in the alliance portfolio. In addition, portfolio metrics ideally capture portfolio synergies including learning, financial, strategic and coordination costs pertaining to contracting, monitoring and safeguarding. A comprehensive performance metric system including milestones that allow partners to evaluate and track alliance and portfolio performance easily enables managers to intervene immediately if expectations are not met.

Step 7: Alliance termination

An alliance portfolio approach complicates alliance termination. Consistent with generic guidelines, under-performance of a single alliance may prompt premature termination. However, the dissolution of a single alliance may adversely impact portfolio performance, which suggests that a termination decision should be postponed until the negative repercussions have been resolved appropriately. For example, a partner may provide critical knowledge to other high-performing partners. In this case, the provision of knowledge needs to be secured before dissolving the relationship. If the termination trajectory is continued, firms need to communicate the termination to other partners in the portfolio in a timely manner if they are to avoid damaging their own reputations.

Summary

Driven by the proliferation and increasing diversity of alliances, firms that embrace an alliance portfolio approach often find themselves in a tangled web of interdependent alliances. Whereas governance of single alliances can be challenging, governance of the partners embedded in an alliance portfolio that encompasses multiple alliance relationships tends to be more complex and demanding. A proactive alliance portfolio approach enables firms to exploit interdependencies between partners and generate synergies beyond what would have been possible through single alliances. However, these interdependencies may also constrain a firm's ability to create portfolio synergies, as some partners are unwilling to collaborate with other partners under certain circumstances. Firms can resolve this situation through efficient alliance portfolio design and active portfolio management. In other words, an alliance portfolio can enhance a firm's competitive advantage only when the portfolio design fits with the portfolio strategy and is supported by portfolio management.

Case: General Electric

General Electric[1] (GE) is a diversified infrastructure, finance and media company. From aircraft engines and power generation to financial services, health care solutions, and television programming, GE operates in more than 100 countries and employs about 300,000 people worldwide. One of the company's business units, GE Energy, serves the energy sector by developing and deploying technology that helps make efficient use of natural resources. With nearly 85,000 global employees and revenues of $37 billion in 2009, GE Energy is one of the world's leading suppliers of power generation and energy delivery technologies. The businesses that comprise GE Energy (GE Power and Water, GE Energy Services and GE Oil and Gas) work together to provide integrated product and service solutions in all areas of the energy industry, including coal, oil, natural gas and nuclear energy; renewable resources such as water, wind, solar and biogas; and other alternative fuels. Collaboration with a variety of partners is an important building block in GE Energy's long-term growth strategy. Some of GE Energy's alliance initiatives in 2010–2011 are outlined below.

GE Energy has built on its growing technology presence in China's thriving chemical production industry by signing new agreements to license its gasification technology to five Chinese companies, for a variety of applications. The licence agreements grant customers the right to utilize GE's proprietary gasification technology, which converts coal and other carbon-based fuels into synthesis gas (syngas) for use in chemical production and other applications. GE's gasification technology is one of the most widely applied technologies of its kind in China, with more than 40 licensed facilities.

GE Energy signed a service alliance with the Tennessee Valley Authority (TVA), the largest public power provider in the United States, which covers four TVA power plants and is valued at $116 million over the next five years. The alliance helps the TVA meet its strategic needs by ensuring the long-term reliability, efficiency and cost-effective operation of its power generation equipment. Under the agreement, GE will provide a core team that offers on-site expertise and experience at the various plant locations to help TVA manage outages and respond quickly to specific project requirements.

GE has signed a cooperation agreement with Norwegian energy companies Statoil and Lyse to carry out technical and environmental feasibility studies jointly regarding the construction of an offshore wind demonstration project in Rogaland County, off the southwest coast of Norway. The agreement includes the installation of up to four 4.0-megawatt offshore, direct-drive wind turbines. Subject to successful completion of the feasibility studies and the appropriate investment and funding decisions, the installation of the wind turbines will start in 2012.

GE and Indian-based Ramky signed emergency water and industrial wastewater treatment agreements designed to address India's industrial wastewater treatment and recycling needs. Such water reuse initiatives can play a major role in helping improve overall water supplies in areas where water issues are critical, such as India. The agreement involves Ramky using GE's industry-leading ultra filtration (UF) and membrane bioreactor (MBR) technology for wastewater treatment and recycling in India's industrial sector. Ramky and GE will also bring the innovative concept of mobile water treatment plants to the Indian water sector.

GE Energy and wind energy developer Iberwind Group SA have signed a 10-year operational and maintenance (O&M) services agreement to cover two Iberwind wind farms in Portugal. Following a complete service agreement for the units that begun in 2005, Iberwind chose to continue using GE as its preferred service provider for the next 10 years. Working closely with Iberwind, GE has customized a complete service programme that will offer Iberwind operational and maintenance support, technology and engineering expertise, and GE Energy will deliver parts to support corrective maintenance activities.

An $18 million outsourcing agreement and facility upgrade for Yara S.p.A.'s Ferrara (Italy) plant with industrial water treatment leader GE Energy has helped Yara meet increasing customer demands. The Ferrara plant supplies ammonia and urea liquids fertilizers to agricultural markets. While production of these products requires large amounts of clean water, the plant must rely on brackish, low-quality surface water sources. Yara outsourced its Ferrara water treatment operations to GE in 2005 to reduce costs, increase reliability and focus on its main businesses. With the recent contract expansion, GE will continue to build, own and operate the water treatment plant with onsite GE personnel until 2020. The facility currently produces up to 320 m^3/hr of demineralized water using two proprietary GE technologies: brackish water reverse osmosis filtration (BWRO) and electro-deionization (EDI).

GE Energy also participates in the Smart Energy Alliance (SEA). The SEA was created in February 2006 to focus on solution development, field services engagement and industry marketing around a business vision of 'next-generation' distribution based on a services-oriented enterprise and a technological vision of open, standards-based solutions. The SEA combines the industry strengths of Capgemini, Cisco Systems, GE Energy, Hewlett-Packard, Intel and Oracle to help utilities transform their transmission and distribution operations. Using a flexible, modular framework, the SEA's open collaboration model delivers innovative solutions that leverage extensive industry expertise, technology leadership and complementary capabilities to help customers achieve greater productivity and profitability.

Questions

1. Given GE Energy's objective to build and maintain a competitive advantage in the global energy industry, what are the important considerations in designing and improving GE Energy's alliance portfolio?
2. What portfolio management initiatives can GE Energy develop to ensure inter-firm learning and coordination between its alliance partners?

17

ALLIANCE NETWORKS

The network view on alliances states that firms are embedded in a set of inter-firm linkages between multiple parties. Whereas alliance portfolios only consider the set of direct relationships between a firm and its partners, alliance networks also involve indirect relationships: the set of relationships between a firm and third parties intermediated by the firm's alliance partners. An alliance network functions as a repository of knowledge, resources and information, and can potentially enhance a firm's competitive advantage. However, an alliance network also involves (social) obligations, interdependencies and lock-in effects, which threaten a firm's autonomy and control. Therefore, from the perspective of a focal firm, an alliance network increases management complexity and coordination costs. The extent to which network benefits outweigh costs depends on a firm's strategic intent, its position in the alliance network and its ability to influence network processes and outcomes. As the opening two sections of this chapter explain, this cost–benefit balance makes it critical to understand the nature of alliance networks, as well as the role of a firm's network position and how a firm can leverage its position to its advantage. Taking the alliance network view as a reference point, the third section also presents managerial guidelines, and concludes with a summary and a case illustration.

The meaning of an alliance network

An alliance network view comprises a firm's direct alliances and its indirect relationships (see Table 17.1). Whereas a direct relationship entails a single alliance between partners, an indirect relationship connects two parties (such as firms) through a third party. For example, a supplier alliance directly connects a manufacturer to a supplier, but the supplier can also be indirectly connected to a manufacturer's wholesaler if the manufacturer and the wholesaler are connected through an alliance of their own. According to alliance network logic, despite the

TABLE 17.1 Examples of alliance networks

Focal firm	Description	Network type*
General Motors	General Motors is organized through internal market units, each of which is expected to have expertise in an area related to an automotive system and be able to sell its products on the open market.	**Internal market network** with interdependent profit centres; compliance with firm policies and collaborative culture.
Nike	Nike's core competence is the design of sport shoes and equipment. It maintains an extensive network of suppliers and retailers, which enables it to reduce manufacturing costs and respond flexibly to customer demands.	**Vertical market network** with independent organizations; upstream suppliers and downstream distributors around one company (integrator).
Toshiba	Toshiba is a diversified manufacturer and marketer consisting of more than 200 companies, 600 'grandchild' companies, and numerous direct and indirect exchange relationships across markets, products, and countries.	**Inter-market network** with independent organizations; institutionalized affiliation among firms in unrelated industries and linked in vertical direct and indirect relationships.
Tata Group	The Tata Group is a conglomerate operating in a wide range of industries, such as consumer products, steel, services and embedded in a large network of direct and indirect exchange relationships.	**Opportunity network** with independent organizations; organized around a central broker and temporal productions and services to execute particular projects.

*Taking a focal firm as reference point, firms can participate in different types of alliance networks
Source: Achrol (1997).

lack of a formal partnership between the supplier and the wholesaler, all three firms may possess relevant technologies, knowledge and/or expertise that could be beneficial to all of them. Essentially, these relationships could take multiple forms, such as informal relationships (for example, regular meetings at professional associations) and formal relationships (such as supplier alliances). However, to stay consistent with the scope of this book, the focus here is on alliance relationships.

An alliance network can enhance a firm's competitive advantage, as its set of direct relationships provides access to a pool of resources that might not otherwise be easily available (Gulati 1998), including financial capital, research and development facilities, and human resources. The network also functions as a source of valuable information through its indirect relationships, by means of referrals, contacts, and knowledge and reputational spillovers (Baum *et al.* 2000). Firms can use this access to resources and information to compete more effectively, to access markets with high entry barriers, to lower their reliance on others, to create innovative products and services, to realize economies of scale and scope and to obtain legitimization. An alliance network also provides a firm with strategic manoeuvrability (Powell 1990). It represents a more efficient form of governance than hierarchies and markets, particularly in uncertain and competitive environments, as it allows a firm to be more flexible and enhance its control over external parties. For example, an alliance network enriches a firm's repertoire of strategic actions, as it provides managers with greater access to industrial intelligence and other types of information than they would generate operating autonomously. Moreover, an alliance network reduces behavioural uncertainty concerning a firm's network partners. Although not all network partners are formally connected through an alliance, the presence of indirect relationships may promote solidarity and collective norms regarding how to operate within an alliance network.

However, alliance networks also present firms with risks and hazards (Gulati and Gargiulo 1999). First, the exchange of resources, information and knowledge in an alliance network often entails obligations for future transactions, as network members may expect receiving firms to reciprocate their efforts. Expected obligations from network partners, as well as the resulting costs for switching to other partners, could cause a firm to be locked-in, which hinders the firm's strategic manoeuvrability. Second, an alliance network creates interdependencies between network members, which reduces their autonomy and therefore constrains their decision making. A firm whose partners have extensive control of key resources cannot exclude those partners from its alliance network without jeopardizing access to those resources; this is a resource constraint that enhances the partners' power over the firm. As other parties in an alliance network obtain more power, concerns also arise over the extent to which value is equally and equitably distributed. Third, firms that are not part of the core of an alliance network may not receive new information or may receive it too late, and may be subject to blind-spot biases. For example, when technological changes occur frequently in an industry, access to new and/or different types of information becomes critical. Consequently, firms that are disconnected from the alliance network are at a considerable disadvantage.

In summary, an alliance network can provide a firm with substantial benefits. However, it also brings a degree of managerial complexity that extends beyond the governance of single alliances and alliance portfolios. The challenge for one firm participating in an alliance network is to capture network benefits while curbing the negative implications of alliance networks. This requires a holistic approach that encompasses an understanding of the effectiveness of a firm's position in an alliance network and the degree to which a firm can exercise influence over network processes and outcomes.

Alliance network governance

The governance of alliance networks (from a focal firm perspective) is more complex than the governance of single alliances and alliance portfolios, owing to the greater

TABLE 17.2 Alliance network governance

	Network position	Network management
Objective	Achieve a position in the alliance network in support of a firm's strategic intent	Capitalize on network position and execute network functions and roles
Approach	Support exploration intent with a closure position; support exploitation intent with a structural hole position; or reconcile strategic intents via temporal separation, structural separation or parallel configuration	Engage in framing, activating, mobilizing, and/or synthesizing functions supported by network management roles, including information-broker, coordinator, relationship broker and network structuring agent
Concern	Trade-off between strengths and weaknesses of network position	Trade-off between costs and benefits of network management

Sources: Burt (1982); Coleman (1990); Jarvensivu and Moller (2009).

number of direct and indirect relationships to be considered. Nevertheless, as with alliance portfolio governance, firms can control their network position in light of their network strategy and initiate corrective actions by creating, changing and maintaining their set of alliances (see Table 17.2).

Alliance network position

A firm's network position refers to the number and pattern of structural linkages between a firm and other parties in a network (Gulati and Gargiulo 1999). Prior studies have assessed a firm's network position by focusing on the structural configuration of an alliance network; their key argument was that a firm's position influences its resources and information availability, as well as how much control a firm has over resource flows in the network (Yli-Renko and Autio 1998). An alliance network view extends beyond an alliance portfolio view (also referred to as an egocentric alliance network) by encompassing indirect relationships. Consequently, the alliance portfolio design parameters can be extended to include indirect relationships in order to explain the relationship between a firm's network position and its performance.

The size dimension pertains to the boundary of the alliance network. Academic studies often set this boundary arbitrarily, which implies that their results need to be interpreted with caution (Scott 2000). The key advantage of larger networks is that they tend to improve a firm's innovative performance, as partners within an alliance network can align resources and information more easily, while created knowledge becomes more easily available to all partners. However, it is also more difficult for a firm to influence resource and information flows in a larger network because of its greater complexity. The partner dimension pertains to partner characteristics within the alliance network, including the partner's industries, functional orientation, and countries of origin. The greater the partner diversity in an alliance network (e.g. different kinds of resources, information, technologies, etc.), the better the access a firm generates to more sources of critical resources (Yli-Renko and Autio 1998). However, indirect relationships mean that firms have less control over the adverse impact of constraining interdependencies, or are less able to leverage facilitating interdependencies than they would be in an alliance portfolio. The governance (or relational) dimension pertains to the strength of the relationship (Granovetter 1973). From an alliance network point of view, strong ties (e.g. equity based) suggest that a firm is embedded in a web of highly integrated direct and indirect relationships. The reciprocal nature of these relationships means that information flows easily through the alliance network. However, whereas partners may initially supply novel information, their contributions may become known over time, thereby reducing the benefits of strong ties. In contrast, weak ties (e.g. non-equity based) suggest that a firm is connected loosely to the other firms in the alliance network. Although the distribution of information is less predictable, weak ties are better suited to the rapid diffusion of new ideas between a variety of parties. The structural dimension pertains to the level of redundancy (that is, overlap) between direct and indirect relationships within an alliance network. To capture redundancy in an alliance network, multiple parameters have been identified. However, it is beyond the scope of this book to discuss them all; therefore, the two prominent parameters in the alliance network literature that are discussed are (1) density and (2) centrality.

Network density (or closure) refers to the extent to which firms in an alliance network are directly connected, as opposed to being connected through a series of indirect relationships (Coleman 1990). Density tends to make inter-party interactions observable to others because those parties have known and common contacts, which increases their willingness to share information freely amongst each other. Firms participating in a dense alliance network can rely on relational norms to promote collaboration and social sanctions (that is, negative reputation) to reduce opportunism. Consequently, network density enhances a firm's performance because it reduces monitoring costs, spreads risk and encourages collective risk-taking. It also enhances reputation, facilitates rapid dissemination of information, improves direct access to resources and facilitates collaboration between network members. However, the fact that partners in the network have similar expectations means that a dense network also decreases a firm's flexibility. For example, social obligations and operating rules may constrain a firm from forging new alliances outside the network.

Network centrality is the relative proximity of firms to the core of the alliance network's inter-firm linkages (Coleman 1990) and is regarded as a measure of network power. A central position in a network is a strategic location, because it enables a firm to exercise influence over resource flows and the diffusion of information. For example, obtaining some control over network processes and outcomes provides a firm with preferential access to resources, such as market information, customer information and technological developments. A case in point is Super Bakery, a food service broker that maintains control over its order-filling cycle, not by direct supervision of the work of the contractors, but by maintaining control over communication with its customers and serving as a communications and coordination centre for the contractors (Williams 2005). Consequently, network centrality enhances a firm's performance because it provides a firm with control over resource and information flows.

When the network dimensions are considered together, it follows that a firm can occupy different network positions, each of which enables the firm to acquire different types of network benefits (Ahuja 2000). This heterogeneity in various network positions also indicates that a network position is only beneficial to a firm when it is aligned with the firm's strategy. The next section draws on two prominent views on alliance networks, those of Burt (1982) and Coleman (1990), to present two prototypical network positions that, respectively, support a firm's exploitation and exploration intents (see Figure 17.1).

In terms of a firm's exploitation intent, favourable outcomes (that is, performance) stem from occupying a structural hole position in an alliance network that is characterized by centrality, relatively few strong direct and indirect relationships, non-redundant relationships and partner homogeneity. A structural hole position suggests that a firm functions as a broker between two otherwise disconnected groups of intertwined parties. Although the two disconnected groups that are connected by a broker are not necessarily unaware of one another, information, resources and knowledge are exchanged through the intermediate firm. Because different information flows within each group, a broker firm has the opportunity to control exchanges between the groups providing it with informational advantages. For example, brokers have the advantage of being able to bring together disconnected firms, which provides them with an opportunity to determine whose interests are served and when contact is established. The structural hole position is best suited

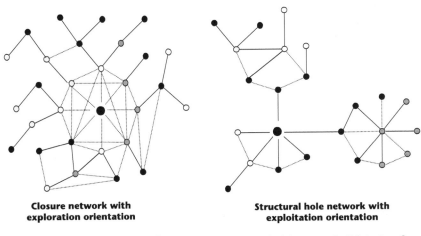

**Closure network with
exploration orientation**

**Structural hole network with
exploitation orientation**

·········· Weak tie ——— Strong tie ● Focal firm ○ Actor type A ◎ Actor type B ● Actor type C

FIGURE 17.1 Alliance network configurations

to an exploitation strategy, as it enables a firm to organize the flow of resources in an efficient manner. That is a broker's function in an alliance network supports the exploitation of existing resource endowments to reduce variety, increase stability and enhance performance. For ease of coordination, a firm will also preferably occupy a prominent position in the centre of the alliance network.

In terms of a firm's exploration intent, favourable outcomes (that is, innovation) stem from the firm's closure position in an alliance network that is characterized by density, multiple weak direct and indirect relationships, redundant relationships and a high diversity of partners. Closure suggests that a firm is embedded in a network of highly coupled, yet loosely coupled, interconnected parties. Closure provides a firm with informational advantages, as it possesses access to multiple sources increasing reliability, timing and early acquisition of information. In addition, network parties tend to interact based on a set of relational norms, which stimulates collaborative behaviour. These network characteristics best suit an exploration strategy. This is because a firm in a network position that is loosely connected to a variety of parties with diverse organizational backgrounds and resources is well positioned to develop new knowledge, see new opportunities and create those capabilities necessary for survival. Furthermore, the rapid diffusion of information in closure networks, and diversity in the cognitive focus of network partners, reinforces innovation. The openness in a closure network also reduces the risk of uneven distribution of network outcomes. For example, closure offers protection against misappropriation, because a firm and its counterparts are better able to act together against a party that violates relational norms and conduct.

The closure and structural hole positions depict two prototypical network positions. As exploitation and exploration can be considered opposing strategies, a firm may seek to obtain either a closure or structural hole position. However, high-performing firms tend to reconcile exploration and exploitation intents, which requires them to adjust their network position accordingly. Despite the absence of any universal prescriptions, the following three implications can be offered, building on the logic that the optimal network position of a firm is contingent on its strategic intent:

- A firm may alternate between exploration and exploitation intents over time, suggesting that its network position also needs to be adapted. A focus on exploration requires a closure network to obtain informational benefits, whereas a focus on exploitation requires a structural hole network to obtain resource benefits. By entering and exiting alliances, a firm can change its network position over time in accordance with its strategic focus.
- A firm may seek to realize its exploration and exploitation intents concurrently, suggesting that its network position needs to accommodate both strategic intents at the same time. Although the closure and the structural hole views on alliance networks have opposing implications, a firm may attempt to configure a position that combines both perspectives.

- A firm may accommodate both strategic intents by separating the organization into two 'parts', each of which pursues its own strategy. For example, by dividing research and development and production into two different business units, the R&D business unit with a focus on exploration may benefit from a closure position, whereas the production business unit with a focus on exploitation may benefit from a structural hole position.

Network management

Firms engage in network management in order to attain and support their position in an alliance network (McGuire 2002). Network management involves restructuring the existing network and improving the conditions of cooperation within the existing structure. Whereas restructuring involves adding or removing alliances, improving the conditions of cooperation involves various network activities to facilitate cooperation between network partners. However, there is a degree of controversy regarding the extent to which alliance networks can be intentionally managed (Jarvensivu and Moller 2009). On one hand, building on the logic that alliance networks constitute a source of a firm's competitive advantage, one view suggests that firms can and should manage an alliance network actively and purposefully. On the other hand, another view indicates that, from a focal firm's perspective, alliance networks are surrounded by uncertainty, as firms cannot manage the behaviour of other parties in the network. The position of this book is that although firms can manage their direct alliance relationships and their alliance portfolios, they can at best, and only to a certain degree, influence network processes and outcomes. To realize network management, we suggest that a firm must fulfil the four functions described below and take on associated network management roles (Jarvensivu and Moller 2009; Knight and Harland 2005).

Framing entails a firm's attempts to influence the roles that each participant may play at any given time, and perceptions about the common purpose of the alliance network. Separate missions, distinct constituencies and competition for resources in alliance networks make it increasingly difficult to achieve some form of overall coordination. A firm may set an agenda and develop initiatives to support joint value creation in an alliance network. Its task is then to create awareness about the agenda and plans among key participants within the alliance network. In order for parties to collaborate and not compete, they should recognize the complementarity of their needs and have mutually understood definitions of the issues to be addressed. To this end, a firm may adopt the role of an information broker, which means that it gathers, analyses and disseminates information to various parties in the network; sometimes this is in response to a request, but it is usually done proactively. A firm may seek to establish an identity and culture for the alliance network, even if it is temporary. Collective sense making helps to develop a working structure for the network, and aligns the perceptions of participants without mechanisms based on authority relations. An alliance network does not need to have completely aligned goals in order to create value, but a certain level of shared planning is required among at least some of the networked actors. If actors believe that they can achieve greater value as network members, then they may be willing to share part of their autonomy to the network and operate like a quasi-organization.

Activating involves identifying potential network participants and assessing the extent to which their skills, knowledge and resources improve network performance. It also includes the process of structuring the alliance network. Building on the overall network objectives, required partners, resources and activities are identified and an attempt is made to install some form of coordination. For example, a firm may fulfil a coordinator role and engage in activities like facilitating inter-partner activities, bringing together representatives of the different firms and facilitating communication and other network practices. A firm can organize meetings between all relevant network participants in order to align perceptions and strengthen linkages. Coordination in alliance networks is maintained increasingly through informal open-ended contracts rather than hierarchical control and authority. Thus, the interactions between network members are neither random nor uniform, but patterned so that they engage in a complicated dance of mutual alignment and adjustment.

Mobilizing involves building commitment among parties in an alliance network to carry out the necessary activities. This is a common and ongoing task for achieving network outcomes. A firm may fulfil the role of advisor, which involves advising parties in the network on various topics, such as policies and alliance activities. In addition, a firm may act as a relationship broker, attempting to initiate and facilitate new alliances between different parties in order to create new opportunities and, if needed, it may mediate in conflicts. In addition, a firm acting as an innovation sponsor tries to mobilize organizations in the network to innovate, with the goal of motivating and stimulating parties to recognize new opportunities for innovation and facilitate potential alliances.

Synthesizing relates to organizing and controlling, and involves creating conditions for productive interaction while preventing, minimizing and removing obstacles to collaboration. The activities are carried out so as to produce effective and efficient network outcomes vis-à-vis expectations. If this does not occur, corrective measures are taken to improve the alliance network. Synthesizing entails facilitating and furthering interaction and facilitating linkages among participants, and reducing complexity and uncertainty by promoting information exchange. For example, a firm may fulfil the role of a network-structuring agent, which monitors and influences the structure of alliance relationships. In this role, a firm may focus on such areas as restructuring the alliance network by initiating new alliances, seeking ways to reduce the costs of resource exchange and enforcing protection mechanisms against misappropriation. The objective is to achieve cooperation among actors while minimizing and removing informational and interactional blockages to the cooperation. This steering of network processes is inherently difficult, in that the result of the network process is derived from the interaction between the strategies of all actors involved.

The way in which a firm can fulfil these management functions depends partially on the intent and structural configuration of an alliance network (Jarvensivu and Moller 2009). First, while some alliance networks are based on more emergent cooperation, others are based on a more deliberately set strategic intent. In emergent alliance networks, management tasks tend to be characterized by ongoing negotiation and renegotiation, adaptation, and re-adaptation. In contrast, alliance networks with a few strong players are more likely to set clear strategies based on the strategy of these players, which means that coordination is more likely to be imposed on other network participants. Second, the distribution of power in an alliance network (that is, centrality) impacts a firm's ability to influence network processes and outcomes. As a firm occupies a central position in an alliance network, it may adopt a more power-driven, hierarchical-type managing style. In contrast, a firm with low centrality must adopt more subtle negotiation approaches. Third, the density of inter-partner linkages affects how well network participants are able to make sense of the current, potential and future partners in their alliance network. High density suggests that network partners frequently interact, which requires less managerial effort to negotiate the framing of the network and allows efforts to focus on activating, mobilizing and synthesizing the network. In contrast, low density indicates that network partners are more distant, which demands more effort to align parties' perceptions and interests.

Alliance network: Decision-making steps

Many firms are unaware of their network positions, let alone the fact that they engage intentionally in network management activities. In contrast, high-performing firms tend to recognize the importance of their alliance networks and consider the formation and management of single alliances in the context of the entire alliance network. Their holistic visualization of the alliance network broadens their range of strategic actions. This section connects the stages of the alliance development framework to an alliance network view (see Figure 17.2), in order to provide insights into the efficient governance of single alliances in an alliance network.

Step 1: Alliance strategy formulation

The decision to establish an alliance is not only influenced by strategic, resource-led and economic imperatives, but also by how a firm is embedded in an alliance network. In addition to generic guidelines, a governance mode decision should thus also incorporate the extent to which certain governance modes help to align a firm's strategic intent to its network position. Where market exchange and internal development are unlikely to affect a firm's network position, mergers and acquisitions and alliances may. For example, merging with a prominent party in the alliance network may enhance a firm's centrality, whereas acquiring a competitor may create a structural hole position. Similarly, entering (or exiting) an alliance

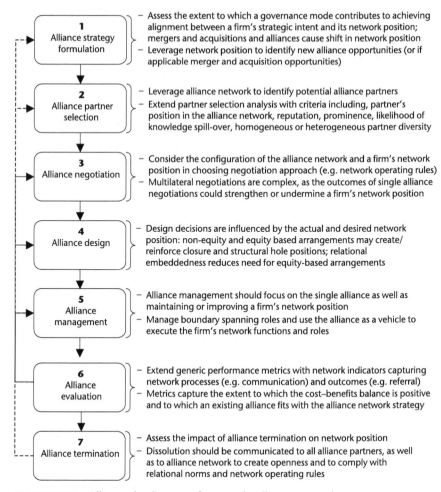

FIGURE 17.2 Alliance development framework: Alliance network

causes a shift in a firm's network position from closure to structural hole and vice versa.

In addition, the firm's position in an alliance network either helps or hinders its identification of new opportunities. For example, through its indirect relationships, a firm receives information about potential alliance partners (or merger and acquisition targets), which may affect its ability to forge viable alliances. A network position may also constrain the extent to which potential partners are aware of potential partner firms, thereby limiting its set of choices. For example, informational advantages tend to enable firms with more central and prominent network positions to establish more new alliances, and to do so with greater frequency. As the available information grows, firms seeking to forge alliances become less reliant on external conditions and more influenced by the alliance network in which they are embedded.

Step 2: Alliance partner selection

An alliance network can reduce what it costs a firm to find and select partners. Through indirect relationships, an alliance network may provide a firm with information about the availability and reliability of potential partners. Moreover, alliance network partners may have a certain status and reputation, which makes them more attractive as partners. Specifically, status and reputation are critical in uncertain environments because they signal that a potential partner has valuable resources and unique skills, and is able to maintain alliance relationships successfully. An alliance network also provides information about the predictability of a potential partner's behaviour. Prior successful experiences with other alliance partners may increase a partner's trustworthiness, which is disseminated in an alliance network through referrals. Within an alliance network, firms with prior alliances tend to forge new alliances with the same partner. The alliance partners have established prior working relationships, are aware of their skills and needs and are therefore more likely to realize high performance levels. In addition, unconnected firms are more likely to ally if they have common partners or are closer in an alliance network. Thus, a firm that leverages its alliance networks actively may reduce costs related to partner search, selection and monitoring. However, a firm may wish to consider the following questions when selecting a partner:

- To what extent does a potential partner enhance or undermine the network position?
- To what extent does a potential partner change the power position of a firm?
- To what extent do network-operating rules tolerate an alliance partner outside the existing alliance network?

Step 3: Alliance negotiation

When taking an alliance network view, generic alliance negotiations guidelines are sufficient to realize favourable negotiation process and outcomes. However, negotiators should be aware of two points. First, when starting alliance negotiations with a partner that is embedded in a firm's alliance network, a negotiator should be aware that the alliance network itself might function as a safeguard against unbalanced negotiation outcomes. If the partners have a history of shared experiences, negotiations are more likely to be characterized by integrative negotiation strategies. In addition, to avoid negative reputational spillovers, negotiations are more likely to occur in a collaborative climate. Second, single-alliance negotiations tend to become more complex when the alliance network view is incorporated. The negotiation bandwidth becomes extended, as a firm's value creation potential comprises the value of the single alliance and the value of the single alliance within the alliance network. Awareness of potential network contributions and constraints may affect negotiation process and outcomes. For example, while identifying and discussing opportunities to create a joint business proposition generates constructive interactions, attempts to resolve opposing interests within the alliance network may result in resistance, conflicts and tensions. In addition, when network-level decisions are part of the negotiation, multi-lateral negotiations (that is, multiple partners) require a careful negotiation approach.

Step 4: Alliance design

Firms tend to approach alliances as stand-alone transactions, which means that they often neglect the influence of a firm's alliance network on alliance design decisions. That is, a firm changes the configuration of the alliance network through alliance design decisions. Whereas partner selection constitutes a critical decision as it affects the homogeneity of heterogeneity of partner diversity, the adopted governance form affects the strength of the tie and thus the network position. For example, forging a non-equity-based learning alliance with a university may strengthen a closure position, whereas establishing a joint venture with a supplier may reinforce a structural hole position.

An important implication of relational embeddedness in an alliance network is the enhanced relational capital between firms. Relational capital promotes collaborative behaviour and increases a partner's awareness that the other has a lot to lose from behaving opportunistically. Social sanctions extend beyond the alliance and may include loss of reputation, loss of business with the alliance partner and deteriorated relationships with other network partners. Consequently, rather than relying on equity-based arrangements and complete contracts, firms may opt for self-enforcing safeguards, which mitigates the risk of opportunism, misappropriation and unpredictable partner behaviour. In other words, familiarity between alliance partners generates relational capital, which enables the partners to use less quasi-hierarchical structures (i.e. non-equity) in the design of the partnership.

Step 5: Alliance management

When firms embrace a proactive approach towards alliance network management, the management of a single alliance extends beyond regular activities, which include building relational norms and capital, initiating corrective measures, resolving conflicts and stimulating inter-firm learning. More specifically, boundary-spanning individuals become critical, as they have a crucial impact on information exchange and decision-making in their own organization and that of their counterparts. Management may focus on boundary-spanning agents to enhance information exchange and obtain control over network benefits (such as referrals). In addition, management may focus on the role the alliance plays in fulfilling its network management efforts. Examples of such roles include:

- An information-broker role (framing) in the network: a firm uses the alliance as a vehicle to disseminate information to various parties in the network.
- A coordinator role (activating): a firm uses the alliance as a vehicle to bring together representatives of the different firms in the alliance network.

- A relationship broker or innovation role (mobilizing): a firm may use the alliance as a vehicle to initiate and facilitate new alliances between different parties.
- A network structuring agent role (synthesizing): a firm uses the alliance as a vehicle to monitor and influence the structure of relationships in the alliance network.

Step 6: Alliance evaluation

By adopting an alliance network view, the performance metric system should be supplemented by metrics that capture alliance network processes and outcomes. Network processes can be captured through metrics that measure the extent to which information is exchanged within the alliance network. Examples could include the number and quality of referrals and contacts an alliance partner provides. In addition, alliance network metrics may capture outcomes associated with the direct relationship, such as the extent to which an alliance generates knowledge, and outcomes associated with indirect relationships, such as the extent to which third party resources have been used. Metrics should also capture the network maintenance costs imposed on a firm. A comprehensive performance metric system enables a firm to evaluate and track alliance and network performance and, if necessary, it can intervene immediately if expectations are not met.

Step 7: Alliance termination

From an alliance network view, an alliance termination decision becomes more complex. Consistent with generic guidelines, the under-performance of a single alliance may prompt a premature termination. However, because the dissolution of a single alliance may adversely impact a firm's network positions, any decision to dissolve the alliance should perhaps be postponed until the negative repercussions are resolved. For example, a firm's alliance partner may be connected to a prominent network partner, and terminating the partnership may have serious negative knowledge and reputational spillovers. If a termination trajectory is continued, a firm must communicate this decision to other partners in the network in a timely manner. If exiting an alliance violates the relational norms established in an alliance network, a firm's relational capital may be seriously damaged unless it can provide an explanation.

Summary

A network view on alliances states that firms are embedded in a set of inter-firm linkages between multiple parties. The functions of an alliance network can potentially enhance a firm's competitive advantage by providing resource advantages through direct relationships and information advantages through indirect relationships. However, an alliance network also increases management complexity and coordination costs, because it imposes (social) obligations, interdependencies and lock-in effects on a firm. Although we have questioned the extent to which a single firm can manage its alliance networks, such networks can enhance a firm's performance when its network position is aligned with its strategic intent. In general, a closure network enables a firm to realize its exploration objectives, whereas a structural hole network favours exploitation objectives. Furthermore, a firm can fulfil different network functions and roles to support an alliance network. As firms can restructure their network position by means of entering and exiting alliances, this chapter has also discussed how an alliance network view impacts the formation and management of single alliances.

Case: IBM

International Business Machines (IBM)[1] is a multinational American technology and consulting firm. It manufactures and sells computer hardware and software and offers infrastructure, hosting and consulting services in areas ranging from mainframe computers to nanotechnology. Throughout its history, IBM has operated at the forefront of computing technology. In the 1930s, IBM's tabulating equipment enabled its customers to process unprecedented amounts of data. In the 1950s and 1960s, IBM developed self-learning programmes to play draughts (IBM 704). It also developed FORTRAN, a scientific programming language, and built a reservation system for American Airlines called SABRE. IBM's computing power even helped NASA track space flights and provided support to the NASA moon missions. In 1973, IBM developed the Universal Product Code, also known as the barcode, which can still be found on virtually every product in the world. The development of mainframe computing, which allowed businesses to upgrade their computing power and run more sophisticated applications, proved pivotal to IBM's performance. IBM was able to build a strong and virtually unchallenged competitive position, primarily due to its innovative capacity, its focus on process optimization and its control over the supply chain.

Due to its internal focus, IBM failed to recognize the change in the markets in the 1980s. One critical threat to IBM's position was the partnership between Sun and Hewlett Packard, which developed an alternative operating system called UNIX; this was the first real alternative to IBM's mainframe operating systems. The public started to become interested in personal computers and, despite IBM's conviction that mainframes would remain the primary source of computing power for business and enterprises, the company entered the 'microcomputer' market in 1981. IBM did not enter the PC market using its standard vertically integrated approach; instead, it used external sources to provide components and operating software that fit IBM requirements. However, due to their open architecture, Intel and Microsoft were able to achieve market dominance. In addition, Intel and Microsoft both supplied new hardware manufacturers like Fujitsu and Compaq in the early 1990s. In addition, in response to increasing complexity, customers were looking for system integration, which was an indication that the IT market was about to change from being technology-oriented to service-oriented. IBM's once comfortable competitive position was fading rapidly. This required IBM to change its internal focus and adopt an external focus.

In 1991/1992, IBM forged a total of 55 alliances, 23 of which focused on further developing its operating system and another 23 of which focused on improving its microprocessor technology. In addition, 42 of the 55 alliances were related to research and development activities, whereas nine partnerships involved joint ventures and research consortia. An example was IBM's long-term alliance with Intel to develop microprocessors and its collaboration with Microsoft to cross-license Windows New Technology. IBM also developed software for third parties, including a flight reservation system and CAD/CAM applications. IBM was also engaged in 10 alliances with Apple, primarily aimed at developing microprocessors and software architecture. These bilateral partnerships enabled IBM to advance its existing technologies. However, to remain competitive, IBM had to discover new markets and technologies.

From 1996 onwards, IBM engaged increasingly in multi-partner collaboration, the objectives of which changed from further development of existing technologies to development of new areas of expertise. For example, the pioneering work of the IBM Internet group was reinforced by its partnering strategies. An initial joint venture with parties such as Netscape and Oracle to develop Internet browsing software was followed by the introduction of various Internet-related products (such as ThinkPad), which were generated through IBM's alliance network. The relatively strong market position that IBM established in 2000 resulted from alliances in the telecom and ICT consultancy industries. By the end of the 1990s, IBM had transformed itself from a hardware manufacturer to a global service provider by changing its internal organizations.

During the first years of the new millennium, IBM further intensified its focus on software development and service provision. Whereas alliances with hardware manufacturers Motorola and Sun had enabled IBM to exploit existing technologies, partnerships with Microsoft, PeopleSoft and Citrix enabled IBM to explore a wide variety of software development projects. IBM also explored the telecommunications industry through network developers and phone manufacturers, such as Cisco and Nokia. IBM has also released code under various open-source licences, such as the platform-independent software framework Eclipse, the three-sentence International Components for Unicode (ICU) licence and the Java-based relational database management system (RDBMS) Apache Derby. By 2001, IBM's revenue stream from its global services outstripped its traditional revenue stream from hardware.

Following these successes, IBM continued its network-based service strategy. For example, IBM sold its hardware division to Lenovo in 2005, but forged a multi-year agreement whereby Lenovo is the leading provider of personal computers to IBM clients, and IBM provides financing and end-user support services for those PC solutions. Building on this success, the agreement was expanded into a global alliance to develop and deliver industry-specific, integrated technology solutions for enterprises, small- and mid-market businesses and individuals. In addition, virtually all of the latest-generation console gaming systems use microprocessors developed by IBM. The Xbox 360 contains a PowerPC tri-core processor, which IBM designed and produced in less than 24 months. Sony's PlayStation 3 features the Cell BE microprocessor, which was designed jointly by IBM, Toshiba and Sony. IBM will provide the microprocessors that serve as the heart of Nintendo's new Wii U system, which will debut in 2012.

Questions

1. Explain how IBM's network strategy and position changed as a result of changes in its strategy.
2. Explain how, at different points in time, IBM's alliance network helped or hindered it realize its strategic objectives.

18

ALLIANCE CO-EVOLUTION

As organizational entities, alliances are inherently complex to manage, and they are continually under threat from external contingencies that originate either in the partners' own organization or in the external environment. The preceding chapters have discussed how these internal and external forces drive alliance development and the instruments alliance managers can use to develop win–win alliances. However, establishing and maintaining alliances also causes changes in partners' organizations and environments, which in turn could force managers to modify their alliance design and management in an effort to maintain fit between the alliance, the alliance partners and the environment. A misfit could lead to deteriorating efficiency or effectiveness and, in an extreme situation, could decrease the viability of the alliance or even decrease the viability of one or all alliance partners in the environment. Together, these relationships between the alliance, the alliance partner organizations and the environment constitute an alliance system. The dynamic interaction within an alliance system has been referred to as alliance co-evolution. This chapter starts by explaining what is meant by a co-evolutionary view on alliances, as well as why, when and how alliance co-evolution occurs. The third section uses the alliance development framework to present managerial guidelines, and the following two sections conclude with a summary and a case illustration.

A co-evolutionary view

The idea of co-evolution is rooted in the tradition of population ecology and evolutionary theory (Hannan and Freeman 1977), and refers to the simultaneous development of organizations and their environment, both independently and interactively (Wilson and Hynes 2009). Co-evolution assumes that change may occur in all interacting populations of organizations, which allows changes to be driven by direct interaction and by feedback. The theory of alliance co-evolution suggests that natural selection (that is, the argument that an alliance that fits with its environment has a greater chance of survival) does take place, but that the simultaneous change in organizations connected through an alliance results in favourable inherited traits that bestow certain advantages, both at an individual level and at a dyadic level. Alliance co-evolution occurs in a population consisting of heterogeneous firms that have adaptive learning capability and are able to interact and mutually influence each other, and where at least two firms have formed an alliance (Volberda and Lewin 2003). In addition, some initiating event, which can either be internal (within the alliance) or external (within one or both alliance partner organizations and or the environment), is present to trigger the co-evolutionary process (see Table 18.1). This dynamic interaction between alliance, partner organizations and environment implies that organizations and the alliance itself represent adaptive entities that, based on learning and experience, engage in a continuous and interrelated self-renewal processes in an attempt to seek and maintain fit.

In order to understand why alliance co-evolution occurs, it is important to elaborate on three overarching principles that underpin co-evolution (Volberda and Lewin 2003). First, self-renewing organizations focus on managing variety by regulating internal rates of change so that they equal or exceed relevant external rates of change. For example, firms reorganize their organizations in response to unforeseen moves by competitors, changes in technology and customers' demands. Second, self-renewing organizations seek to optimize self-organization, which

TABLE 18.1 Driving and inhibiting forces of alliance adaptation

	Driving forces	*Inhibiting forces*
Alliance environment	Governments changing foreign direct investment policies, competitors introducing new technologies, and companies entering or exiting industries may prompt adaptation.	Governments raising legal and other barriers to exit or entry markets, competitors forming multi-partner alliances, and a lack of legitimacy in an environment may create inertia.
Partner firms	Internal reorganizations, a shift in corporate strategy, a shift in resource needs, a shift in financial position, and changes to the board of directors may prompt adaptation.	Existing alliances with other firms, lack of necessary resources, internal political games, and administrative policies and procedures may create inertia.
Alliance	Worse-than-expected performance, partners updating their expectations, the governance form appearing to be inefficient, and differential learning may prompt adaptation	Sunk costs due to non-recoverable investments in technology, machinery, and personnel; the dynamics of political coalitions; and a lack of partner interactions may create inertia.

suggests that they are continuously engaged in learning and adaptive processes to improve their ability to maintain a fit between themselves and their environment. Thirdly, self-renewing organizations synchronize concurrent exploitation and exploration. In this context, exploitation refers to the strategic intention to enhance performance by leveraging existing capabilities, while exploration refers to the strategic intent to enhance by performance by discovering new potential useful capabilities. Alliances represent a way of evoking organizational self-renewal; they enable firms to align flexibly with environmental requirements, they trigger internal optimization, and firms contemplating an alliance may use it to exploit and explore while avoiding competence traps (too much exploitation) and learning traps (too much exploration) (March 1991).

Though four co-evolutionary generative mechanisms have been distinguished (see Table 18.2) to illustrate the wide range of evolutionary paths that can occur, within the context of alliances, managed selection provides the foundation for the underlying principles of co-evolving in an alliance system (Volberda and

TABLE 18.2 Four co-evolutionary trajectories

	Description
Naïve selection	Co-evolution through naïve selection proceeds through a continuous cycle of variation, selection and retention, and causes a firm (or organization) to evolve towards a better fit with the environment. Variations emerge through blind or random change initiatives, while selection occurs principally through competition for scarce resources and retention involves forces that perpetuate and maintain selected initiatives.
Managed selection	Co-evolution through managed selection suggests that managers develop preferences for certain responses or variations. Instead of blind variations, variations become more deliberate or intelligent, based on past experience. Management may develop forms of anticipatory control system in which prior knowledge functions as a selector, blocking perceived dangerous or inadequate actions before they are executed.
Hierarchical renewal	Co-evolution through hierarchical renewal suggests that managers can shape their environment and that strategy-making involves multiple levels of management. In this context, co-evolution is driven primarily by the strategic intent of senior management. Adaptation results from the top-down administrative decisions and the resulting outcomes are highly idiosyncratic. Successful trajectories are highly dependent on senior management's decision rationality and industry foresight.
Holistic renewal	Co-evolution through holistic renewal focuses on collective sense-making and suggests a close link between collective cognitions processes of co-evolution. Periods of stability and convergence, as opposed to those of upheaval and change, are mirrored in similar changes in beliefs and ideologies. Interpretations give meaning to data and precede learning and action.

Source: Volberda and Lewin (2003).

Lewin 2003). Managed selection suggests that self-renewing organizations can use alliances to manage internal rates of change, optimize self-organization and balance concurrent exploration and exploitation. Moreover, managed selection implies that alliance governance is a mixture of market selection mechanisms and managerial adaptation processes, which makes this view less path-dependent and deterministic than, say, the naïve selection mechanism. More specifically, when selection is applied to alliance management, it suggests that devising partnerships is one way that firms adapt to a changing environment.

Whereas evolution suggests that change initially occurs at the firm level, co-evolution considers simultaneous changes with firms and their environment, or dyadic pairs of firms. In addition, a co-evolutionary view captures multi-directional causalities over a long period of time, in which the outcomes of co-evolution are emergent and in which changes in any one variable (for example, at the micro or macro level) may be caused endogenously by changes in the other (Das and Teng 2002). Consequently, a co-evolutionary view is made up of dynamic trajectories evoked by drivers that enable and restrict change within an alliance system. For example, economic, social, technological, environmental and political macro-variables may change over time and influence firms' micro-level alliance decisions. This, in turn, influences the broader alliance environment, including alliance partners' organizations (Wilson and Hynes 2009). Because firms are able to change themselves proactively, their alliances, and, to a certain degree, their environment (that is, they can select the 'best' alternative), alliance co-evolution occurs through a deliberate approach rather than via random chance-like processes.

Drivers of alliance co-evolution

The literature on alliance co-evolution has emerged only recently, which means that conclusive evidence on alliance co-evolution is virtually non-existent (Volberda and Lewin 2003). However, the alliance studies that examined alliance co-evolution did identify drivers of alliance co-evolution operating at three levels of analysis: the alliance, the partner organizations and the alliance environment.

Alliance level

At the alliance level, outcome and process discrepancies may prompt adaptation in alliance conditions and processes (Kumar and Nti 1998), including changes in the governance, the alliance contract, the division of activities, decision making and performance expectations. In turn, these modifications affect the development and outcomes of the alliance, which creates a continuous cycle of learning and adaptation (Büchel 2002). Although multiple drivers of adaptation have been identified (see Table 18.1), these tend to operate through three key mechanisms (Koza and Lewin 1998): (1) relative absorptive capacity, (2) control and (3) identity.

A partner's relative absorptive capacity is a critical driver of alliance adaptation and development (Koza and Lewin 1998). Relative absorptive capacity refers to the

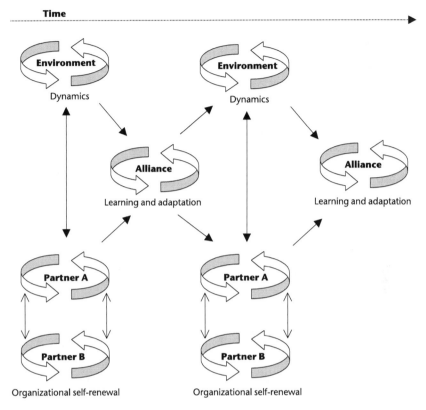

FIGURE 18.1 Alliance system

extent to which partners have a similar ability to value, assimilate and commercialize knowledge within their own organization (Lane and Lubatkin 1998). The extent to which alliance partners are similar (or different) in their ability to learn from and with one another may cause partners' resources endowments to diverge or converge over time, which creates different managerial responses (Nakamura *et al*. 1996). Resource convergence eliminates the initial motives to establish the alliance, which requires managers to dissolve the alliance or seek alternative ways to create value. In contrast, resource divergence increases partners' dependence on one another, which encourages them to increase efforts to acquire each other's valuable resources. In addition, learning about each other's capabilities may cause partners' strategic intentions to diverge or converge (see Box 18.1). For example, examining co-evolution in the banking industry Ul-Haq (2005) identifies three development patterns: (1) 'differential parallel co-evolution', in which the evolution of the strategic intents of the two firms are at different rates but in a broadly similar direction; (2) 'differential convergent co-evolution', in which the strategic intents of the two firms evolve at different rates but in a convergent direction; and (3) 'differential divergent co-evolution', where the strategic intents of the two firms

---

BOX 18.1   NEXIA'S CO-EVOLUTION

Nexia is a professional service network in the public accounting industry and was intentionally forged and formally organized in order to produce cross-border referrals. It selected members by means of two criteria: potential members are independent national players and they lack the ability or desire to internationalize. However, as time passed, some members discovered and became attracted to opportunities beyond their national market. In addition, unfair distribution of outcomes led individual members to bypass the original intention of the network by entering each other's markets independently. To cope with this unintended consequence Nexia developed two initiatives. First, it imposed a variety of coordinating, integrating, and formalizing mechanisms to support its referral work and it invested in building a collective network identity. The expectation was that enhancing a network identity would attenuate the member firms' incentives to defect. However, as tensions rose, Nexia realized that nurturing and institutionalizing one identity was not enough to deal with competitive behaviours. Second, Nexia's control mechanisms were not highly elaborated initially because of the perceived need to minimize overhead costs. The controls were primarily developed to facilitate cooperation in international referrals. However, as the potentially opportunistic intent of some member firms began to emerge, Nexia developed more stringent mechanisms and procedures to counteract and control the behaviour of participants.

Source: Koza and Lewin (1999).

evolve at different rates, but in a divergent direction. Although, partners' absorptive capacity functions as a driver for alliance adaptation, the impact is, to a certain degree, conditioned by the exploitation or exploration intent of the alliance. In exploration alliances, partners' ability to acquire knowledge is critical, whereas the role of absorptive capacity is of minor concern in exploitation alliances. Therefore, asymmetry between partners·in terms of absorptive capacity is likely to trigger adaptation in exploration alliances to control the emergence of learning races (Hamel 1991).

Control mechanisms enable alliance partners to monitor alliance progress and emerging outcome and process discrepancies (Kumar 2010). These mechanisms function as an important driver of alliance adaptation and development (Koza and Lewin 1998). For example, Ariño and de la Torre's (1998) detailed account of the development of an international joint venture suggests that assessments of efficiency and equity conditions prompt partner firms to address dissatisfying situations in various manners, such as by improving relational governance, engaging in contractual renegotiations, doing nothing, and terminating the alliance. However, alliances vary in their use of control mechanism and, for example, match the choice of output and behaviour control with the exploration and exploitation intents (Koza and Lewin 1998). In exploitation alliances, output controls are predominantly used to capture short-term results, whereas exploration alliances employ behavioural and process control to tap into time-dependent activities such as learning. When the intended outcome is uncertain or vague, as is the case in exploration-oriented alliances, an alliance is more receptive to adaptation as managers change their initial conditions once the outcomes become clearer.

Identity also functions as a mechanism that enables alliance learning and adaptation (Koza and Lewin 1998). Identity may prompt processes of collective sense making, which creates a sense of shared fate among alliance members. For example, creating a common identity in a joint venture eases decision making, conflict resolution and learning, as individuals share similar values and norms. In contrast, identifying with one's partners could be counter-productive due to identity conflicts. Therefore, identification with the alliance functions as an integrating mechanism within the alliance, and as a differentiating mechanism that demarcates the alliance itself from the partners. Identity integration is more critical in exploitation alliances, because it enables partners to exploit existing capabilities jointly. In exploration alliances, identification tends to be with the partners, as identifying with an alliance partner may inhibit knowledge acquisition and result in alliances that extend beyond the intended time horizon. However, a certain degree of identification can serve to moderate conflict.

Partner firm level

Changes in partner organizations, both foreseen and unforeseen, may prompt alliance adaptations (Koza and Lewin 1998). A shift in corporate strategy, internal reorganizations, changing resource requirements, a shift in financial position, changes in required technology, and even a change in the board of directors may encourage managers to modify alliance design and management (Blodgett 1992; Shortell and Zajac 1988). For example, the alliance between Liz Claiborne and Avon encountered difficulty when Avon acquired an upscale cosmetics company in an effort to enhance its image (Stafford 1994). Because the acquisition increased the market commonality of the two partners, Liz Claiborne began to view Avon more as a competitor than a partner, which led to the termination of the alliance. To deal with conflicting pressures for exploration and exploitation, a firm's alliance portfolio is likely to evolve continuously (Lavie and Rosenkopf 2006), with existing alliances terminated and new ones established. In addition, the pursuit of exploration and exploitation may cause alliance partners to impose changes to their alliances, such as modifications in governance form, incentive systems and monitoring systems, in an attempt to maintain consistency between their corporate/business strategies and the alliance objectives. A shift in a partner firm's experience managing alliances as an alliance progresses may also trigger alliance adaptations (Das and Teng 2002). A firm that increases its institutionalized alliance experience may enhance its reputation and function as a signal for trustworthiness, which reduces the need for (costly) contractual governance.

As an alliance develops, it may also cause changes within the partner firms' organizations. Alliance outcomes and processes are likely to affect alliance partners as, in most cases, the alliance is at least partially integrated into the organization. Reciprocal financial and organizational relationships facilitate the transfer of resources, information and routines, which are not necessarily part of the alliance agreement, from the alliance to the partner organizations. An exploration alliance designed to develop new products is often organized through an equity-based arrangement that is characterized by high levels of involvement and integration. Consequently, an alliance partner is likely to absorb valuable knowledge elements of the initial alliance agreement and may also acquire additional knowledge and information about areas such as markets, production technologies and operating procedures. The assimilation of this knowledge changes a firm's resource endowment, which means it is also likely to cause changes in a firm's strategy, systems and operations. Although exploitation alliances tend to be organized through non-equity-based arrangements (that is, with relatively little integration) a similar transfer of resources, information and routines may occur. For example, successful supplier alliances are characterized by alliance-specific investments, such as co-production locations, which often require partner organizations to adjust their operations to accommodate one another's needs. For example, Wilson and Hynes (2009) show that a firm seeking access to the fresh produce market in the UK through an international alliance experienced changes in its technical skills, new product development and networking opportunities as a result of the alliance.

Alliance environment level

The alliance environment affects a firm's decisions to form and manage alliances (Koza and Lewin 1998). In a stable environment, a firm may enhance its competitive position by establishing exploitation alliances to use existing capabilities with the aim of achieving cost reductions and economies of scale, for example. Exploration alliances are more suitable in a dynamic environment, as a heterogeneous resource endowment contributes to a firm's ability to respond in an appropriate and timely manner to new circumstances. For example, the results of Lampel and Shamsie's (2003) study of the US motion picture industry indicate that changes in the environment caused a transition to flexible hub organizations supported by alliances. Practices and routines that speed up mobilizing capabilities became more important to box office success than practices and routines that make up the transforming capabilities associated with a studio era dominated by integrated hierarchies. Jacobides and Winter (2005) report on co-evolution trajectories in American mortgage banking and Swiss watch manufacturing. Their results indicate that, within an industry, differential profitability, arising from heterogeneous capabilities across firms, promotes distinct vertical structures. Whereas incremental innovation provides access to specialization gains and produces a secular drift toward vertical disintegration, radical changes in technology require new and integrated capabilities, leading to a phase of vertical reintegration. Therefore, firms are sensitive to changing environmental conditions, such as shifts in customer preferences and technological developments, and this prompts them to adapt their alliance strategies.

Changes in the alliance environment may also require partners to adapt alliance design and management, and to renew the conditions under which the collaboration takes place. For example, if competitors intend to introduce a new technology that renders existing technologies obsolete, partners engaged in a learning alliance may need to speed up their own development process, search for possibilities to collaborate with these competitors or decide to dissolve the alliance. Tjemkes and Furrer (2011) argue that industry conditions also affect managerial responses to adversity within alliances. Firms that operate in industries with high technological turbulence tend to prefer destructive response strategies, unlike those firms that operate in industries characterized by low technological turbulence, whose response strategies aim to maintain and preserve their alliance relationships. In contrast, when firms operate in industries characterized by low competitive intensity, the relative importance of preserving existing alliances diminishes, as alternative suppliers could be required to respond satisfactorily to customers' preferences. Conseqüently, these firms are more willing to put the alliance relationship at risk and more likely to prefer destructive response strategies, such as exit, opportunism and neglect.

In turn, an alliance may impact its environment, as alliance formation and outcomes could impact industry and market dynamics. For example, the announcement of the Star Alliance, a multi-partner airline alliance involving United Airlines, Lufthansa, Scandinavian Airlines, Air Canada and Thai Airways, led non-members to immediately look for partners, such as Air France with Air India and American Airlines with Aerolineas Argentinas (Guidice *et al.* 2003). Firms respond to alliance competition by seeking and forming countervailing alliances with similar partners as a way of duplicating the benefits their rivals are gaining (Gimeno 2004). A firm could seek entry into its rivals' networks by creating alliances with its rivals' partner, or it could seek to match the rivals' advantage by creating countervailing alliances with other partners that also face the same competitive threat. For example, Wilson and Hynes (2009) report that the formation of alliances within the fresh produce industry in the UK changed the power dynamics across the value chain, which prompted other parties in the value chain to form new alliances.

Alliance system

The linkages between alliance, alliance partner organizations and alliance environment create an alliance system in which alliance co-evolutionary processes occur (see Figure 18.1). Each level represents a unit of change, but also depicts the object of change (Wilson and Hynes 2009). Therefore, drivers associated with each level generate learning and adaptation directly, interactively and reciprocally within the alliance system. This dynamic pattern of interactions, both within and between different levels of the system, generates co-evolutionary alliance processes in which all elements progress. However, a state of equilibrium is never likely to be achieved owing to converging and diverging patterns of positive and negative feedback. Taking the perspective of one firm participating in an alliance system, this chapter also proposes that proactive management of an alliance system is beyond the ability of any manager. Owing to bounded rationality and cognitive limitations, it is unlikely that a single alliance manager could comprehend the relationships between drivers of change, intermediary mechanisms or the consequences of change across the alliance, partner firm and environmental levels of analysis. Nevertheless, we suggest that when firms are viewed as self-renewal entities, they have a certain degree of managerial control over co-evolutionary processes:

- Based on continuous assessment of efficiency and equity conditions, alliance partners may initiate modifications to alliance design and alliance management, thereby generating continuous cycles of learning and adaptation.
- Based on continuous assessment of alliance (portfolio) outcomes, alliance partners may experience and initiate modifications to their firm's strategy and organization.
- Based on continuous assessment of alliance environment, alliance partners may experience and initiate modifications to their firm's strategy and organization, as well as to alliance design and management.

A firm can enhance the viability of an alliance system by installing buffering mechanisms and boundary-spanning agents. Buffering refers to the regulation and/or insulation of alliance activities, functions, resources and individuals from the effects of changes in environment and/or partner organization (Lynn 2005). Different buffering mechanisms can be integrated into the core activities of the alliance. A buffer of financial resources within an alliance functions as a cushion when unforeseen circumstances threaten the alliance's viability. Appointing a manager who is responsible for finding, hiring and training new alliance employees can reduce the potential uncertainty of not having the right experts with the right collaborative mindset. Another example of buffering is allocating surplus resources to stimulate radical innovation in response to anticipated external changes, while simultaneously allocating resources to achieve the immediate alliance objectives. Boundary-spanning agents link and coordinate alliance activities with key elements of the environment and partner organizations (Jemison 1984). These agents are concerned primarily with the exchange of information to detect and bring into the alliance information about changes in the environment and alliance partner organizations, as well as send information into the environment that presents the alliance in a favourable light. For example, in order to detect and bring relevant information about alliance partner organizations, an agent could hold regular meetings with people from relevant parts of the corporate and business levels of each alliance partner organization.

Alliance co-evolution: Decision-making steps

Drawing on a co-evolutionary view, alliances are complex adaptive systems that have far from optimal performance. Changes at the alliance, partner firm and alliance environment level require managers to learn and adapt their alliances continuously. To provide some insights into alliance co-evolution and the governance of a single alliance, the insights outlined above are applied to the alliance development framework (see Figure 18.2).

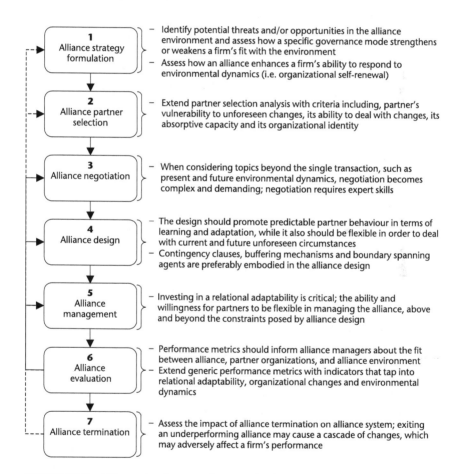

1
Alliance strategy formulation
– Identify potential threats and/or opportunities in the alliance environment and assess how a specific governance mode strengthens or weakens a firm's fit with the environment
– Assess how an alliance enhances a firm's ability to respond to environmental dynamics (i.e. organizational self-renewal)

2
Alliance partner selection
– Extend partner selection analysis with criteria including, partner's vulnerability to unforeseen changes, its ability to deal with changes, its absorptive capacity and its organizational identity

3
Alliance negotiation
– When considering topics beyond the single transaction, such as present and future environmental dynamics, negotiation becomes complex and demanding; negotiation requires expert skills

4
Alliance design
– The design should promote predictable partner behaviour in terms of learning and adaptation, while it also should be flexible in order to deal with current and future unforeseen circumstances
– Contingency clauses, buffering mechanisms and boundary spanning agents are preferably embodied in the alliance design

5
Alliance management
– Investing in a relational adaptability is critical; the ability and willingness for partners to be flexible in managing the alliance, above and beyond the constraints posed by alliance design

6
Alliance evaluation
– Performance metrics should inform alliance managers about the fit between alliance, partner organizations, and alliance environment
– Extend generic performance metrics with indicators that tap into relational adaptability, organizational changes and environmental dynamics

7
Alliance termination
– Assess the impact of alliance termination on alliance system; exiting an underperforming alliance may cause a cascade of changes, which may adversely affect a firm's performance

FIGURE 18.2   Alliance development framework: Alliance co-evolution★

★An alliance co-evolutionary perspective entails a holistic view on an alliance system, making it virtually impossible to develop normative and prescriptive guidelines. The managerial guidelines are thus indicative and entail how an alliance manager may deal with alliance co-evolutionary processes.

Step 1: Alliance strategy formulation

During the alliance strategy formulation stage, firms decide whether an alliance is their preferred governance mode, as opposed to internalization or market exchange. Taking a co-evolutionary alliance view, the generic guidelines for governance mode decisions still apply. However, in addition to factors such as economic, strategic and learning motivations, a co-evolutionary view stresses the importance of environmental conditions. For example, a firm may prefer an alliance when resources are not readily available in a market and its environment is volatile, as it provides a firm with the required strategic flexibility. An alliance then functions as a strategic way for a firm to cope with external uncertainties. However, when developing an alliance strategy, it is important to consider implications that extend beyond the alliance's direct value creation potential. Forging an alliance may affect environmental dynamics, which may have positive or negative consequences for the firm. For example, allying with a competitor to achieve economies of scale may prompt other rivals to form partnerships. An alliance may also trigger changes in the firm's organization as knowledge, resources and organizational routines are transformed through the alliance relationship. During strategic analysis, therefore, managers must recognize that a single alliance is embedded in a complex alliance system. In order to assess the potential dynamic interactions between an alliance, partner organizations and the alliance environment, managers could use scenario planning to assess the potential impact that the alliance could have on the firm's long-term performance.

Step 2: Alliance partner selection

When co-evolutionary processes in an alliance system are taken as a reference point, partner selection constitutes a crucial activity. Consistent with generic guidelines, it is critical to select a partner with similar resource and organizational attributes, as partner misfit is a primary source of alliance adaptation. However, a firm should also focus during partner selection on the relative absorptive capacity and partner's identity. A differential ability to learn combined with diverging organizational identities, specifically in exploration alliances, may trigger a learning race and an escalating cycle of modifications that could potentially lead to the termination of the alliance. More specifically, supplemental partner selection criteria include:

- Relative absorptive capacity captured by the extent to which partners possess similar learning practices, knowledge transfer mechanisms, a knowledge foundation and incentive systems.
- The organization's identity (or culture), which can be captured, for example, by indicators that tap into an individual's values and norms, working practices and perceived reputation.
- Partner's vulnerability to changes in the environment, which may include financial strength, portfolio of alliances and innovative capacity.

Step 3: Alliance negotiation

Co-evolutionary alliance processes involve repetitive cycles of learning and adaptation. Therefore, alliance negotiations should focus on how to deal with internal and external dynamics that challenge alliance stability. Although negotiators may, by interchangeably using integrative and distributive negotiation strategies, arrive at negotiation outcomes that specify the alliance's value creation potential and pay-off structure, negotiating adaptation and contingency provisions require excellent negotiation skills, including an ability to encourage dialogue and constructive interactions. Different perceptions about internal and external developments must be reconciled before negotiators are likely to agree on the nature, the timing and the cause of an alliance adaptation. For example, they must reach consensus about the conditions under which a firm is allowed to increase its equity stake in a joint venture. Furthermore, negotiations may focus on the nature of the buffering mechanism and the role of boundary-spanning agents. For example, having a partner comply with excess funding in order to create a financial buffer requires expert negotiation tactics and skills.

Step 4: Alliance design

For an alliance co-evolutionary view, the generic guidelines for governance form decisions are applicable. For example, when alliance partners establish an exploratory alliance, equity-based arrangements are preferable to non-equity arrangements. One primary objective of an alliance design is to promote predictable partner behaviour. From a co-evolutionary perspective, this means that an alliance design shapes how learning and adaptation in response to unforeseen circumstances occurs as the alliance progresses. More specifically, partners designing an alliance must consider, to the best of their ability, the impact and consequences of co-evolutionary processes within the alliance system. In other words, governance form, alliance contracts and control mechanisms need to be tailored to the (expected) alliance environment, the partner firms' conditions and the alliance objectives. Given the complexity of alliance co-evolution, an exhaustive list of design implications is virtually impossible. However, consider the following illustrations:

- A learning alliance could be organized through a non-equity-based arrangement (as opposed to an equity-based one), supplemented with process and behavioural control mechanisms, as partners operate in a relative dynamic environment, which increases the need for flexibility.
- Standard alliance contracts could be supplemented with contingency provisions, which are particularly relevant in volatile environments as they specify procedures for how to react and/or initiate changes in the alliance proactively.
- The assignment of dedicated boundary-spanning agents functions as an early warning system. Based on early signals, alliance managers can take timely measures to deal with changes, such as establishing a financial buffer.

Step 5: Alliance management

The generic guidelines are applicable for managing an alliance on a day-to-day basis. From a co-evolutionary perspective, however, the significance of relational adaptability increases. This refers to the willingness and ability of partners to be flexible when conducting the relationship, above and beyond the constraints posed by alliance design (if necessary). This causes partners to treat the relationship as an adjustable framework, in which changes will occur to redress imbalances in the relationship if either party is adversely affected by changing circumstances. Moreover, partners are willing to make these adaptations without resorting to expensive and time-consuming contractual renegotiations. In addition to promoting adaptive behaviour, managers must pay attention to changes in their partner's organization, as well as the environment and their potential impact on alliance design and management. Information about changes in the alliance system is critical to prepare adaptations in alliance design and management.

Step 6: Alliance evaluation

While the performance metric system should be tailored to the objectives of the alliance, additional metrics could be incorporated to account for the co-evolutionary processes in the alliance system. Alliance managers would like to know the extent to which there is sufficient fit between the alliance partners, the alliance and the environment, both now and in the future. Some of the indicators that should be included or require specific attention are:

- Alliance process indicators that tap into relational adaptability, such as the degree of trust, commitment, flexibility and inter-firm learning, etc.
- Indicators that tap into partner firms' organization, such as shifts in strategy; shifts in organizational structure, culture and routines; product and service innovations; etc.
- Indicators that tap into the alliance environment, such as technological advancements, industry dynamics, political and economic developments, etc.

Step 7: Alliance termination

From a co-evolutionary perspective, exiting an alliance is as critical as forging one. Although a firm may shift its focus away from the single transaction, termination could cause a series of changes within an alliance system. The firm and its partner must act and secure the provision of resources via alternative arrangements, which may include a new alliance, an acquisition or a market exchange. In addition, competitors, suppliers and customers may respond, as the termination may either present new opportunities or restrict their range of strategic actions. Paradoxically, terminating one under-performing alliance to improve a firm's performance may actually harm the firm due to unpredictable co-evolutionary processes.

Summary

Alliance co-evolution occurs when different parts of an alliance system evolve simultaneously and interact with each other in such a way that learning and adaptations in the alliance, the partners' organization and the alliance environment influence interactively the performance of the alliance, and thus the performance of the partner firms. As such, alliances depict the outcome, object and trigger of change in the alliance system. However, it is most likely that a state of equilibrium will never be achieved, owing to the converging and diverging patterns of positive and negative feedback across the alliance system levels. Owing to ongoing co-evolutionary processes, the purposeful management of an alliance system is beyond the ability of any manager. However, taking the viewpoint of a single alliance, managers should attempt to take account of the triggers and consequences of co-evolutionary processes in alliance decision-making.

Case: Personal care appliances

The world market for personal care appliances is forecast to maintain a compound annual growth rate (CAGR) of over 2.52 per cent over the years 2000–2010 and reach in excess of 460 million units by the end of the decade.[1] Asia-Pacific is the fastest growing market, with a CAGR of about 4.01 per cent between 2000 and 2010. The growing popularity of personal care appliances is mainly attributed to increased consumer awareness related to improving appearance, and also to personal wellness. There is intense competition in the personal care electrical appliances market due to the presence of a limited number of players, including Colgate-Palmolive, Helen of Troy, Johnson & Johnson, Matsushita Electric Industrial Company, Royal Philips Electronics, Procter and Gamble, Braun, Sanyo Electric Company and Wahl Clipper Corporation. A sub-segment in the personal care market is oral care appliances.

The global market for oral care appliances is largely driven by electric toothbrushes, the sales value of which increased by approximately 15 per cent in 2005. Greater efficiency and lower prices improved the position of electric toothbrushes relative to other oral care products. Increasing demand for power toothbrushes was initially driven by consumer curiosity, as well as the promise of delivering a simple and effective brushing experience. Compared to manual toothbrushes, however, the power toothbrush segment is characterized by a high degree of fragmentation, primarily due to high-cost and high-end models. Between 2000 and 2010, several key events occurred in the fast growing oral care market.

In 2000, Proctor and Gamble (P&G) invested more than $200 million in global sales, helping Crest become the consumer-product maker's twelfth billion-dollar brand. This investment also helped Crest reclaim the title as the number-one oral care brand in the US, a position it lost to Colgate in 1998. However, a small company called SpinBrush developed a new electric toothbrush and sold it for only $5, at a time when most electric brushes were priced at more than $50.

In 2000, SpinBrush became the best-selling toothbrush in the United States. In 2001, Proctor and Gamble (P&G) acquired SpinBrush, which helped P&G's Crest oral care business grow rapidly. Following the acquisition, P&G sold SpinBrush in around 35 countries, marking its quickest global rollout ever. It also added a multitude of models, including ones with replaceable heads. SpinBrush also marked a dramatic departure for the 165-year-old P&G. For once, P&G did not insist on controlling every step, from product development to pricing. Instead, it harnessed its greatest strength: its ability to market and distribute products.

In 2000, in response to customer demand, competitor Colgate launched Motion, a SpinBrush look-alike, at the same price. In 2004, Philips and P&G announced a joint venture to co-develop and co-market the IntelliClean System so they could take on their largest competitors in the US oral care market: Gillette and its Oral-B brand. The alliance combined the best companies in the oral health industry, the technological competence of Philips and P&G in the area of oral care, and added Crest's toothpaste expertise. Initially, the IntelliClean was available only through the American Dental Association (ADA), but was launched in the US consumer market in 2005.

In 2005, P&G embarked on its largest acquisition to date, a $57 billion deal for Gillette that would create the world's largest consumer-products company. P&G added Duracell batteries, Right Guard deodorant and Gillette razors to its more than 300 consumer brands. P&G's acquisition of Gillette further intensified competition in the oral care market. In 2005, the SpinBrush product line was acquired by Church & Dwight from P&G, the latter divesting its SpinBrush toothbrush business because it competed with Gillette's Oral-B brand, which had a better position in the electric toothbrush market. In addition, Gillette was very competitive, and probably had the best power-brushes in the world at that time. However, P&G's acquisition of Gillette conflicted with its partnership with Philips for the IntelliClean brand, as Oral-B and IntelliClean competed heavily. Moreover, the US market for rechargeable toothbrushes was highly concentrated, with Gillette and Philips accounting for virtually all sales of these products. The acquisition would have allowed P&G to acquire the only significant competitor to its joint venture partner – Philips – which would have reduced P&G's incentives to support the IntelliClean product. Therefore, the agreement between Philips and P&G was revised to contain non-compete provisions to protect customers' interests. For example, P&G and Philips agreed to limit joint activities to the US market only.

Since the Gillette acquisition, P&G has continued its proactive marketing of the Oral B brand. For example, it has established multiple relationships with professional dentists and associated organizations that endorsed the Oral B brand. In turn, in 2008 Philips Sonicare partnered with Oral Health America (OHA) to conduct a public opinion survey to reveal the state of oral health in America. In 2010, Philips Sonicare also formed an alliance with Susan G. Komen to raise funds for the fight against breast cancer. The power-toothbrush brand donated $100,000 to the organization and agreed to release a commemorative Sonicare toothbrush with a pink power button (pink is the official colour of the Komen organization).

Questions

1. Explain how Proctor & Gamble and Philips use acquisitions and alliances to enhance their competitive positions? What are their different motives?
2. What changes took place on the alliance, partner firm and alliance environment levels and how do they affect the alliance system?

19

ALLIANCE CAPABILITIES

A firm's alliance capability refers to its ability to design, manage and terminate alliances successfully. An alliance capability thus can enhance the overall performance of a firm's alliances, in that it enables the firm to purposefully create, extend or modify the routines it uses to inform its alliance decision making. Firms develop alliance capabilities over time, but they also tend to capture only minimal knowledge or develop just a few best practices. In an environment with few alliances, such an ad hoc approach may be effective; however, the increasing importance of alliances implies that an unstructured approach will ultimately produce frustrating, unsatisfactory results. In contrast, a structured approach that embeds the alliance capability in the organizational design, culture and minds of employees enables the firm to build and deploy its expansive alliance capabilities more effectively. To adopt such a structured approach, alliance managers first need to understand what alliance capabilities are (first section) before they can gain insights into capability building and deployment (second section) and their own necessary competences (third section). In the next two sections we provide a systematic framework with a set of decision-making steps regarding alliance capabilities and a summary. We conclude with a case illustration.

The meaning of alliance capabilities

One of the main factors contributing to strong alliance performance is the development of specific managerial routines to address (sets of) alliances – that is, a firm's alliance capability (Kale and Singh 2007). With alliance capabilities, firms can standardize and optimize the partner selection process, then make appropriate alliance design and management decisions. A highly developed alliance capability also assists firms in choosing performance indicators that are consistent with their specific alliance strategy, then evaluate and, if needed, terminate under-performing alliances while still ensuring favourable outcomes. Beyond the direct effect of alliance capabilities, firms also vary in their degree of capability, such that those with superior competences have a competitive edge over their peers that lack them. To comprehend the performance implications of possessing alliance capabilities, and their varying levels, it becomes important to distinguish between (1) alliance capability routines and (2) alliance capability instruments.

Alliance capability routines

The dynamic capability view (Teece *et al.* 1997) suggests that alliance capabilities constitute a set of managerial routines designed to improve firm performance by optimizing the governance of its alliance. Thus routines relate to the governance of a single alliance, in the form of coordination and transformation routines, or else target the management of a firm's alliance portfolio through alliance proactiveness and alliance portfolio coordination.

Alliance coordination routines coordinate activities and resources with a specific alliance partner (Schilke and Goerzen 2010). They thus provide firms with the ability to formulate an alliance strategy, select an alliance partner, negotiate and design an efficient structure, and then manage, evaluate and terminate that specific alliance. If a firm possesses alliance coordination routines, it will also have developed a standardized approach to guide and inform its decisions about each new alliance. Each alliance development stage demands different alliance capabilities, but their coordination routines enable firms to deal readily with potential deal breakers as the alliance progresses. For example, the routines might centre on developing partner profiles, building long and short lists of potential partners and formulating a partner fit framework to support partner fit analyses. In contrast, in the alliance management stage, the routines pertain to the firm's ability to coordinate, communicate and bond with its counterpart (Schreiner *et al.* 2009). Thus they ensure that any single alliance is governed as efficiently as possible, and that the legitimacy of the transaction is maximized.

Alliance transformation routines instead pertain to a firm's ability to modify alliances over the course of the alliance process (Niederkofler 1991). Where alliance coordination routines inform decision making, transformation routines reflect the recognition that it is unrealistic to expect a perfect fit between partners from the very beginning (Schilke and Goerzen 2010). Interaction and adaptation between partners are prerequisites, as the alliance develops, for establishing and maintaining high partner fit; the transformation routines include contract amendments, fluctuations in alliance-related personnel or changes in alliance-related governance mechanisms that encourage such adaptations. Flexibility in alliance design is frequently mentioned as a critical element of win–win alliances, but transformation routines actually facilitate firms' ability to act flexibly and initiate timely corrective measures during the progression of their partnerships.

Alliance proactiveness pertains to a firm's ability to discover and act on new alliance opportunities before its competitors can (Sarkar *et al.* 2009); it therefore applies beyond individual alliances. By institutionalizing sensing routines, firms can readily identify potential partners and enjoy first-mover advantages over their competitors. The potential scarcity of suitable alliance candidates may leave late movers with sub-optimal partnering options; firms with proactiveness routines enjoy an advantageous position in the market for partners. In a market with limited high-quality partnering options, routines to identify potentially valuable partnering opportunities constitute a source of strategic advantage.

Finally, the potential interdependencies between individual alliances may enable the firm to develop routines for coordinating its alliance portfolio. An alliance portfolio coordination capability helps the firm identify interdependencies, avoid duplicate actions and produce synergies among its individual alliances (Schilke and Goerzen 2010). By systematically identifying and creating synergies, alliance portfolio coordination also can turn an alliance portfolio into more than just the sum of its parts. These routines minimize risks by lowering the resource investments needed to achieve gains and diminish conflicts across different relationships in the firm's alliance portfolio. Supplemental benefits may derive from the firm's ability to identify, assimilate and use knowledge within and across alliance partners. Alliance portfolio coordination also improves the firm's performance, because it implies the coordination of knowledge across otherwise disconnected alliance partners. Routines and practices targeted at knowledge management across alliance partners provide firms with a competitive advantage.

Alliance capability instruments

The performance-enhancing qualities of an alliance capability depend not just on routines but also on the instruments that are at the disposal of the firm (see Table 19.1). For example, an alliance function refers to all systems of communication, authority and workflow surrounding the alliance. It thus provides a focal point for capturing and storing alliance management lessons and best practices, whether in the form of a part- or full-time position or even a specialized department. Firms such as Hewlett-Packard, Eli Lilly and Philips have established separate organizational units to manage their alliances. The alliance department thus functions as a link, a coordinator and a bond within the organization that supports the extensive use and development of alliance capabilities.

Generally an alliance function fulfils five roles: expert, advisor, knowledge manager, coach, and network facilitator (Kale *et al.* 2001). The expert role means it identifies potential partners and governs the ins-and-outs of the alliance relationships. The advisor role refers to providing line management with expertise, tools and operating procedures and, when necessary, mediating in alliances that are suffering escalating conflicts. The knowledge management role requires collecting, codifying and communicating alliance best practices. In the role of coach, it develops and offers training, education and advice to alliance managers and partner firms. Finally, as a network facilitator, the function initiates gatherings to enable alliance managers to meet and share experiences. Firms with such an alliance function tend to enjoy superior performance (Dyer *et al.* 2001).

TABLE 19.1 Alliance capability instruments

Instruments	Description	Tools
Alliance function	Specialized support staff offers (standardized) know-how and know-what, contributing to efficient alliance design, management and assessment.	Alliance department, specialists, designated top executives, designated alliance managers, gatekeepers.
Alliance training	Training and learning enable managers to identify problems, develop solutions, and implement them skilfully and responsibly.	Internal training, external training, alliance handbooks, alliance best practices, cross-alliance evaluation, formal learning structures, training in intercultural management.
Alliance managers	Integrating the function of alliance managers with human resource management practices provides alliance managers with incentives to achieve excellence.	Management programs, competency framework, rewards and bonuses.
Alliance tools	Developing supportive decision-making tools helps alliance managers make better informed decisions.	Alliance database, Intranet, generic template alliance metrics, standardized tools, joint business planning, joint alliance evaluation, country specific management, partner programs.
Third parties	Overcoming deficiencies in alliance capabilities by hiring external parties increases the chances of alliance success.	Consultants, financial/legal experts, mediators for conflict resolution.

Sources: Heimeriks and Duysters (2007); Heimeriks *et al.* (2009).

Alliance training refers specifically to managers' acquisition of the knowledge, skills and mindset required to perform different activities related to each distinct alliance development stage (Heimeriks *et al.* 2009). Firms may engage in different forms of training and learning, including in-house and external alliance training, developing an alliance handbook, cross-alliance evaluations or interdepartmental learning. For example, Hewlett-Packard (HP) developed a two-day course on alliance management, which it offers three times a year. The company also provides shorter, three-hour courses on alliance management and makes all its alliance materials available on the internal HP alliance website. Such offerings are not trivial when it comes to the success of the partnership, because alliance governance often does not come naturally to traditional managers, who prefer decision autonomy.

To effectuate alliance capabilities among alliance managers, firms may develop management development programmes (Lambe *et al.* 2002) to organize alliance manager competences systematically in a competency framework that also includes reward and bonus systems. Participating in such programmes enhances managers' ability to keep track of and coordinate a vast number of partners, and as alliances grow increasingly important for business, such practical alliance management experience is likely to become a standard criterion for managerial careers. Thus HP created opportunities for internal networking among its managers, not just through internal training programmes but also through company-wide alliance summits and virtual meetings with executives. The company also regularly sends alliance managers to alliance management programmes at various business schools to develop their competences.

The standardized alliance tools that firms might develop include alliance databases, intranet access, performance metrics and tools tailored to each alliance development stage (see Table. 19.2). The application of alliance tools indicates that firms have codified and leveraged methodically their alliance knowledge and best practices gained from previous alliances (Kale and Singh 2007). A database provides access to others' past experiences, tools, checklists and information about partners, all of which can support alliance managers in their daily functions. Hewlett-Packard again offers a prime example: it has developed 60 different tools and templates, all of which are included in a 300-page manual for decision making in specific alliance situations. The manual includes, for example, a template for making a business case for an alliance, a partner evaluation form, a negotiation template that outlines the roles and responsibilities of different departments, a list of ways to measure alliance performance and an alliance termination checklist (Dyer et al. 2001). Such alliance tools not only support managerial decision making, but also enhance alliance performance.

Firms may also use third parties, such as consultants, legal/financial experts and mediators, who provide specialized knowledge related to legal issues, conflict resolution, financing and alliance governance. Because alliance capabilities foster firms' alliance (portfolio) performance, third parties might be helpful for developing and supplementing internal alliance capabilities (Heimeriks and Duysters 2007). For example, during the alliance design stage, firms are likely to rely on outside financial, legal and alliance specialists to secure their investments. They often use external financial experts to perform due diligence or valuation services, as well as to give them advice on investment structures. Legal experts might substitute for a firm's lack of knowledge regarding contractual agreements, especially if the firm is relatively small. When conflicts arise, external experts can assist in conflict resolution by acting as independent mediators. Thus, access to external knowledge decreases the constraints imposed on firms by a scarcity of internal resources and enables them to deal better with their capability deficiencies.

Overall then, firms with alliance capabilities (i.e. routines and instruments) tend to outperform their peers that lack those capabilities (Ziggers and Tjemkes 2010). In particular, they experience more positive effects on their stock prices after alliance announcements (Anand and Khanna 2000), enjoy stronger value creation and profit generation in single alliances (Lambe et al. 2002) and achieve higher overall rates of goal achievement (Heimeriks and Duysters 2007). Institutionalized management processes aimed at coordinating, communicating and bonding the alliance partners

TABLE 19.2 Alliance tools

Alliance strategy formulation	Alliance partner selection	Alliance negotiation	Alliance design	Alliance management	Alliance evaluation	Alliance termination
Value chain analysis	Partner screening form	Negotiation matrix	Alliance governance form guidelines	Alliance contact list	Generic performance metric template	Termination checklist
Resource need checklist	Partner selection protocol	Needs-vs.-wants checklist	Alliance contract template	Alliance communication infrastructure	Evaluation form	Termination planning work sheet
Resource vulnerability checklist	Partner fit framework	Negotiation procedure checklist	Alliance management control guidelines	Trust building worksheet	Checklist metric procedures	Best practice template
	Partner database	Negotiation team checklist		Response strategy framework		

Source: Dyer *et al.* (2001); Kale and Singh (2009).

positively affects performance at both alliance and firm levels (Schreiner *et al.* 2009). Furthermore, processes related to alliance proactiveness, relational governance and strategy or resource coordination by the alliance partners enhance alliance portfolio performance (Sarkar *et al.* 2009). Most companies engage in multiple alliances, so a firm's capability to govern its portfolio alliances constitutes another important competitive advantage.

Building and deploying alliance capabilities

Before a firm can deploy its alliance capabilities, it must obtain access to or develop them. Although firms learn by doing, alliance experience cannot ensure superior alliance performance by itself (Simonin 1997). Lessons must be translated into know-how, which needs to be actively managed and dispersed throughout the organization (Anand and Khanna 2000). Alliance learning processes provide a key mechanism for enabling the alliance function to lead to greater alliance success (Kale and Singh 2007). Deliberate learning mechanisms allow alliance experience to produce enhanced performance in future alliances (Kale *et al.* 2002).

Developing alliance capabilities in particular requires four learning mechanisms: (1) capture, (2) codify, (3) communication and (4) coaching (Dyer *et al.* 2001; Kale and Singh 2007). Drawing on prior experience with alliance relationships, a firm should initiate activities to capture its managers' experiences. For example, debriefing can reveal managers' tacit know-how about the design, management and termination of an alliance. Furthermore, a firm might stimulate the codification or recording of experiences by providing guidelines, checklists and worksheets and encouraging managers to revise them. With such codified knowledge, the firm can encourage activities that facilitate communication among staff members. Knowledge sharing in the form of networks and fora contributes to the development of routines and new insights. Routinization and increasing know-how enable managers to provide coaching that further diffuses alliance knowledge. When these learning mechanisms are employed simultaneously, alliance capabilities become institutionalized.

However, depending on the number and purposes of the alliances they undertake, firms might work to achieve varying competence levels (see Table 19.3). A Level 1 competence suggests that a firm primarily uses a reactive alliance strategy that excludes efforts to build partnerships. Alliances get stimulated by single champions with limited responsibilities. Initial alliance management is chaotic and ad hoc; alliance problems get solved as they arise. No tools support diagnoses or solutions, even if some of these Level 1 firms build on their prior experience to make decisions.

A Level 2 competence suggests that firms recognize that alliances represent viable growth alternatives, so they have standardized their important alliance processes. For example, a firm might have developed a partner fit tool to select the right alliance partner(s) and use it systematically throughout the organization. In addition, it works to develop its efforts in different functional areas, such as R&D, production, marketing, or distribution. Firm-wide, management invests in a

TABLE 19.3 Alliance capability competence levels

	Level 1: Ad hoc	*Level 2: Extended*	*Level 3: Institutionalized*
Alliance	Few alliances; reactive approach disconnected from corporate strategy	Reasonable number of alliances; alliance are strategic alternatives; becoming a partner of choice	Large number of alliances; systematic reengineering of the value chain to develop and sustain competitive advantage
Learning	Non-deliberate and ad hoc	Informal knowledge sharing and codification of best practices	Creation of knowledge structure, processes, and routines to build and leverage alliance capabilities
Champion	Individual, single champion with a vision	Alliance team, responsible for capability building and deployment	Organization, company-wide awareness to build and leverage alliance capabilities
Authority	Line management	Middle management	Top management
Activities	Legal and financial skills; hands-on tools; partner selection; performance assessment	Develop alliance community; standardization of tools across alliance development stages; training, best practice handbook; balanced metrics	Corporate strategy–driven; integrate with firm's strategic analysis, alliance portfolio management; alliance function, alliance programs; intranet

Source: Harbison and Pekar (1998); Pekar and Allio (1994).

corporate architecture and strategy, so to some degree, a Level 2 firm can measure, monitor and perhaps even manage the quality of the alliance process.

A Level 3 competence suggests that firms systematically reengineer the value chain to achieve the close integration of their operational activities. The coherent, integrated alliance strategy gets embedded in the corporate strategy. The firm possesses widespread alliance capabilities and thus can obtain and leverage a competitive advantage through partnerships. Procedures are standardized, often with dedicated staff that engage in significant sharing to develop best practices. Some repository of knowledge has been established for future use; alliance knowledge gets periodically disseminated through training and education. To exploit their alliance knowledge, these firms commit to process discipline; that is, their alliance processes, methods and tools are well organized and finely tuned. On this level alliance management tools are used consistently and developed systemically. At this high level of alliance maturity, one or more specialists are at work within the organization; with greater maturity, this specialist takes a greater role, and the criteria for selecting the specialist become more stringent.

Effective alliance capability building and deploying is conditional on the firms' need and ability to forge alliances. Resource allocation decisions must reflect the size of the firm and its tendency to use alliances as a competitive strategy. For relatively small firms with few alliances, Level 1 alliance capabilities are sufficient. To enhance their alliance capability over time, however, these firms might search for partners with institutionalized alliance capabilities or hire third parties. Relatively large firms with numerous alliances may want to invest to develop a Level 2 competence and eventually progress to Level 3, because for them, alliance capabilities constitute a source of significant competitive advantage.

Alliance managers' competences

Alliances are governed by alliance managers, not partner firms, who are responsible for the design, management and evaluation of the partnerships. Critical to any successful alliance is the designation of a champion who will organize internal support and secure resources, with the confidence and support of top management. A champion also has unconditional faith in the potential success of the alliance and possesses a clear view of its future. Effective champions tend to be senior managers who can adopt a multidisciplinary view on problems and solutions, have been working for the organization for a long time, are familiar with different operational disciplines and have informal internal and external networks. However, because alliances are dynamic entities, each development stage also demands different competences.

Preparing an alliance requires managers with vision and strategic skills. They must be able to communicate how an alliance fits within the firm's corporate strategy. Their aim is to ensure that the collective effort is coherent and that initiatives are communicated vertically and horizontally throughout the organization. In addition, this manager should be able to translate a firm's requirements into a coherent alliance strategy and create constructive perceptions about the alliance's future. The manager also must decide where to direct efforts and energies. With such skills and competences, managers can conduct a proper strategic and partner analysis, which probably requires that they have achieved a senior management position.

The next steps – negotiation and designing – require competences pertaining to advocacy and facilitation. First, the alliance manager must sell the alliance internally to senior and operational managers. Second, an alliance must sell the potential partnership to its counterpart. An alliance manager thus acts as a networker who oversees boundary conditions and disseminates information, both internally and externally. A manager also needs negotiation and political skills to align conflicting interests and explore potential tensions creatively to find common ground and solutions.

The actual management of the alliance requires managers with coordinative and social skills. Coordinative skills pertain to a manager's flexibility, endurance and patience. A manager must be flexible enough to accommodate partners' interests, possess competences to rebuild damaged interpersonal relations and have tolerance for unfamiliar or uncomfortable situations. In addition, endurance and patience will help managers build the honest and reliable personal relationships needed to foster relationship progress. Sensitivity, defined as an ability to listen and observe, is also important with regard to building relational norms and capital. Curiosity is vital: an interest in others contributes to an open climate. Thus, in the management stage, an alliance manager needs the competences to act as both an operational manager and a disturbance handler.

Finally, the alliance termination stage demands different skills to extract value from the relationship and avoid unintended repercussions. A manager should be able to communicate the termination intention and possess mediation skills to deal effectively with the virtually inevitable conflicts. As in the negotiation and design stages, negotiation and political skills are required to organize an exit with favourable outcomes.

Any individual alliance manager is unlikely to have such a comprehensive set of competences, which leads many firms to set up alliance teams. The team comprises a group of diverse people who together personify the managerial competences required for each alliance development stage. It should include some top management representatives to embed the alliance in the organization and provide support when necessary. In addition, operational managers should be part of the alliance team. Their tasks pertain to the daily management of a partnership, and their input is critical during the design and negotiation stage, so they can share their knowledge about the possibilities and adversities associated with operational integration. An alliance team may also benefit from the presence of third-party specialists. Working in an alliance team enables team members to provide and obtain feedback, which means they are likely to avoid adverse decisions that are guided solely by personal interests or hubris. An effective alliance team adopts effective decision-making processes to reduce the probability of failed partnerships.

Alliance capabilities: Decision-making steps

To develop and use alliance capabilities effectively, firms need a systematic, structured approach that allows them to consider a variety of issues. For example, firms must decide on the importance of alliance activity for realizing their strategic objectives and consistently organizing their alliance capabilities. Conditional on this decision, other choices that inform alliance (portfolio) success follow: the use of advanced management techniques, formalization of procedures, dedicated staff, establishment of knowledge repositories, dedicated alliance functions, best practices and alliance training. To facilitate these choices, we organize them into three decision-making steps (see Figure 19.1).

Step 1: Determine the criticality of alliance capabilities

To determine the criticality of an alliance capability, firms must understand how and to what extent their alliances contribute to their competitive advantages. For example, if realizing its long-term strategy depends primarily on a firm's

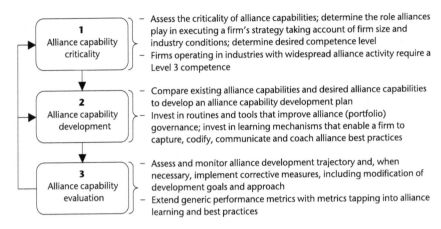

FIGURE 19.1 Decision making steps: Alliance capabilities

autonomous growth, alliances and alliance capabilities will play a limited role. In contrast, if a firm focuses on its core competences and perceives alliances as strategic instruments that help it remain competitive and flexible, building and using alliance capabilities becomes critical. In the latter case, alliances are integral to firms' corporate strategies and embodied in their corporate strategies and policies. That is, even if modern alliances tend to underpin a firm's competitive advantage, the actual alliance capabilities may fulfil three roles:

- Critical success factor: an alliance capability is a critical success factor if it contributes to alliance success but alliances themselves are not key to gaining competitive advantages. To make these alliances work, firms require a Level 1 alliance competence.
- Core competence: an alliance capability constitutes a core competence when the firm obtains a distinctive competitive position through its smart alliance management. Firms leverage their alliance capability to outperform that of their competitors; therefore, they should invest in obtaining Level 2 alliance competence.
- Qualifier: in many industries, allying has become so pervasive that it is virtually impossible to operate successfully without alliances – such as the automotive industry with its manufacturer–supplier dyads, the pharmaceutical industry with its biotechnology links, and the airline industry with its multi-partner coalitions. Thus an alliance capability is a prerequisite for firm survival, and failing to attain Level 3 competences will impose a severe disadvantage on a firm.

Step 2: Formulate and execute alliance capability development plans

Depending on the criticality of its alliance capabilities, a firm should formulate and execute an alliance capability development plan. First, it should identify which alliance capability routines are required to achieve its desired competence level. For example, a firm may develop routines to optimize the governance of single alliances, such as alliance coordination and transformation routines. It also could invest in alliance portfolio routines, including alliance proactiveness and alliance portfolio coordination, or it might seek a combination of single and portfolio alliance routines. Second, the firm should decide which alliance capability instruments are required: is it really necessary to establish an alliance function (see Box 19.1), offer alliance training, initiate a management development programme, build alliance tools and source third parties? Third, by comparing the desired routines and instruments with its existing alliance capabilities, the firm's managers can formulate alliance capability development goals and plan to organize and manage the development trajectory. In other words, managers determine how to capture experience with existing alliances, codify it, communicate the information throughout the organization and coach and facilitate appropriate processes.

BOX 19.1 DESIGNING AN ALLIANCE OFFICE

When an alliance office is centralized, it often represents an integral part of the firm's top management team. The key advantages of centralization include:
- Clustered know-how
- Diffusion throughout operational departments
- Development of best practices
- Specialized expertise and routines
- Ongoing repetition of standardized processes.

Thus a centralized office requires senior executive champions, relationship managers, well-defined tools and practices, consistent and sufficient assistance to business units, coordination across partners, centralized knowledge, and monitoring and management. The contributions of a centralized alliance office to value creation, as perceived by business units, can be limited.

It might be useful instead to consider integrating an alliance office into the operational structure, such that alliance activity is organized within a business unit, which reports to headquarters. The key advantages of such decentralization are:
- Integration into the operational/business strategy
- Ability to adapt to local knowledge of customers and partners
- Direct accountability
- Flexibility and speed in design, decision making, and execution.

In terms of organizational design, decentralization requires informal cross-linkages, limited formalization and bureaucracy, and fast decision making. However, it also makes building and leveraging alliance know-how and know-what across the company more difficult.

Step 3: Evaluate the alliance capability development trajectory

To sustain effective alliance capability developments, managers must continuously monitor the development process. Monitoring provides the necessary information to take appropriate actions, whether that means changing alliance capability development goals, altering the development approach, or organizing and managing the learning processes differently. The criticality of evaluating alliance-learning processes means that firms often should extend their alliance performance metric system with indicators that capture the degree to which they engage in alliance learning and develop and use best practices.

Following the three steps for alliance capability development and deployment does not provide a clear-cut recipe for instant success, but by adopting these insights, alliance managers can enhance their firm's long term alliance capabilities.

Summary

Firms that possess an alliance capability tend to outperform those that lack institutionalized alliance know-how and know-what. An alliance capability can enhance the performance of a firm's (portfolio of) alliances, because it leads to the purposeful creation, extension or modification of the routines and tools that inform alliance decision making. In this context, routines pertain to alliances and alliance portfolio practices that inform decision making; tools constitute the instruments that firms can deploy to manage their partnerships. Conditional on achieving a required level of alliance capabilities – determined by the contribution of the alliance activity to the firm's competitive advantage – firms should engage in a more or less structured approach to build and deploy their alliance capabilities. In short, the firm articulates a clear alliance strategy that is supported by senior management, establishes a dedicated structure to manage and coordinate alliances, facilitates decision making and learning in alliances, invests in building a culture that encourages growth through alliances and provides training to create partnership mindsets and skills. To conclude, alliance capabilities are a means to an end. The various routines, tools, and practices are not designed to impose rigid standardization or corporate dictates, nor should they be objectives in and of themselves. Rather, these practices are intended to improve management skills.

Case: Philips

Founded in 1891 as an electric lamp manufacturer, Royal Philips[1] (Philips) has become a global player in the consumer electronics, healthcare and lighting industries. Throughout its successful history Philips has been known for its innovative capacity to introduce industry- and market-changing products. During the late 1990s Philips engaged increasingly in various partnerships in its attempts to respond to changing global markets. Alliances with companies such as Sara Lee, InBev and Nike enabled Philips to create new product categories that fuelled its growth. Philips also forged multiple alliances with similar partners; companies like Dell, Nokia and Sony were not only Philips customers but also supplied it with many of their own products and services. To deal with the increasing complexity of its relationships and take a more structured approach to dealing with them, Philips established an Alliance Office: a dedicated department tasked with developing and implementing a proactive, systematic, company-wide approach to managing alliances.

The Alliance Office started as a centre of expertise on alliance management and then became a vehicle for developing, spreading, and institutionalizing alliance know-how and know-what. To prioritize its work, the Alliance Office classified Philips' alliances into four categories, based on the level of synergy with the alliance partner and the alliance's potential value. Alliances with low synergy and low potential value represented business alliances, whereas corporate alliances had high value and high synergy. Philips thus focused initially on the management of its most important alliances; for each corporate alliance, it assigned a dedicated alliance manager, created a 'corporate partner team' across divisions with executive sponsorship and organized support by the managerial board. This alliance team interacted frequently to exchange information and develop plans for approaching the partner company.

After enjoying some initial successes, the Alliance Office moved on to tackle strategic alliances, characterized by their high potential value but little apparent synergy with Philips. Strategic alliances typically implied the development of a new product or service and thus demanded high involvement by operational managers. The Alliance Office refrained from active alliance management in this case; instead, it offered support for any consideration of new strategic alliances. Operations and Alliance Office delegates worked together to evaluate systematically the business rationales for each alliance and the extent of partner fit. If the alliance was executed, the Alliance Office provided support, advice and tools for managing it.

The Alliance Office also developed multiple alliance tools to enhance alliance management throughout the organization. For example, its partner selection tool tapped the degree of partner fit between Philips and any potential partner. The tool emphasized the importance of cultural fit: Even if partners contributed complementary resources and shared the same strategic vision, their alliance could still fail if they simply could not work effectively together due to the huge or insurmountable differences in their cultures. The alliance office created other tools for individual managers; for example, a Health Check tool evaluated the performance of any alliance using both hard and soft metrics. The logic behind all these tools was not to prescribe decisions but rather to generate systematic analyses, debate and dialogue to support the decisions that managers must make at every stage of an alliance.

In line with Philips' decentralized management structure, each alliance was formed and managed independently by various divisions or businesses. In this setting, however, it was difficult to share best practices, which led to some repeated alliance mistakes. Therefore, a main objective of the Alliance Office was to institutionalize alliance capabilities and lead the implementation of systematic processes that would guide alliance management decisions. In addition to developing routines, providing tools and advocating their use in individual alliances, the Alliance Office sought to capture and disseminate knowledge to improve the competences of alliance managers. To this end, it organized quarterly alliance meetings and pushed for periodic alliance reviews.

Since establishing the Alliance Office Philips has entered into several successful alliances with companies from a variety of industries, including but not limited to fast-moving consumer goods, telecom, IT and pharmaceuticals. Although initially business managers resisted asking the Alliance Office for help, they quickly acknowledged the value it offered to their business and its performance.

Questions

1. To what extent has the structured approach Philips adopted to govern its alliances contributed to its competitive position?
2. During the establishment of the Alliance Office, Philips' management structure was decentralized. How might this management structure have impeded and/ or reinforced the effectiveness of the Alliance Office?

20

STRATEGIC ALLIANCE MANAGEMENT
Science and Art

A thorough understanding of strategic alliance management is a prerequisite for the twenty-first century, when successful alliances are, and will continue to become increasingly, critical strategic tools in firms' competitive arsenals. They appear in many forms and offer a wide range of benefits – economies of scale, reduced competition, innovation, and profits, to name just a few. Paradoxically, even as firms increase their focus on and use of alliances, failure rates seem to keep climbing. To disentangle the difference between alliance success and failure, we have connected existing theoretical and practical insights to present a much needed, coherent, academically grounded development framework of strategic alliance management that comprises seven separate but related development stages: alliance strategy formulation, partner selection, alliance negotiation, alliance design, alliance management, alliance evaluation and alliance termination. We also have elaborated on rationales for decision-making steps for each stage. Failure might also be attributed to an unawareness of the challenges associated with establishing alliances with unique objectives, diverging partner characteristics, and distinct contexts. Consequently, we have supplemented the generic insights with specific decision-making rationales and steps. Because alliance failure is more likely when firms fail to embed alliance experience in their organizational processes, we have finally detailed how firms can build and deploy their alliance capabilities.

As a whole, this book suggests that alliances can be purposively and almost scientifically designed and managed to achieve success. By applying the alliance development framework, managers will be able to organize their alliance decision making systematically. Yet alliances are dynamic organizational arrangements, and decision makers still confront a wide range of contingencies that often affect alliance processes and outcomes adversely. The insights in this book deal with a substantial number of contingencies, but no list can be exhaustive. In addition, as alliances evolve, managers must address seemingly contradictory, or even mutually exclusive, forces. To resolve these paradoxes, alliance managers should attempt to reconcile the opposing forces creatively; there is no logical way to put the opposites together in an internally consistent pattern. To elaborate on our view that strategic alliance management constitutes both a science and an art, we conclude this book by detailing the science of alliance management, followed by a discussion of its art. We end by outlining several future themes that we expect to become salient to the field of strategic alliance management.

The science of strategic alliance management

A scientific approach to strategic alliance management entails the development of a coherent set of theories that inform objective and systematic decision making. The raison d'être of theory is to reduce the complexity of the empirical world by developing and testing theoretical explanations and predictions (Bacharach 1989). A rigorous theory can be generalized beyond the specific context in which it originated. The alliance development framework presented in this book thus draws on wide-ranging theoretical perspectives used by various academics to explain alliance phenomena. That is, the framework and derived decision-making guidelines are well grounded academically.

Yet there are some limitations to the framework. Some theories aim to explain the same alliance phenomena, but their different approaches and assumptions make the related research findings difficult or even impossible to compare (Bell et al. 2006). For example, transaction cost economics predicts the conditions, such as asset specificity, frequency or uncertainty, in which certain governance forms are most efficient (Williamson 1981). Thus the theory is normative and prescriptive. The institutional approach is incompatible with such normative assumptions (Teng 2005), because its underlying notion that alliances are inherently behavioural responses to external pressures means there is no need for an efficient governance form. Studies from these two distinct theoretical perspectives are therefore essentially incomparable. In addition, many theories provide only partial explanations. For example, the resource-based view states that an alliance should be terminated if the missing resources or capabilities have been captured or are no longer needed. However, little guidance exists regarding the possibility of changing resource needs in relation to a particular alliance. Although a co-evolutionary view on alliances provides some insights into the relationships between learning and adaptation within an alliance system, the explanations are often confined to specific elements (e.g. environmental dynamics, alliance design or alliance management). No single, unique theoretical perspective can provide a coherent set of explanations for deriving systematic guidelines for successful strategic alliance management.

To overcome these limitations, we have drawn on multiple (though certainly not all) theoretical perspectives to arrive at a coherent set of guidelines for alliance decision making. Because alliances depict socially and economically complex organizational entities operating in a continuously changing environment, consisting of members whose mindsets and interests are likely to shape the relationship, the implications of our academically grounded framework can go only so far. One important implication is that strategic alliance management necessitates, in addition to academic knowledge, the experience, expertise and creativity of alliance managers.

The art of strategic alliance management

The foundation for our claim that strategic alliance management constitutes an art that is informed by science is our recognition of alliances as inherently complex organizational arrangements. To reduce this complexity, we have disentangled alliance development systematically into separate and manageable parts; however, we also note that alliance managers confront opposing, and occasionally mutually exclusive, forces that if left unattended will destroy the alliance. Our alliance development framework implicitly details various opposing forces, though we postulate here that three alliance paradoxes permeate all strategic alliance management. We use the label 'paradox' to refer to opposing forces that appear irreconcilable, yet we also argue that through intelligent and creative alliance management, such forces may be resolved (Wit and Meyer 2004). Accordingly, we discuss three key alliance paradoxes: (1) the cooperative versus competitive, (2) the economic versus social and (3) the deliberate versus emergent paradoxes.

The cooperative versus competitive alliance paradox

Cooperation and competition are opposing forces (Das and Teng 2000a). Throughout the alliance development process, any collaboration between partners balances against the competitive aspects of their partnership. Each partner seeks to reconcile joint alliance activities with its own interests. Cooperation consists of the parties' efforts to implement value-creating conditions and processes (Das and Teng 2003). For example, as the alliance progresses, partners may contribute complementary resources (Das and Teng 2000b), make alliance-specific investments (Madhok and Tallman 1998), initiate reciprocal learning (Lubatkin et al. 2001), or invest in relational capital (Ariño and de la Torre 1998) to support the collaborative logic. In contrast, competition implies efforts to appropriate value from the alliance, if necessary, at the expense of the partner firm (Dyer et al. 2008). As the alliance evolves, the partners' focus shifts to realizing a favourable pay-off structure (Parkhe 1993), opportunism (Wathne and Heide 2000), knowledge acquisition (Hamel 1991), and the use of bargaining power (Lax and Sebenius 1986) to support their individual interests. Cooperative and competitive forces thus are at odds, differing in both philosophy and spirit. To realize high-performing, sustainable alliances, such forces are indispensable though and must be reconciled.

A possible way to approach alliances involves considering value creation and appropriation as unrelated, so the alliance depicts a zero-sum situation. Attempts to appropriate more value from the alliance have no effect on value creation. This logic can apply to pure transaction-based alliances with financial objectives, but it appears less valid for more complex alliance relationships that pursue multiple objectives (Tjemkes 2008). Alternatively, considering alliances as positive-sum situations and acknowledging their temporal interrelatedness can help resolve the cooperative–competitive alliance paradox. Initiatives to appropriate excessive value from the alliance hinder subsequent value creation, superior value creation reduces incentives to appropriate excessive value; therefore, value creation and appropriation are interrelated. For example, exercising a bargaining power advantage to reap additional financial benefits may increase a firm's performance temporarily, but it also undermines the counterpart's collaborative effort and jeopardizes joint value creation. Similarly, exploiting an absorptive capacity advantage to obtain additional knowledge may enhance a firm's resource endowment, but it may also ignite a learning race that undermines the alliance's long-term knowledge creation. In contrast, when a firm refrains from exploiting a bargaining power and/or absorptive capacity advantage, it signals commitment to its partner, which increases the chances of greater value creation. Then the firm may appropriate more absolute value, because it focuses on cooperation rather than solely pursuing competition.

The economic versus social alliance paradox

The second alliance paradox comprises the opposing pair of economic and social forces (Faems *et al.* 2008). An economic exchange view focuses on the structural design of single transactions and emphasizes the importance of alliance design (i.e. contracts) as effective and efficient governance mechanism. Alliance managers thus appear rational, purposeful and calculative. In contrast, a social exchange view centres on relational processes in ongoing alliances, and emphasizes the importance of relational norms and capital for coordinating alliances and safeguarding partners' interests. Social bonds and individual entanglements act as social control mechanisms that encourage managers to reciprocate cooperative behaviours (Ring and Van de Ven 1994). Although both economic and social forces drive alliance development and permeate all development stages, they constitute contending forces. Thus a primary focus on the economic aspects of an alliance implies an under-socialized view of managerial action, which is problematic because social interactions in an alliance constitute a critical prerequisite of win–win partnerships. A primary focus on social exchange is also undesirable, in that an over-socialized view neglects alliances' economic purposes. To create a high-performance alliance, the contrasting forces must be reconciled.

Because alliances serve to contribute to firm performance, one way to approach this paradox would be simply to ignore the social side of alliances. Here again though, the logic applies better to simple transactions (i.e. market exchanges) than to complex alliance relationships (Dwyer *et al.* 1987). Economic exchanges are embedded in social relationships (Granovetter 1985), and the way in which decision makers reconcile economic and social forces determines alliance processes and outcomes. Alternatively, resolutions of the alliance paradox could focus on temporal interrelatedness between economic and social forces. For example, Faems and colleagues (2008) show that contracts with a similar degree but different nature of formalization trigger different kinds of trust dynamics. Tjemkes (2008) demonstrates that, conditional on the alliance objective, alliance design directly or indirectly through relational governance influences performance. Therefore, initial alliance design functions as an architecture that either catalyses or impedes social interactions. However, economic and social forces may also become manifest in unison in various distinct development stages. Douma and colleagues (2000) argue that partner selection demands assessments of both economic and social aspects, and Poppo and Zenger (2002) find that formal contracts and relational governance reinforce each other in effective explanations of alliance performance. According to Kumar and Nti (1998), combined assessments of outcome and process discrepancies shape the developmental path of alliances, such that each combination requires different managerial actions. To resolve the alliance paradox then, it is critical to consider economic and social forces simultaneously. That is, decision makers need – in addition to an in-depth understanding of how economic and social forces interrelate, the contingencies that affect them, and their direct and combined impacts on alliance progress – to make use of their experience, expertise and creativity to develop viable solutions.

The deliberate versus emergent alliance paradox

In this third alliance paradox, deliberate and emergent forces come into apparent conflict (Wit and Meyer 2004). Deliberateness suggests that alliances are organizational arrangements that can be designed and managed purposively. Firms can impose controls on and generate predictable patterns of behaviours and actions: they can formulate a set alliance strategy and then develop a plan to execute it. The alliance contract results and they expect partners to behave consistently with the stipulations in that contract. Yet unforeseen events often prompt learning, change and adaptation, which generate necessary patterns of emergent (strategic) actions to recover the relationship. For example, the introduction of a new product by a competitor may prompt partners to re-evaluate their initial plans and develop an alternative course of action. A primary focus on deliberate forces thus suggests that decision makers have a mechanistic understanding of alliance management, which conflicts with the inherently unstable nature of these relationships. A primary focus on emergent forces instead implies a reactive approach to alliance management, which is likely to result in under-performance due to a lack of direction.

To resolve this paradox, alliance partners could simply ignore one force. If they ignore emergence, partners depend solely on a blueprint to form and execute their alliance, which often creates structural and contractual rigidities and restrains partners from responding to internal and external unforeseen circumstances (Das and Teng 2000a). Moreover, partners may become locked into a repeated mode of interaction, with little learning, which initiates greater frustration for both partners in terms of the lack of progress. In contrast, when emergent forces receive too much emphasis, the alliance tends to evolve without direction or control. Even if the alliance objectives have been planned intentionally, progress in the alliance allows new objectives to emerge (Ariño 2003). Without a clear strategy and aligned system, it is difficult to evaluate the potential value of each new objective.

Thus another option arises: to focus on the temporal interrelatedness between deliberate and emergent forces. To achieve short-term results, decision makers set milestones and execute a straightforward project plan, while they also consider their formulated long-term objectives. As the alliance progresses, they use their new insights to deal with emergent circumstances. However, deliberateness and emergence may appear simultaneously, in which case the solution requires some form of separation. For example, it may be beneficial to disconnect exploration and exploitation activities in the alliance (Koza and Lewin 2000). Exploration requires flexibility, whereas exploitation benefits from a more rigid approach. Similarly, the alliance might distinguish decision-making at strategic versus operational levels. In the former, decision-making processes should account for emergent circumstances, whereas in the latter, deliberateness helps the partners achieve efficiency. In any case, it requires skilful, experienced alliance managers to reconcile the tension between deliberate 'stick to the plan' and emergent 'open to adaptation' approaches.

To conclude, although strategic alliances can improve a firm's competitive advantage, they are also inherently fragile, unstable and difficult to manage. Whereas the 'science' element of strategic alliance management advances informed and systematic decision making, alliance managers need to trust their competences to resolve the three alliance paradoxes. Not understanding or neglecting to seek creative solutions may upset the status quo, leading to premature alliance dissolution. Moreover, the alliance paradoxes also become manifest within and between alliance development stages; strategic alliance management thus consists of consecutive and repetitive decisions propelled by interactive forces, namely, cooperative versus competitive, economic versus social and deliberate versus emergent. An in-depth understanding, obtained from long experience, of these contending forces will help alliance managers better predict, prevent and even deal with specific tensions in their own alliance situations. By combining the alliance development framework in this book with their own managerial experience, expertise and creativity, alliance managers can formulate and implement the right decisions for each unique alliance situation they confront (see Figure 20.1).

The future of strategic alliance management

In this book we provide a coherent and comprehensive understanding of strategic alliance management. During the writing process though, novel ideas kept emerging, both in academia and in practice. Unfortunately, we have not been able to incorporate all these brand-new insights in our book, although on the positive side, this trend suggests a bright future for strategic alliance management. We detail four especially promising areas of interest.

First, mainstream alliance research focuses primarily on alliance design, with the argument that design constitutes the primary antecedent of superior alliance performance. However, as we have argued throughout this book, alliance processes

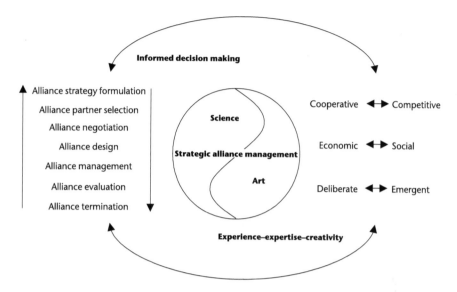

FIGURE 20.1 Strategic alliance management

and managers' behaviours constitute equally important predictors of alliance success. Research on alliance processes and behaviour is advancing (Salk 2005), but several topics remain open as potentially fruitful research avenues:

- *Alliance teams.* Following in the steps of some recent studies (Li and Hambrick 2005), research should explore the relationships among alliance teams, alliance processes and team outcomes, such as decision making and conflicts. In addition, alliances constitute a system of teams from both partners and the alliance. Research should explore the dynamics across this set of teams, as well as among individual team members.
- *Negotiations behaviour.* Building on emerging alliance negotiations research (Das and Kumar 2010), future studies could explore a variety of topics: How can alliance managers achieve favourable processes and outcomes during alliance (re)negotiations? What causes firms to initiate renegotiations? What effect do distinct negotiations behaviours have on alliance development? How does opportunistic behaviour manifest itself during alliance negotiations?
- *Alliances and ICT.* The information and communication technology (ICT) revolution already has affected how alliances function, and it will continue to do so in the future. Yet only a few studies have adopted an ICT lens to examine strategic alliance management (Yang *et al.* 2007). So how might ICT provide opportunities for employees in geographically dispersed locations to communicate, share and collaborate so as to achieve private and common goals? How should partners optimize work-flows in alliances? How can ICT tools enable social activities in alliances, including finding and getting in contact with people, sharing information, and working together?

Second, most alliance research has adopted a static approach (i.e. cross-sectional) (cf. Ariño and de la Torre 1998; de Rond and Bouchikhi 2004). To advance understanding about strategic alliance management, we need a dynamic perspective to disentangle presumed causal relationships, resolve inconclusive results, and unravel multilevel explanations. The following topics may provide inputs for research endeavours:

- *Alliances as multilevel entities.* Studies should explore the dynamics between different levels of analysis (Faems *et al.* 2008), including strategic, tactical, and operational, while focusing on varied, alliance-related phenomena: how do communication, trust and contracting within and between different levels of partner organizations enable or hinder collaborative activities across partners? How do changes at different levels within partner organizations, as well as within the alliance, affect one another? What are the differences and tensions in alliance management between alliances initiated at operational or strategic levels?
- *Alliance as co-evolution.* Although several studies have detailed alliance co-evolution (Volberda and Lewin 2003), numerous questions remain unexplored: how do changes in the partner's alliance portfolio influence a firm's portfolio? How and where should particular buffering systems and boundary-spanning agents be located to deal with disturbances from the environment or alliance partner organizations? To what extent, in what conditions, and how do alliance outcomes affect the alliance environment?
- *Under-performing alliances.* Alliance research tends to focus on alliance performance, neglecting ways in which under-performance is not always the same (Patzelt and Shepherd 2008). Questions that warrant answers include the following: to what extent do antecedents of performance differ from under-performance? What type of intervention (e.g. response strategies) is likely to revitalize an alliance? When should an alliance be terminated, such that dissolution does not occur before objective realization or continues after objective realization?

Third, alliances have become increasingly popular, so new alliance types keep emerging. It is important to understand the motives and governance of these new forms: the quality of alliance decision making is likely conditioned by the type of alliance chosen:

- *Transitional alliance.* In dynamic industries, such as the Internet sector, transitional alliances seem to have replaced traditional partnerships as the most dominant form (Duysters and Man 2003). This type of alliance centres on learning, speed, short planning horizons, network fit and a focus on relatively few specialized tasks. When and how should partners use transitional alliances? What would constitute an efficient design and effective alliance management approach? How are value creation and value appropriation interrelated?

- *Service alliance.* Consistent with the development of servitization (Baines *et al.* 2009), firms increasingly forge alliances to attain service provision benefits. Unlike production, services reach outcomes through co-production with customers, so alliances based on services tend to be highly interactive, short-term focused, and project-based. In which conditions does such a service alliance support a business strategy? How do organizational identity and customer identity interrelate, and what is their impact on alliance performance? How is it possible to manage the alliance–customer interaction?

- *Acquisition alliances.* Although studies have produced insights in the choice between acquisition and alliances, they have tended to neglect the occasional use of an alliance as the predecessor of an acquisition (Hagedoorn and Sadowski 1999). To date, it remains unclear why firms initiate such a trajectory. In what conditions is an alliance transformed into an acquisition? How does an integration trajectory progress, how does alliance management differ from traditional acquisitions, and what are performance implications?

- *Crowdsourcing and crowdfunding.* Technology makes it possible to communicate easily with customers and suppliers and to use their resources for different purposes, such as innovation, policy making and marketing. The notion of crowdsourcing (Howe 2008) is increasingly becoming a tool that firms depend on to accelerate their innovation processes and outcomes. Instead of raising funds from a very small group of sophisticated investors, firms seek increasingly to secure financial resources from a large audience, often through social media, or crowdfunding. Research needs to address several questions, such as how to mobilize, motivate and reward a crowd for funding. How should firms monitor crowdsourcing processes and outcomes (e.g. intellectual property)? How can they best distribute the generated value?

Fourth, moving beyond the single alliance perspective, several developments require attention, especially with regard to their effects on the management of single alliance relationships. Three key themes are:

- *Open innovation.* In response to an environment becoming increasingly dynamic and demanding, firms shift from organizing innovation internally to mobilizing and integrating external resources – that is, open innovation (Chesbrough 2003). How can these firms organize co-creation among producers, customers, suppliers, competitors and so on? How should they leverage and protect critical resources?

- *Alliance portfolio.* Alliance portfolios constitute a source of competitive advantage and recent studies offer insights in portfolio design and management (Hoffmann 2007). However, numerous questions remain unanswered. How do alliance portfolios develop over time? In what conditions are alliance portfolios effective? How is it possible to capture and measure portfolio performance?

- *Alliance capabilities.* Research tends to converge on the salience of alliance capabilities (Schilke and Goerzen 2010) but not on the answers to several remaining issues. In what conditions do internally (e.g. alliance) and externally (e.g. consultants) sourced functions become substitutes or complements? How do alliance capabilities develop over time? How can firms optimize the deployment of alliance capabilities?

Academics should explore these research themes and develop rigorous theories, which then can inform alliance decision making. Studies also need to build on prior research to develop a conceptually sound and empirically validated body of knowledge. The accumulation of such knowledge will allow for verification, falsification and replication, which can help build a theoretically consistent, integrated and logical structure of ideas. These theoretical advances may benefit managers by enhancing their ability to deal with their strategic alliances – which means in turn that research output must be practically applicable, incorporate explanations and guidelines for managers, provide counter-intuitive insights and apply to practitioners at an appropriate time. With this book, we hope to have made one such a relevant contribution.

NOTES

Chapter 1

1 Williamson (1985) calls the three governance modes hierarchy, market, and hybrid.
2 *Financial Times* (2010); *Guardian* (2010).

Chapter 3

1 Interview with a senior executive of Grolsch.

Chapter 4

1 Lewis (2004); Renault (2010); Weis (2011); corporate website: http://www.nissan-global.com/EN/index.html (accessed 2 August 2011).

Chapter 5

1 Microsoft News Center (2001); Nokia (2011); *PC World* (2009); Today in Windows (2001); Fried (2011).

Chapter 6

1 This section builds on prior research with Olivier Furrer (Radboud University Nijmegen), whom we acknowledge for his contribution.
2 Interviews with two senior executives of TNO and two senior executives of Hoogendoorn.

Chapter 7

1 See Innovarno Pharma Licensing (2006); Schering Plough (2004); Verhoeven (2009).
2 See Frincu (2007); corporate websites: http://www.lg.com/nl/over-lg/index.jsp (accessed 2 August 2011); http://www.philips.nl/ (accessed 2 August 2011).
3 See Beauty King (2005); Beauty Packaging (2010).

Chapter 8

1 Dickinson and Moure (2008); Zhou (2009); Yu (2009); Dickinson (2007).

Chapter 9

1 Interview with senior executives of NAM.

Chapter 10

1 Interview with a senior executive of Holst Centre.

Chapter 11

1 Gamerslifeline.com (2010); Capcom (2010).

Chapter 12

1 *China Business Review* (2008); *Shenzhen Daily* (2007); *Alternate Medic* (2007); *Sidney Morning Herald* (2008).

Chapter 13

1 This section builds on prior research with Anoop Madhok (Schulich School of Business), whom we acknowledge for his contribution.
2 CNNMoney (2004); ICMR (2006); Pixar Planet forum (2008); Fonda (2006); corporate website: http://www.pixar.com/companyinfo/ (accessed 2 August 2011).

Chapter 14

1 Interview with a senior executive of TNT.

Chapter 15

1 Interview with a senior executive of KLM.

Chapter 16

1 Business Wire (2011b); Capgemini (2007); Deutsch (2007).

Chapter 17

1 Adapted from Dittrich *et al.* (2007). See also IBM (2007); TechScoop (2011); IBM (2011a); IBM (2011b).

Chapter 18

1 Businessweek Online (2002); Federal Trade Commission (2006); *HFN Daily News* (2010); Oral Health America (2008); Philips (2004); and PR Web (2008).

Chapter 19

1 Bell and Lemmens (2007); Bell *et al.* (2010); Singh *et al.* (2008).

REFERENCES

Achrol, R.S. (1997) 'Changes in the theory of interorganizational relations in marketing: Toward a network paradigm'. *Journal of the Academy of Marketing Science*, 25: 56–71.

AFX News Limited (2007) 'Anheuser–Busch in alliance to import Budejovicky Budvar's Czechvar into VS'. Forbes Online. Available online at http://www.forbes.com/feeds/afx/2007/01/08/afx3309265.html (accessed 2 August 2011).

Ahuja, G. (2000) 'Collaboration networks, structural holes, and innovation: A longitudinal study'. *Administrative Science Quarterly*, 45: 425–455.

Albanese, R. and Van Fleet, D.D. (1985) 'The free-riding tendency in organizations'. *Scandinavian Journal of Management Studies*, 2: 121–135.

Aldrich, H.E. and Pfeffer, J. (1976) 'Environments of organization'. *Annual Review of Sociology*, 2: 79–105.

Algeanews (2011) 'Solazyme and Bunge sign JDA partnership for production of renewable triglyceride oils'. Available online at http://algaenews.com/?p=384 (accessed 2 August 2011).

Alternate Medic (2007) 'Even Coca-cola is looking into Chinese herbal medicines'. Available online at http://www.alternatively-healthier.com/chinese-herbal-medicines.html (accessed 2 August 2011).

Alvarez, S.A. and Barney, J.B. (2001) 'How entrepreneurial firms can benefit from alliances with large partners'. *Academy of Management Executive*, 15: 139.

Anand, B.N. and Khanna, T. (2000) 'Do firms learn to create value? The case of alliances'. *Strategic Management Journal*, 21: 295–315.

Anderson, E. (1990) 'Two firms, one frontier: On assessing joint venture performance'. *Sloan Management Review*, 31: 19–30.

Ariño, A. (2003) 'Measures of collaborative venture performance: an analysis of construct validity'. *Journal of International Business Studies*, 34: 66–79.

Ariño, A. and De la Torre, J. (1998) 'Learning from failure: Towards an evolutionary model of collaborative ventures'. *Organization Science*, 9: 306–325.

Ariño, A. and Reuer, J.J. (2004) 'Designing and renegotiating strategic alliance contracts'. *Academy of Management Executive*, 18: 37–48.

Ariño, A., de la Torre, J. and Ring, P.S. (2001) 'Relational quality: Managing trust in corporate alliances'. *California Management Review*, 44: 109–131.

Arla (2011) 'Vitamin D: The effect of vitamin D enrichments in Danish families'. Available online at http://www.arla.com/about-us/research-and-innovation/research-strategy/research-partnerships/vitamin-d/ (accessed 2 August 2011).

Arora, A. and Ceccagnoli, M. (2006) 'Patent protection, complementary assets, and firms' incentives for technology licensing'. *Management Science*, 52: 293–308.

Arya, B. and Salk, J.E. (2006) 'Cross-sector alliance learning and effectiveness of voluntary codes of corporate social responsibility'. *Business Ethics Quarterly*, 16: 211–234.

Aulakh, P.S., Kotabe, M. and Sahay, A. (1996) 'Trust and performance in cross-border marketing partnerships: A behavioral approach'. *Journal of International Business Studies*, 27: 1,005–1,032.

Austin, J.E. (2000) *The Collaboration Challenge: How Nonprofits and Business Succeed Through Strategic Alliances*. San Francisco, CA: Jossey-Bass.

Bacharach, S.B. (1989) 'Organizational theories – Some criteria for evaluation'. *Academy of Management Review*, 14: 496–515.

Baines, T.S., Lightfoot, H.W., Benedettini, J.M. and Kay, J.M. (2009) 'The servitization of manufacturing: A review of literature and reflection on future challenges'. *Journal of Manufacturing Technology Management*, 20: 547–567.

Bamford, J.D. and Ernst, D. (2003) 'Growth of alliance capabilities'. In Bamford, J.D., Gomes-Casseres, B. and Robinson, M.S. (eds.), *Mastering Alliance Strategy: A Comprehensive Guide to Design, Management, and Organization*, San Francisco: Jossey-Bass, pp. 321–333.

Barkema, H.G., Bell, J.H.J. and Pennings, J.M. (1996) 'Foreign entry, cultural barriers, and learning'. *Strategic Management Journal*, 17: 151–166.

Barney, J.B. (1991) 'Firm resources and sustained competitive advantage'. *Journal of Management*, 17: 99–120.

Barney, J.B. and Hansen, M.H. (1994) 'Trustworthiness as a source of competitive advantage'. *Strategic Management Journal*, 15: 175–190.

Barringer, B.R. and Harrison, J.S. (2000) 'Walking a tightrope: Creating value through interorganizational relationships'. *Journal of Management*, 26: 367–403.

BASF News (2011) 'Plant biotechnology'. Available online at http://www.basf.com/group/corporate/en/products-and-industries/biotechnology/plant-biotechnology/index (accessed 2 August 2011).

Baum, J.A.C., Calabrese, T. and Silverman, B.S. (2000) 'Don't go it alone: Alliance network composition and startups' performance in Canadian biotechnology'. *Strategic Management Journal*, 21: 267–294.

Beamish, P.W. (1993) 'Characteristics of joint ventures in the people's Republic of China'. *Journal of International Marketing*, 1: 29–48.

Beauty King (2005) 'International: Seizing the potential in all markets'. Available online at http://www.reveal-thegame.com/docs/International-Seizing_the_potential_in_all_markets.pdf (accessed 2 August 2011).

Beauty Packaging (2010) '2009 company of the Year L'Oréal: Believable Beauty'. Available online at http://www.beautypackaging.com/articles/2010/01/2009-company-of-the-year-loreal-believable-beauty/ (accessed 2 August 2011).

Beer (2006) 'Keycorp in Latin America MasterCard Paypass partnership'. Available online at http://www.itwire.com/it-industry-news/listed-techs/6905-keycorp-in-latin-america-mastercard-paypass-partnership (accessed 2 August 2011).

Bell, J. and Lemmens, C.E.A.V. (2007) 'Alliantievaardigheden als kerncompetentie: een verdiepende case study'. *Tijdschrift voor Management en Organisatie*, 61: 129–138.

Bell, J., den Ouden, B. and Ziggers, G.W. (2006) 'Dynamics of cooperation: At the brink of irrelevance'. *Journal of Management Studies*, 43: 1,607–1,619.

Bell, J., Singh, H. and Kale, P. (2010) 'Making strategic alliances work: How Royal Philips tries to build alliance capability'. In Tjemkes, B., van den Hout, T. and Schrijver, I. (eds.), *Strategie in verhouding: Netwerken, stakeholders, samenwerken*, Den Haag: Lemma, pp. 165–174.

Berthon, P., Pitt, L.F., Ewing, M.T. and Bakkeland, G. (2003) 'Norms and power in marketing relationships: Alternative theories and empirical evidence'. *Journal of Business Research*, 56: 699–709.

Biotechnology and Biological Sciences Research Council News (2010) 'Public–private research partnership to develop improved crops for food security'. Available online at http://www. alphagalileo.org/ViewItem.aspx?ItemId=70268&CultureCode=en (accessed 2 August 2011).

Blankenburg Holm, D., Eriksson, K. and Johanson, J. (1999) 'Creating value through mutual commitment to business network relationships'. *Strategic Management Journal*, 20: 467–486.

Blau, P.M. (1964) *Exchange and Power in Social Life*. New York: Wiley.

Blodgett, L.L. (1991a) 'Partner contributions as predictors of equity share in international joint ventures'. *Journal of International Business Studies*, 22: 63–78.

Blodgett, L.L. (1991b) 'Toward a resource-based theory of bargaining power in international joint ventures'. *Journal of Global Marketing*, 5: 35–54.

Blodgett, L.L. (1992) 'Factors in the instability of international joint ventures – An event history analysis'. *Strategic Management Journal*, 13: 475–481.

Boersma, M.F., Buckley, P.J. and Ghauri, P.N. (2003) 'Trust in international joint venture relationships'. *Journal of Business Research*, 56: 1,031–1,042.

Bonaccorsi, A. and Piccaluga, A. (2000) 'A theoretical framework for the evaluation of university–industry relationships'. *R&D Management*, 24: 229–247.

Bradford, K.D., Stringfellow, A. and Weitz, B.A. (2004) 'Managing conflict to improve the effectiveness of retail networks'. *Journal of Retailing*, 80: 181–195.

Brouthers, K.D. and Bamossy, G.J. (2006) 'Post-formation processes in eastern and western European joint ventures'. *Journal of Management Studies*, 43: 203–229.

Brown, T.J. and Dacin, P.A. (1997) 'The company and the product: Corporate associations and consumer product responses'. *Journal of Marketing*, 61: 68–84.

Browning, L.D., Beyer, J.M. and Shetler, J.C. (1995) 'Building cooperation in a competitive industry: SEMATECH and the semiconductor industry'. *Academy of Management Journal*, 38: 113–151.

Büchel, B. (2002) 'Joint venture development: Driving forces towards equilibrium'. *Journal of World Business*, 37: 199–207.

Büchel, B. and Thuy, L.X. (2001) 'Measures of joint venture performance from multiple perspectives: An evaluation by local and foreign managers in Vietnam'. *Asia Pacific Journal of Management*, 18: 101–111.

Burt, R.S. (1982) *Toward a Structural Theory of Action: Network Models of Social Structure, Perception, and Action*. New York: Acadamic Press.

Business Week (2010) 'Balfour Beatty Rail, Inc. wins construction of Denver's multi-billion dollar Eagle P3 commuter rail project'. Available online at http://investing.business week.com/research/stocks/private/snapshot.asp?privcapId=6461704 (accessed 2 August 2011).

Businessweek Online (2002) 'Why P&G's smile is so bright: With the fast-growing SpinBrush, the company bent its own rules – and won'. Available online at http://karlulrich. pbworks.com/f/P&G-spinbrush.pdf (accessed 2 August, 2011).

Business Wire (2011a) 'Solazyme and Dow form an alliance for the development of micro algae-derived oils for use in bio-based dielectric insulating fluids'. Available online at http:// www.businesswire.com/news/home/20110309005503/en/Solazyme-Dow-Form-Alliance-Development-Micro-Algae-Derived (accessed 2 August 2011).

Business Wire (2011b) 'GE Energy Financial Services expands gas-fired lending portfolio with $73 million for LS power merchant plant'. Available online at http://www.businesswire. com/news/home/20110613006238/en/GE-Energy-Financial-Services-Expands-Gas-Fired-Lending (accessed 2 August 2011).

Buss (2003) 'Happily ever after'. Available online at http://www.brandchannel.com/features_ effect.asp?pf_id=151 (accessed 2 August 2011).

Caniëls, M.C.J. and Gelderman, C.J. (2010) 'The safeguarding effect of governance mechanisms in inter-firm exchange: The decisive role of mutual opportunism'. *British Journal of Management*, 21: 239–254.

Capaldo, A. (2007) 'Network structure and innovation: The leveraging of a dual network as a distinctive relational capability'. *Strategic Management Journal*, 28: 585–608.

Capcom (2010) 'Capcom partners with playboy for dead rising'. Available online at http:// www.capcom-unity.com/jgonzo/blog/2010/06/11/capcom_partners_with_playboy_ for_dead_rising_2! (accessed 2 August 2011).

Capgemini (2007) 'Smart energy alliance: Planning next generation distribution with the distribution roadmap'. Available online at http://www.capgemini.com/insights-and-resources/by-publication/distribution_roadmap/ (accessed 2 August 2011).

Chai, K.H. (2003) 'Bridging islands of knowledge: A framework of knowledge sharing mechanisms'. *International Journal of Technology Management*, 25: 703–727.

Chang, W.L. (2009) 'Using multi-criteria decision aid to rank and select co-branding partners: From a brand personality perspective'. *Kybernetes*, 38: 954–969.

Chang, W.L. and Chang, K.C. (2008) 'A taxonomy model for a strategic co-branding position'. In Hawamdeh, S., Stauss, K. and Barachini, F. (eds.), *Knowledge Management: Competencies and Professionalism*, Series on Innovation and Knowledge Management World Scientific Publishing, Singapore. Vol. 7, pp. 355–366.

Chen, C.J. (2004) 'The effects of knowledge attribute, alliance characteristics, and absorptive capacity on knowledge transfer performance'. *R&D Management*, 34: 311–321.

Chen, D., Park, S.H. and Newburry, W. (2009) 'Parent contribution and organizational control in international joint ventures'. *Strategic Management Journal*, 30: 1,133–1,156.

Chesbrough, H. (2003) *Open Innovation: The New Imperative for Creating and Profiting from Technology*. Boston, MA: Harvard Business School Press.

Chi, T. (1994) 'Trading in strategic resources – necessary conditions, transaction cost problems, and choice of exchange structure'. *Strategic Management Journal*, 15: 271–290.

Child, J. (2002) 'A configurational analysis of international joint ventures'. *Organization Studies*, 23: 781–815.

Child, J. and Faulkner, D. (1998) *Strategies of Cooperation: Managing Alliances, Networks, and Joint Ventures*. Oxford: Oxford University Press.

Child, J. and Yan, Y.N. (1999) 'Investment and control in international joint ventures: The case of China'. *Journal of World Business*, 34: 3–15.

China Business Review (2008) 'Coca Cola in China: Quenching the thirst of a billion'. Available online at http://www.chinabusinessreview.com/public/0107/weisert.html (accessed 2 August 2011).

Cisionwire (2001) 'Sony Ericsson Mobile Communications established today'. Available online at http://www.cisionwire.com/ericsson/r/sony-ericsson-mobile-communications-established-today,c48602 (accessed 2 August 2011).

CNNMoney (2004) 'Pixar dumps Disney'. Available online at http://money.cnn.com/2004/01/29/news/companies/pixar_disney/ (accessed 2 August 2011).

CNN News (2008) 'Royal Dutch Shell forms biofuel research'. Available online at http://www.csnews.com/top-story-royal_dutch_shell_forms_biofuel_research_partnership-54425.html (accessed 2 August 2011).

Coff, R.W. (1999) 'When competitive advantage doesn't lead to performance: The resource-based view and stakeholder bargaining power'. *Organization Science*, 10: 119–133.

Cohen, W.M. and Levinthal, D. (1990) 'Absorptive capacity: A new perspective on learning and innovation'. *Administrative Science Quarterly*, 35: 128–152.

Coleman, J.S. (1990) *Foundations of Social Theory*. Cambridge: Harvard University Press.

Contractor, F. J. (2001) 'Intangible assets and principles for their valuation', in Contractor, F.J. (ed.), *Valuation of Intangible Assets in Global Operations*, pp. 3–24.

Contractor, F. J. (2005) 'Alliance structure and process: Will the two research streams ever meet in alliance research?'. *European Management Review*, 2: 123–129.

Contractor, F. J. and Ra, W. (2000) 'Negotiating alliance contracts – Strategy and behavioral effects of alternative compensation arrangements'. *International Business Review*, 9: 271–299.

Cravens, K., Piercy, N. and Cravens, D. (2000) 'Assessing the performance of strategic alliances: Matching metrics to strategies'. *European Management Journal*, 18: 529–541.

CSIS News (2011) 'CARE and Cargill: An innovative NGO–private sector partnership to fight global poverty'. Available online at http://csis.org/event/care-and-cargill-innovative-ngo-private-sector-partnership-fight-global-poverty (accessed 2 August 2011).

Cullen, J.B., Johnson, J.L. and Sakano, T. (1995) 'Japanese and local partner commitment to IJVs: Psychological consequences of outcomes and investments in the IJV relationship'. *Journal of International Business Studies*, 26: 91–115.

Cummings, J.L. and Teng, B.-S. (2003) 'Transferring R&D knowledge: The key factors affecting knowledge transfer success'. *Journal of Engineering and Technology Management*, 20: 39–68.

Dacin, M.T., Hitt, M.A. and Levitas, E. (1997) 'Selecting partners for successful international alliances: Examination of US and Korean firms'. *Journal of World Business*, 32: 3–16.

Das, T.K. and Kumar, R. (2010) 'Inter-partner negotiations in the alliance development', in Das, T.K. (ed.), *Researching Strategic Alliances: Emerging Perspectives*. Charlotte, NC: Information Age Publishing, pp. 207–258.

Das, T.K. and Rahman, N. (2001) 'Partner misbehaviour in strategic alliances: Guidelines for effective deterrence'. *Journal of General Management*, 27: 43–70.

Das, T.K. and Teng, B.-S. (2000a) 'Instabilities of strategic alliances: An internal tensions perspective'. *Organization Science*, 11: 77–101.

Das, T.K. and Teng, B.-S. (2000b) 'A resource-based theory of strategic alliances'. *Journal of Management*, 26: 31–61.

Das, T.K. and Teng, B.-S. (2001) 'Trust, control, and risk in strategic alliances: An integrated framework'. *Organization Studies*, 22: 251–283.

Das, T.K. and Teng, B.-S. (2002) 'The dynamics of alliance conditions in the alliance development process'. *Journal of Management Studies*, 39: 725–746.

Das, T.K. and Teng, B.-S. (2003) 'Partner analysis and alliance performance'. *Scandinavian Journal of Management*, 19: 279–308.

D'Aunno, T.A. and Zuckerman, H.S. (1987) 'A life cycle model of organizational federations: The case of hospitals'. *Academy of Management Review*, 12: 534–545.

David, R.J. and Han, S.K. (2004) 'A systematic assessment of the empirical support for transaction cost economics'. *Strategic Management Journal*, 25: 39–58.

Deeds, D.L. and Hill, C.W.L. (1998) 'An examination of opportunistic action within research alliances: Evidence from the biotechnology industry'. *Journal of Business Venturing*, 14: 141–163.

Dekker, H.C. (2004) 'Control of inter-organizational relationships: Evidence on appropriation concerns and coordination requirements'. *Accounting Organizations and Society*, 29: 27–49.

de Man, A.P. (2005) 'Alliance capability: A comparison of the strength of European and American companies'. *European Management Journal*, 23: 315–323.

Den Hartigh, E., Ortt, G., Van de Kaa, G. and Stolwijk, C. (2010). 'Technology standards battles and business networks during the technology life cycle: A comparative case study'. *Economics and Management of Innovation: EMI Discussion Paper Series*: #2009–04.

de Rond, M. and Bouchikhi, H. (2004) 'On the dialectics of strategic alliances'. *Organization Science*, 15: 56–69.

Deutsch, C.H. (2007) 'New York Times, the venturesome giant'. *New York Times*. Available online at http://www.nytimes.com/2007/10/05/business/worldbusiness/05venture.html (accessed 2 August 2011).

de Wulf, K. and Odekerken-Schroder, G. (2001) 'A critical review of theories underlying relationship marketing in the context of explaining consumer relationships'. *Journal for the Theory of Social Behaviour*, 31: 73–101.

Dickinson, S. (2007), 'Danone v. Wahaha: On the lessons to be learned from the tensions within China's largest beverage joint venture'. *China Economic Review*. Available online at http://www.chinaeconomicreview.com/cer/2007_09/Danone_v_Wahaha.html (accessed 2 August 2011).

Dickinson, S. and Moure, H. (2008) 'Danone v. Wahaha: Lessons for joint ventures in China'. Chinalawblog.com. Available online at http://www.chinalawblog.com/Danone WahahaLessons.pdf (accessed 2 August 2011).

DiMaggio, P.J. and Powell, W.W. (1983) 'The iron cage revisited – Institutional isomorphism and collective rationality in organizational fields'. *American Sociological Review*, 48: 147–160.

Ding, D.Z. (1997) 'Control, conflict, and performance: A study of US–Chinese joint ventures'. *Journal of International Marketing*, 5: 31–45.

Dittrich, K., Duysters, G. and de Man, A.P. (2007) 'Strategic repositioning by means of alliance networks: The case of IBM'. *Research policy*, 36: 1,496–1,511.

Douma, M.U., Bilderbeek, J., Idenburg, P.J. and Looise, J.K. (2000) 'Strategic alliances – Managing the dynamics of fit'. *Long Range Planning*, 33: 579–598.

Doz, Y.L. (1996) 'The evolution of cooperation in strategic alliances: Initial conditions or learning processes?' *Strategic Management Journal*, 17: 55–83.

Doz, Y. and Hamel, G. (1998) *Alliance Advantage: The Art of Creating Value through Partnering*. Boston, MA: Harvard Business School Press.

Duysters, G. and Man, de, A.P. (2003) 'Transitory alliances: An instrument for surviving turbulent industries?'. *R&D Management*, 33: 49–58.

Duysters, G., Kok, G. and Vaandrager, M. (1999) 'Crafting successful strategic technology partnerships'. *R&D Management*, 29: 343–351.

Dwyer, F.R., Schurr, P.H. and Oh, S. (1987) 'Developing buyer–seller relationships'. *Journal of Marketing*, 51: 11–27.

Dyer, J.H. (1996) 'Specialized supplier networks as a source of competitive advantage: Evidence from the auto industry'. *Strategic Management Journal*, 17: 271–291.

Dyer, J.H. (1997) 'Effective interfirm collaboration: How firms minimize transaction costs and maximize transaction value'. *Strategic Management Journal*, 18: 535–556.

Dyer, J.H. and Nobeoka, K. (2000) 'Creating and managing a high-performance knowledge-sharing network: The Toyota case'. *Strategic Management Journal*, 21: 345–367.

Dyer, J.H. and Singh, H. (1998) 'The relational view: Cooperative strategy and sources of interorganizational competitive advantage'. *Academy of Management Review*, 23: 660–679.

Dyer, J.H., Kale, P. and Singh, H. (2001) 'How to make strategic alliances work: Developing a dedicated alliance function is key to building the expertise needed for competitive advantage'. *Sloan Management Journal*, 42: 37–43.

Dyer, J., Singh, H. and Kale, P. (2008) 'Splitting the pie: Rent distribution in alliances and networks'. *Managerial and Decision Economics*, 29: 137–148.

Economist (1998) 'The science of alliance'. Available online at http://www.economist.com/node/361379?story_id=E1_PGTPSJ (accessed 2 August 2011).

EE Times (2006) 'IBM, Sony, Toshiba tip 32-nm alliance'. Available online at http://www.eetimes.com/electronics-news/4057811/Updated-IBM-Sony-Toshiba-tip-32-nm-alliance (accessed 2 August 2011).

Eneco Nieuws (2011) 'Samen voor schone energie en natuurbescherming'. Available online at http://thuis.eneco.nl/nieuws/eneco-en-wereld-natuur-fonds-partners/ (accessed 2 August 2011).

Energyboom (2011) 'Solazyme and Dow Chemicals form algae partnership'. Available online at http://www.energyboom.com/biofuels/solazyme-and-dow-chemical-form-algae-partnership (accessed 2 August 2011).

Erevelles, S., Stevenson, T.H., Srinivasan, S. and Fukawa, N. (2008) 'An analysis of B2B ingredient co-branding relationships'. *Industrial Marketing Management*, 37: 940–952.

Eurekalert (2011) 'Optiqua–NTU partnership to develop the next-generation sensor technology'. Available online at http://www.eurekalert.org/pub_releases/2011-02/ntu-opt021411.php (accessed 2 August 2011).

Evangelista, F. and Hau, L.N. (2009) 'Organizational context and knowledge acquisition in IJVs: An empirical study'. *Journal of World Business*, 44: 63–73.

Faems, D., Janssens, M., Madhok, A. and Van Looy, B. (2008) 'Toward an integrative perspective on alliance governance: Connecting contract design, trust dynamics, and contract application'. *Academy of Management Journal*, 51: 1,053–1,078.

Farrell, D. (1983) 'Exit, voice, loyalty, and neglect as responses to job dissatisfaction – A multidimensional-scaling study'. *Academy of Management Journal*, 26: 596–607.

Faulkner, D. (1995) *International Strategic Alliances: Co-operating to Compete*. Maidenhead, UK: McGraw-Hill.

Federal Trade Commission (2006) 'Analysis of agreement containing consent orders to aid public comment: In the matter of the Procter & Gamble company and the Gillette company, file no. 051-0115'. Available online at http://www.ftc.gov/os/caselist/0510115/050930ana0510115.pdf (accessed 2 August 2011).

Financial Times (2010) 'Shell and Gazprom in oil and gas alliance'. Available online at: http://www.ft.com/intl/cms/s/0/97988602-fcb4-11df-bfdd-00144feab49a.html#axzz1TtIy9xAE (accessed 2 August 2011).

Fink, R.C., Edelman, L.F., Hatten, K.J. and James, W.L. (2006) 'Transaction cost economics, resource dependence theory, and customer–supplier relationships'. *Industrial and Corporate Change*, 15: 497–529.

Finkelstein, S. (1997) 'Interindustry merger patterns and resource dependence: A replication and extension of Pfeffer (1972)'. *Strategic Management Journal*, 18: 787–810.

Fonda, D. (2006) 'Who gains from a Pixar–Disney merger?' Available online at http://www.time.com/time/business/article/0,8599,1150674,00.html (accessed 2 August 2011).

Ford Media Company (2009) 'Ford and Magna form electrifying alliance'. Available online at http://media.ford.com/article_display.cfm?article_id=29673 (accessed 2 August 2011).

Franko, L.G. (1971) *Joint Venture Survival in Multinational Corporations*. New York: Praeger.

Fried, I. (2011) 'Nokia's Microsoft partnership: Does the new strategy add up?' Available online at http://allthingsd.com/20110211/live-from-nokias-investor-meeting-does-the-new-strategy-add-up/ (accessed 2 August 2011).

Frincu, D. (2007) 'LG and Philips, the beginning of a beautiful partnership'. Available online at http://news.softpedia.com/news/LG-and-Philips-the-Beginning-of-a-Beautiful-Partenership-49607.shtml (accessed 2 August 2011).

Fryxell, G.E., Dooley, R.S. and Vryza, M. (2002) 'After the ink dries: The interaction of trust and control in US-based international joint ventures'. *Journal of Management Studies*, 39: 865–886.

Furrer, O., Tjemkes, B.V., Adolfs, K. and Ulgen Aydinlik, A. (In press) 'Responding to adverse situations within exchange relationships: The cross-cultural validity of a circumplex model'. *Journal of Cross-Cultural Psychology*.

Galapagos (2010) 'Galapagos en Roche gaan strategische alliantie aan op gebied van COPD'. Available online at http://www.glpg.com/press/2010/1'.pdf (accessed 2 August 2011).

Gamerslifeline.com (2010) 'Capcom teams up with playboy magazine to bring sexy back to dead rising'. Available online at http://www.gamerslifeline.com/capcom-teams-up-with-playboy-magazine-to-bring-sexy-back-to-dead-rising-2/ (accessed 2 August 2011).

Ganesan, S. (1993) 'Negotiation strategies and the nature of channel relationships'. *Journal of Marketing Research*, 30: 183–203.

García-Canal, E., Duarte, C.L., Criado, J.R. and Llaneza, A.V. (2002) 'Accelerating international expansion through global alliances: A typology of cooperative strategies'. *Journal of World Business*, 37: 91–107.

García-Canal, E., Valdes-Llaneza, A. and Ariño, A. (2003) 'Effectiveness of dyadic and multi-party joint ventures'. *Organization Studies*, 24: 743–770.

Gelfand, M.J., Major, V.S., Raver, J.L., Nishii, L.H. and O'Brien, K. (2006) 'Negotiating relationally: The dynamics of the relational self in negotiations'. *Academy of Management Review*, 31: 427–451.

Geringer, J. M., and Hebert, L. (1989) 'Control and performance of international joint ventures'. *Journal of International Business Studies*, 20 (2): 235–254.

Geylani, T., Inman, J.J. and Ter Hofstede, F. (2008) 'Image reinforcement or impairment: The effects of co-branding on attribute uncertainty'. *Marketing Science*, 27: 730–744.

Geyskens, I. and Steenkamp, J. (2000) 'Economic and social satisfaction: Measurement and relevance to marketing channel relationships'. *Journal of Retailing*, 76: 11–32.

Ghoshal, S. and Moran, P. (1996) 'Bad for practice: A critique of the transaction cost theory'. *Academy of Management Review*, 21: 13–47.

Giller, C. and Matear, S. (2001) 'The termination of inter-firm relationships'. *Journal of Business and Industrial Marketing*, 16: 94–112.

Gimeno, J. (2004) 'Competition within and between networks: The contingent effect of competitive embeddedness on alliance formation'. *Academy of Management Journal*, 15: 584–602.

Glaister, K.W. and Buckley, P. J. (1996) 'Strategic motives for international alliance formation'. *Journal of Management Studies*, 33: 301–332.

Glaister, K.W., Husan, R. and Buckley, P. J. (2003) 'Decision-making autonomy in UK international equity joint ventures'. *British Journal of Management*, 14: 305–322.

Granovetter, M.S. (1973) 'The strength of weak ties'. *American Journal of Sociology*, 78: 1,360–1,380.

Granovetter, M. (1985) 'Economic action and social structure: A theory of embeddedness'. *American Journal of Sociology*, 91: 481–510.

Greenberg, J. (1987) 'A taxonomy of organizational justice theories'. *Academy of Management Review*, 12: 9–22.

Grooms, L. (2008) 'Grainnet Exclusive: Mercedes and algae?'. *Biofuels Journal*. Available online at http://www.biofuelsjournal.com/articles/Mercedes___Algae__Solazyme_Road_Testing_Algae_based_Biodiesel_In_Mercedes-54315.html (accessed 2 August 2011).

Guardian (2010) 'Shell and Gazprom sign "global co-operation" pact'. Available online at http://www.guardian.co.uk/business/2010/nov/30/shell-gazprom-global-cooperation-pact (accessed 2 August 2011).

Guidice, R.M., Vasudevan, A. and Duysters, G. (2003) 'From "me against you" to "us against them": Alliance formation based on inter-alliance rivalry'. *Strategic Management Journal*, 19: 135–152.

Gulati, R. (1995a) 'Does familiarity breed trust – The implications of repeated ties for contractual choice in alliances'. *Academy of Management Journal*, 38: 85–112.

Gulati, R. (1995b) 'Social structure and alliance formation patterns: A longitudinal analysis'. *Administrative Science Quarterly*, 40: 619–652.

Gulati, R. (1998) 'Alliances and networks'. *Strategic Management Journal*, 19: 293–317.

Gulati, R. and Gargiulo, M. (1999) 'Where do interorganizational networks come from?' *American Journal of Sociology*, 104: 1,439–1,493.

Gulati, R. and Nickerson, J.A. (2008) 'Interorganizational trust, governance choice, and exchange performance'. *Organization Science*, 19: 688–708.

Gulati, R. and Singh, H. (1998) 'The architecture of cooperation: Managing coordination costs and appropriation concerns in strategic alliances'. *Administrative Science Quarterly*, 43: 781–814.

Gulati, R. and Sytch, M. (2007) 'Dependence asymmetry and joint dependence in interorganizational relationships: Effects of embeddedness on a manufacturer's performance in procurement relationships'. *Administrative Science Quarterly*, 52: 32–69.

Gulati, R., Khanna, T. and Nohria, N. (1994) 'Unilateral commitments and the importance of process in alliances'. *Sloan Management Review*, 35: 61–69.

Gulati, R., Sytch, M. and Mehrotra, P. (2008) 'Breaking up is never easy: Planning for exit in a strategic alliance'. *California Review Management*, 50: 147–163.

Hagedoorn, J. and Hesen, G. (2007) 'Contract law and the governance of inter-firm technology partnerships – An analysis of different modes of partnering and their contractual implications'. *Journal of Management Studies*, 44: 342–366.

Hagedoorn, J. and Sadowski, B. (1999) 'The transition from strategic technology alliances to mergers and acquisitions: An exploratory study'. *Journal of Management Studies*, 36: 87–107.

Halinen, A. and Tahtinen, J. (2002) 'A process theory of relationship ending'. *International Journal of Service Industry Management*, 13: 163–180.

Hamel, G. (1991) 'Competition for competence and inter-partner learning within international strategic alliances'. *Strategic Management Journal*, 12: 83–103.

Hannan, M.T. and Freeman, J. (1977) 'Population ecology of organizations'. *American Journal of Sociology*, 82: 929–964.

Harbison, J. and Pekar, P. (1998) *Smart Alliances: A Practical Guide to Repeatable Success*. San Francisco: Jossey-Bass.

Harrigan, K.R. (1988) 'Strategic alliances and partner asymmetries', in Contractor, F. J. and Lorange, P. (eds.), *Cooperative Strategies in International Business*. Lexington: Lexington Books.

Harrington, S. J. (1991) 'What corporate America is teaching about ethics'. *Academy of Management Executive*, 5: 21–30.

Heide, J.B. and John, G. (1992) 'Do norms matter in marketing relationships?' *Journal of Marketing*, 56: 32–44.

Heide, J.B. and Miner, A.S. (1992) 'The shadow of the future – Effects of anticipated interaction and frequency of contact on buyer–seller cooperation'. *Academy of Management Journal*, 35: 265–291.

Heide, J.B., Wathne, K.H. and Rokkan, A.I. (2007) 'Interfirm monitoring, social contracts, and relationship outcomes'. *Journal of Marketing Research*, 44: 425–433.

Heimeriks, K.H. and Duysters, G. (2007) 'Alliance capability as a mediator between experience and alliance performance: An empirical investigation into the alliance capability development process'. *Journal of Management Studies*, 44: 25–49.

Heimeriks, K.H., Klijn, E. and Reuer, J.J. (2009) 'Building capabilities for alliance portfolios'. *Long Range Planning*, 42: 96–114.

Hennart, J.F. (1988) 'A transaction costs theory of equity joint ventures'. *Strategic Management Journal*, 9: 361–374.

Hennart, J.F. (2006) 'Alliance research: Less is more'. *Journal of Management Studies*, 43: 1,621–1,628.

Hennart, J.F. and Zeng, M. (2005) 'Structural determinants of joint venture performance'. *European Management Review*, 2: 105.

Hennart, J.F., Kim, D.J. and Zeng, M. (1998) 'The impact of joint venture status on the longevity of Japanese stakes in US manufacturing affiliates'. *Organization Science*, 9: 382–395.

Hennart, J.F. and Zeng, M. (2005) 'Structural determinants of joint venture performance'. *European Management Review*, 2: 105.

HFN Daily News (2010) 'Philips Sonicare Partners with Susan G. Komen for the Cure'. Available online at http://www.hfnmag.com/housewares/philips-sonicare-partners-susan-g-komen-cure (accessed 2 August 2011).

Hill, R.C. and Hellriegel, D. (1994) 'Critical contingencies in joint venture management – Some lessons from managers'. *Organization Science*, 5: 594–607.

Hirschman, A.O. (1970) *Exit, Voice and Loyalty: Responses to Decline in Firms, Organizations and States*. Cambridge, MA: Harvard University Press.

Hitt, M.A., Dacin, M.T., Levitas, E., Arregle, J.L. and Borza, A. (2000) 'Partner selection in emerging and developed market contexts: Resource-based and organizational learning perspectives'. *Academy of Management Journal*, 43: 449–467.

Hoang, H. and Rothaermel, F.T. (2005) 'The effect of general and partner-specific alliance experience on joint R&D project performance'. *Academy of Management Journal*, 48: 332–345.

Hoffmann, W.H. (2007) 'Strategies for managing a portfolio of alliances'. *Strategic Management Journal*, 28: 827–856.

Hoffmann, W.H. and Schlosser, R. (2001) 'Success factors of strategic alliances in small and medium-sized enterprises: An empirical survey'. *Long Range Planning*, 34: 357–381.

Hofstede, G. (1991) *Cultures and Organizations: Software of the Mind*. London: McGraw Hill.

Hofstede, G. and Bond, M.H. (1988) 'The Confucius connection: From cultural roots to economic growth'. *Organizational Dynamics* 16: 5–21.

House, R.J. (2004) *Culture, Leadership, and Organizations: The GLOBE study of 62 societies* Thousand Oaks, CA: Sage Publications, Inc.

Howe, J. (2008) *Crowdsourcing: Why the Power of the Crowd Is Driving the Future Business*. New York: Three Rivers Press.

HP (2009) 'HP and Microsoft expand Alliance in Unified Communications and Collaboration'. Available online at http://www.hp.com/hpinfo/newsroom/press/2009/090519xa.html (accessed 2 August 2011).

HP Technology@work (2011) 'Microsoft'. Available online at http://h41112.www4.hp.com/events/taw-2011/ww/en/sponsors.html (accessed 2 August 2011).

Hwang, P. and Burgers, W.P. (1997) 'The many faces of multi-firm alliances: Lessons for managers'. *California Management Review*, 39: 101–117.

IBM (2007) 'Lenovo and IBM expand global alliance'. Available online at http://www-03.ibm.com/press/us/en/pressrelease/21589.wss (accessed 2 August 2011).

IBM (2011a) 'Our history of progress, 1890s to 2001'. Available online at http://www-03.ibm.com/ibm/history/interactive/ibm_ohe_pdf_13.pdf (accessed 28 September, 2011).

IBM (2011b) 'Louis V. Gerstner, Jr. CEO 1993–2002'. Available online at http://www-03.ibm.com/press/us/en/biography/10153.wss (accessed 28 September, 2011).

IBS Center for Management Research (ICMR) (2006) 'Disney's acquisition of Pixar, case # BSTR203'. Available online at http://www.icmrindia.org/casestudies/catalogue/Business%20strategy/Business%20Strategy%20Disney's%20Acquisition%20of%20Pixar.htm) (accessed 2 August 2011).

Inkpen, A.C. (2000) 'Learning through joint ventures: A framework of knowledge acquisition'. *Journal of Management Studies*, 37: 1,019–1,043.

Inkpen, A.C. and Beamish, P.W. (1997) 'Knowledge, bargaining power, and the instability of international joint ventures'. *Academy of Management Review*, 22: 177–202.

Innovarno Pharma Licensing (2006) 'Grupo Uriach launches Palau Pharma with the collaboration of several investors'. Available online at http://pharmalicensing.com/public/press/view/1195558350_4742c5cea677d/grupo-uriach-launches-palau-pharma-with-the-collaboration-of-several-financial-investors (accessed 2 August 2011).

Iphone Magazine (2010) 'How Apple–Google partnership turned sour'. Available online at http://freeiphonehacks.com/how-apple-google-partnership-turned-sour/ (accessed 2 August 2011).

Ireland, R.D. and Webb, J.W. (2007) 'A multi-theoretic perspective on trust and power in strategic supply chains'. *Journal of Operations Management*, 25: 482–497.

Ireland, R.D., Hitt, M.A. and Vaidyanath, D. (2002) 'Alliance management as a source of competitive advantage'. *Journal of Management*, 28: 413–446.

Jacobides, M.G. and Winter, S.G. (2005) 'The co-evolution of capabilities and transaction costs: Explaining the institutional structure of production'. *Strategic Management Journal*, 26: 395–413.

Janowicz-Panjaitan, M. and Noorderhaven, N.G. (2008) 'Formal and informal inter-organizational learning within strategic alliances'. *Research Policy*, 37: 1,337–1,355.

Jap, S.D. (1999) 'Pie-expansion efforts: Collaboration processes in buyer–supplier relationships'. *Journal of Marketing Research*, 36: 461–475.

Jap, S.D. (2001) '"Pie sharing" in complex collaboration contexts'. *Journal of Marketing Research*, 38: 86–99.

Jap, S.D. and Ganesan, S. (2000) 'Control mechanisms and the relationship life cycle: Implications for safeguarding specific investments and developing commitment'. *Journal of Marketing Research*, 37: 227–245.

Jarvensivu, T. and Moller, K. (2009) 'Metatheory of network management: A contingency perspective'. *Industrial Marketing Management*, 38: 654–661.

Jemison, D.B. (1984) 'The importance of boundary spanning roles in strategic decision making'. *Journal of Management Studies*, 21: 131–152.

Jiang, R.J., Tao, Q.T. and Santoro, M.D. (2010) 'Alliance portfolio diversity and firm performance'. *Strategic Management Journal*, 31: 1,136–1,144.

Joshi, A.W. and Arnold, S.J. (1997) 'The impact of buyer dependence on buyer opportunism in buyer–supplier relationships: The moderating role of relational norms'. *Psychology and Marketing*, 14: 823–845.

Joskow, P.L. (1985) 'Vertical integration and long term contracts: The case of coal burning electric generation plants'. *Journal of Law, Economics and Organization*, 1: 33–80.

Kale, P. and Singh, H. (2007) 'Building firm capabilities through learning: The role of the alliance learning process in alliance capability and firm-level alliance success'. *Strategic Management Journal*, 28: 981–1,000.

Kale, P. and Singh, H. (2009) 'Managing strategic alliances: What do we know now, and where do we go from here?'. *Academy of Management Perspectives*, 23: 45–62.

Kale, P., Dyer, J.H. and Singh, H. (2001) 'Value creation and success in strategic alliances: Alliancing skills and the role of alliance structure and systems'. *European Management Journal*, 19: 463–471.

Kale, P., Dyer, J.H. and Singh, H. (2002) 'Alliance capability, stock market response, and long-term alliance success: The role of the alliance function'. *Strategic Management Journal*, 23: 747–767.

Kale, P., Singh, H. and Perlmutter, H. (2000) 'Learning and protection of proprietary assets in strategic alliances: Building relational capital'. *Strategic Management Journal*, 21: 217–237.

Kang, N.H. and Sakai, K. (2001) 'New patterns of industrial globalization: Cross-border mergers and acquisitions and strategic alliances'. *Report of the Industry Division of the OECD*: 1–174.

Kanter, R.M. (1994) 'Collaborative advantage – the art of alliances'. *Harvard Business Review*, July: 96–108.

Kaplan, R.S., Norton, D.P. and Rugelsjoen, B. (2010) 'Managing alliances with the balanced score card'. *Harvard Business Review*, January-February: 114–120.

Katila, R., Rosenberger, J.D. and Eisenhardt, K.M. (2008) 'Swimming with sharks: Technology ventures, defense mechanisms and corporate relationships'. *Administrative Science Quarterly*, 53: 295–332.

Kaufmann, J. and O'Neill, H.M. (2007) 'Do culturally distant partners choose different types of joint ventures?'. *Journal of World Business*, 42: 435–448.

Kersten, G.E. (2001) 'Modeling distributive and integrative negotiations: Review and revised characterization'. *Group Decision and Negotiation*, 10: 493–514.

Khanna, T. (1998) 'The scope of alliances'. *Organization Science*, 9: 340–355.

Khanna, T., Gulati, R. and Nohria, N. (1998) 'The dynamics of learning alliances: Competition, cooperation, and relative scope'. *Strategic Management Journal*, 19: 193–210.

Killing, J.P. (1983) *Strategies for Joint Venture Success*. New York: Praeger.

Kipnis, D. and Schmidt, S. (1985) 'The language of persuasion'. *Psychology Today*, 19: 40–46.

Klein, B., Crawford, R.G. and Alchian, A.A. (1978) 'Vertical integration, appropriable rents, and the competitive contracting process'. *Journal of Law and Economics*, 21: 297–326.

Knight, L. (2002) 'Network learning: Exploring learning by interorganizational networks'. *Human Relations*, 55: 427–454.

Knight, L. and Harland, C. (2005) 'Managing supply networks: Organizational roles in network management'. *European Management Journal*, 23: 281–292.

Kogut, B. (1988) 'Joint ventures – theoretical and empirical – perspectives'. *Strategic Management Journal*, 9: 319–332.

Kogut, B. (1989) 'The stability of joint ventures: Reciprocity and competive rivalry'. *Journal of Industrial Economics*, 38: 183–198.

Kok, G. and Wildeman, L. (1997) 'Succesvolle allianties'. *Nijenrode Management Review*, 4: 78–84.

Koka, B.R. and Prescott, J.E. (2008) 'Designing alliance networks: The influence of network position, environmental change, and strategy on firm performance'. *Strategic Management Journal*, 29: 639–661.

Kotabe, M., Martin, X. and Domoto, H. (2003) 'Gaining from vertical partnerships: Knowledge transfer, relationship duration, and supplier performance improvement in the U.S. and Japanese automotive industries'. *Strategic Management Journal*, 24: 293–316.

Kotler, P. (1991) *Marketing Management: Analysis, planning, and Control*. Englewood Cliffs, NL: Prentice-Hall.

Koza, M.P. and Lewin, A.Y. (1998) 'The co-evolution of strategic alliances'. *Organization Science*, 9: 255–264.

Koza, M.P. and Lewin, A.Y. (1999) 'The coevolution of network alliances: A longitudinal analysis of an international professional service network'. *Organization Science*, 10: 638–653.

Koza, M. and Lewin, A. (2000) 'Managing partnerships and strategic alliances: Raising the odds of success'. *European Management Journal*, 16: 146–151.

Kumar, M.V.S. (2010) 'Differential gains between partners in joint ventures: Role of resource appropriation and private benefits'. *Organization Science*, 21: 232–248.

Kumar, R. and Nti, K.O. (1998) 'Differential learning and interaction in alliance dynamics: A process and outcome discrepancy model'. *Organization Science*, 9: 356–367.

Kumar, N., Scheer, L.K. and Steenkamp, J. (1995) 'The effects of perceived interdependence on dealer attitudes'. *Journal of Marketing Research*, 32: 348–356.

Kwak, Y.H., Chih, Y.Y. and Ibbs, C.W. (2009) 'Towards a comprehensive understanding of public–private partnerships for infrastructure development'. *California Management Review*, 51: 51–78.

Lambe, C.J., Spekman, R.E. and Hunt, S.D. (2002) 'Alliance competence, resources, and alliance success: Conceptualization, measurement, and initial test'. *Journal of the Academy of Marketing Science*, 30: 141–158.

Lampel, J. and Shamsie, J. (2003) 'Capabilities in motion: New organizational forms and the reshaping of the Hollywood movie industry'. *Journal of Management Studies*, 40: 2,189–2,210.

Lane, P.J. and Lubatkin, M. (1998) 'Relative absorptive capacity and interorganizational learning'. *Strategic Management Journal*, 19: 461–477.

Lane, P.J., Salk, J.E. and Lyles, M.A. (2001) 'Absorptive capacity, learning, and performance in international joint ventures'. *Strategic Management Journal*, 22: 1,139–1,161.

Lavie, D. (2006) 'The competitive advantage of interconnected firms: An extension of the resource-based view'. *Academy of Management Review*, 31: 638–658.

Lavie, D. (2007) 'Alliance portfolios and firm performance: A study of value creation and appropriation in the US software industry'. *Strategic Management Journal*, 28: 1,187–1,212.

Lavie, D. and Rosenkopf, L. (2006) 'Balancing exploration and exploitation in alliance formation'. *Academy of Management Journal*, 49: 797–818.

Lavie, D., Lechner, C. and Singh, H. (2007) 'The performance implications of timing of entry and involvement in multipartner alliances'. *Academy of Management Journal*, 50: 578–604.

Lax, D.A. and Sebenius, J.K. (1986) *The Manager as Negotiator: Bargaining for Cooperation and Competitive Gain*. New York: Free Press.

Lee, S.-C., Chang, S.-N., Liu, C.-Y. and Yang, J. (2007) 'The effect of knowledge protection, knowledge ambiguity, and relational capital on alliance performance'. *Knowledge and Process Management*, 14: 58–69.

Lee, Y. and Cavusgil, S.T. (2006) 'Enhancing alliance performance: The effects of contractual-based versus relational-based governance'. *Journal of Business Research*, 59: 896–905.

Lewicki, R.J., Weiss, S.E. and Lewin, D. (1992) 'Models of conflict, negotiation and 3rd party intervention – A review and synthesis'. *Journal of Organizational Behavior*, 13: 209–252.

Lewis, R. (2004) 'Renault/Nissan: A successful partnership'. Available online at http://www.carkeys.co.uk/features/renaultnissan-successful-partnership (accessed 2 August 2011).

Li, J.T. and Hambrick, D.C. (2005) 'Factional groups: A new vantage on demographic faultlines, conflict, and disintegration in work teams'. *Academy of Management Journal*, 48: 794–813.

Lin, X.H. and Germain, R. (1998) 'Sustaining satisfactory joint venture relationships: The role of conflict resolution strategy'. *Journal of International Business Studies*, 29: 179–196.

Lin, Z., Yang, H.B. and Arya, B. (2009) 'Alliance partners and firm performance: Resource complementarity and status association'. *Strategic Management Journal*, 30: 921–940.

Litwak, E. and Hylton, L.F. (1962) 'Interorganizational analysis – a hypothesis on coordinating agencies'. *Administrative Science Quarterly*, 6: 395–420.

London, T., Rondinelli, D.A. and O'Neill, H. (2006) 'Strange bedfellows: Alliances between corporations and nonprofits'. In Shenkar, O. and Reuer, J.J. (eds.), *Handbook of Strategic Alliances*, Thousand Oaks: Sage Publications, Inc., pp. 353–366.

Lorenzoni, G. and Baden-Fuller, C. (1995) 'Creating a strategic centre to manage a web of partners.' *California Management Review*, 37: 1–18.

Loza, J. (2004) 'Business–community partnerships: The case for community organization capacity building'. *Journal of Business Ethics*, 53: 297–311.

Lubatkin, M., Florin, J. and Lane, P. (2001) 'Learning together and apart: A model of reciprocal interfirm learning'. *Human Relations*, 54: 1,353–1,382.

Lui, S.S. and Ngo, H.Y. (2004) 'The role of trust and contractual safeguards on cooperation in non-equity alliances'. *Journal of Management*, 30: 471–485.

Luo, Y.D. (2002) 'Contract, cooperation, and performance in international joint ventures'. *Strategic Management Journal*, 23: 903–919.

Luo, Y.D. (2005) 'How important are shared perceptions of procedural justice in cooperative alliances?' *Academy of Management Journal*, 48: 695–709.

Luo, Y.D. (2002) 'Contract, cooperation, and performance in international joint ventures'. *Strategic Management Journal*, 23: 903–919.

Lyles, M.A. and Salk, J.E. (1996) 'Knowledge acquisition from foreign parents in international joint ventures: An empirical examination in the Hungarian context'. *Journal of International Business Studies*, 27: 877–904.

Lynn, M.L. (2005) 'Organizational buffering: Managing boundaries and cores'. *Organization Studies*, 26: 37–61.

Lyons, T.F., Krachenberg, A.R. and Henke, J.W. (1990) 'Mixed motive marriages – What's next for buyer–supplier relations?' *Sloan Management Review*, 31: 29–36.

Macdonald, S. and Chrisp, T. (2005) 'Acknowledging the purpose of partnership'. *Journal of Business Ethics*, 59: 307–317.

McGuire, M. (2002) 'Managing networks: Propositions on what managers do and why they do'. *Public Administration Review*, 62: 599–609.

Macneil, I.R. (1978) 'Contracts – Adjustment of long-term economic relations under classical, neoclassical, and relational contract law'. *Northwestern University Law Review*, 72: 854–905.

Madhok, A. (1995) 'Opportunism and trust in joint venture relationships: An exploratory study and a model'. *Scandinavian Journal of Management*, 11: 57–74.

Madhok, A. and Tallman, S.B. (1998) 'Resources, transactions and rents: Managing value through interfirm collaborative relationships'. *Organization Science*, 9: 326–339.

Makhija, M.V. and Ganesh, U. (1997) 'The relationship between control and partner learning in learning-related joint ventures'. *Organization Science*, 8: 508–527.

Makino, S., Chan, C.M., Isobe, T. and Beamish, P.W. (2007) 'Intended and unintended termination of international joint ventures'. *Strategic Management Journal*, 28: 1,113–1,132.

March, J.G. (1991) 'Exploration and exploitation in organizational learning'. *Organization Science*, 2: 71–78.

Marketwire (2011) 'NovAtel Inc. and Raven Industries announce new supplier agreement'. Available online at http://www.marketwire.com/press-release/novatel-inc-and-raven-industries-announce-new-supplier-agreement-1415754.htm (accessed 2 August 2011).

Martino, M. (2010) 'Galapagos, Roche enter $588.7m COPD alliance'. Available online at http://www.fiercebiotech.com/story/galapagos-roche-enter-588-7m-copd-alliance/2010-01-11?utm_medium=rss&utm_source=rss&cmp-id=OTC-RSS-FB0 (accessed 2 August 2011).

Masten, S.E., Meehan, J.W. and Snyder, E.A. (1991) 'The cost of organization'. *Journal of Law, Economics and Organization*, 7: 1–25.

Mayer, K.J. and Argyres, N.S. (2004) 'Learning to contract: Evidence from the personal computer industry'. *Organization Science*, 15: 394–410.

Meier, M. (2011) 'Knowledge management in strategic alliances: A review of empirical evidence'. *International Journal of Management Reviews*, 13: 1–23.

Mellewigt, T. and Das, T.K. (2010) 'Alliance structure choice in the telecommunications industry: Between resource type and resource heterogeneity'. *International Journal of Strategic Change Management*, 2: 128–144.

Meschi, P.X. (1997) 'Longevity and cultural differences of international joint ventures: Toward time-based cultural management'. *Human Relations*, 50: 211–228.

Meschi, P.-X. (2005) 'Environmental uncertainty and survival of international joint ventures: The case of political and economical risk in emerging countries'. *European Management Review*, 2: 143–152.

Meyer-Krahmer, F. and Smoch, U. (1998) 'Scientific based technologies university–industry interaction in four fields'. *Research Policy*, 27: 835–851.

Microsoft News Center (2001) 'Microsoft and Nokia form global alliance to design, develop and market mobile productivity solutions'. Available online at http://www.microsoft.com/presspass/press/2009/aug09/08-12pixipr.mspx (accessed 2 August 2011).

Morgan, R.M. and Hunt, S.D. (1994) 'The commitment-trust theory of relationship marketing'. *Journal of Marketing*, 58: 20–38.

Mowery, D.C., Oxley, J.E. and Silverman, B.S. (1996) 'Strategic alliances and interfirm knowledge transfer'. *Strategic Management Journal*, 17: 77–91.

Mowery, D.C., Oxley, J.E. and Silverman, B.S. (1998) 'Technological overlap and interfirm cooperation: Implications for the resource-based view of the firm'. *Research Policy*, 27: 507–523.

Muthusamy, S.K. and White, M.A. (2005) 'Learning and knowledge transfer in strategic alliances: A social exchange view'. *Organization Studies*, 26: 415–441.

Nair, A., Narasimhan, R. and Bendoly, E. (2011) 'Coopetitive buyer–supplier relationship: An investigation of bargaining power, relational context, and investment strategies'. *Decision Sciences*, 42: 93–127.

Nakamura, M., Shaver, J.M. and Yeung, B. (1996) 'An empirical investigation of joint venture dynamics: Evidence from US–Japan joint ventures'. *International Journal of Industrial Organization*, 14: 521–541.

Neurocrine (2002) 'Pfizer announce worldwide agreement to develop, promote insomnia treatment'. Available online at http://phx.corporate-ir.net/phoenix.zhtml?c=68817&p=irol-newsArticle&ID=613269&highlight= (accessed 2 August 2011).

Neurocrine (2006) 'Neurocrine and Pfizer terminate collaboration agreement for Indiplon'. Available online at http://phx.corporate-ir.net/phoenix.zhtml?c=68817&p=irol-newsArticle&ID=875459&highlight= (accessed 2 August 2011).

Niederkofler, M. (1991) 'The evolution of strategic alliances – Opportunities for managerial influence'. *Journal of Business Venturing*, 6: 237–257.

Noble, G. and Jones, R. (2006) 'The role of boundary-spanning managers in the establishment of public–private partnerships'. *Public Administration*, 84: 91–117.

Nokia (2011) 'Nokia and Microsoft sign definitive agreement ahead of schedule'. Available online at http://press.nokia.com/2011/04/21/nokia-and-microsoft-sign-definitive-agreement-ahead-of-schedule/ (accessed 2 August 2011).

Nonaka, I. (1994) 'A dynamic theory of organizational knowledge creation'. *Organization Science*, 5: 14–37.

Nooteboom, B. (2004) 'Governance and competence: How can they be combined?' *Cambridge Journal of Economics*, 28: 505–525.

Norman, P.M. (2002) 'Protecting knowledge in strategic alliances: Resource and relational characteristics'. *Journal of High Technology Management Research*, 13: 177–202.

Olekalns, M., Smith, P.L. and Walsh, T. (1996) 'The process of negotiating: Strategy and timing as predictors of outcomes'. *Organizational Behavior and Human Decision Processes*, 68: 68–77.

Oneworld Trust (2009) '2008 Global Accountability Report'. Available online at http://oneworldtrust.org/publications/doc_view/270-2008-cargill-accountability-profile?tmpl=component&format=raw (accessed 2 August 2011).

Open Source IP PBX (2010) 'Panasonic announces new distribution alliance with leading distributor NETXUSA'. Available online at http://www.asterisk-digium.com/panasonic-announces-new-distribution-alliance-with-leading-distributor-netxusa.html (accessed 2 August 2011).

Oral Health America (2008) 'Philips Sonicare partners with OHA to conduct public opinion survey of oral health in America'. Available online at http://www.orthodontic productsonline.com/news/2008-05-16_01.asp (accessed 2 August 2011).

Osborn, R.N. and Baughn, C.C. (1990) 'Forms of interorganizational governance for multinational alliances'. *Academy of Management Journal*, 33: 503–519.

Oxley, J.E. (1997) 'Appropriability hazards and governance in strategic alliances: A transaction cost approach'. *Journal of Law Economics and Organization*, 13: 387–409.

Oxley, J.E. (1999) 'Institutional environment and the mechanisms of governance: The impact of intellectual property protection on the structure of inter-firm alliances'. *Journal of Economic Behavior and Organization*, 38: 283–309.

Oxley, J. and Wada, T. (2009) 'Alliance structure and the scope of knowledge transfer: Evidence from US–Japan agreements'. *Management Science*, 55: 635–649.

Oxley, J.E. and Sampson, R.C. (2004) 'The scope and governance of international R&D alliances'. *Strategic Management Journal*, 25: 723–749.

Palmatier, R.W., Dant, R.R. and Grewal, D. (2007) 'A comparative longitudinal analysis of theoretical perspectives of interorganizational relationship performance'. *Journal of Marketing*, 71: 172–194.

Panasonic USA Pressroom (2010) 'Panasonic announces new distribution alliance with leading distributor NETXUSA'. Available online at http://www2.panasonic.com/webapp/wcs/stores/servlet/prModelDetail?storeId=11301&catalogId=13251&itemId=413577&modelNo=Content05262010045658083&surfModel=Content05262010045658083 (accessed 2 August 2011).

Pangarkar, N. and Klein, S. (1998) 'Bandwagon pressures and inter-firm alliances in the global pharmaceutical industry'. *Journal of International Marketing*, 6: 54–73.

Panteli, N. and Sockalingam, S. (2005) 'Trust and conflict within virtual inter-organizational alliances: A framework for facilitating knowledge sharing'. *Decision Support Systems*, 39: 599–617.

Parise, S. and Casher, A. (2003) 'Alliance portfolios: Designing and managing your network of business-partner relationships'. *Academy of Management Executive*, 17: 25–39.

Park, C.W., Jun, S.Y. and Shocker, A.D. (1996) 'Composite branding alliances: An investigation of extension and feedback effects'. *Journal of Marketing Research*, 33: 453–466.

Park, S.H. and Russo, M.V. (1996) 'When competition eclipses cooperation: An event history analysis of joint venture failure'. *Management Science*, 42: 875–890.

Park, S.H. and Ungson, G.R. (1997) 'The effect of national culture, organizational complementarity, and economic motivation on joint venture dissolution'. *Academy of Management Journal*, 40: 279–307.

Parkhe, A. (1991) 'Interfirm diversity, organizational learning, and longevity in global strategic alliances'. *Journal of International Business Studies*, 22: 579–601.

Parkhe, A. (1993) 'Strategic alliance structuring: A game theoretic and transaction cost examination of interfirm cooperation'. *Academy of Management Journal*, 36: 794–829.

Partnership Shell (2011) 'Shell Biofuels brochure: Sustainable low CO_2 fuel today'. Available online at http://www-static.shell.com/static/environment_society/downloads/alternative_energies_transport/shell_biofuels_brochure_2011.pdf (accessed 2 August 2011).

Patzelt, H. and Shepherd, D.A. (2008) 'The decision to persist with underperforming alliances: The role of trust and control'. *Journal of Management Studies*, 45: 1,217–1,243.

PC World (2009) 'Microsoft, Nokia target 'Crackberry' crowd with Mobile Office'. Available online at http://www.pcworld.com/businesscenter/article/170091/microsoft_nokia_target_crackberry_crowd_with_mobile_office.html (accessed 2 August 2011).

Pekar, P. and Allio, R. (1994) 'Making alliances work – guidelines for success'. *Long Range Planning*, 27: 54–65.

Peng, M.W. and Shenkar, O. (2002) 'Joint venture dissolution as corporate divorce'. *Academy of Management Executive*, 16: 92–105.

Perkmann, M., Neely, A. and Walsh, K. (2011) 'How should firms evaluate success in university–industry alliances? A performance measurement system'. *R&D Management*, 41: 202–216.

Pfeffer, J. and Nowak, P. (1976) 'Joint ventures and interorganizational interdependence'. *Administrative Science Quarterly*, 21: 398–418.

Pfeffer, J. and Salancik, G.R. (1978) *The External Control of Organizations: A Resource Dependence Perspective*. New York: Harper and Row.

Philips (2004) 'Philips en Procter & Gamble kondigen alliantie aan voor de introductie van de Intelliclean van Philips' Sonicare® en Crest®'. Available online at http://www.newscenter.philips.com/nl_nl/standard/about/news/press/article-14525.wpd (accessed 2 August 2011).

Ping, R.A. (1993) 'The effects of satisfaction and structural constraints on retailer exiting, voice, loyalty, opportunism, and neglect'. *Journal of Retailing*, 69: 320–352.

Pisano, G.P. (1989) 'Using equity participation to support exchange – Evidence from the biotechnology industry'. *Journal of Law Economics and Organization*, 5: 109–126.

Pixar Planet forum (2008) 'The truth about the Disney/Pixar partnership ... many answers'. Available online at http://www.pixarplanet.com/forums/viewtopic.php?f=6&t=2945&start=0 (accessed 2 August 2011).

Poppo, L. and Zenger, T. (2002) 'Do formal contracts and relational governance function as substitutes or complements?' *Strategic Management Journal*, 23: 707–725.

Porter, M.E. (1987) 'From competitive strategy to cooperative strategy'. *Harvard Business Review*, 65: 43–59.

Powell, W.W. (1990) 'Neither market nor hierarchy – Network forms of organization'. *Research in Organizational Behavior*, 12: 295–336.

Powell, W.W., Koput, K.W. and SmithDoerr, L. (1996) 'Interorganizational collaboration and the locus of innovation: Networks of learning in biotechnology'. *Administrative Science Quarterly*, 41: 116–145.

Pruitt, D.G. (1983) 'Strategic choice in negotiation'. *American Behavioral Scientist*, 27: 167–194.

Pruitt, D.G. and Lewis, S.A. (1975) 'Development of integrative solutions in bilateral negotiation'. *Journal of Personality and Social Psychology*, 31: 621–633.

PR Web (2008) 'Worldwide market for personal care appliances to reach 460 million units by 2010, according to a new report by Global Industry Analysts, Inc.'. Available online at http://www.prweb.com/releases/appliances_personal_care/hair_care_oral_care/prweb765894.htm (accessed 2 August 2011).

PR Web (2011) 'Leading card manufacturer CPI Expands contactless portfolio with new partnerships: Industry leaders debut next generation Mastercard approved mobile payment sticker'. Available online at http://www.prweb.com/releases/2011/4/prweb8297504.htm (accessed 2 August 2011).

Rao, A. and Schmidt, S.M. (1998) 'A behavioral perspective on negotiating international alliances'. *Journal of International Business Studies*, 29: 665–693.

Renault (2010) 'The Renault–Nissan alliance'. Available online at http://www.renault. com/en/groupe/l-alliance-renault-nissan/pages/l-alliance-renault-nissan.aspx (accessed 2 August 2011).

Reuer, J.J. and Ariño, A. (2007) 'Strategic alliance contracts: Dimensions and determinants of contractual complexity'. *Strategic Management Journal*, 28: 313–330.

Reuer, J.J. and Zollo, M. (2005) 'Termination outcomes of research alliances'. *Research Policy*, 34: 101–115.

Revilla, E., Sarkis, J. and Acosta, J. (2005) 'Towards a knowledge management and learning taxonomy for research joint ventures'. *Technovation*, 25: 1,307–1,316.

Reynolds, M. and Yuthas, K. (2008) 'Moral discourse and corporate social responsibility reporting'. *Journal of Business Ethics*, 78: 47–64.

Ring, P.S. and Van de Ven, A.H. (1994) 'Developmental processes of cooperative interorganizational relationships'. *Academy of Management Review*, 19: 90–118.

Robson, M.J., Leonidou, L.C. and Katsikeas, C.S. (2002) 'Factors influencing international joint venture performance: Theoretical perspectives, assessment, and future directions'. *Management International Review*, 42: 385–418.

Rochemont, M.H. (2010) *Opening up for innovation: The Antecedents of Multi-partner Alliance Performance*, Technical University Eindhoven, Eindhoven.

Rondinelli, D.A. and London, T. (2003) 'How corporations and environmental groups cooperate: Assessing cross-sector alliances and collaborations'. *Academy of Management Executive*, 17: 61–76.

Rusbult, C.E., Zembrodt, I.M. and Gunn, L.K. (1982) 'Exit, voice, loyalty, and neglect – Responses to dissatisfaction in romantic involvements'. *Journal of Personality and Social Psychology*, 43: 1,230–1,242.

Russo, M.V. (1992) 'Power plays – Regulation, diversification, and backward integration in the electric utility industry'. *Strategic Management Journal*, 13: 13–27.

SAAB Newsroom (2010) 'Saab Automobile and BMW enter agreement for supply of gasoline engines'. Available online at http://newsroom.saab.com/news/news/saabauto mobileandbmwenteragreementforsupplyofgasolineengines.5.6a0ed975128ec1d13f17f fe2487.html (accessed 2 August 2011).

Salk, J.E. (2005) 'Often called for but rarely chosen: alliance research that directly studies process'. *European Management Review*, 2: 117–122.

Sampson, R.C. (2004a) 'The cost of misaligned governance in R&D alliances'. *Journal of Law Economics and Organization*, 20: 484–526.

Sampson, R.C. (2004b) 'Organizational choice in R&D alliances: Knowledge-based and transaction cost perspectives'. *Managerial and Decision Economics*, 25: 421–436.

Sampson, R.C. (2005) 'Experience effects and collaborative returns in R&D alliances'. *Strategic Management Journal*, 26: 1,009–1,031.

Sarkar, M.B., Aulakh, P.S. and Madhok, A. (2009) 'Process capabilities and value generation in alliance portfolios'. *Organization Science*, 20: 583–600.

Sarkar, M.B., Echambadi, R., Cavusgil, S.T. and Aulakh, P.S. (2001) 'The influence of complementarity, compatibility, and relationship capital on alliance performance'. *Journal of the Academy of Marketing Science*, 29: 358–373.

Saxton, T. (1997) 'The effects of partner and relationship characteristics on alliance outcomes'. *Academy of Management Journal*, 40: 443–461.

Schaan, J.L. (1983) 'Parent control and joint venture success: The case of Mexico'. Unpublished doctoral dissertation. University of Western Ontario.

Scheer, L.K., Kumar, N. and Steenkamp, J. (2003) 'Reactions to perceived inequity in US and Dutch interorganizational relationships'. *Academy of Management Journal*, 46: 303–316.

Schering Plough (2004) 'Uriach and Organon enter into collaboration to discover and develop therapeutics for inflammatory disorders'. Available online at http://schering-plough.se/pressrum/organon-ab/internationellt-pressmeddelandebruriach-and-organon-enter-into-collaboration-to-discover-and-develop-therapeutics-for-inflammatory-disorders/ (accessed 2 August 2011).

Schifrin, M. (2001) 'Is your company magnetic?' *Forbes*, May 21: 16.

Schilke, O. and Goerzen, A. (2010) 'Alliance management capability: An investigation of the construct and its measurement'. *Journal of Management*, 36: 1,192–1,219.

Schneider, S.C. and Barsoux, J.-L. (1997) *Managing across cultures*. London Prentice-Hall.

Schoenmakers, W. and Duysters, G. (2006) 'Learning in strategic technology alliances'. *Technology Analysis and Strategic Management*, 18: 245–264.

Schreiner, M., Kale, P. and Corsten, D. (2009) 'What really is alliance management capability and how does it impact alliance outcomes and success?' *Strategic Management Journal*, 30: 1,395–1,419.

Scott, J. (2000) *Social Network Analysis: a Handbook*. London: Sage Publications Ltd.

Scott, W.R. 2003, *Organizations: Rational, Natural and Open Systems*. Upper Saddle River, NJ: Prentice Hall.

Segil, L. (1998) *Measuring the Value of Partnering: How to use metrics, to plan, develop, and implement successful alliances*. New York: Amacom.

Shan, W.J., Walker, G. and Kogut, B. (1994) 'Interfirm cooperation and startup innovation in the biotechnology industry'. *Strategic Management Journal*, 15: 387–394.

Shenkar, O. and Zeira, Y. (1992) 'Role-conflict and role ambiguity of chief executive officers in international joint ventures'. *Journal of International Business Studies*, 23: 55–75.

Shenzhen Daily (2007) 'Coca-Cola sets up Chinese research center for herbal drinks'. Available online at http://www.china.org.cn/health/2007-10/25/content_1229650.htm (accessed 2 August 2011).

Shortell, S.M. and Zajac, E.J. (1988) 'Internal corporate joint ventures – Development processes and performance outcomes'. *Strategic Management Journal*, 9: 527–542.

Sidney Morning Herald (2008) 'Chinese herbal coke: can't beat the healing'. Available online at http://www.smh.com.au/business/chinese-herbal-coke-cant-beat-the-healing-20080801-3onw.html (accessed 2 August 2011).

Simonin, B.L. (1999) 'Ambiguity and the process of knowledge transfer in strategic alliances'. *Strategic Management Journal*, 20: 595–623.

Simonin, B.L. and Ruth, J.A. (1998) 'Is a company known by the company it keeps? Assessing the spillover effects of brand alliances on consumer brand attitudes'. *Journal of Marketing Research*, 35: 30–42.

Singh, H., Bell, J. and Kale, P. (2008) *Philips: Building alliance capabilities*. Wharton, University of Pennsylvania.

Stafford, E.R. (1994) 'Using co-operative strategies to make alliances work'. *Long Range Planning*, 27: 64–74.

Stafford, E.R., Polonsky, M.J. and Hartman, C.L. (2000) 'Environmental NGO–business collaboration and strategic bridging: A case analysis of the Greenpeace–Foron alliance'. *Business Strategy and the Environment*, 9: 122–135.

Star Alliance (2011) 'TAM Airlines joins Star Alliance: Star Alliance network enhanced with more destinations and flights across Brazil and South America'. Available online at http://www.staralliance.com/en/press/tam-launch-prp/ (accessed 2 August 2011).

Steensma, H.K., Marino, L. and Weaver, K.M. (2000) 'The influence of national culture on the formation of technology alliances by entrepreneurial firms'. *Academy of Management Journal*, 43: 951–973.

Sterling (2010) 'Saab in talks with BMW over potential partnership'. Available online at http://www.csmonitor.com/Business/Latest-News-Wires/2010/0927/Saab-in-talks-with-BMW-over-potential-partnership (accessed 2 August 2011).

Stuart, T.E. (2000) 'Interorganizational alliances and the performance of firms: A study of growth and innovation rates in a high-technology industry'. *Strategic Management Journal*, 21: 791–811.

Swait, J., Erdem, T., Louviere, J. and Dubelaar, C. (1993) 'The equalization price: A measure of consumer-perceived brand equity'. *International Journal of Research in Marketing*, 10: 23–45.

Szulanski, G. (1996) 'Exploring internal stickiness: Impediments to the transfer of best practice within the firm'. *Strategic Management Journal*, 17: 27–43.

Takeda (2007) 'Lilly and Takeda to terminate joint development/co-marketing agreement on ruboxistaurin mesylate, an agent for the treatment of diabetes microvascular complications'. Available online at http://www.takeda.com/press/article_27436.html (accessed 2 August 2011).

Tan, K.C. (2001) 'A framework of supply chain management literature'. *European Journal of Purchasing and Supply Management*, 7: 39–48.

Taras, V., Rowney, J. and Steel, P. (2009) 'Half a century of measuring culture: Review of approaches, challenges, and limitations based on the analysis of 121 instruments for quantifying culture.' *Journal of International Management*, 15: 357–373.

Technicolor Press Center (2011) 'Technicolor and Canon USA form strategic alliance to leverage technicolor color science for Canon EOS DSLR cameras'. Available online at http://www.technicolor.com/en/hi/about-technicolor/press-center/2011/technicolor-canon-usa-form-strategic-alliance-to-leverage-technicolor-color-science-for-canon-eos-dslr-cameras (accessed 2 August 2011).

TechScoop, The (2011) 'IBM processors power Wii U'. Available online at http://www.thetechscoop.net/2011/06/11/ibm-processors-power-wii-u/ (accessed 2 August 2011).

Teece, D.J., Pisano, G. and Shuen, A. (1997) 'Dynamic capabilities and strategic management'. *Strategic Management Journal*, 18: 509–533.

Teng, B. (2005) 'The emergence and popularization of strategic alliances: Institutional and entrepreneurial views'. *International Entrepreneurship and Management Journal*, 1: 61–82.

Thibaut, J.W. and Kelley, H.H. (1959) *The Social Psychology of Groups*. New York: Wiley.

Thompson, L. (1990) 'Negotiation behavior and outcomes – Empirical-evidence and theoretical issues'. *Psychological Bulletin*, 108: 515–532.

Tjemkes, B. (2008) 'Growing and sharing the pie: A study of performance in strategic alliances'. Nijmegen: Radboud University Nijmegen.

Tjemkes, B. and Furrer, O. (2010) 'The antecedents of response strategies in strategic alliances'. *Management Decision*, 48: 1,103–1,133.

Tjemkes, B. and Furrer, O. (2011) 'Behavioral responses to adverse situations in strategic alliances'. In Das, T.K. (ed.), *Behavioral Perspectives on Strategic Alliances*, Charlotte, NC: Information Age Publishing Researching Strategic Alliances, pp. 227–249.

Today in Windows (2001) 'What does the Nokia–Microsoft partnership mean?' Available online at http://www.todayinwindows.com/2011/04/what-does-the-nokia-microsoft-partnership-mean/ (accessed 2 August 2011).

Trompenaars, F. (1993) *Riding the Waves of Culture: Understanding cultural diversity in business.* London: The Economist Books.

Ul-Haq, R.U.-H. (2005) *Alliances and Co-Evolution: Insights from the banking sector.* Basingstoke: Palgrave Macmillan.

Van Voorhis, V. (2011) 'BASF plant Science in Kekaha'. GardenIsland.com. Available online at http://thegardenisland.com/business/local/article_4e0481f0-634b-11e0-86aa-001cc 4c03286.html (accessed 2 August 2011).

Venkatraman, N., Koh, J. and Loh, L. (1994) 'The adoption of corporate governance mechanisms: A test of competing diffusion models'. *Management Science*, 40: 496–507.

Verhoeven, J. (2009) 'Initial steps in establishing technology development in China, experiences from Organon'. Available online at http://www.science-alliance.nl/ publiceren/Initial%20steps%20in%20establishing%20technology%20development%20 in%20China%20(Verhoeven).pdf (accessed 2 August 2011).

Villalonga, B. and McGahan, A.M. (2005) 'The choice among acquisitions, alliances, and divestitures'. *Strategic Management Journal*, 26: 1,183–1,208.

Vlaar, P.W.L. (2006) 'Making sense of formalization in interorganizational relationships: Beyond coordination and control'. Rotterdam: Erasmus Universiteit Rotterdam.

Vlaar, P.W.L., Van den Bosch, F.A.J. and Volberda, H.W. (2007) 'Towards a dialectic perspective on formalization in interorganizational relationships: How alliance managers capitalize on the duality inherent in contracts, rules and procedures'. *Organization Studies*, 28: 437–466.

Volberda, H.W. and Lewin, A.Y. (2003) 'Guest editors' introduction – Co-evolutionary dynamics within and between firms: From evolution to co-evolution'. *Journal of Management Studies*, 40: 2,111–2,136.

Votolato, N.L. and Unnava, H.R. (2006) 'Spillover of negative information on brand alliances'. *Journal of Consumer Psychology*, 16: 196–202.

Walter, G.A. and Barney, J.B. (1990) 'Research notes and communications management objectives in mergers and acquisitions'. *Strategic Management Journal*, 11: 79–86.

Washburn, J.H., Till, B.A., Priluck, R. and Boughton, P.D. (2000) 'The effect of co-branding on search, experience, and credence attribute performance ratings before and after product trial'. American Marketing Association Summer Marketing Educators' Conference, Chicago IL, Volume 11, 117.

Wassmer, U. (2008) 'Alliance portfolios: A review and research agenda'. *Journal of Management*, 36: 141–171.

Wassmer, U. (2010) 'How to manage alliance better than one at a time'. *MIT Sloan Management Review*, 51: 77–84.

Wathne, K.H. and Heide, J.B. (2000) 'Opportunism in interfirm relationships: Forms, outcomes, and solutions'. *Journal of Marketing*, 64: 36–51.

Weis, S.E. (2011) 'Negotiating the Renault–Nissan alliance: Insights from Renault's experience'. In Benoliel, M. (ed.), *Negotiation Excellence*, World Scientific Publishers Company, pp. 315–340.

Weitz, B.E. and Jap, S.D. (1995) 'Relationship marketing and distribution channels'. *Journal of the Academy of Marketing Science*, 23: 305–320.

White, G.O., Joplin, J.R.W. and Salama, M.F. (2007) 'Contracts and conflict resolution strategies in foreign ventures: A transaction cost perspective'. *International Journal of Conflict Management*, 18: 376–390.

Wilson, J. and Hynes, N. (2009) 'Co-evolution of firms and strategic alliances: Theory and empirical evidence'. *Technological Forecasting and Social Change*, 76: 620–628.

Williams, T. (2005) 'Cooperation by design: Structure and cooperation in interorganizational networks'. *Journal of Business Research*, 58: 223–231.

Williamson, O.E. (1975) *Markets and Hierarchies: Analysis and Antitrust Implications*. New York: Free Press.

Williamson, O.E. (1981) 'The economics of organization – The transaction cost approach'. *American Journal of Sociology*, 87: 548–577.

Williamson, O.E. (1985) *The Economic Institutions of Capitalism*. New York: Free Press.

Williamson, O.E. (1991) 'Comparative economic organization – Analysis of discrete structural alternatives'. *Administrative Science Quarterly*, 36: 269–296.

Wit, de, Bob and Meyer, R. (2004) *Strategy Process, Content, Context: An International Perspective*. London: Thomson Learning.

Wittmann, C.M. (2007) 'Strategic alliances: What can we learn when they fail?' *Journal of Business-to-Business Marketing*, 14: 1–19.

Wojciszke, B., Brycz, H. and Borkenau, P. (1993) 'Effects of information-content and evaluative extremity on positivity and negativity biases'. *Journal of Personality and Social Psychology*, 64: 327–335.

Wolfe, R.J. and McGinn, K.L. (2005) 'Perceived relative power and its influence on negotiations'. *Group Decision and Negotiation*, 14: 3–20.

Wood, G. (2002) 'A partnership model of corporate ethics'. *Journal of Business Ethics*, 40: 61–73.

Yan, A.M. and Gray, B. (1994) 'Bargaining power, management control, and performance in United States – China joint ventures: A comparative case study'. *Academy of Management Journal*, 37: 1,478–1,51.

Yan, A.M. and Gray, B. (2001) 'Antecedents and effects of parent control in international joint ventures'. *Journal of Management Studies*, 38: 393–416.

Yan, A.M. and Zeng, M. (1999) 'International joint venture instability: A critique of previous research, a reconceptualization, and directions for future research'. *Journal of International Business Studies*, 30: 397–414.

Yang, M.-H., Liao, C.-H. and Liu, S.-C. (2007) 'Applying internet-based information systems to facilitate business alliance activities'. *Internet-based Information Systems*, 107: 125–140.

Yeheskel, O., Zeira, O., Shenkar, Y. and Newburry, W. (2001) 'Parent company dissimilarity and equity international joint venture effectiveness'. *Journal of International Management*, 7: 81–104.

Yin, X.L. and Shanley, M. (2008) 'Industry determinants of the "merger versus alliance" decision'. *Academy of Management Review*, 33: 473–491.

Yli-Renko, H. and Autio, E. (1998) 'The network embeddedness of new, technology-based firms: Developing a systemic evolution model'. *Small Business Economics*, 11: 253–267.

Yli-Renko, H., Autio, E. and Sapienza, H.J. (2001) 'Social capital, knowledge acquisition, and knowledge exploitation in young technology-based firms'. *Strategic Management Journal*, 22: 587–613.

Yodel (2008) 'Yodel to take Google AdWords service to three countries'. Available online at http://www.yodel.co.nz/blog/fulfilnet-secures-alliance-with-google-to-sell-adwords (accessed 2 August 2011).

Yu, X. (2009) 'Danone, Wahaha reach a settlement in beverage dispute'. *China Daily*. Available online at http://www.chinadaily.com.cn/bizchina/2009-10/05/content_8764096.htm (accessed 2 August 2011)

Zahra, S.A. and George, G. (2002) 'Absorptive capacity: A review, reconceptualization, and extension'. *Academy of Management Review*, 27: 185–203.

Zajac, E.J. and Olsen, C.P. (1993) 'From transaction cost to transactional value analysis – Implications for the study of interorganizational strategies'. *Journal of Management Studies*, 30: 131–145.

Zeng, M. and Chen, X.P. (2003) 'Achieving cooperation in multiparty alliances: A social dilemma approach to partnership management'. *Academy of Management Review*, 28: 587–605.

Zeng, M. and Hennart, J.F. (2002) 'From learning races to cooperative specialization: towards a new framework for alliance management'. In Contractor, F.J. and Lorange, P. (eds.), *Cooperative Strategies and Alliances*, Amsterdam: Pergamon International Business and Management Series, pp. 189–210.

Zhang, Y. and Li, H. (2001) 'The control design and performance in international joint ventures: a dynamic evolution perspective'. *International Business Review*, 10: 95–113.

Zhou, J. (2009) 'Trademark disputes between Danone and Wahaha Group'. China-business-law.com. Available online at http://www.china-business-law.com/trademark-disputes-between-danone-and-wahaha-group/ (accessed 2 August 2011).

Ziggers, G.W. and Tjemkes, B.V. (2010) 'Dynamics in inter-firm collaboration: The impact of alliance capabilities on performance'. *International Journal of Food System Dynamics*, 1: 151–166.

Zinn, W. and Parasuraman, A. (1997) 'Scope and intensity of logistics-based strategic alliances – A conceptual classification and managerial implications'. *Industrial Marketing Management*, 26: 137–147.

INDEX

Bold type refers to Figures, Tables and Boxes